Understanding the World Economy
Third edition

D0219502

The world economy is in a constant state of flux and understanding the changing nature of world economic affairs can prove a daunting task. Tony Cleaver, in the third edition of this internationally successful text, comprehensively examines and illuminates all major global economic developments.

Key topics include:

- China's rapid economic growth
- increasing concerns over the direction of Russia's transition
- the recent financial crisis in Argentina
- the enlargement of the European Union
- concerns over the economics of oil and the environment
- current research in New Institutional Economics and property rights
- foundations of markets and the problems of economic development.

Understanding the World Economy combines current world case studies with the accessible style and structure of the previous editions, ensuring that this book remains essential reading for all students studying economics and for lay readers.

Tony Cleaver is Vice Master at Grey College and lectures in the Department of Economics at the University of Durham.

DOUGLAS COLLEGE LIBRARY

Understanding the World Economy

Third edition

Tony Cleaver

Routledge
Taylor & Francis Group

LONDON AND NEW YORK

DOUGLAS COLLEGE LIBRARY

First published 1997
by Routledge
2 Park Square, Milton Park, Abingdon, Oxon, OX14 4RN

Simultaneously published in the USA and Canada
by Routledge
270 Madison Ave, New York, NY 10016

Reprinted 1997, 1998, 1999, 2001, 2002

Third edition 2007

*Routledge is an imprint of the Taylor & Francis Group,
an informa business*

© 1997, 2007 Tony Cleaver

Typeset in Times New Roman by
Keystroke, 28 High Street, Tettenhall, Wolverhampton
Printed and bound in Great Britain by
TJ International Ltd, Padstow, Cornwall

All rights reserved. No part of this book may be reprinted or reproduced
or utilised in any form or by any electronic, mechanical, or other means,
now known or hereafter invented, including photocopying and recording,
or in any information storage or retrieval system, without permission in
writing from the publishers.

British Library Cataloguing in Publication Data
A catalogue record for this book is available from the British Library

Library of Congress Cataloging in Publication Data
A catalog record for this book has been requested

ISBN10: 0–415–77106–4 (hbk)
ISBN10: 0–415–77105–6 (pbk)

ISBN13: 978–0–415–77106–1 (hbk)
ISBN13: 978–0–415–77105–4 (pbk)

Contents

List of illustrations   vi
Preface to the third edition   ix

Introduction   1

1 Command, market and mixed economies   9

2 The transition economies   32

3 Microeconomics and macroeconomics   56

4 Unemployment and inflation   71

5 Free trade, regional agreements and strategic policies   91

6 Customs unions and common markets   107

7 Money, banking and international finance   125

8 Exchange rates and currency union   143

9 The economics of oil   165

10 Foreign debt, financial crises and international policemen   188

11 Development, growth and Asian dragons   206

12 Environmental economics: sustaining spaceship earth   233

13 Conclusion: into the twenty-first century   253

Index   259

Illustrations

FIGURES

0.1	The themes of the introduction	7
1.1	The themes of chapter 1	28
2.1	Shares of Chinese industrial output, 1978 and 1993	45
2.2	% annual growth of per capita GDP 1978–95	46
2.3	Income per head in US$, 1995	46
2.4	Russia: GDP and investment in the 1990s	47
2.5	Net capital flows, 1992–7 (1994–7 in the case of Russia)	48
2.6	Cross-country comparisons of investment, 1998	49
2.7	The themes of chapter 2	52
3.1	Circulation of money: incomes and spending	63
3.2	Incomes leak out as savings	63
3.3	All spending goes through firms	63
3.4	The circular flow of incomes and expenditure	64
3.5	The themes of chapter 3	69
4.1	% unemployed in the United Kingdom and United States, 1900–90	75
4.2	UK Phillips curve, 1862–1958	77
4.3	Chile: economic growth, 1961–98	79
4.4	Chile: unemployment, 1960–99	79
4.5	The expectations-augmented Phillips curve	80
4.6	UK: inflation and unemployment, 1978–2005	85
4.7	USA: inflation and unemployment, 1978–2005	85
4.8	Germany: inflation and unemployment, 1978–2005	85
4.9	France: inflation and unemployment, 1978–2005	86
4.10	Italy: inflation and unemployment, 1978–2005	86
4.11	The themes of chapter 4	89
5.1	Index of world trade and growth, 1950–99	93
5.2	The themes of chapter 5	105
6.1	The most mobile, employable resources move out of the periphery	115
6.2	The themes of chapter 6	122
7.1	The themes of chapter 7	139

8.1	Exports to the European Union as a % of GDP, 1996	158
8.2	US and UK: unemployment and wage growth, 1995–2005	159
8.3	Spain and Italy: unemployment and wage growth, 1995–2005	160
8.4	The Netherlands and Belgium: unemployment and wage growth, 1995–2005	160
8.5	Germany and France: unemployment and wage growth, 1995–2005	161
8.6	The themes of chapter 8	163
9.1	World oil consumption, 1960–2004	167
9.2	World oil reserves, 2004	174
9.3	Oil production (mbd), 1994–2004	178
9.4	2004 trade in oil (mbd)	179
9.5	The spot price of oil (Dubai light), 1964–2004	182
9.6	The themes of chapter 9	185
10.1	Total external debt for selected countries	201
10.2	The themes of chapter 10	203
11.1	India: real GDP per capita in constant prices, 1950–2000	219
11.2	Neoclassical growth theory	221
11.3	Average growth in GNP per capita, 1965–90	224
11.4	The themes of chapter 11	230
12.1	The relationship between economic activity and the environment	237
12.2	How the rate of regeneration of a species varies with its population/stock size	242
12.3	The themes of chapter 12	251

TABLES

2.1	Growth rate of the Soviet Union	37
2.2	Growth rates of Soviet inputs and productivity	37
2.3	Growth rates of Chinese income per head and export trade	45
6.1	European nations, selected data	117
10.1	South East Asian economies in trouble	197
10.2	Debt indicators for heavily indebted poor countries compared to other less developed countries	204
11.1	GNP *per capita*, selected countries, 2003	207
11.2	Development indicators, selected countries, 2003	208
11.3	Natural resources and the environment	214
11.4	The Asian 'dragons', selected data	225

BOXES

1.1	Getting the mix right in the Brazilian rainforest	27
3.1	Microeconomics and cigarettes	61
3.2	Macroeconomics and the case of Japan	66
4.1	Supply-side policies in action (1) Chile	77
4.2	Supply-side policies in action (2) the UK	82
8.1	Currency boards	148
10.1	Long-term capital management: a hedge fund that got clipped	190
11.1	Turning round the 'permit raj'	219
11.2	The informal sector and property rights	222
12.1	Pollution permits and global warming	245

Preface to the third edition

To understand the world economy requires identifying the major events taking place, analysing their causes and consequences and setting them in the context of more slowly moving global forces.

In the attempt to illuminate various issues of international scope and appeal, the first edition of this text sought to explain why the command economic systems that controlled the destiny of Eastern Europe and most of Asia had so quickly collapsed. This was undoubtedly *the* monumental economic change of the late twentieth century. Whilst this is still important to understand for anyone seeking a grasp of world affairs, chapter 2 in this third edition shifts the emphasis onto how and why the transition experiences of the major powers involved – Russia and China – have been so different: the Chinese economy has taken off and its incomes, investments and trade are rapidly growing, whereas the former Soviet Union still struggles to find direction. Meanwhile the European Union has increased in size again as a number of nations formerly tied to Moscow shift their allegiance westward.

The major concerns of globalisation, the plight of poorer peoples and the environment have not undergone any revolutionary transformation. They remain as important today as ever. Data on these topics have been revised and, to widen the perspective, brief explanations of the problems experienced in Argentina and of the resurgence of India are added.

The various theories in the discipline of economics which attempt to explain inflation, unemployment, finance, trade and growth still underpin the analyses but the astute reader will also notice an increasing emphasis on the institutional foundations of market systems. This reflects recent research and my own appreciation that it is the slow-moving, underlying forces that shift beneath economies which can best explain why some countries experience economic progress whilst others suffer financial crisis. Headlines in the media may grab the attention and identify the events needful of analysis but more penetrating texts are required – I hope like this one – to provide for somewhat deeper understanding.

There are many injustices in the world. The existing unequal distribution of global incomes is one of the more urgent causes for concern and is a major theme of this text. It must be strongly emphasised at the outset, however, that all the evidence to date shows that, *in general*, world trade is not harmful to the interests of the poorest of the poor. Look further in the pages that follow to seek justification for this claim. Global capitalism is not played out as a zero-sum game in a world of fixed resources where for one party to grow richer it means another party must grow poorer.

This does not imply that in some specific instances exploitation does not take place. Sadly, economic power can be abused just as efficiently and ruthlessly as political and military might. How such power might be controlled is the central investigation of this study and it would be premature to summarise conclusions here. But is the solution to strive for the complete collapse of market systems built on private capital? To be overtaken by what – state control? This would be an ironic message to send to Eastern European states emerging from the constraints of central planning.

It is not the aim of this preface, however, to launch straight into an examination of the rival forms of economic organisation. This matter, amongst others, is considered within. But it *is* the intention to awaken the interest of the reader in the all-pervasive reach of simple economics.

Despite the monumental political events that marked our entry into the new millennium, it is asserted here that all of the economic forces at work in shaping global relations remain basically unchanged. It is only the current outcomes that differ. Today, as in the last decades of the twentieth century, a pro-market economic philosophy still dominates public policy-making – both in national governments as well as in international economic institutions. Given the alternatives, examined in chapter 1, some will say that is just as well – though it does not mean that this is an excuse for letting private enterprise have its own way everywhere.

The desire for all peoples to enrich themselves, to undertake trade and to develop their economies is as great as ever – as are all the problems that this brings with them. The speed at which money changes hands round the globe, the speed at which industry and employment grows and declines and the speed at which environmental resources are exploited still threatens to overtake the speed at which humankind can adjust its institutions and practices to cope. Some of the social and economic impacts of these latest conflicts are analysed within – including their effect on academic thinking.

But the *raison d'etre* for this book stays the same. We all share the same planet. The economic, cultural and ecological diversity it supports is precious, unique – and *interconnected*. Though some of us may exercise more control over it than others, we all have a responsibility to study where our spaceship is going, to cast our vote – either through the ballot box or through the pattern of our spending – and not to pollute nor provoke anarchy in our communal living quarters. Our destinies are all entwined and the pace at which global forces now operate means this will increasingly be so.

Tony Cleaver

Introduction

Economics is not always easy to get on with. It is not that the subject matter is dry, soulless and confusing – just that many textbooks seem to present it that way.

The reality is that people actually care passionately about economic issues. Too passionately: there have been more revolutions, killings and 'disappearances' caused by disputes over rival systems of economic organisation than due to disagreements of any other kind. Nonetheless, students do not usually turn to economics books for stimulating reading or to resolve problems in passionate debate.

So there is a dilemma in studying this subject. People know intuitively that economic affairs are important and that more knowledge in this field is desirable; but, at the same time, many complain after long hours of study that what can be gained from mastering all the difficult analysis involved seems to be very little. In the jargon of the textbooks, the rate of return seems to be too low to fully repay the investment.

This is a justifiable complaint. Students live very crowded lives. An hour or two's study in the evening has a very real *opportunity cost* – you lose the opportunity to do so many other entertaining things; take three months out of a year to cram in a course of study and the sacrifice is enormous – the pay-off had better be worth it; extend that course to cover two or three years and we are talking about what seems a lifetime.

Time is very precious. As Einstein knew, it is not a constant. It flies by faster when you are a student; it slows down and crawls along as you get older and are presented with fewer life-changing decisions. An economist might wryly remark that there is diminishing marginal utility involved here: the more years you consume, the less precious each one seems!

What it all amounts to is that newcomers to economics are understandably impatient to learn how to use the subject to unlock some of the mysteries, conundrums and injustices of everyday life. For those with eyes to see, such problems are all around us – on the streets, on the television, in the newspapers. Will the poor always be with us? Is unemployment *natural*? Why are prices rising? Doesn't anyone care about the environment? These are difficult questions, every one; all good reasons for turning to economics. The very first book ever written on the subject was *An Inquiry into the Nature and Causes of the Wealth of Nations*. It is a good title. These things are all worthy of study – providing you gain in learning, not confusion.

This book is an attempt to help. It does not promise to provide the solutions to all or any of the world's problems – if these solutions were so easy to come by they would already be in place – but it is designed to make some of the ideas, theories and arguments more accessible to the general reader. If you can understand these a little better you can then understand why certain politicians, business executives and other practical people put into effect some of the policies they do. You should thus be able to argue with a little knowledge – rather than with a lot of prejudice – why you think certain actions are right or wrong.

But beware: a little knowledge is a dangerous thing. Complex problems can easily be oversimplified. Reducing issues of world importance to a few pages is necessary to begin with – this is a taster in economics, after all – but further understanding requires commitment to longer study. Quick, short-term returns are necessary to keep investors happy and 'hanging-on in there', but long-run profits and sustainable growth are not bought so easily. A textbook or two may be necessary – and, hopefully, you will in time be able to see through the dry logic into the passionate implications of what this subject is all about . . .

ECONOMICS, SOCIAL SCIENCE AND THE THEORY OF KNOWLEDGE

Let me emphasise at the beginning one particular feature of economics that is common to all forms of learning, whether it be science, languages, art or whatever. This is perhaps more obvious in economics than in many other subjects, but it is true for all: *we can never know anything with absolute certainty*. Do not deduce from this that economics is therefore not worth bothering about. Just because 'final answers' are unattainable, that knowledge is a time-consuming pathway without end, it does not mean we might as well give up at the start. Be assured that a certain amount of profit can be gained fairly quickly and, if you invest your time wisely, returns can magnify with compound interest as you go along.

Economists know only too well the fallibility of their science. Like weather forecasters, we make predictions about what we think might happen. Since there are so many variables to consider, so many things that can change, we have to assume that some will remain constant (in the 'short run') and base our predictions on what is expected to happen to others. Past experience helps. If we observe that every time in the past when a wind blew from the West it brought rain then we can induce a general law that can be applied to the future – it will rain when the West wind blows next, assuming all other things remain the same.

With the weather, of course, just as in economics, we can never be absolutely sure. Storms from a totally unexpected quarter can blow all our calculations adrift. Things never stay constant for very long.

The analogy with meteorology can be pressed too far, however. This is because it can never be emphasised enough that economics is first and foremost a social science – the product of a set of analytical tools that attempts to make sense of society. It concerns itself with different issues than, say, sociology, anthropology, history, etc., but its subject of study is very much the same: humankind – and economics shares with these other disciplines, therefore, the same difficulty of applying scientific methodology.

This assertion – that economics is essentially a scientific inquiry into social activity – is the second most important feature of the subject worthy of note. In my view, a thorough grasp of all the implications of this statement is absolutely essential if the time-pressed student is really to profit from study of the subject. The more I teach economics, the more I become concerned that the bulk of esoteric analysis that fills our textbooks is nowhere near as useful to the average student as this fundamental. It is so easy to spend your time struggling to make sense of complex theoretical arguments that you lose sight of what it is all for.

You may be surprised to learn that this can be as true for long-term practitioners of the subject as it is for newcomers. There is much criticism within the profession that academic economists are increasingly limiting their research to fields that may be susceptible to precise mathematical treatment, but which are of limited relevance to the 'big questions' at large. Because these questions are difficult to fathom, therefore, mainstream economics is being accused of the error outlined above: of burying itself in impressive computation and being unwilling or, worse, unable to see what is important on the pathway to knowledge.

There is a perverse comfort in this discovery. We all make mistakes. If you feel occasionally overwhelmed by the complexity of it all and nervous in claiming any special insights about society then you are not alone. But do not be put off. Keep on asking awkward questions. If reputable experts and the hefty, authoritative tomes they produce, cannot answer you in a mean-ingful way then it is not necessarily you that is wrong. Maybe you are on to something.

This point is worth emphasising. I see economists engaged in investigating social phenomena, employing scientific methodology where they can as objectively as possible, but at the same time working within a specific social and historical context. Inevitably, this context influences the objectivity and scientific validity of the economist's product.

Every scientist possesses a certain world view and works with a given body of knowledge to back him/her up. We all attempt to contribute towards the advancement of knowledge but, consciously or otherwise, in so doing we may be promoting one particular perspective in place of another. In the evolution of science a number of schools of thought can be identified. Many may coexist together, though usually one 'paradigm' may predominate. If one such paradigm becomes a lasting, unquestioned research tradition then there is a danger of science stagnating. Knowledge advances best when new minds are continually challenging, re-interpreting the dominant tradition. Young students impatient with their teachers are to be welcomed!

The philosophy that underpins this text is a personal interpretation like any other. It should not go unchallenged. It is born of an emphasis on 'Positive Economics' – that is, we must attempt to scientifically test all claims to economic knowledge – but it also accepts that any assertion about society must be treated with caution, in the knowledge that all economists are subjective, value-ridden individuals, no matter how hard we might try to be unbiased.

There are problems in attempting to be 'scientific' about society. Any systematic, rigorous investigation of phenomena involves the tried and tested formula of scientific method. This methodological approach involves a strict and time-honoured procedure that must be satisfied if research findings at the end of it are to have any acceptance by the scientific community. But the searchlight of scientific method has its limitations: it can illuminate certain areas better than others. As a tool of investigation it is extremely useful, but the technical demands of this instrument of inquiry should not be the sole determinant of the goals of social investigation. It is a means to an end only. If there are important places where it sheds little light we must still continue to search, albeit rather tentatively. In the end, what the economist can unearth must be presented with all humility. Any pretensions to uncovering the truth will be set about with qualifications, since this is in the nature of social science.

Scientific method involves observation of phenomena; generalising of hypotheses; deduction of predictions and testing them for corroboration or falsification of theory. These are the essential steps involved in any scientific investigation from Galileo to Einstein; from Hippocrates to Sherlock Holmes. At all stages in this process, however, there are problems endemic to the social – as distinct from the natural – sciences.

Objective recording of data is an immense difficulty when people are studying people. What one observer perceives from a given social phenomenon another will not. The cultural values the observer brings to the scene are inextricably bound up with his/her allegedly objective report.

Take the example of a worker who considers that the wage rate paid for a job is insufficient compensation for the sacrifice involved. Is this a case of exploitation of the labour force? Other observers might say it is merely someone 'pricing themselves out of work'. If unemployment results here, is this 'voluntary' or 'involuntary'? It depends on your point of view. (What you perceive to be happening here has very important policy implications – see chapters 3 and 4.)

Everyone has prejudices. We cannot avoid them since we make judgements every day based on our (inevitably limited) perception of others. It is essential for the student of social science to realise that it is thus impossible to be completely value-free, but if we can make just a little progress towards greater objectivity in our observations then this will be immensely more valuable to us than memorising whole bookshelves of algebraic theory.

In addition to the difficulty of defining and measuring certain phenomena in principle, this problem is compounded in practice by vagaries in the statistical record. Even supposing there was agreement between countries on what constitutes unemployment – or, say, how we might evaluate capital – the efficiency of data gathering can be questionable. In some places, just counting the population is difficult enough, let alone calculating what they do or what they produce.

What we observe to be happening in the world at large, therefore, is inevitably blinkered, right at the start. Our access to information is limited by scarce and/or unreliable data and even where our viewpoint is crystal clear our own perception is never uncluttered. What face do you first see in a crowd? Your own. All observation is to some degree subjective: you see what you best recognise.

Generating universal laws – the next stage in the scientific process – becomes more difficult the greater the complexity of the subject under the microscope. A fundamental difference between natural science and social science worth mentioning here is the distinction between what has been termed homogenous evidence and heterogeneous evidence. In certain natural sciences you are dealing with pieces of data that are identical and behave the same way under similar circumstances (one hydrogen atom is the same as another). In social sciences the different bits of data (people) are not alike. As a result we can make extremely complex statements about the world in physics based on relatively few experiences. And we hold these views with something close to certainty: we know, for example, when Halley's Comet will return for thousands of years into the future, thanks to a very few observations. But we cannot make quite such confident claims about the world in biology (plants and animals constitute heterogeneous data also) and even less so about humans. Who knows, for example, when unemployment in Europe will return to low, pre-1980 levels?

There are numerous general laws in physics, that most respectable, fore-castable of sciences. These are accepted by the scientific community and are of universal applicability throughout the cosmos. All such laws will tend to have a 'sell-by' date; that is, there comes a time as our knowledge improves when they are revised and a new scientific paradigm is formulated – Newtonian physics was superseded by Einstein, for example – but the point is that in the meantime, given our limited vision, our laws of light, gravity, etc., are upheld everywhere we look, without exception. They are general, universal axioms, infallible enough to build spaceships to the moon and back. Natural sciences based on more complex building blocks (e.g. organic chemistry) will have substantially fewer such laws. In biology there is only one: the theory of evolution. But in social science there are none. In economics, which perhaps uses more scientific techniques of inquiry than the other humanities, there are many attempts at general laws, but all are only statistical tendencies where exceptions abound. General 'laws' in economics apply only if certain assumptions are maintained. (If workers ask for more wages, then assuming their motivation, efficiency and productivity in work does not change, businesses may employ fewer . . .)

Deducing specific predictions from general laws in social science is not too easy either. Predictions may be precise, but they cannot be used to falsify or corroborate hypotheses with a great degree of certainty, since – unlike laboratory experiments – other factors in society can never be held constant. (Did the fall in UK and US inflation throughout the 1980s confirm or confound monetarist theory?)

This is a problem that laboratory science knows well enough (you may have done the experiment wrong!) but whereas the pure scientist can do it again (though at cost) and isolate the variables better next time, the social scientist has to take the world as he/she finds it, along with all its 'imperfections'. Unravelling what has been going on in society – whether particular changes have had more or less influence than others on subsequent events – is thus extremely difficult to determine when all sorts of things are happening all the time. Some scholars have asserted that since falsification/corroboration of general laws in economics is impossible to achieve, so the whole attempt to apply Popperian scientific methodology is pointless. This seems a bit extreme – we can rely on the scientific searchlight in some areas, if not all.

As a result of these difficulties, in comparison to the natural sciences, social scientists recognise the need for much larger and more representative samples, and much greater care in their interpretation, in order to make reasonable claims to knowledge. They are increasingly turning to more sophisticated computational techniques to assist them. Even then there is an inevitable lack of precision: as the price of oil rises, people will generally buy less of it – a 'law' in economics with a lot of statistical support – but how much they will actually buy next time is more difficult to say. Contrast this statement with what can be asserted if the *temperature* of oil rises: chemical engineers in oil refineries can predict to a calculable degree exactly what will happen to it.

A final point of caution: humankind has an insatiable curiosity and a capacity to theorise in the search for causes. If, for example, it is noted that on a number of occasions after a flash of lightning there follows a clap of thunder then not only can a general law be induced, but there is a natural impulse to ask: why?

Most people cannot accept not knowing why things happen and will rush into any causal explanation – from magic to the influence of gods, gurus and aliens – rather than be left with uncertainty. In the case of economics and social science, however, it is the purpose of this emphasis on the Theory of Knowledge to stop the drift into narrow-minded use and abuse of science, where nice theories impede rather than illuminate our vision. We should ask ourselves continually: 'Which is the most worthwhile area to investigate?'; 'How reasonable are my beliefs?'; and 'Am I certain that I'm not being selective in my choice of data?'

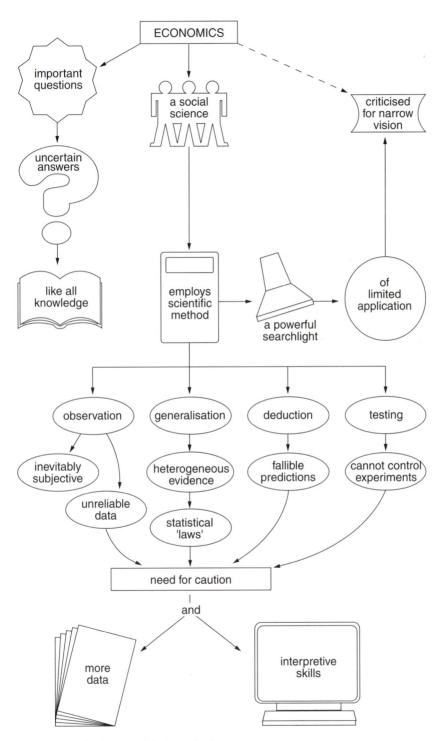

Figure 0.1 The themes of the introduction

It is too easy to leap to erroneous conclusions when investigating urgent social problems. One of the world's most famous (fictional) social scientists, Sherlock Holmes, knew what he was up against: 'It is a capital mistake, Watson, to theorise before one has sufficient data' (from *Scandal in Bohemia*). It is advice we should all take note of: suspending judgement is better than slipping into prejudice.

KEY WORDS

Opportunity cost   This is perhaps the most fundamental concept in economics. The true cost of doing anything is giving up the opportunity to do something else you would really like. This is as relevant to the student who chooses to bury him/herself in a textbook and tries to forget about the party that everyone else is going to, as it is to the speculator who invests a small fortune in one company's shares and hopes that the other one that looked attractive turns out to be as buoyant as a flat tyre. A choice has to be taken whenever scarce resources are employed – if time and money are no object then it does not matter what you do, but in the real world consumers, business executives and government officials are frequently confronted with difficult decisions as to what actions to take. The cost of opting for one course of action is losing the opportunity to follow another.

FURTHER READING

Bastian, Sue. 'What to do with logic: inductive inferences', *International Quarterly*, winter, 1986–7.
Ormerod, Paul. *The Death of Economics*. Faber & Faber, 1994.

1 Command, market and mixed economies

Topics to be considered in this chapter:

- The functions of all economic systems – what, how and for whom goods and services are produced.
- Five questions in building an economic system:

  1 Where is decision-making located?
  2 What is the economic philosophy?
  3 What signalling mechanism allocates resources?
  4 Who owns resources?
  5 Is it cooperation, competition or collusion in industry?

- System failures: the inefficiencies and inequities of government, corporate and free market 'solutions'.
- Getting the mix right.

INTRODUCTION

During the twentieth century, the world witnessed a contest between two contrasting engines of economic development: one powerhouse being led by central command; the other being ruled by markets. One operated in Eastern Europe and the old Soviet Union; the other was championed by the West.

You could say that the last century therefore hosted humankind's greatest-ever experiment in social, political and economic organisation and, according to many commentators, the great ideological battle between the two opposing economic systems has finally been settled – with victory allegedly going to the market model.

Other observers might remark that the whole East–West conflict was a massive irrelevance. Opposite economic philosophies fuelled a struggle for supremacy between two superpowers which trampled on the interests of billions of poor bystanders, not to mention all other life on the planet. Resources were diverted in rich and poor countries alike into an ideological dispute to win 'hearts and minds' that destroyed lives, impoverished economies and polluted the biosphere. Confusion, continuing conflict and environmental contamination are our inheritance in this new millennium.

Such differences in perspective on the evolution and current practice of economic systems run through this book and you are encouraged to evaluate these arguments. But we need first of all to understand what economic systems *are*, how countries construct them and what are the choices embodied in their design. This is the objective of this opening chapter.

ECONOMIC SYSTEMS

Economics studies the way societies organise resources to satisfy their needs. Economic organisation in this context refers to the ownership and control of the means of production, how decisions of consumption and production are made and communicated to others and how efficiently economic changes are effected.

Fundamental economic decisions face all societies. Any community must decide *what* goods and services it should produce; *how* it should best employ its resources to secure these ends; and finally, *for whom* in society, and in what number, these benefits should be provided. We can therefore classify any given economic system by the way – either by accident or design – it resolves these issues.

There is a wealth of options involved in building a modern economy to make these decisions and they can be assessed in five dimensions. I have chosen to categorise economies into three types in each dimension, although this is a purely personal interpretation – you may like to think of others.

The first dimension: the location of decision-making

• Where are the economic decisions made in society, and by whom?

The power to decide what, how and for whom goods and services are produced may be centralised in the hands of political dictators; it may be controlled by the boards of a number of giant industrial and financial empires, or it may depend upon the collective authority of millions of ordinary individuals dispersed throughout society.

A command economic system is characterised by **central control** – all major decisions regarding the community's organisation are made at the centre and communicated by command via a bureaucracy of subordinates. The leaders of a command system may inherit power, be elected, appointed, or seize it by force. They may be communist or fascist; a monarchy or republic. The political colour and constitutional validity of the organising authority is not at issue; the key aspect of this form of organisation is that the major economic decisions are taken centrally and are not dispersed.

No other country exhibited such centralised control of its economic affairs as much as did the old Soviet Union – where the range of goods produced, the production methods and locations and, in many cases, individuals' wages and places of employment could all be decided by the central planning committee, *Gosplan*.

Such concentration of economic power stands in stark contrast to **consumer sovereignty**, which describes decision-making in a perfectly competitive market system, free from government intervention. Here, the consumer is king. All decisions regarding what goods should be produced in a free-market system are taken in accordance with individual demand. If consumers in aggregate want more of one product than another then their purchasing power will drive producers to comply. Nobel prize-winning economist Paul Samuelson likened the process to individuals casting dollar votes in an open contest (market) for the goods and services they prefer. Those commodities that receive the most 'votes' will inevitably be supplied.

How business is conducted, how society's resources are employed to produce what consumers want, is decided by independent managers throughout the economy who are free to choose production methods, and employ labour and capital as they so wish. They will make profits only insofar as they respond to consumer demand.

Decisions as to who benefits most in this economic system are spread widely and are made in accordance with those who have participated most productively in serving consumer needs. The popular football player may earn more than the doctor or social worker, but that is what people pay for. All decision-making is thus decentralised: the authority to organise and control resources is dispersed throughout society. The consumer is the sovereign decision-maker.

Such a dispersed system of making decisions is a theoretical ideal – an economic 'democracy' that takes no account of the fact that in reality many people may be disenfranchised whereas a few may dominate the 'voting'. Consumer sovereignty may exist only in an underdeveloped form in many countries where society instead exhibits **dualism**. This is an economic structure where great wealth sits side by side with widespread poverty. A few national or multinational corporations and their employees may possess significant economic power and exercise this with the (in some cases, conditional) approval of government whilst all around them millions of the poor struggle to survive in a subsistence economy which can only barely provide for basic needs.

In one dimension of this schizophrenic society, decisions as to what goods and services are supplied are taken in boardrooms where the long-term interests of the corporate empire are considered in the context of national and international economic forecasts, the behaviour of business rivals and the relationship with government policy-makers. In the other, less fortunate dimension, people make do with whatever resources are unclaimed or cast aside by the wealthy – farming marginal lands, recycling waste materials: not so much taking decisions and exercising control over their destiny as clinging on the best they can to the residue that is left to them.

In the wealthy, modern sector, how production is organised and who is employed at what wage will depend on the corporation's bargaining strength in different market places – high-tech inputs may be developed in one location, cheap labour contracted in another and overall profits declared in a third. In the poor, traditional sector, production techniques are determined by the availability of whatever resources are left over – typically a large pool of relatively unskilled labour and native enterprise plus whatever capital equipment can be scrounged second-hand.

The location of much decision-making in dualistic, less-developed countries therefore resides in wealthy enclaves from which the poor are generally excluded.

The second dimension: the economic philosophy

- What is the code of values that underpins social and economic organisation? What is it that drives individuals and institutions to perform their particular economic functions?
- Do people act to serve their own interests first above all others? Do the needs of society take precedence over the individual? Or perhaps a tribal or community-based ethic dominates all social interaction?

Such questions can be answered by studying the nature and conduct of the main producing and consuming agents in the economy.

For some countries there is a well-articulated **communal ethic** embodied in all main institutions, emphasising the prior needs of the state. Such an ethic will be revered as the unique, unifying code that gives meaning and identity to the state and society and dictates the role of the individual within it. Although most often associated with communist or fundamentalist Islamic states, many countries of different philosophical persuasions have also exhorted the responsibilities of the people for the collective good as a means of consolidating and promoting nationhood. (Calls to patriotism are especially urgent, of course, during wartime.)

In the command economy, resources are mobilised according to a coherent set of values; clearly set out with practical applications for subordinates to follow at all levels within the society. As an extreme example, the East German border guard was thus legally empowered to shoot anyone trying to flee from the country: there can be no clearer demonstration of the view that the state has supremacy over individual rights.

An opposite ethic to the one above is that which insists on the primacy of **self-interest**. Margaret Thatcher once claimed that 'there is no such thing as society', implying that the market society is best understood as an agglomeration of individuals. Often, the name of Adam Smith is reverently quoted in this regard, and the following passage is perhaps the most famous in all economics:

> Every individual endeavours to employ his capital so that its produce may be of greatest value. He generally neither intends to promote the public interest, nor knows how much he is promoting it. He intends only his own security, only his own gain. And he is in this led by an 'invisible hand' to promote an end which was no part of his intention. By pursuing his own

interest he frequently promotes that of society more effectually than when he really intends to promote it.

(Adam Smith, *The Wealth of Nations*, 1776)

Smith wrote this over 200 years ago as the professor of moral philosophy at Glasgow University, and was well aware of the ethical and institutional foundations upon which this assertion is based. The individual's right to property ownership, laws of contract and of fair and equal exchange requires rigorous protection. The state is the guardian of the individual, and the power of princes, politicians or monopolies to usurp these rights must be limited. Assured of protection, therefore, the consumer acts to increase wealth and welfare (what economists call 'utility'); the producer aims to maximise profits. The value system that pervades the free market is thus the pursuit of individual well-being.

Anthropologists argue that humankind has tribal origins and that, inevitably, the **extended family ethic** still remains a basic instinct. In poorer countries in particular, where the reach of public services may be restricted and unreliable and where the private sector is under-developed, it is the extended family that provides for most social and economic organisation. If, in a modern market society, you want to buy a used car you might pick up the phone book or look in the local newspaper. Such behaviour is unthinkable in less developed economies. It would certainly be unproductive. If you wish to know where to get the best deal in buying or selling anything, if you are looking for a job, if you want a guide in another part of the country, if you are in trouble and need help – you ask someone in the extended family. It is the oldest form of economic organisation and it is still the *only* form of organisation in some parts of the world. No wonder then that it is to the family that the individual's first allegiance lies in these countries.

For those newly industrialised countries that have experienced rapid economic growth in the last quarter-century, the extended family ethic still permeates the economy – albeit that it sits less well with the requirements of the market place. Jobs are supposed to be widely advertised, not reserved for offspring. Loans should be allocated to investments according to strict commercial criteria, not given at a discount to friends and family. 'Cronyism' has been accused of causing the 1997 financial crisis in East Asia.

In modern market economies, family and local community ties have loosened considerably. That is what an efficient market demands. Even so, the family or tribal ethic is still important and, in their desire to survive the competitive jungle of modern economies, people are sometimes driven to form their own tribal groups if their energies are not harnessed by existing organisations. Tribal bonding which is *not* coherently developed can express itself in gangland warfare or football hooliganism, but where codified into a unifying team philosophy or mission statement – most often designed to differentiate one group from its rivals – it can be a highly effective means of organising, motivating, disciplining and giving direction to collective resources.

Individuals who are recruited by rich and powerful corporations may come to see their personal goals as inextricably linked to those of the business they serve and, as they rise up within the management hierarchy, the institution repays this loyalty with reciprocal commitment. This was the traditional employment-for-life ethic in Japanese business (not so certain now) and it is observed in modern multinationals locking in their executives with stock options, health and pension plans and other company perks. (Indeed, I have even heard it said that multinationals prefer to hire senior executives who are into their third or fourth marriage. Such individuals have demonstrated that the *corporate* family is their first priority!) All such practices are economic expressions of the extended family ethic.

The third dimension: the allocative mechanism

- How are economic decisions signalled to all the relevant institutions throughout society?
- By what means are productive resources – skilled labour, capital equipment and enterprising management – all brought together in the desired locations and set to work in the most efficient way possible?

How is it organised that the right quantities of agricultural output are produced on the farms, sent to the factories, processed into foods and then delivered to all the outlets in the country just at the correct time and place so that we can all enjoy fresh milk, bread and cereals for breakfast? We take this highly efficient arrangement for granted, yet any breakdown in what is actually a tremendously complex economic interaction between millions of participants would mean that these perishable foodstuffs would go rotten before they got to us. The organising mechanism used to allocate these resources – goods and services to all the various destinations in an economy – will typically be a system of planning, or prices.

Under a system of **central planning**, all economic activity is subordinate to a strict, institutionalised logic. Anyone who has served in a large, hierarchical organisation (such as in the armed services) will know all about this, but as a means of administering a whole economy the former Soviet Union provided the example *par excellence*.

First, a systematic process was employed to formulate long-term goals for the entire country. This required review of past performance, contemplating future ambitions and relating these to present resources. The highest decision-making authority – in the ex-USSR, the Politburo – was involved here. Once these national goals were agreed upon, they were handed down to the planning committee – the Gosplan – to be translated into specific targets for all sectors of the economy. Research was next undertaken into alternative strategies for achieving these targets. Having considered all the options, the decision was then made to implement the chosen strategy and to give the go-ahead to (typically) the next five-year plan. Once underway, planners were responsible for monitoring progress throughout the economy, in order to feed back results ready for the next planning phase.

Administering central planning in the Soviet Union was obviously a tremendously complex and important responsibility, and its success depended on high professional standards upheld by key officers – the nomenklatura. These bureaucrats played an important part in issuing orders and allocating key resources throughout the economy but, even in a command organisation as extensive as the old Soviet Union, not everything could be planned (especially in the distribution of consumer goods). The task was simply too big.

According to John Kenneth Galbraith (*The New Industrial State*, London: Hamilton, 1967), *Corporate* planning determines the allocation of resources in big business empires. A price mechanism may well be used for internal accounting purposes but these prices are likely to be administered by the corporation and are not freely determined in a balanced, competitive market. This typically occurs where the corporation's own departments or subsidiaries act as both buyer and seller (for example where an oil company produces crude oil in one country and 'sells' it to its refining subsidiary in another) or where it dominates one side of the market in dealing with outsiders (for example, a US sportswear giant buying tennis shoes from a small Indonesian factory).

Corporate planning arises where the application of technology in sophisticated production processes requires high degrees of (human and capital) specialisation and the investment of large sums of money over considerable periods of time. If research and development into new products and the training and development of new skills and production processes must be undertaken years ahead of eventual sales then corporations must think long term. Consumer tastes, government policies, the state of technology and the behaviour of business rivals cannot therefore be allowed to change as freely as the wind. Considerable energy and corporate muscle will be devoted to influencing them. The last thing the head of Megacar Corp wants is an unexpected change in, say, petroleum duty or transport technology that makes his latest product unsaleable. Much investment will therefore take place in marketing and persuasive advertising; in contributions to party political funds; in research and development of new technologies, and in negotiations and/or mergers with other corporations. This is undertaken on a continuing basis to help reduce the business uncertainties and to aid the progress of corporate planning.

The **price mechanism** is the dominant means of allocating resources in a competitive market economy. It operates wherever buyers and sellers of commodities meet freely to conduct trade on an equal basis. It requires that all traders operate according to agreed rules, no one gains excessive influence, information is freely available to all and each individual market place negotiates its own outcome. Prices thus reflect real (not prejudiced) forces operating in society and signal to all parties what activities are most (or least) in demand, most (or least) profitable.

If growing numbers of consumers decide that smoking cigarettes is bad for them and eating organic foods is healthy, then they will reduce consumption of one and increase purchases of the other. Reduced demand for tobacco will cause market prices to fall and producers will start to lose profits. Conversely, farmers of soya beans, nuts and lentils will be enjoying rising demand and prices. Over the long term, if these market trends persist, then in the factories and fields, cigarette packers and tobacco pluckers will face falling demand, falling wages and fewer hours of work whilst wages and work conditions on farms producing organic foodstuffs via environmentally friendly methods will steadily improve. Workers will move; the allocation of resources will change; the pattern of production throughout the economy will adjust. All this is signalled by the movement of prices: in consumer-goods markets (for cigarettes and vegetables), in land and capital markets (rent, interest and profits), and in labour markets (wages).

In a perfect market system, therefore, all resources are priced in relation to their relative scarcity, are employed accordingly, and move their employment in response to price and profit signals from consumer markets. Social organisation is thus automatic, self-adjusting: Smith's 'invisible hand'.

Tradition remains the allocative mechanism in some of the poorest communities in the world:

- What crops and animals are raised on the peasant smallholdings that patchwork the land? Those that have stood the test of time and have proven to be reliable and of least risk.
- What technology is employed in production? That which is handed down from father to son (wooden ploughs still in use on fields in the Nile valley are unchanged in design from those over 3,000 years older).
- Who inherits the land when a peasant farmer dies? It is divided amongst his family survivors according to tradition.

Such practice is resistant to change not because people know no better – it is because they know only too well what works given their limited resources, often unreliable climate and the (tragically) unpredictable political environment that defines their world. Traditional practice therefore evolves over time thanks to generations of learning by trial and error. It may eventually become institutionalised in the religion and/or culture of the society such that economically efficient and rational choices may acquire a veneer of quaint custom and costume but this should not fool the observer into thinking that economic organisation is primitive or absent. There is no explicit signalling mechanism in much of the less developed world. There is no all-embracing planning nor price system that dictates who does what – but tradition functions in ways more important than first meets the eye.

The fourth dimension: the ownership of resources

- Should private individuals be free to own and employ all the means to produce wealth in an economy? If so, up to what (if any) limit? Or should this economic power be entrusted to the state?

Ownership of productive assets imparts a vested interest in their use and in the distribution of the rewards that they earn.

Command systems that are communist, not fascist, in political make-up insist on **state ownership** of resources. The exact pattern differs according to the country concerned: in the old Soviet Union and in communist China, for example, agricultural land was forcibly collectivised since the traditional, feudal pattern of former ownership was considered a direct impediment to economic development. In countries such as Poland and Hungary, however, the practice of collective farming was abandoned as unworkable.

With regard to industrial capital, in all of these economies it was state owned. Factory managers were appointed by the authorities and charged with running the enterprises consistent with planned instructions. Public ownership ensures that managers who control day-to-day operations have no entitlement to any profits made, beyond what is their due in salaries. There is no quarrel either as to the amount and nature of employment, nor to any changes in policy goals – state ownership of the means of production confers controlling influence to the leaders of the political administration, not to individual factory heads. There can be no independent operators marching to a different tune. Full employment can be guaranteed; all production plans can be implemented; use of resources for any ends not sanctioned by the state is theoretically impossible.

In a pure market economy there is no state ownership of the means of production, all are subject to **private enterprise**. Individuals are free to own and employ whatever resources they can command. Decisions on how to produce what consumers demand are thus taken by independent entrepreneurs, who, if they calculate correctly, are then entitled to pocket any rewards left after paying off their costs. If incorrect, they are free to go bust.

Private ownership thus ensures that business practices are determined by those with a vested interest in successful outcomes. If entrepreneurs get it wrong, then – with no state support – they must move quickly to change their production plans. Going bust means they will have to sell out to someone else who will have different ideas on how best to employ their resources and how to spend any profits made.

The size to which privately owned enterprises can grow depends on the amount of capital that can be accumulated. Although many may start as one-man businesses, they will never grow to enjoy the advantages of large-scale production unless a means can be found to pool the resources of a large number of wealth holders or capitalists. Corporate enterprise first became really successful in the time of Europe's merchant adventurers -when a number of private traders would raise enough funds between them to equip a ship, hire a captain and crew and then send it out to the Indies to return laden with spices for sale. The enterprising merchants would all then share in the profits in accordance with the size of their original capital contribution.

The idea caught on. Individual investors might only contribute a limited amount of capital, but large numbers together could share in a multi-million dollar corporation that could grow to make massive profits. Two safety features of shareholding encouraged the expansion of this form of enterprise: If the small investor wanted to get his money out then he didn't have to apply to wind up the business, he could simply sell his share to a third party (in a stock exchange); also, if disaster happened and the company incurred massive debts then, at worst, the small investor would lose only his share. With *limited liability*, he could not be forced to pay any more.

Given this security, incorporated enterprises could thus grow over time to exploit *economies of scale* – becoming big enough to drive down prices and costs of their inputs, to invest in new technologies and to position themselves with respect to business rivals and governments so as to maximise profits.

Any dispute in the market place as to what, how or for whom the means of production should be employed is thus decided by the power of profits. Private property rights confer on the most successful corporation the power to outbid others and thus to determine the direction and purpose of economic activity. What style of football should the national team play? What repertoire will be featured in theatres, music halls and on the air-waves?

Who will be employed doing what in the industrial heartlands? Those who have guessed or manipulated the public mood correctly and most consistently in the past will have the deepest pockets and thus the economic power to make these decisions. The state will not.

Communal ownership distinguishes many parts of the less-developed world. Individual *property rights* are absent or not formally recognised in law and instead there may exist an informal entitlement for all to share common resources in an agreed way. In nomadic native communities far from the reach of the money economy there may be no need nor understanding of property rights beyond the possession of a few personal belongings. Such people may no more own the land than the animals that roam upon it. But such communities are increasingly rare today; a more common explanation for the absence of property rights is that they are too difficult to acquire. Poorer people therefore survive on (continually threatened) communal property such as traditional farmlands, reservations, urban shanty towns and informal employment since they cannot gain access to legal entitlement.

The absence of property rights protected by law has become recognised as *the* prime cause of continuing poverty and underdevelopment. A family may have constructed and lived in their own house on the margins of a big city for generations. The local community may well recognise and accept this fact but the law may not. As such, therefore, the family will find it impossible to use their property as security to raise a loan. Without savings and investment the family – and by extension all communities like them – cannot prosper. Without property rights, no individual business can protect itself from those who back out on a deal nor those who (legally) can buy their land, capital and ideas out from under them. Communal ownership condemns the community to economic powerlessness.

The fifth dimension: the pattern of industry

- What is the nature of interaction between institutions in the economy? Are they partners or rivals? Is it cooperation, competition or collusion?

- Is the pattern of production across the community characterised by a few giant monopolies or is it instead atomised into numerous smaller operatives?

Businesses can work in league with others; or independently and at odds with them. They can be large or small; many or few. The network of institutions within the economy may display a variety of such patterns.

An economy based on central command will create **state monopolies** in each and every sector of industrial activity. The production of steel, locomotives, energy and transport will all have to be coordinated to meet state requirements, for example – there is no economic sense in producing more locomotives than the country's transport network can handle. Efficient communication and cooperation between all producers is essential since all are performing complementary tasks. There is no economic rationale for competition in industry, given these circumstances. Indeed, it would militate against any sensible and efficient means of conducting business if different producers insisted on independence and tried to outdo, rather than assist, each other.

In command systems there is additionally and inevitably the incentive – in order to facilitate planning and to exploit cost-reducing economies of scale – to concentrate the resources of specific industries on one site, or at least on very few sites. State monopolies lead naturally to giantism in the heavy industries, therefore.

In contrast, the pure market economy cannot function efficiently without **competition**. Any coordination of decision-making between different producers is not designed, not planned for, but is instead the evolutionary outcome of unregulated market forces.

Since there is no restriction on who can employ resources and make profits (or losses), competitive industry is characterised by the freedom of entry and exit of independent agents. The free market reigns: all are out to make money – ultimately at the expense of rivals. Such a situation ensures only the most efficient survive, and also that all consumers have alternative goods and services to choose between – all resources have alternative employments.

The need to succeed, and the fear of failure, makes it imperative to improve resources all the time in a competitive environment. Labour must continually upgrade its skills, capital must incorporate the very latest technology, land must be improved to increase its productivity and entrepreneurs must be ever more enterprising. From the point of view of society, such business practices are indeed to be welcomed but the irony is that competition may promote its own eventual corruption: the most efficient, innovative and profitable enterprises grow at the expense of the rest such that *oligopoly* results. A few large, rival corporations come to dominate most markets.

Now, where each enterprise disputes market control with two or three well-known rivals, business behaviour is characterised by caution, *tacit collusion* and, only on rare occasions, aggressive competition.

A given market place may once have been inhabited by many competing businesses but, as the least successful go broke or get taken over, a few large corporations evolve. Typically, there will be an informal hierarchy amongst them according to the market share each commands but every enterprise will be painfully aware that its own economic fortunes are dependent to a significant extent on the behaviour of the others. With so few players remaining, any increased growth for one is likely to be at the directly observable expense of another. Such provocation is unlikely to go unanswered! Generally speaking, the smaller the number of rivals, the more similar they are in size and the more stable is market demand, then the greater the sensitivity of all operators – the greater the reluctance to disturb the status quo. Oligopolists will prefer to collude in maintaining prices at a profitable level, limiting competition to the realms of advertising and marketing gimmicks, rather than initiate a damaging price war. When one rival undercuts the others in the attempt to win sales it only results in everyone else following suit such that the same market shares result for all but everyone earns less. This may be good news for consumers but it is no way for the corporations to maximise profits.

A relatively rich, noisy and flamboyant market sector may coexist with a much poorer but economically tenacious **informal sector** that thrives alongside it. The scale of operation is typically small (one-man or family based); such enterprise is neither recognised nor regulated by the law but start-up costs are minimal so entry and employment is barred to no one.

The informal sector is nonetheless economically important. In poor countries, well over half of the population in the cities may work there. Scarce capital is used efficiently and economically and much native enterprise is displayed. People live on their wits to provide goods and services across their entire spectrum of economic activity: from foodstuffs to personal services; from low-tech, capital goods to manufactured products (typically made from recycled materials). Trade in legitimate items such as fast foods, jewellery, clothing, furniture, transport and tourist services is plied on the streets as well as the less legitimate supply of pirated CDs, stolen goods, illicit drugs and prostitution.

In less-developed countries, the informal sector has a complex inter-relation with the formal market sector: a corporate or government employee can buy his lunch, have his shoes shined and get his car fixed by informal street traders. As the formal economy grows and expands, it can thus generate more business also for the informal sector. At the same time, at times of economic downturn when the formal sector employee loses his job, where does he go? The informal sector acts as the residual economy that takes up the slack. With little social security provision, those cast out by big business or public office must take to the streets also.

SYSTEM FAILURE

So much for theory. The above identifies the various options taken up in the creation of an economic system but, whatever the choices a community makes, it is in the nature of economics that there are costs involved. The brief accounts given so far have glossed over the many problems involved in the way different economic systems operate.

The failures inherent in centrally planned, command economies have thundered around the world – they have been significant enough to bring down the old Soviet Union and precipitate the transition to more market-based structures throughout all of the former socialist countries of Eastern Europe. But alternative economic systems have their difficulties as well, in more subtle and pervasive ways, and those who live by the dictates of consumer or corporate sovereignty may often be too close to see the problems with any clarity. There are lessons to be learnt from studying the shortcomings of all types of economic system.

It was mentioned earlier that all economic systems have to solve the fundamental problems of *what*, *how* and *for whom* in society production takes place. We can use this classification, therefore, in examining system failures.

The command model is based on the premise that the central authorities know what is best for their country. Planning is undertaken to mobilise all necessary resources, issuing clear commands to all sectors in order to bring about desired ends.

Where a country is at a very primitive stage of its development, when there is little quarrel about what goods and services are needed for all, and where natural resources remain dormant awaiting exploitation, then command systems can be remarkably effective in securing economic growth. Corrupt and entrenched political institutions may be swept aside and living standards for all may be rapidly improved.

Problems arise, however, as soon as economies develop and become more sophisticated. The premise that the centre knows best can be challenged. What consumers want beyond bare essentials is really only known to themselves, yet the entire rationale of planning is that orders are sent from the centre, above, rather than from individuals, below. It was the supreme arrogance of Communist philosophy to assume that central planners could direct the economic organisation of the entire Soviet Union (and extend their influence also into Eastern Europe). But central control over such a vast empire could not hope to make efficient decisions over every issue down to the last detail. Waste and social injustice were rampant. In the end, how goods and services were produced and for whom they were destined had more to do with political influence than any social or economic rationale. It was only because this command model was centred on the largest, most resource-rich country on earth that they could cover up the monumental inefficiencies for so long.

An investigation into the demise and reform of the centrally planned command model follows in the next chapter but just because this extreme example of state control has not withstood the test of time it does not necessarily mean that *all* forms of government involvement in economic organisation are suspect. In fact, we shall go on to see that it is the absence of controls on market systems of whatever complexion – consumer sovereignty or corporate capitalism – which brings all sorts of problems.

There are two issues here: those relating to equity and *normative economics* (i.e. the economic system works OK, but do we like what it delivers?); and those relating to efficiency and *positive economics* (the economic system fails to work properly).

With respect to **what** goods and services are produced, there are some commodities which individual consumers may demand – such as hard drugs or offensively racist or sexist publications – but which society may prefer to outlaw. Consumer sovereignty will be prohibited in these cases. Similarly, there are other products on which corporate empires may devote enormous expense but which governments will want to closely supervise – research and development of new weapons systems, for example.

Millions and millions of dollars are spent each year on these commodities and there are undoubtedly enormous profits involved in the international trade of drugs and armaments. We can predict that the more money is forthcoming for these goods, the more of the world's resources will be devoted to producing them. But can this really go unchallenged? The fact that governments seek (not always successfully) to control these trades is an indication of the unacceptability of free markets for such products.

With regard to communal interests, markets fail to provide essential *public* or *merit goods* like decent roads, defence and police forces, sufficient health and educational services. A mind-boggling variety of cars, guns, cigarettes, breakfast cereals and glossy magazines can be attractively promoted and sold across the counter to the willing customer, but the market has no means of reaching out and demanding payment from everyone who benefits from street-lighting, or national security, for example. There is an in-built bias to produce anything (no matter how trivial or harmful) for which demand can be stimulated and access restricted to individual fee-payers. Other goods and services which bring immense benefits to all the public and for which demand cannot be necessarily restricted only to those who pay for them will find few producers.

This leads us to consider more carefully **how** markets organise production, and particularly how efficiently prices function. The price mechanism is lauded as an automatic and unprejudiced signalling device which communicates consumer and producer decisions to all parties so as to promote the most economically efficient outcomes. For example, a change in consumer tastes away from genetically modified foods will cause profit-seeking farmers to invest in organic products; the competition between computer software companies will bring more sophisticated games onto the market at affordable prices.

But efficient markets require perfect information and perfect competition and there are plenty of instances when one or the other of these conditions are missing. The progress of science shows us that information is never 'perfect'. Are technological breakthroughs in the production of genetically modified foods helpful or harmful? In the time it takes to conduct conclusive research, rumours abound. Meanwhile, consumer demand swings from one extreme to another and valuable investments are wasted. Herd-like behaviour is particularly notorious in financial markets where doubts over a particular currency can cause panic selling and whole countries can suffer the consequences. (A 75 per cent devaluation of the Indonesian rupiah in the space of a few days in 1997 indicates over-reaction in the markets and a catastrophic loss of income for millions of Indonesians.)

In these examples, neither buyers nor sellers have perfect knowledge and thus rumours and false information determine what happens. There are other cases where one side of the market knows far more than the other and with this asymmetry, again, the free market 'solution' will be neither efficient nor equitable. Consumers are particularly vulnerable in the case of private medicine. Someone who is sick, worried and fearful about his/her medical condition is at the mercy of the doctor who alone has access to specialist knowledge. If profit maximisation is the only motive in the market place, without a code of ethics enforceable in law, then the ignorant and frightened patient can be scared out of every penny he or she owns.

Markets can partly safeguard against such exploitation if consumers have choice. But as already demonstrated, competition between the many can evolve into dominance by the few. Market prices then do not move much. They come to signal neither changes in consumer demands nor breakthroughs in producer technology but simply collusion and corporate power. It is preferable for oligopolists in these circumstances to limit competition to advertising and marketing campaigns – meanwhile stabilising prices at levels as high as the market will bear without causing consumer outrage.

Not only do market prices reflect some things they should not (corporate power, above), but they also leave out other important elements that ought to be included.

For example, in a market system the low price of travelling by car compared to rail transport into a city should be a reflection of the relative efficiency of the two services: if the cost to the private consumer of taking the car eventually increases (say due to rising fuel consumption, or time lost in traffic jams) then there will come a point when rail transport is preferred instead. But such calculation of private costs and benefits – which is at the heart of the free-market society – takes no account of the costs imposed on society. Cars kill and maim. They pour out pollution. They impose major transformations on urban landscapes. Lifestyles and social interaction are subtly but importantly affected.

The most efficient way to daily transport thousands of individuals from rural and suburban areas into city centres is not in separately cocooned and powered steel and metal death traps along massive land-gobbling superhighways. That is how consumers will choose to travel, however, so long as the price of car travel does not include the social costs of funeral and hospital bills, land purchase orders and environmental blight that such private decisions impose on others.

The price mechanism is thus not an automatic, objective, value-free device to organise an economy since the free market inevitably brings into the price calculus all sorts of hidden prejudices. The implications here are massively important. Not only will each and every price signal fail to some extent to reflect all the costs and benefits involved in its market determination, but by extension the sum total of these distorted market interactions will bring about an economy-wide outcome that must be far from optimum.

One result worth emphasising is the impoverishment of the environment. Priceless (literally!) natural assets such as clean air and seas are plundered without limit in unregulated markets and the long-term consequences for the planet are extremely worrying. Of course, command economies run by governments that care little about the environment can cause the same, if not worse, problems. The point is, however, that free markets embody no mechanism that is responsive to all the needs of the planet. Informed regulation is therefore essential to ensure sustainable development.

Another far-reaching implication is that market systems are chronically unstable. Decentralised decision-making allows millions of consumers and producers the freedom to organise (distort) economic resources as they so wish, but the cumulative total of their market-revealed preferences may lead to a level of aggregate demand that is either too great or too little for society to sustain. Boom and slump, inflation or unemployment results, therefore. The cyclical pattern of economic disturbance to free-market societies is well-observed but still seemingly unavoidable – related perhaps to what the famous UK economist John Maynard Keynes called 'animal spirits': the herd instinct.

Enthusiasts for market economics have argued that the system is self-adjusting and that, rather than suffer the botched attempts of governments to improve matters, the free market should simply be left to find its own equilibrium. Unfortunately, swings in economic fortune like the Great Depression of the 1930s, the inflationary 1970s and the 1990s East Asian crisis imposed penalties too great for most countries to ignore. **For whom** in society are market systems designed to serve? Only the wealthy and powerful? If property rights and the distribution of resources is heavily concentrated in the favour of a few then leaving the market to find its own solution is for many too passive and painful a policy recommendation. Where is the evidence that free markets will bring employment and personal development to the poor? Billions of Africans, Asians and Americans are still waiting.

Not only is it inequitable but some market 'solutions' might simply fail. The classic remedy for unemployment, for example, is a cut in wages – people can thus price themselves back into jobs, it is argued. But low-paid jobs are perceived as low-skilled/poor-quality work and both buyers and sellers of this form of labour may not wish to trade in it. Unemployment will become entrenched. Additionally, as Keynes famously demonstrated, if businesses follow one another and impose wage cuts across all labour markets then the level of aggregate demand – and thus employment – will fall further. Markets *need* government to regulate them.

Lastly, market systems require labour and capital to be mobile – to move out of declining industries and areas and into growing ones. The very efficiency of this process, however, causes social distress, and in the extreme, cumulative economic divergence.

Resources flow from poorer regions into richer ones in pursuit of higher rewards. Society polarises and those that lose out find it ever harder to catch up and close the economic gap that separates them from success. Without international guardians to prevent it, globalised free trade between unequals may institutionalise mechanisms that only serve to widen the gulf between richer and poorer countries.

Prices, profits and the growth performance of high-tech products tend to be high and determined within the ambit of rich countries and corporations. Meanwhile, poorer countries become stuck in the role of providers of low-tech primary products to the wealthy. Prices and prospects of these goods are fixed outside their reach in international commodity markets where individual producer countries are powerless 'price-takers'. Moreover in such a context, the interests of poorer countries are set against each other – if Brazil's coffee harvest fails, Kenya benefits; if Zambian copper production slows down, Chile earns more.

Meanwhile, multinational banks and businesses can become conduits for the exodus of capital and skilled labour from the poor world into the rich. It pays to sell goods, incur indebtedness, recruit personnel and make off with the profits. Those who praise free market mobility are usually the ones who want to take advantage of it.

There are social as well as economic consequences. Highly mobile societies lead to a decline in personal contacts and an erosion of social responsibility. Families break up; crime increases; concern for the disadvantaged fades. Physical barriers reinforce the social separation – richer people lock the doors of their cars and homes and employ security guards to protect their workplaces and shopping and leisure complexes. Market efficiency is gained at the expense of equity; individual material success is pursued in preference to social cohesion and the welfare of the community.

Through an accumulation of influences, therefore, the dynamics of the modern, competitive, atomistic market place bring about a growing malaise in lifestyles. The pursuit of self-interest; the increasing economic liberation of both women and men; the market's need for geographical and occupational mobility and its lack of adequate valuation for a sense of community and of permanence all operate to assign a low price and priority to long-term social relationships. *Short-termism* – the requirement to pay back investments quickly or face closure – is a profit horizon that rewards the break-up and sale of assets rather than putting in the time necessary to mend troubled relationships. This impairs not only the long-term health of businesses, it cripples also the development of communities, families and individual health. Statistics on crime and vandalism, divorce, suicide and mental disorder have all accelerated in the Western, market economies of North America and Europe. The numbers of divorces, single-parent families, old people living alone or apart from caring relatives continue to increase. A market system that slowly, relentlessly, robs us of our humanity is not a system we can triumphantly celebrate. It can destroy the very fabric of society.

CONCLUSION: GETTING THE MIX RIGHT

Building an economic system is a practical problem, not a theoretical exercise. No command system ever functioned without the presence of some markets; nor has any market economy ever operated without state intervention of some kind.

We have seen that normative and positive economic problems exist at either social extreme: in command and market economies conditions are created that we find both distasteful and economically inefficient. Solving these problems, getting the mix right between how far markets should be left to themselves and how far central authorities should intervene, is the business of political economy – it is for each country to decide in accordance with its own political and economic institutions.

The end of the twentieth century has seen a marked shift in the world away from extensive government intervention and towards increasing resort to decentralised markets as a means of solving problems of economic organisation. This change has been most revolutionary in the case of the former Soviet Union and Eastern Europe (see following chapter), but it has also occurred on the mainland of China and has been a feature of deregulating and privatising governments all round the globe from South America to East Asia. There are very few countries which have not felt the impact of this shift in economic philosophy.

But has the pendulum swung too far? By letting the wealth-creators have their head has this not been to the cost of the poor and powerless? This has certainly been the claim of many who participate in violent protests against the effects of free trade and global capitalism. Are they correct? The debate continues and its focus changes with the march of time. Questions asked today are outdated with the onset of the next crisis: Can either private financial institutions or public authority be trusted to invest people's money wisely? Is trade and growth at the expense of equity? How can environmental degradation be halted, if not actually reversed? And finally – even if we could get the degree of government control about right for one country, how can we secure the same for the world economy as a whole?

There is no one mixed economy solution that is ideal for all communities, nor for one country for all time. The blend of government, corporate or consumer sovereignty; state or self-interest; planning and prices; public or private ownership; monopoly or competition must be kept continually under review by governments and individuals so as to maximise efficiency gains and guard against abuses. Changing internal or external circumstances bring unforeseen social costs or benefits, and so the mix must change again. For the world as a whole, the balance of economic gain versus pain will seem to favour some communities at some times before it then moves elsewhere. This book is an attempt to examine some of these issues but note that whatever conclusions we come to, they are certain to be short lived. The world economy never stands still for long.

BOX 1.1 GETTING THE MIX RIGHT IN THE BRAZILIAN RAINFOREST

Over 14 per cent of the Amazon rainforest in Brazil has been lost over the last thirty years or so thanks to the greedy pursuit of profit. But this is not just the result of the unrestricted operation of free market economics – it has been encouraged by misguided incentive schemes of the government.

Grants were provided for those interested in developing the jungle for farming – even though the land, when cleared, was unproductive. Some businesses therefore just grabbed the grants, sold what commercial timber could be quickly felled and then abandoned the land they had plundered.

Other enterprises would desecrate the forest but use the useless land to declare incomes earned in business ventures made elsewhere – thereby cashing in on the tax-free status of 'farming'.

In the meantime, 15,000 square kilometres of Amazon forest per year would be slashed and burnt and lost forever – together with the infinite variety of species that is so diverse that biologists cannot catalogue the half of it.

Brazil is a huge country which contains some of the poorest people on earth as well as immensely rich eco-diversity. The trick is to improve the wealth of the nation at the same time as not impoverishing their environmental heritage – but getting the mix right between private markets and government controls has not been easy.

The irresistible force of consumer sovereignty, however, can be employed to the good. As incomes rise, 'green' consumers are increasingly demanding products of environmentally friendly practice and are prepared to pay the premium for this choice. In forestry this means producers can earn more for hardwoods that are certified as coming from sustainable forestry practice.

Public authority must therefore exercise careful control of certification. Instead of rushing into the jungle, hacking down the big trees, destroying the forest canopy and then letting the ecological cancer so released degrade the rest of the land around, loggers can thus learn ways of felling trees that avoid damaging everything else in the vicinity. Carefully managed, the forest can be harvested in a way that allows for healthy regeneration – leaving a critical minimum of big trees per hectare – and thus private enterprise is assured of profits that continue in the long term. This is both good for private incomes and good for species survival.

Source: *The Economist*, 12 May 2001, p. 117

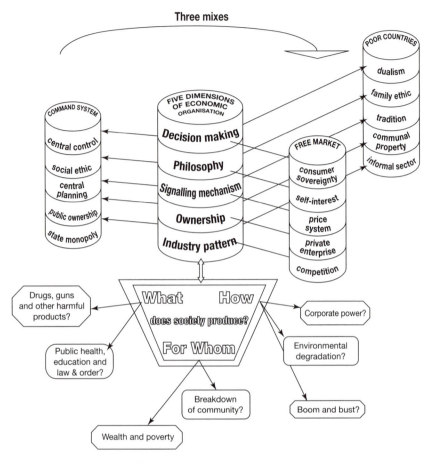

Figure 1.1 The themes of chapter 1

KEY WORDS

Command system   This is an economic system where most decisions about what, how and for whom goods and services are produced are taken by a central authority. Planning, rather than prices, tends to be the organising mechanism in such communities. (Note that the political character of the central authority is indeterminate: it may be left or right wing; such governments may inherit power, seize it or be voted in. The key to economic organisation, however, is that most decisions are taken by command.)

Dualism   exists when extremes of wealth and poverty seem to live side by side in formal and informal sector business. It results when access to development is denied to many – usually because it is very costly to exploit opportunities, gain official recognition and capitalise on a business idea. Foreign or domestic elites can accumulate wealth and invest in impressive buildings, businesses and lifestyles whereas poorer peoples with little property and less protection in law can rely only on their own underdeveloped ingenuity and very limited capital to construct their futures.

Economies of scale   If a business can increase its scale of operations by, say, doubling all inputs it may make cost savings such that it can more than double its outputs. Take a simple box. If you double its dimensions you will need four times as much material to make it, but its volume will increase by eight times. The average cost of storing the box's contents falls, therefore, by half. All businesses involved in storing processing and transporting large volumes can exploit this economy of scale. There are a number of other advantages of bigness – for example, a large firm can bargain for discounts on all its purchases – though a business can only benefit from these economies of scale if it has a big market it can sell to.

Formal and informal sectors   exist in all countries and refer to those economic activities which are recognised by the state and those which are not. The former are subject to the law, official measurement, regulation, taxation and, in consequence, they figure in official statistics. They vary in size from small, one-person businesses to multinational corporations. Informal sector businesses are unofficial, they may or may not attempt to evade detection, they tend to be small, family-and-friends enterprises but can extend to large networks of contacts across a country and overseas. Informal sector enterprise ranges from subsistence farmers to urban stall-holders, workshops, repair services and drug-running cartels. Such operations can be very productive, extremely economic in their use of capital and may offer much employment, albeit at low wages. The informal sector *can* act as a residual pool of resources to formal sector employment that shrinks in size as booming conditions mean regular businesses are looking for talent and then takes up the slack in times of recession when formal enterprise is cutting back – though such a straight-forward relationship between the two sectors is probably an over-simplification.

Limited liability   If you own a small share of a business that gets seriously into debt then – if other owners cannot pay – you may be called upon to pay all the bills. Such unlimited liability would frighten off anyone thinking of investing in business! But if your liability is *limited* only to the extent of your shareholding and no more (that may anyway be quite enough) then this is much more likely to inspire confidence in investment. Large corporations or public limited companies (PLCs) can thus be built up with millions and millions of shareholders each contributing a relatively small fraction of the total capital.

Market system   A market economy is one in which goods and services are freely exchanged for one another and prices are determined by individual traders – the impersonal forces of supply and demand. People sell their labour to private industry and use their incomes so earned to purchase whatever goods and services they desire. The economic organisation of society is thus decentralised, invisible and automatic – the movement of prices indicates to producers and consumers where they can best employ their resources.

Merit goods   are those which carry substantial external benefits, like education and health. Such services can be provided privately through the market place, but all of society gains if everyone has access to these at low cost. You benefit if you live in an educated community where all your neighbours are inoculated against disease – irrespective of their incomes.

Monopoly   A monopoly is a large, single supplier that dominates an industry. Private monopolies can make huge profits by charging higher prices than a competitive firm would demand – for this reason they tend to be either outlawed in market societies or taken over by the state. Public monopolies are common, intending to provide public services (e.g. postal services, transport, etc.) at low cost. The lack of competition for such giants, however, whether privately or publicly owned, tends to breed inefficiency: there is no incentive to serve the public well since consumers have no other choice of producer to buy from.

Oligopoly   This is an industry dominated by a few, large, economically powerful businesses. Monopoly – a single giant that has no rivals – is outlawed in many private market places since such operators inevitably charge exploitative prices with no fear of competition. Oligopolies are common, however, and where rivalry is confined to power plays between a select few big enterprises then marketing hype becomes a sophisticated, multi-billion-dollar activity dedicated to manipulating consumer tastes.

Positive and normative economics   A positive economics statement is one which is theoretically testable: it can be proven true or false. A normative statement involves a value judgement, the expression of a preference or opinion, and as such is not testable.

Property rights   Private property rights form the foundation stone upon which market systems are built. Trade can only be possible if sole rights to the property to be exchanged are guaranteed. You wouldn't exchange hard-earned cash to purchase any item if you weren't sure it was yours to keep. Similarly, both the labourer and the capitalist will invest in the future if they are assured of receiving the gains produced but if they are denied that right then neither will make the effort. Economic progress stands or falls on this principle.

Public goods   Some goods and services must be provided communally or not at all – like national defence. Consumers do not line up to pay for such services because if I enjoy freedom from foreign invasion so too does my neighbour. If I could buy such defence, therefore, my non-paying neighbour could not be excluded from enjoying it. No market system will supply such commodities if people will not pay the price. They have to be provided via public taxation.

Short-termism   This is the get-rich-quick attitude that discounts the future and wants rewards now rather than later. Without denying that cash in the hand today is better than cash in the hand tomorrow, it all depends on the price. Would you prefer $100 today or $101 next year? How about $110? Or $1000? What price is worth the wait? Investments of uncertain return that take a very long time to bear fruit are likely to be ignored in markets that take a short term view – but note that this means that there will be very little, if any, investment in education, having children, getting married even . . .

Tacit collusion   Rival corporations may come to an understanding not to rock the boat when there are mutual gains to be had from relative inaction. There may be no overt communication between us – especially if the law actually forbids this – but you and I both know that we if can cut our internal costs yet leave market prices standing we will see our profits increasing. Similarly, it suits us both if we can keep other competitors from sharing in our good fortune. So if I play a few dirty tricks to frustrate some young upstart company trying to break into our market – you wouldn't blow the whistle on me, would you?

QUESTIONS

1 Examine the claim that increasing international trade leads to a widening gap of global incomes between rich and poor countries.
2 'The planet cannot survive the corrupting influence of the politician's lust for power nor the capitalist's greed for profits.' Is the environment best protected by the actions of governments, corporations or individual members of the public?
3 What are the normative and positive economic criticisms of unrestricted growth in corporate capitalism? What role of the government would you recommend in the light of these criticisms?
4 Market prices do not reflect the true economic costs of production. Why? What are the implications for market societies?

5 Contrast the suitability of planning and price mechanisms in organising the allocation of a nation's school students to university places.

FURTHER READING

Crouch, Colin and Marquand, David (eds). *Ethics and Markets*. Blackwell, 1993.
Nove, Alec. *The Economics of Feasible Socialism Revisited*. Allen & Unwin, 1991.
Ravallion, M. 'Growth, inequality and poverty: looking beyond averages', The World Bank Development Research Group (March 2001), http://www.worldbank.org/.
The Economist magazine, 'Poverty and property rights', 31 March 2001.

2 The transition economies

Topics to be considered in this chapter:

- The institutional foundations for trade.
- The inefficiencies of command systems.
- The package of market reforms.
- Quick or slow reform? Different starting points and strategies.
- Chinese and Russian transition pathways.

INTRODUCTION

Pre-industrial Europe possessed a feudal social order where resources were employed according to tradition. Ownership of land was the key source of wealth; labour followed occupations determined by custom and social hierarchy. Neither land nor labour was marketed freely, though the product of these resources that was surplus to needs would have been.

The aristocracy owned large estates, a fraction of which would be rented out to tenant farmers, and the majority of the population would be serfs or vassals working in the fields, with rights determined by the lord in his manor, and they were tied to the land by poverty, ignorance and the law.

Over the years, populations did not grow much since both birth and death rates were high. Agriculture was the dominant employment. Before the factory age, manufacturing was limited to craft guilds and cottage industry.

Factors of production stayed in their traditional employments and so long as there was peace and social stability there was no change in these affairs. Such free trade that did take place was the exchange of produce from the farms, villages and workshops, sold in market centres across the continent, especially when harvests were plentiful.

In traditional societies, technology is slow to change and economic growth is minimal. There is little incentive to allocate resources more efficiently, cut costs and pursue profits: not at the top of the social order, since aristocrats already enjoy superior status, and not at the bottom of society either, since any increase in workers' output becomes the property of the landlord, not the labourer.

The only way to reallocate resources – that is, to redistribute the employment of land and labour in a feudal economy – would be to resort to seizing what belonged to others. In fact, over generations, intermittent conflicts had tended to produce a competitive equilibrium with title to land vested in many well-established families, so any disturbance of such tradition would be costly and unpredictable.

Rivalries and the threat of armed conflict institutionalised the relationship between those that owned and governed the land and their subjects. In order to defend their lands against invasion or wage war against outsiders, rulers need to raise armies, feed them and fit them with weapons. For this they had to administer taxes. Rulers need the economic support of their subjects therefore and they are likely to gain more, with the costs of administration likely to be lowest, if cooperation is negotiated, agreed and codified in the law. In return, all subjects can enjoy safety from predation. The lowliest and most powerless subject can be free from exploitation by the powerful if he plays his part in the bargain, pays his dues and marches off to war when called to do so. Tradition allies with a command economy: part of feudal society's output is yielded to the centre in return for protection. Peace, order and stability suit everyone.

This does not produce economic progress, however. Stability does not induce innovation, yet innovation is essential for growth and development (see chapter 11). The only endogenous source of social change (that is, apart from random natural disasters like the Black Death) came from the relatively small class of merchants and travellers like the Venetian Marco Polo (1254–1324) who went east and Christopher Columbus (1451–1506) a Genoan who sailed West.

THE INSTITUTIONAL FOUNDATIONS FOR TRADE

By modern standards, merchant ventures in feudal times were small scale, infrequent and they induced painfully slow transformations in attitudes and economic practice. With the hindsight of history they appear momentous but, in the context of relatively settled agricultural societies where monarchies were in command and customs and futures were certain, sailing off on long journeys into the unknown were mostly not very profitable nor very popular.

Firstly, the source of funds for such enterprise was limited to wealthy nobles – the more costly the expedition, the wealthier the patron needed to be (Columbus needed the backing of Ferdinand and Isabella of Spain after first being turned down by the king of Portugal). Secondly, journeying beyond the military protection of their champions necessitated the diversion of much resource to defend the expeditionaries from predation.

Institutions in traditional and unsophisticated command economies did not exist to pool capital and allocate it to competent, risk-taking entrepreneurs, nor could they meaningfully assess the dangers involved and make a calculated estimation of the rate of return. One of the most important social inventions that allowed enterprise to escape from feudal economic organisation was the joint stock company or corporation – a legal device that allows many owners of small property to band together, and creates a legal entity with the potential to be greater than the sum of its individual parts. This also facilitates a growing market in capital: businesses can raise funds from a wider base than just one family or group of friends and successful stock holders can buy out loss makers. Capital resources thus transfer from less efficient to more efficient employments, winning businesses are motivated to employ managers on the basis of merit, not nepotism, and meanwhile individual stock holders enjoy protection from uncertainty by the promise of limited liability.

Uncertainty militates against enterprise, innovation and growth. *Uncertainty*, by definition, refers to unquantifiable unknowns but it can be transformed by the systematic accumulation of relevant data into more measurable *risk*. Today, developed market economies have evolved a vast range of financial institutions that have come into existence in order to gather information, break down uncertainty, calculate risk and help people hedge against it (see chapter 7). People in economically advanced societies can now respond positively to the presence of risk by marketing it, sharing it and reducing it to manageable proportions. Such practice fails, however, in poorer traditional and command economies where these institutions do not exist or are underdeveloped.

Modern economics recognises that a fundamental determinant of any country's long-run economic performance is the quality of its institutions and social infrastructure. Where such institutions promote incentives to abide by the law, respect property and invest in the future then trade, technologies and incomes will grow. Alternatively, social structures may promote the incentive to pay bribes, seek official favours and exploit the less fortunate. Such actions are essentially short term and destructive of longer-term economic progress.

Settled agriculture is vulnerable to predation. If a farm cannot be protected from theft, then thievery may be easier and more profitable than farming. A large fraction of society will thus resort to predation and those that do farm the land will have to devote increasing resources to protecting their livelihoods. Much output is thereby lost since, at the local level, many resources are firstly devoted to thieving and secondly this only ensures that even more resources are devoted to try and counter it. Potentially the worst thieves will be the most powerful in society, unless social structures have evolved to hold them in check.

There are economies of scale to be realised if kings, rulers or governments organise collective security. It is more efficient for the laws to be policed nationally by a recognised official agency which treats all the same, than by every household trying to enforce its own agenda. Providing those in power protect everyone's property equally – from the peasant's chickens to the lord's manor house – then there can be no favour unfairly purchased from any of the king's men. Business risk becomes measurable rather than dependent on the uncertain whim of fickle rulers. Further, if a trader's word becomes enforceable in law there is incentive to invest in the future delivery of a contract. Buyers can be guaranteed a future harvest or shipment of goods, safe in the knowledge that non-compliance of contracts will be punished.

If society's institutions reward trust and can calculate risk then the economy will prosper. If social customs and constructs reward political favour, corruption and theft then resources will be diverted away from productive employment to the long-term detriment of all.

There is no greater illustration of these themes than the in the experience of the old Soviet empire and communist China through the twentieth century and into the twenty-first. These former command systems are undergoing a far-reaching overhaul of their economies with the objective of building more efficient, productive market societies. The transition the component countries involved are undergoing, however, differs in just about every case: for some in Eastern Europe, they suffered a relatively short, though undoubtedly painful, shock – but recovery has been secured and the future is now looking better. Much further to the east, the Chinese route to market has been one of long-drawn-out, gradual and a gradually accelerating transition. In between, for the old Soviet Union, there has certainly been momentous change but old habits of sucking up to political superiors and exploiting the powerless still hamper coherent and consistent economic progress.

But before analysing their different pathways to market, it is first important to study why command systems themselves were unable to deliver the economic progress that so many millions wanted and worked for.

THE INEFFICIENCIES OF MODERN COMMAND SYSTEMS

The continent of Asia is the largest and most resource-rich land mass on the planet. The command system of the former Soviet Union and its satellite states in Eastern Europe controlled the largest part of this continent for the latter half of the twentieth century and, in addition, much of the rest of Asia was admin-istered by a similar organisation of central planning – that of the communist republic of China.

Had the command systems of these countries been economically efficient in the times that they ruled, then the destiny of the world and the geo-political realities we face today in the twenty-first century would have been radically different to what we know now. However, potentially the biggest concentra-tion of economic power on the planet employed a system of organisation that hamstrung its development and condemned it to only a second-best performance compared to the West. Central planning that dominated the life of billions and provided a radically different political ideology to that prevailing in the capitalist countries proved to be monumentally wasteful. Since it could not produce rates of growth comparable to market systems, the peoples and governments of (nearly all) Asia have dispensed with it. (North Korea is holding out but even there the government cannot fool all of its people all of the time . . .)

The reasons behind the collapse of the former communist bloc countries were predominantly economic – triggering the political and social revolutions in 1989 and thereafter which brought down the old 'Iron Curtain'. Although founded on idealistic and ideological principles that still continue to win converts to this day, the waste and economic inefficiency of the command system which was supposed to embody them proved, in the end, terminal.

The key to the unravelling of Eastern Europe and the former Soviet Union lies in the systemic failures of command structures. In the 1980s, when it became apparent that Soviet President Mikhail Gorbachev was preoccupied with his own country's internal seizures and would not intervene in the social upheavals of Eastern Europe then the governments in each satellite country lost all effective power to continue. Thus the inexorable process of cumulative economic decline that had been underway for decades facilitated a sudden and sweeping chain reaction throughout the region. One regime after another was brought down in quick succession.

The abandonment of central planning in the Peoples Republic of China follows a different, and uniquely Chinese, path but the fundamental reason was the same – bit by bit, the country jettisoned an allocative mechanism that was failing to perform satisfactorily and changed it for one that worked better.

ECONOMIC DECLINE OF THE SOVIET UNION

The weaknesses of the Soviet economic engine had existed for years, indeed they were endemic, although the sheer size and power of the machine had blinded many twentieth-century observers to the problems of its inefficiency and its failing capacity for growth.

The Soviet economic slowdown had in fact been apparent in the 1970s, and despite world economic traumas such as the oil price shocks and the international financial crises which tended to obscure the picture, informed commentators were predicting that difficulties would increase a decade or more before the eventual collapse. *The Economist* in a typically partisan editorial said that: 'Economic crisis is stalking not only Poland but the whole communist world. For the Soviet Union it could be terminal. There must be increasing hope that the Soviet system will not outlast this century' (*The Economist*, 1 January 1980, p. 14).

Evidence of this economic decline is given in Table 2.1. (It should be noted that data on past Soviet performance are always quoted with reservation: official statistics require interpretation due to ideological differences in definition, quite apart from problems of political manipulation. Data available from Western sources may meanwhile not be fully complete. Whatever their source, however, in this case the overall trend is quite clear.)

Abel Aganbegyan, chief economic advisor to M. Gorbachev and main architect of his *perestroika* (restructuring) programme, stated that the data do not take into account hidden price rises and the falling quality of consumer goods. A more realistic picture is to assume that *no* GNP growth took place in

Table 2.1 Growth rate of the Soviet Union (%)

Period	GNP	GNP/head
1950–60	5.7	3.9
1960–70	5.2	3.9
1970–75	3.7	2.7
1975–80	2.6	1.8
1980–85	2.0	1.1

Source: G. Ofer, 'Soviet economic growth', *Journal of Economic Literature*, December 1987.

the period 1980–5. Indeed 'unprecedented stagnation and crisis occurred during the period 1979–82 when production of 40 per cent of all industrial goods actually fell. Agriculture declined – throughout this period it failed to reach 1978 levels' (*The Challenge: Economics of Perestroika*, Hutchinson, 1988).

REASONS FOR DECLINE

The paramount reason for such decline is the inefficiency of central planning as an allocative mechanism for advanced societies.

As a system, planning has an inherent bias towards producing quantity rather than quality. Planned targets to produce specific quantities are identifiable and enforceable. That such outputs be of good quality is a much vaguer, non-enforceable notion. Good quality cannot be adjudged by planners, administrators; it can only be determined by end-users, i.e. customers. It is for this reason, it was said, that you could only get shoes either for dwarfs or for hefty policemen – any suitable footwear had gone long before you got to the head of the queue. But 'how can this problem be overcome if plans are orders of superior authority (the central planners or ministries) and not those placed by users?' (Alec Nove, *The Economics of Feasible Socialism*, Allen & Unwin, 1983).

A look at the determinants of Soviet economic growth reinforces the impression of planning's inherent bias for quantity rather than quality and efficiency (see Table 2.2). *Throughout its entire history* as a command

Table 2.2 Growth rate of Soviet inputs and productivity (%)

Period	Combined factor inputs	Total factor productivity	
1928–40	4.0	1.7	*CIA estimate*
1950–60	4.0	1.6	1.4
1960–70	3.7	1.5	0.9
1970–75	3.7	0.0	1.5
1975–80	3.0	–0.4	–0.8
1980–85	2.5	–0.5	–1.2

Source: G. Ofer, 'Soviet economic growth', *Journal of Economic Literature*, December 1987.

economy, the Soviet Union grew due to the increased employment of labour, capital and land inputs, whilst the productivity of these inputs steadily declined. (This is diametrically opposed to the experience of all modern, market economies which have grown predominantly due to advancing technological progress applied to fixed or slow-growing inputs.)

Such a growth model cannot be sustained, of course, not even in the former Soviet Union – which was the biggest and most resource-rich country on earth. There are limits to continually expanding employment, and in the 1970s, as is evidenced above, the Soviet Union ran up against them. With the developed world's highest rates of capital investment and participation rates of population in the labour force, there was little potential left for increasing inputs. Without improvements in productivity, *diminishing returns* were inevitable.

Despite all the efforts of Soviet political leaders to reverse this trend, productivity stubbornly declined. Indeed insistence on catching up with the West served only to compound the inefficiency of the planning process. Too often unrealistic demands provoked confusion and chaos in production units. One example was the tragedy of Chernobyl, the nuclear power station that blew apart and polluted great swathes of the Ukraine and further West. A month before the disaster, a letter appeared in a Kiev newspaper from Lyubov Kovalevska, a senior manager at the plant. She wrote to complain that Soviet ministries had created chaos by advancing the completion of the construction project by one year. Lack of building materials had made it impossible to meet the new deadlines at the required standards, she wrote. Of 45,500 cubic metres of concrete purchased for the facility, 3,200 cubic metres never arrived and 'much of the rest' was substandard and unfit for its purpose.

According to economist G. Ofer, the 'strategy of haste' systematically constrained managers to meet current planned targets at the expense of making more beneficial long-term investments. In the extreme, future projects were plundered in order to deliver existing orders. Such practice was confirmed by Martin Walker, quoted in *The Economist*, 28 April 1990. He describes 'storming' in a Lithuanian TV factory – the rush to meet planned production targets in the last few days before the deadline. According to the workers involved, the incentive is to satisfy The Plan, not the customer:

> We never use a screwdriver in the last week. We hammer the screws in. We slam solder on the connections, cannibalise parts from other televisions if we have run out of the right ones, use glue or hammers to fix switches that were never meant for that model. And all the time the management is pressing us to work faster, to make the target so we all get our bonuses.

Hungarian economist Janos Kornai characterised the centrally planned countries as economies of shortage (J. Kornai, *The Economies of Shortage,* Amsterdam: North Holland, 1980), where there was high priority to invest in capital equipment in order to maintain growth and catch up the West, and inevitably lower priority attached to producing consumer goods. Allied to this there was an ideological insistence on a high defence posture and economic self-sufficiency (autarky).

Such a political/economic structure could not allow for failure to meet production targets in high priority sectors. Hence such production units operated with 'soft budget constraints' (i.e. the government bailed them out if they squandered any inputs) and lower priority sectors had to go without. *It should be apparent that there is no incentive for an economy so organised to strive to be efficient.* Although there were steadily lengthening queues to obtain basic essentials, no mechanism existed to ensure producers met consumers' needs.

Parallel with the growing incapacity of the command economies to supply their own needs was an increasing indebtedness to the West. When money was cheap after the first oil shock in the mid-1970s, communist governments – along with those in many other countries around the world – considered incurring debt was a sound policy. But it was not so much the soaring interest rates of 1979–80 that prompted their eventual debt crisis; it was more the chronic incapacity of these autarkic, inward-looking and corrupt economies to utilise their borrowed funds efficiently. In particular, the inability of the Soviet Union to help its satellite countries in Eastern Europe severely damaged its image as the strong, infallible leader of the region. On the contrary, falling deliveries of Soviet oil and other raw materials to its partners undermined any economic rationale for a COMECON pattern of trade and development and provoked more, not less, indebtedness to the West.

None of these developments escaped the notice of politicians, planners and bureaucrats of the countries involved, and every variety of economic reform consistent with Soviet dominated central authority was tried. But the message of those years is that partial economic liberalisation did not work. There was no 'third way' between a command system and a market economy. Despite all the efforts of Gorbachev's presidency to implement 'perestroika' and (in his own words) 'the union of centralism and independence of economic organisation', nothing could prevent the eventual collapse of the command economies in the massive upheavals of 1989–90. All the former Eastern bloc countries have now implemented policies to establish free-market systems within their territories. Soviet central planning is dead.

THE REFORMS

The contrasting features of command and market systems give the key to the reforms required in the transformation from one form of economic organisation to the other. I have earlier characterised the two economic systems as opposing extremes in the following spectra:

Central control   Consumer sovereignty
State doctrine   Self-interest
Planning mechanism   Price mechanism
State ownership   Private enterprise
State monopoly   Competition

The institutional changes required to move the various command economies from the left side of this range towards the right are huge, costly and time-consuming, though there is general agreement on what needs to be done. *How* this should be managed differs enormously from one country to another. It is one thing knowing where you want to get to. It is quite another to find a navigable pathway that leads you there. In the end, each country's starting conditions and the political and economic realities they faced determined the route they took.

1 Privatisation of land and capital is the most difficult yet most fundamental and important reform required. Within the pattern of ownership of society's resources are embodied issues such as the relationship of the individual to the state; freedom to pursue private, rather than communal interests; rights to employ others; the establishment of contracts; systems of law; etc. Establishing property rights is central also to changing attitudes of the people from being passive dependants to becoming entrepreneurial participators of social evolution with vested interests in future outcomes.

The Chinese agricultural revolution from the mid-1960s to the 1980s – where market incentives were introduced into the farms – showed that great increases in productivity are possible by giving the tillers of the soil the fruits of their own labour. Employing the same principle in industry means selling off the factories, setting up stock markets (to facilitate transfers of ownership), and allowing individual businessmen to decide for themselves which companies to form, which goods and services to supply, what resources to employ and how to spend any profits they make.

Only by allowing and protecting private property, with the right to retain profits, will investment in new technologies occur – ensuring that accumulated wealth is employed to society's benefit rather than being uselessly stockpiled, fleeing the country or funding corruption or extravagance.

There is one essential proviso here, however. Privatisation requires the exchange of information in open and transparent capital markets. The general public must be able to assess the potential profits to be realised in buying shares in former state enterprises. If not, gold mines will be snapped up by a greedy few: *asymmetric information* will be exploited by those with inside knowledge. Similarly, uninformed share ownership cannot keep management efficient and on their toes. Those appointed to run privatised industries may use them to enrich themselves rather than distribute profits to the owners. (This is the *principal–agent problem*, well known in market economies).

2 Price reform is essential to open up markets in all consumer and producer goods. Eliminating all subsidies and controls may be painful but 'sensible market prices are vital for efficient resource allocation' (Jeffrey Sachs: Harvard professor and advisor to the Polish and Russian governments; quoted in *The Economist*, 13 January 1990).

For too long state enterprises in the command economies were nurtured on underpriced oil, raw materials and labour. The result was that vast segments of industry were 'value subtractors' producing outputs with a net real value of less than their inputs, measured at world prices. Poland, for example, had become by the late 1980s an exporter of semi-tropical flowers as a result of an absurdly low price of energy which made it possible to heat vast glasshouses at a fraction of their true cost. Similarly, a Kazakh woman could fly thousands of subsidised miles to sell her water melons in Kiev since the value of her product was officially greater than her air ticket! Only a realistic and dynamic pricing system can prevent such monumental waste.

This implies large price increases in precisely those goods that have been in shortage for decades, but this must occur if supplies are ever to increase. Farmers will only produce more wheat, and industrialists more textiles, if their selling prices and profits move up in response to demand.

Realistic prices imply a *convertible currency* at free-floating exchange rates, thus ensuring domestic goods are valued appropriately in world terms. Industries will export those goods in which they have a comparative advantage and import those which are too costly to produce at home. Inefficient firms unable to compete with foreign products will go bust, freeing up their resources to be more productively and profitably employed elsewhere.

3 Free entry of new businesses must be ensured by breaking up the old state monopolies and providing the legal and institutional framework for new start-ups, take-overs and the accumulation and investment of profits. Privatisation and free prices are not enough – that would only convert state monopolies into private ones which would then exploit their power. Only competition can guarantee that costs and prices will be kept down and businesses will be efficient.

Stock market prices will then correctly signal which businesses best cater for consumer demand and are deserving of more investment, and which businesses are less successful in following the market and less worthy of financial support. Capital will thus flow from declining to growing sectors – providing such mobility is facilitated and not obstructed by the state.

4 Tight control of the money supply is essential if any of the above measures are to work, but it is perhaps the most difficult short-run policy for pro-market governments to implement. If governments give in to public demands for wage increases; for unemployment benefits; for subsidies to huge, ailing state enterprises producing things that nobody wants to buy, then government deficits will get out of control, money supplies will increase and inflation will result. Resources will remain tied up in all the wrong employments; deadbeat firms will remain alive; productivity, public confidence and the real value of money will all be sacrificed. It is too easy for governments to create more paper money and distribute this to those sectors of the economy with the most political clout, but since real output is unaffected this can only be at the expense of others in the economy with little or no bargaining power.

IMPLEMENTATION: SHOCK THERAPY OR GRADUAL CHANGE?

Despite similarities of economic organisation – thanks to the straitjacket of central planning – the component states that used to make up the former Soviet Union (FSU) and the Eastern European bloc were all different. The collapse of power in Moscow triggered independence movements throughout the former communist empire and this has meant that the transition towards the market model has been piloted by many different governments – each a representative of countries with their own set of political, cultural and economic characteristics.

In China, the path to transition did *not* include the overthrow of government. Instead the introduction of market mechanisms has been managed by the state and has been *de*centralised with the guiding hand of local authorities very much involved. Never as comprehensively planned, nor as industrially developed as the former Soviet Union, the delegation of Chinese economic decision-making away from the centre and down to the level of villages and individual market places has been allowed to grow according to what seemed to work best. As a result the story of gradual transition in this country varies markedly from what took place further West.

A strong sense of separate nationality exists throughout Eastern Europe and the Baltic states which were taken over by communists after World War II. These Europeans still remembered market forms of economic organisation and were united in their desire to forge links, if not become full members, with the European Union. In contrast, an independent political and economic identity is still very new in many FSU states further to the East, which tend to be more agrarian, possess lower per capita incomes and culturally, economically and politically were more locked into command rule from the Kremlin.

For some countries – e.g. Poland – sudden shock therapy was considered the most appropriate transition strategy, all the required policy reforms thus being implemented in a 'big bang' on 1 January 1990. For others – e.g. Hungary – somewhat slower change occurred. Hungary was the most market-oriented economy of them all and a mad dash to accelerate the process was judged unnecessary. Meanwhile Czechoslovakia, neither as crisis-ridden as Poland nor as liberalised as Hungary, chose an intermediate, 'minimum bang' approach, albeit involving the separation of the Czech and Slovak Republics.

The case for shock therapy in Poland was based on the advice that all the necessary reforms listed above must be introduced simultaneously since the success of any one requires success of them all. (Polish experts and advisors such as Jeffrey Sachs were convinced of this after the failure of earlier piecemeal reforms – e.g. economic liberalisation had proved incompatible with centralism: devolving management control without ownership meant industry bosses voted for pay increases and starved factories of new investment. This 'reform' did nothing, therefore, to prevent the ageing of East European capital.)

In the FSU, more rapid transition was possible in the Baltic countries which geographically and historically are closer to the West. Other states from

Armenia to Tadzhikistan – more distant from Europe, only recently politically independent and with almost no experience of free market organisation – have inevitably progressed much more slowly.

The transition record in China has been surprisingly different. Its success over the last two decades has been impressive: achieving rates of economic growth that far outstrip any other country. But the reform path it has followed differs strikingly from the standard prescriptions outlined above. That is because the piecemeal, gradual changes introduced *worked* in the Chinese case, just as they failed in East European attempts. Why? Because the transitional institutions created in China embodied incentives compatible with those in power and this therefore enabled continuing change, increasing the pace of reform.

CHINA'S ROAD TO THE MARKET: A UNIQUE STORY OF SUCCESS

In the 1970s, China was a poor, centrally planned, overpopulated country hostile to outsiders and opposed to radical reform. Its population was three times greater than that of the old Soviet Union and Eastern Europe combined but crammed into half the land area. After the self-inflicted economic disasters of the (misnamed) 'Great Leap Forward' (1958–60) and the 'Cultural Revolution' (1966–76) China's economy was half the size of Russia's and its income per capita represented only 15 per cent. Less than two decades later, however, China's economy had grown tremendously while Russia's had shrunk. In 1995, US economic historian Angus Maddison calculated that China's GDP was almost five times greater than Russia's and its income per capita had reached 60 per cent.

Since the 1980s, China has transformed itself from a poor, sluggish, highly inefficient command economy into a dynamic, emerging market society with the highest growth rate in the world and which has enriched the lives of almost a quarter of the world's population. It has been a staggering success story . . . but China has pursued an entirely unique pathway to progress that challenges all the conventional pronouncements of transition economics. How did it do it?

According to Deng Xiaoping, in charge at the start of the reform period in 1978, China's way forward has been incremental, step-by-step: 'crossing the river by feeling the stones under the feet'. It has nonetheless been consistently followed – innovatively pursued by changing political leadership over the years as the economic gains realised at each step have reinforced the desire to continue the process.

Characteristic of the Chinese way has been the introduction of reforms in a pilot or experimental fashion first of all, usually in restricted localities where results can be observed and lessons learned before broadening the scope of reforms across the country. Secondly, the Chinese have not confused ends with means. Best practice institutions – such as privatisation of all industry, full market pricing and macroeconomic stabilisation – represent the summit of the mountain to be climbed and efforts were thus devoted to finding transitional institutions that would lead to this end eventually – not get there straight away. Thirdly, as already implied in the text above, the development of the economy took place alongside political evolution, not revolution, where the overall reform programme was administered in a coherently managed and controlled socio-political context.

The first examples of such cautious pragmatism were to be found in agriculture with the introduction of *dual track pricing* and the *household responsibility system*. Official farm targets were maintained where outputs were purchased by the state at administered (low) prices. But individual households were allowed to sell any surplus over and above these quotas – grown on strips of land allocated to them – at local market prices.

After the communist revolution in 1949, Chinese agriculture had been collectivised in massive communes – which proved to be massively inefficient. The reallocation of collective land to individual households was started on a pilot basis in Anhwei province in 1978. By 1980, 14 per cent of all collective farm production teams had changed over to the household responsibility system, becoming 80 per cent by 1982 and 99 per cent by 1984.

Annual growth of farm outputs from 1957 to 1978 increased by 2.32 per cent but from 1978 to 1987 this had increased to 5.77 per cent per annum. Even more revealing was the rate of growth of farm labour productivity: *minus* 0.19 per cent a year from 1957 to 1978 but plus 4.99 per cent p.a. from 1978 to 1987 (Maddison). That is, with market incentives now, agricultural labour was working much more efficiently.

More efficient labour meant that increasing food supplies could now be secured and still resources would be left over for employment in non-farm, rural industrial activity. The institutional form this next step led to was small-scale, *township and village enterprises* (TVEs) which were market driven but mostly local authority owned. In the absence of privatisation and with less-than-secure property rights this novel industrial arrangement nonetheless served to increase incentives for profit-seeking entrepreneurs *and* bought the support of local government who could use these TVEs as revenue raising devices. Both private and public sector interests thus earned income from TVEs and, with this, political support for the extension of market practice was won over (see Figure 2.1).

Opening the economy to the stimulus of world trade was similarly begun in a restricted fashion first of all: four coastal special enterprise zones (SEZs), or free trade areas, were set up in 1980 where all imports and exports were duty free, where wages were low by world standards and where new enterprises enjoyed substantial tax holidays. International trade boomed (see Table 2.3). The SEZs increased in economic activity and population to embrace fourteen coastal cities by 1984 and in 1988 a fifth SEZ was created.

In 1978 China was in receipt of virtually no foreign direct investment. By 1996 it had received $174.9 billion. Maddison states that 63 per cent of this came from Hong Kong, Taiwan and Singapore – overseas Chinese who had retained contacts with the mainland, who could see the economic potential and knew how to exploit it. The SEZs thus became important vehicles for the

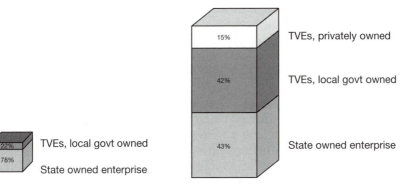

1978: 423.7 bn yuan   **1993: 4,840.2 bn yuan**

Figure 2.1 Shares of Chinese industrial output, 1978 and 1993

transfer of capital, technology, management training and the development of international contacts.

It has not all been a success, however. In China as in all other transition economies further West, the biggest unsolved problem has been what to do with large, state-owned enterprises (SOEs). These huge concentrations of industrial assets were formed under the old command system to facilitate direct political control of the economy and, whilst TVEs and privately owned businesses have been allowed to blossom around them, SOEs still constitute the backbone of the nation. They produce everything from military equipment to children's toys to state hotels. Their contribution to the GDP has fallen now to about one-quarter of industrial output but they still employ millions (inefficiently) and provide a vital source of social benefits to their employees (e.g. health and education services). SOEs provide revenue for over half of the national government's budget and yet they also represent a huge financial burden since they have received enormous sums of state allocated funds from the banking sector and there is little likelihood that these loss-making enterprises can repay them.

Table 2.3 Growth rates of Chinese income per head and export trade

Annual growth of Chinese GDP per capita		
1913–52	*1952–78*	*1978–95*
–0.1%	2.3%	6.0%

Annual growth of exports		
1929–52	*1952–78*	*1978–95*
–1.3%	6.4%	13.5%

Source: Maddison.

In world terms, China is a huge and still relatively poor country which has a long way to go before it can catch up with Western living standards. But partly because of this, its recent growth rate has been rapid (see Figures 2.2 and 2.3) and many observers claim it will not slow down for some time yet. China's success has been in finding transitional institutions, which if not perfect have nonetheless served to help the nation forward in its long journey. Dual track pricing, TVEs and the delegation of economic decision-making from national to local government have satisfied political masters as well as rewarded private enterprise. There is still a long way to go: private ownership of land is still restricted, SOEs have not been privatised and an unreformed financial sector with stubbornly creeping inflation remains a major worry. But measured in terms of the changes so far achieved and in raising the incomes of billions, China's story is one of outstanding success.

TRANSITIONAL INSTITUTIONS IN RUSSIA

Since the 1990s, whereas China's economy has grown at one of the highest rates in the world, Russia's has grown at one of the slowest. The reason for this is related to the different nature of transitional institutions which have evolved to guide private-sector activity.

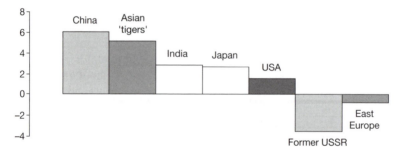

Figure 2.2 % annual growth of per capita GDP 1978–95

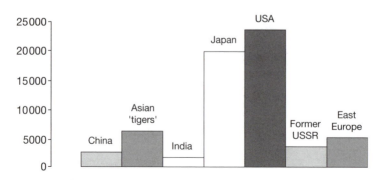

Figure 2.3 Income per head in US$, 1995

Source: World Bank.

The road to reform in Russia began with a big bang in 1992 and a package of measures aimed at spreading privatisation, lifting controls and freeing up the economy to respond to market incentives. With the dismantling of central command came a precipitous drop in output throughout old Soviet industry (see Figure 2.4). It was consumers and not government planners that placed orders now. A rapid rise in inflation occurred as pent-up consumer demand was released onto a market place characterised by shortage. Despite this, many small businesses sprung up in a climate of optimism, even though they could not compensate for the confusion and decline in big state industries.

The extent of the fall in Russian GDP is difficult to calculate for many reasons – political manipulation of the data, no reliable market measures of value, rapid changes in relative prices, unrecorded growth of the informal sector – but best estimates vary from a decline of approximately 40 to 50 per cent of national income from 1989 to 1996. The welfare effect of this collapse was less, however, since much of this decline occurred in heavy capital and military goods production and not in essential consumer goods and services.

The pace of privatisation and liberalisation picked up through the 1990s such that from 100 per cent state ownership in 1989, a smaller Russian industrial sector had attained 60 per cent private ownership by 1998. This progress, though encouraging, was however *not* matched by essential complementary reforms such as establishing an infrastructure of legal, financial and administrative institutions: i.e., an independent judiciary, central bank and government.

In China, transition took place under the tight control of the central government which delegated economic decision-making to local authorities in a clear, unambiguous manner. In contrast in Russia, transition occurred with what some observers have called a dysfunctional democracy where there was neither imposed central control nor clear rules of market operations. In principle,

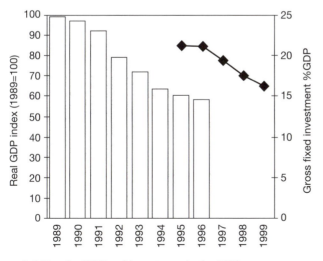

Figure 2.4 Russia: GDP and investment in the 1990s

property rights were better protected in newly enacted laws in Russia than in China, but in practice the spread of corruption, the distortions of Russian banking and finance and the unpredictable actions of both local and central governments have meant that foreign investors have consistently voted China as a safer place to do business than Russia. Figure 2.5 shows Russia as the only transition country to register an *outflow* of funds in the 1990s: domestic and foreign capitalists were, on balance, anxious to get their money out of the country, not into it.

Russia, unlike China, was a fully industrialised country at the outset of transition – dominated by a structure of huge, state owned enterprises (SOEs) which left little room for the private sector to grow up unchallenged. In fact, local authorities were used as a means to *obstruct* the private sector – SOEs paying bribes for protection such that local politicians had a vested interest in blocking market competition rather than (in the Chinese case) promoting private-sector growth and profits.

The distorted evolution of Russia's financial institutions added to the problems. From 1989 to 1998, while the real economy was contracting as indicated above the number of commercial banks increased from around 100 to 2,500. What were these banks up to? Not lending to the private sector. They were doing their best to attract deposits from domestic and foreign savers in order to invest in local and particularly national government securities. *Financial intermediaries* in Western developed nations function to attract funds from individual and corporate savers, to collect financial information and assess risks of potential outlets and thus to allocate finance to the most efficient private sector investors (see chapter 7). In Russia, banks grew up to funnel funds into government, not industry. *Rent-seeking* was more profitable than investing in business. And in the hands of the government, the public allocation of these monies was not going to promote growthful, profitable outlets. Some were propping up loss-making SOEs, paying for welfare and social security programmes and supporting regional aid; other funds were paying off political favours and building up private empires. And all the time, the real economy was faltering and, with it, tax revenues were falling and social security demands rising.

Early in 1998 it became clear that the Russian government's *budget deficit* was unmanageable. Expenditures were outgrowing income. International

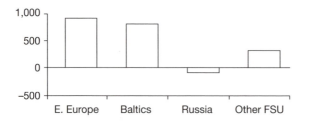

Figure 2.5 Net capital flows, 1992–7 (1994–7 in the case of Russia)

agencies which had loaned vast sums to Russia became worried about the risk of default and the continuing lack of any structural reform in the country. World commodity prices were falling (bad news for a country whose only claim to wealth was its resource base) and interest rates rose. The fragile Russian banking system was stuck with loans to the government which were in danger of never being repaid, plus large foreign currency debts and a seriously over-valued rouble.

On 17 August 1998 meltdown occurred. The government announced a moratorium on all debts it owed to home and foreign creditors. The rouble sunk like a stone on the foreign exchanges; year-on-year inflation rose from a target of 8 per cent to 85 per cent; real incomes contracted 28 per cent compared to 1997. Those living in poverty increased and, yet again, people turned to the streets to barter their belongings. Infant mortality, malnutrition and illness rose. Life expectancy fell.

Ironically, the collapse of Russia's transitional financial infrastructure brought about some reform. Although many commercial banks with large government security holdings collapsed, those that survived the 1998 crash now reallocated more of their loans to the real sector rather than just to the government. Importantly, world commodity prices began to rise, thanks to booming demand from big consumers such as China, India, the USA and Europe. As a result the Russian economy began to recover. The many struggling (but inevitably efficient) firms that had had to rely on their own resources could now attract finance, investment and expansion. Since the bottom of the recession in 1998, Russia has posted positive growth rates.

Political instability continues to be an issue, however. At the time of writing, President Putin's government is seizing oil and gas industry assets and impris-oning executives for alleged tax evasion – yet the break-up and re-structuring of the Russian oil industry is being carried out by political cronies. For whose eventual benefit? Confidence in secure property rights and the rule of law is shaken.

Certainly the culture of tax avoidance and the evasion of regulations and social responsibility must change. The banking system still has some way to go before it becomes a competitive, stable and trustworthy conduit for domestic savings into much needed industrial investment, free from special interests. The rule of law must grow in authority to overcome powerful and corrupting vested interests. Government must serve as an impartial promoter of national interest and not become a vehicle for predation and the abuse of power. A sustained rise

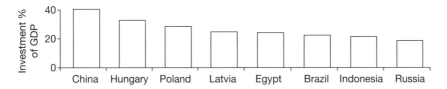

Figure 2.6 Cross-country comparisons of investment, 1998

in the price of oil and gas can bring windfall gains in export incomes but for whose benefit? Without more reform of institutional infrastructure this will not promote competitive and efficient private industry. A successful transition to an equitable and efficient market economy is thus not assured. Too many questions still hang over Russia's future.

CONCLUSIONS

Those countries that started earliest and have been most consistent in following the path to market reform have inevitably come the furthest to date. Political acceptability of the necessary changes has likewise been easiest in those Eastern European countries where central control was always resented as a recent imposition on previously successful and independent societies and where the promise of early entry into the European Community has kept minds focused on the task of building market economies.

Some reforms have gone better than others. Releasing prices from official controls and allowing them to rise or fall as trade dictates is easier than remaining unmoved by the cries of suffering and refusing to print more money. Likewise, removing restraints on private entrepreneurs and allowing the rise of a private sector has been easier in certain countries than limiting the accumulation of economic power released into the hands of a few *oligarchs*.

The winners and losers under a market system are different to those in command economies. The miners, shipbuilders and steelworkers who enjoyed high status and pay under communism – and ironically were in the forefront of those pushing for reforms in Poland and Russia – are those the market has least need for. The future belongs to people with adaptive entrepreneurial skills, not heroic metal-bashers. Small traders, restaurateurs and informal, semi-legal businessmen have experienced a far faster appreciation of their earnings than state-sector stalwarts. The biggest winners of all have been those quickest to play in under-regulated financial markets.

In all markets, sensible prices are vital. Setting the right price for a country's currency is particularly so: if it is overvalued then domestic industry will find it impossible to sell its products abroad. Imports of Western capital and consumer goods may be cheap (helping contain inflation) but the key constraint on restructuring a former command economy is finding markets for what can be produced. Selling rather low-quality products is difficult enough without overpricing them. East German industry's unique access to the immense European Community, for example, served only to drive much of it into early bankruptcy when the Ostmark's union with the Deutschmark was at too high a price. Chinese manufactured exports, on the other hand, have flooded world markets by pegging the yuan at a low price.

A realistic price for labour is important for exactly the same reason. In European terms, the old state industries were overstaffed and underskilled. Employment prospects are best, therefore, if local labour is cheaper than alternatives. Owing to wage demands secured after unification, East German workers cost more than Portuguese and Irish labour but were far less productive. Small wonder they attracted insufficient employment.

A willingness to adapt and experiment, with an unclouded vision of where you want to get to, has proved to be essential in China's success. If state owned enterprises still tie up too much capital, if private property rights are still not formalised, and if all resources are not yet freely tradable then progress will be hampered, but providing public and private decision-makers are nonetheless working together to remove restrictions and promote growth, then the transitional institutions at first constructed may not be perfect – but may evolve that way.

Where there is insufficient protection from predation by those with economic power, where the rules for business conduct are neither drawn up nor implemented to guarantee equal treatment for all, then small enterprises will never thrive. The investment climate is too uncertain. The future of the Russian economy is not dependent on enormous concentrations of resource wealth such as Gazprom – now one of the world's biggest suppliers of natural gas. It depends on small start-ups of innovative entrepreneurs. Market economies need solid foundations to grow healthily: an infrastructure of secure property rights, enforced without favour; an environment where risks are calculable and not dependent on government diktat. Growth requires innovation; innovation requires resources to move freely to efficient employments; rates of return will signal efficient investment opportunities only where competition rules – that is, where small, medium and large businesses can compete on level playing fields. Lastly, in a global market place, countries will attract limitless funds from abroad providing international as well as domestic investors are free from predation.

Fundamentally, the success or failure of the transition process is not therefore dependent on foreign influence. It lies within the grasp of the peoples of Eastern Europe, the former Soviet empire and China – and particularly it rests in the hands of their political leaders. A new economic order needs to be built.

There is no mystery as to what needs to be done, nor any illusion now as to the costs involved. Centralisation, collectivisation and cronyism has to go. For China perhaps – agricultural and less developed than the others – industry did not need to be dismantled, just set free to grow. East Europe has paid a higher price in redeploying labour and capital but has shown the way. What is still lacking in those FSU states that have still to reverse their economic fortunes, however, are the institutions to promote a sense of national will to get the job done, to provide the incentives and to enforce the rule of law. It is a lack of leadership; of good government. Yegor Gaidar, ex-prime minister of Russia and one of the prime advocates of reform, said in 1999 that the old socialist system may have embodied soft budget constraints but it at least exercised rigid administrative control which kept enterprise managers on their toes. Now the country has neither budgetary nor administrative discipline. It has *kleptocapitalism*. Oligarchs in cahoots with government have seized control of enormous assets and Russia has been diverted away from the goal of building

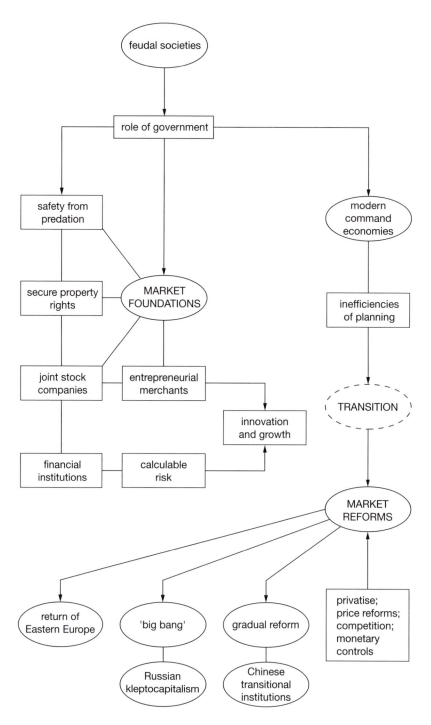

Figure 2.7 The themes of chapter 2

a competitive market environment. The country blunders on with the worst of both worlds in which self-interest, corruption and the abuse of power all flourish. Russia still falters at a crossroads, uncertain as to whether economic activity is to be regulated by law and order or poisoned by political influence, crime and cronyism.

The future of Russia is crucial. Huge, populous, resource rich and still militarily powerful it straddles Asia and provides markets and sources of supplies for a host of neighbour states. If its deep-rooted structural problems are successfully addressed it will drag itself up by its boot-straps and bring most of the continent with it. If it does not, if it continues to tear itself apart by internal crises, then its future will be bleak and its instability will continue to threaten all those nations which have only recently escaped its iron embrace.

KEY WORDS

Asymmetric information   will cause any market to fail. Buyers and sellers must *both* be informed about the real worth of the item traded if a fair and efficient price is to be determined. An efficient allocation of society's resources is impossible in a market economy if one side to a bargain exploits the other. Land, labour and capital will be employed sub-optimally if the most productive deployments are *not* signalled via the price mechanism. See *kleptocapitalism* and *privatisation*.

A **budget deficit**   occurs when a government's spending exceeds its income, thus requiring it to borrow more. A budget surplus is the opposite.

COMECON   stands for Council for Mutual Economic Assistance, set up in 1949, between Eastern European command economies and the Soviet Union with the aim of integrating planning and promoting mutual self-sufficiency. Cuba and Vietnam later joined. It became a means of tying in dependence on the old Soviet Union.

Convertible currency   A currency freely exchangeable for any other, in markets unrestricted by government intervention. Most East European currencies were formerly subject to strict controls that kept their prices artificially high; implementing free convertibility meant their exchange rates plummeted.

Diminishing returns   The law of diminishing returns states that where at least one factor of production is in fixed supply, then increasing production must eventually occur at a steadily decreasing rate. That is, in any given factory or farm, each additional investment in capital and labour will secure additional outputs that progressively decline. This is so because factors of production are not perfect substitutes for each other. So long as one resource is fixed in supply, increased application of all others cannot continually compensate for its absence. More and more sophisticated capital equipment and technical knowledge can secure increasing output of oil and gas from a given production site, for example, but this increased production is subject to diminishing returns (see also chapter 9, p. 165).

Dual track pricing   was the Chinese system of agricultural distribution where target quantities of crops were sold off to public officials at administered prices and any output produced above these quantities was allowed to be sold off privately for whatever the market would pay.

Financial intermediaries   are private, commercial banks and money lenders which act in the market place brokering deals between those who have surplus funds and those who have insufficient. That is, they attract funds from the millions of savers in a community and then loan these on to businesses which wish to invest. See chapter 7 for more detail.

Household responsibility system   China's household responsibility system was the halfway house between collectively owned and farmed lands and private agriculture. On the original communes – huge enterprises employing thousands – there was little economic incentive for one worker to work his hardest since he would never see the reward for his efforts. On the tiny strips of land that families could lease and farm for their own consumption, productivity was very much higher. As soon as it became politically possible, therefore, administrators delegated more land to individual households or families, and reduced the amount communally farmed. Outputs increased accordingly.

Kleptocapitalism   Kleptomania (stealing) with capitalism. Where valuable state assets are offered for sale in an emerging market that few know about, then those who do have inside information can make a killing. The accusation made against many FSU privatisation sales is that it has allowed the rise of a capitalist **oligarchy**: the accumulation, use and abuse of economic power by a few.

Perestroika   Russian for re-structuring. This notion, and *glasnost* – increasing press freedom – were key platforms promoted by Mikhail Gorbachev in reforming the Soviet economy during the 1980s. *Perestroika* was intended to mean devolving decision-making to individual plant managers throughout the old USSR and thus to improve economic efficiency without overthrowing communist rule and state ownership of all resources. Trying to hold onto the tail of the free-market lion such that it could only go halfway out of its cage was doomed, however. Gorbachev got mauled; the lion got away.

The principal–agent problem   Principals employ agents to act on their behalf and to secure them benefits; the problem is that, once empowered, if control mechanisms are not efficient, agents can be more interested in their own gain than that of their principals. Hence the growth of 'Fat Cats' in newly privatised businesses.

Privatisation   A state-owned enterprise is privatised when it is offered for sale to private consumers/investors. The price of shares in such a privatised concern depends on how profitable the business is expected to be: a well-managed enterprise with modern capital equipment and a well-defined customer base is likely to have no problem in selling its shares at a relatively high price. Conversely, no one is likely to want shares in an outdated, inefficient dinosaur. This assumes, however, free access to information to all parties in the market place. One-sided or *asymmetric information* can lead to *kleptocapitalism*.

Rent-seeking   This is where fortunes can be made by petitioning government for special favours: such as inside information on which state assets will be put up for sale when; or gaining a unique subsidy or tax break; or being granted the sole licence to import and sell products that are in high demand. If rent seeking is easier than risk-taking in private business then entrepreneurs will be diverted from investing in productive capital. Resources will be employed in sucking up to government.

Risk   the calculable odds that your business investment will succeed. Note that high-risk ventures will still attract investment if the rate of return is appropriately higher. If you cannot calculate the odds, however, then only a fool will invest. See *uncertainty*.

Town and village enterprises   were the institutional form that profit-seeking business first took in rural China after 1978. These were not originally privately owned, since private property rights were still distrusted at the time, but were owned and controlled instead by local governments. These enterprises were nonetheless devoted to producing and selling products in more or less competitive markets and where revenues so earned returned to those that set up the business. Both local authority *and* private incomes could grow and there thus remained considerable incentive to increase efficiency, sales and future revenues.

Uncertainty   Lack of relevant information on a business venture that makes it impossible to calculate the chances of success.

QUESTIONS

1 Account for the economic collapse of the old Soviet Union.
2 Does making the transition from a command to a market system mean that the government should be removed from all involvement in the economy? If not, what *is* its new role?
3 Compare and contrast the transition successes and failures of China and Russia. What accounts for the wide difference in experiences?
4 What are the financial difficulties involved in making the transition to a market economy? How can (a) a central bank, (b) private commercial banks/intermediaries, and (c) foreign banks help?
5 What policies could the developed, market economies of the world adopt to help the emerging economies in transition? Why should they?

FURTHER READING

Blanchard, Olivier and Shleifer, Andrei. 'Federalism with and without political centralisation: China versus Russia', *NBER Working Paper 7616*, March 2000.

Fischer, Stanley and Sahay, Ratna. 'The transition economies after ten years', *IMF Working Paper*, February 2000.

Gaidar, Yegor. 'Lessons of the Russian crisis for transition economies', *Finance and Development*, 36 (2), IMF, 1999.

Huang, H., Marin, D. and Xu, C. 'Financial crisis, economic recovery and banking development in Russia, Ukraine and other FSU countries', *IMF Working Paper 105*, June 2004.

Maddison, A. *Chinese Economic Performance in the Long Run*, OECD, 1998.

Qian, Y. 'How reform worked in China', ch. 11 in D. Rodrik (ed.), *In Search of Prosperity*, Princeton University Press, 2003.

3 Microeconomics and macroeconomics

Topics to be considered in this chapter:

- Microeconomics: the efficiency of markets.
- Flexibility of prices vs. supplies.
- Agricultural markets and labour markets.
- Macroeconomics: the circular flow of national income.
- The equilibrium level of incomes and spending.
- The supply-side critique.

INTRODUCTION

An understanding of prices is absolutely essential to an understanding of market societies. As was emphasised in chapter 1, the price mechanism is the key organising agency of the modern market economy – the invisible hand that directs the pattern of all consumption, production and distribution. It determines what is produced, which industries and economic practices will succeed or fail, and which resources will, or will not, be employed.

Prices can be considered at the level of the individual market place – the causes and effects of changes in the price of houses or health care, for example – or we can study the operation and influence of the price mechanism for the economy as a whole: the general level of incomes, inflation, employment, etc. The analysis of how individual markets work is microeconomics; the study of the economy as a whole – the behaviour of all individual markets aggregated together – is macroeconomics.

These two branches of theoretical economics have evolved because it has become apparent that economic policies and practices which are workable at the micro-level do not necessarily apply at the macro-level. This is not just a matter of dry, academic debate. When economists' policy recommendations are acted upon, the livelihood of millions is affected. This leads us to the second most famous quotation in economics, from John Maynard Keynes:

> The ideas of economists and political philosophers, both when they are right and when they are wrong, are more powerful than is commonly

understood. Indeed the world is ruled by little else. Practical men, who believe themselves to be quite exempt from any intellectual influences, are usually the slaves of some defunct economist. Madmen in authority, who hear voices in the air, are distilling their frenzy from some academic scribbler of a few years back. I am sure that the power of vested interests is vastly exaggerated compared with the gradual encroachment of ideas.

(J. M. Keynes, The General Theory of Employment,
Interest and Money, 1936)

Certainly these words are true of Keynes' own ideas which have revolutionised economics, government policies and people's lives. Keynes was the founder of modern macroeconomics and the book from which the above quotation is taken caused a fundamental re-think of classical economics. The distinct differences between micro- and macroeconomic theory and policy implications continue to excite controversy today and thus deserve to be more 'commonly understood'.

MICROECONOMICS

Classical economics, as derived from the earliest economists like Adam Smith and others, was and is concerned with the efficiency of individual markets – i.e. how to make the most efficient, economic use of given resources. This is microeconomics: the study of consumer and producer behaviour in the trade for specific goods or services.

In a free market for housing, for example, if consumer demand exceeds supply then prices will rise. Profit-seeking entrepreneurs thus have an incentive to produce more of this higher-priced commodity; they will hire construction workers, building materials and land away from less-profitable employments (farming?) and thus expand production of the homes that more and more people in the market increasingly want.

Prices are therefore vital signalling devices in market systems. They ration out scarce existing supplies between competing consumers and simultaneously induce businesses to mobilise resources, adjust production and thus eradicate any shortages and surpluses.

Let us look more closely at this interaction between prices, demand and supply.

There are many factors that influence consumer and producer decisions, and some markets react differently to others. Take the example of a local newspaper, on sale every day in a particular city. On the occasion of a major news story – perhaps the success of the local football team – there might be a rush in demand and the newspaper sells out, leaving many dissatisfied customers. How is the market likely to respond to this *disequilibrium* situation where demand exceeds supply at the ruling market price? In this example we can predict that on the following day, assuming continuing interest in the story, local shops and stallholders will order more newspapers to meet anticipated demand, and the printers will run off more copies. It is also possible that to avoid disappointment some consumers will leave the market – perhaps following the story on local TV and radio – rather than risk unfulfilled demand a second time.

In these circumstances, if suppliers have guessed correctly, the quantity of newspapers will adjust to secure the necessary equilibrium between demand and supply. Sales increase; all consumers are satisfied; the newspaper price remains unchanged.

A different scenario may operate in the second-hand market for football tickets. On the day of a keenly contested match, those supporters who have been sharp enough to buy tickets early may find that there are many frustrated consumers desperate to pay inflated prices in order to secure entry to the vital football game. The ability of the local club to increase the supply of tickets is limited by the capacity of the ground so in this case the shortfall between supply and demand is closed by a movement in prices, quantity staying the same. Existing tickets are likely to change hands outside the ground, scarce supplies going to the highest bidders.

For many goods and services, a combination of both these movements will ensure demand equals supply: there will be some adjustment in prices and some change in quantities traded to bring about market equilibrium.

The key point necessary to emphasise here is that there are a number of different influences affecting demand and supply. Consumers' incomes change, their tastes and preferences vary, advertising has its impact – all these factors, as well as a change in prices, may influence demand for one product rather than another. In production, costs will alter, technological breakthroughs occur, random shocks (from earthquakes to exchange rates) have their effect. These issues, as well as the prospective price the entrepreneur is seeking, will influence the quantity of the product eventually supplied.

Some of these factors are more variable than others, and the 'art' in the science of economics is to identify – in the case being studied – which is the key variable, and which factors in comparison are relatively unchanging. A theory of demand, supply and price can thus be constructed and, given factor x changes and y remains constant, we can thus predict the market outcome.

Whether, of course, economists' predictions are fulfilled depends on whether or not they guessed right on the variables that changed. If x was constant and y changed – or, worse, x and y stayed the same and z varied – then their theories need revising. Here you can begin to see the source of controversy in the subject.

Some examples will make these issues clearer.

Agricultural markets are typically unstable. Supplies of coffee have been decimated by frost; fine weather can produce unexpectedly good wheat harvests; hailstorms can ruin a wine vintage. Even normally stable demand for basic commodities like beef or corn can be drastically affected by health scares such as 'mad cow' or foot and mouth disease and worries over genetically modified crops.

When random shocks frequently disturb commodity markets and supplies cannot change rapidly (it takes another year to the next harvest) then prices alone must adjust to the new circumstances. As a result, the prices of farm produce in unregulated markets are typically subject to wild swings from one year to another. Farm incomes are similarly affected since the one impacts on the other.

For many countries, such instability is not acceptable in so important an industry as food production. Variability and unpredictability of prices and incomes is a considerable disincentive to agricultural investment and future food supplies. For this reason many governments all around the world intervene to support their farming sectors.

One type of agricultural intervention is to guarantee minimum *price floors* to farmers, as is practised, for example, for cereal markets within the European Community's Common Agricultural Policy (the CAP).

In theory, the best remedy for extreme short-term price variability is to guarantee a median price to farmers that evens out the fluctuations between good years and bad. Surplus supplies can be stockpiled in years of good harvests and sold back into the market when there is a shortfall. Looking back over past years it should be easy enough to pick out the long-term trend in farm outputs, prices and incomes. All that is therefore necessary is to reassure farmers that these prices will be guaranteed into the future. In years where market prices dive below the relevant support price the CAP promises to pay the difference. In years where prices move above this floor the CAP will keep the mark-up. The beauty of this proposal is that if the median price is correctly calculated the scheme pays for itself: support payments made one year are balanced by earnings in another.

The CAP in practice has not found things so easy. In volatile commodity markets, guaranteeing farm price supports creates a certainty where before there was none. This shifts perception and thus behaviour.

With a guaranteed floor, farmers know that whatever they produce they will now be able to sell at a constant price – if not to the market then into a stockpile. Over time, therefore, they will plough up hedgerows, press into service all their marginal land, pile on fertilisers, pesticides and whatever technology is available to increase yields and thereby maximise their incomes. Whatever price level the CAP picks as a middle value between expected market highs and lows they will soon find inappropriate – it will induce quantities supplied far greater than originally estimated. As a result the CAP has had to continually come up with other interventions to correct the tendency for overproduction – taking 'set aside' land out of production, enforcing quotas on farm outputs, re-fixing prices at lower levels, etc.

Whereas before any imbalance between demand and supply was mediated by strong price movements, now price becomes unchanging and supplies inexorably grow to outstrip demand. No automatic mechanism exists to bring about equilibrium.

Critics argue that overproduction – the alleged butter mountains and wine lakes – will be a continuing feature of the CAP until the market is free of intervention and price flexibility is restored. Others say that this does not solve anything and simply returns us to the original problem of instability.

The notion of free markets has a particularly strong hold on classical economics. Price flexibility is considered essential to efficiency and the evolution of an equilibrium price that equates demand and supply and thus 'clears the market' is a theoretical process that has a powerful influence on the mind-set of microeconomics.

It should be noted, however, that to advocate price flexibility in examples like the above is in fact to declare the value judgement that short-term *allocative efficiency* in clearing markets is more worthwhile than other alternative objectives, such as long-term agricultural stability in this case. This important point, that economic policy recommendations embody judgements as to which objectives are more valuable than others, is worth bearing in mind whenever you are trying to disentangle controversies in economics.

Consider the application of microeconomic theory to labour markets: this can provide us with one explanation for unemployment. If there are too many people without jobs it is because supply of labour is greater than demand. To clear this particular market place, the theory states that wages (the price of labour) must fall. Employers would then find hiring workers more attractive; similarly fewer workers would offer their labour to the market. Registered unemployment would decrease.

The notion that people price themselves out of work and that wages must be free to fall is an important tenet of classical (pre-1930s) and modern neoclassical economics. In Britain in the 1920s this policy was enacted – prompting the General Strike in 1926 when coalminers refused to accept this alleged solution to their country's economic ills. Widespread wage cuts were resorted to also in the USA in the attempt to reduce unemployment in the Great Depression in the 1930s, and history repeated itself again recently in the late 1980s/early 1990s recession when certain economists argued for 'flexible labour markets' and politicians urged workers to price themselves back into jobs.

Should wages be flexible (downwards)? Is this an acceptable solution to unemployment? Or, if the supply of labour exceeds demand perhaps some variable other than its price/wage should adjust to secure equilibrium?

The alternative strategy is to accept that low-pay/low-skill jobs attract few dealers in modern, Western economies and rather than encourage wages to move, training and productivity deals should be implemented to enable workers to upgrade skills and become mobile between jobs. The more labour supply becomes flexible the less wages need to be (in which case minimum wage laws can become tenable).

This example therefore illustrates the point that market equilibrium can be closed either by price movements or by adjustment in the quantities traded. Unemployment may perhaps be more quickly reduced if you can persuade

BOX 3.1 MICROECONOMICS AND CIGARETTES

Demand for cigarettes is notoriously unresponsive to price change in the short run – if you are hooked, you're hooked and you have to pay any increase in price the cigarette companies force onto you.

Actually, an increase in the price of cigarettes is more likely to be due to taxation nowadays – governments know as well as producers that sales will not be much affected by an extra 10 per cent on a pack, so why not let the tax authorities benefit from price increases rather than company profits?

Over the longer term, however, the deteriorating public health, bad publicity and government restrictions that smoking attracts means that demand for cigarettes has been shrinking in the developed world. Hence the drive for the big companies like Philip Morris, British American Tobacco (BAT) and R. J. Reynolds to promote sales in the developing world where large-scale advertising and marketing promotions are still relatively free from controls.

Consumer prices are forced up if supplies fall short of demand but they fall if the opposite occurs. How can cigarette companies expand sales in developing markets but still keep prices and profits up?

Cutthroat competition between the big three producers will not help – it serves only to drive down prices in the fruitless search of stealing market share from rivals that are just as determined not to let you get away with it. Better then if you can somehow collude to keep prices up and arrange to 'develop' the market in an 'ordered' way – that is, fix things between you to ensure growth in overall consumer demand and share out the market to an agreed formula.

Such collusive agreements to carve up a country's market are outlawed in most nations but if you meet in, say, London, and casually discuss market arrangements in Africa, Latin America, Eastern Europe or Asia then whose laws are you breaking?

Does such business behaviour take place? Well population growth, incomes and consumerism are growing rapidly in numerous emerging markets – more rapidly than the growth of laws to protect consumers' rights. This is too good an opportunity for profit maximisers to miss . . .

businesses to take on more people to work for less pay, but long-term labour market equilibrium is perhaps better secured if investment in human capital occurs. Job stability is more assured for high-skilled rather than low-skilled workers.

Meanwhile, back in the 1930s Great Depression, governments in Europe and North America followed the classical economic prescription of wage cuts to stimulate more industrial demand for labour. In this case, however, instead of reducing unemployment, this policy only served to make matters worse – to the consternation of governments and the bafflement of their economic advisors. Unemployment in supposedly modern, civilised economies rose to historically unprecedented levels of up to a quarter of all workers and showed no apparent tendency to fall. Why? What had gone wrong?

John Maynard Keynes had to formulate a new general theory of economics to answer this question. In doing so he looked beyond classical microeconomics (the efficiency of one market place as compared to another) and opened up an entirely new field of inquiry: macroeconomics – concerned with the general level of incomes, expenditure and employment in an economy as a whole. It is to this area of economics that we now turn.

MACROECONOMICS

There are many criticisms of market theory (see the previous chapter on command and market systems) but the one we most need to focus on here is that of the *fallacy of composition* – that is, the assumption that what works for the community in an individual market place will work for all market places throughout an economy added together.

Specifically, all the millions of independent decisions by consumers in markets up and down the country may add up to a general level of national demand for resources that is insufficient (or alternatively, too great) for the economy as a whole to sustain. Insufficient aggregate demand will mean unemployment and recession; too much demand means price rises and inflation.

Keynes argued that cutting wages, in the hope of pricing people back into work if implemented on a large scale, only serves to drive down the general level of incomes and consumption, thereby reducing employment prospects still further. Which businesses will take on more workers and produce more goods and services if incomes and spending throughout the economy are falling? Aggregate demand in the 1930s was insufficient to keep the bulk of the labour force in employment, and Keynes argued for expansionary government policies (the very opposite of wage cuts) in order to remedy the situation. Many Keynesian economists all round the world argue precisely the same today.

Let us look at Keynesian macroeconomics in more detail. If we ignore the influence of governments for the time being, we can divide an economy into two sectors: producers and consumers. For the sake of simplicity we can say that all production is located in business firms and all consumption occurs in households (see Figure 3.1). There is thus a *circular flow* of money and incomes between households and firms within the economy. Incomes are earned at work and spent at home on those consumer goods and services produced by business.

All income in a market economy is derived from the production process. It may be earned in the form of wages or salaries for direct work, or it can be earnings from the ownership of capital or land. Either way, these resources of labour, enterprise, capital and land can only generate earnings if they are employed in production. And eventually all these incomes, from whichever source, will find their way into someone's household where they will be spent or not as the case may be.

Looking at the household sector for the moment, we can say that any income received that is not directly spent on consumer goods and services is 'saved', that is, it is not passed on through the market place to producers. It therefore leaks out of the circular flow (see Figure 3.2).

If we consider now all expenditure in the economy, we find that it is made up of spending on consumer goods, plus some fraction spent by firms on business investment – that is, building capital goods to provide for future production. Either way, all spending goes through firms and contributes to the income they generate (see Figure 3.3).

We should add the qualification at this stage that households buy many imported goods and services. Thus some consumer spending will always leak out of the circular flow in one country and enter that of another. By the same argument, every trading country will receive some foreign spending on those exports it sells abroad.

Putting all these elements together, we can thus see the full picture for the whole economy (see Figure 3.4). According to this circular flow model,

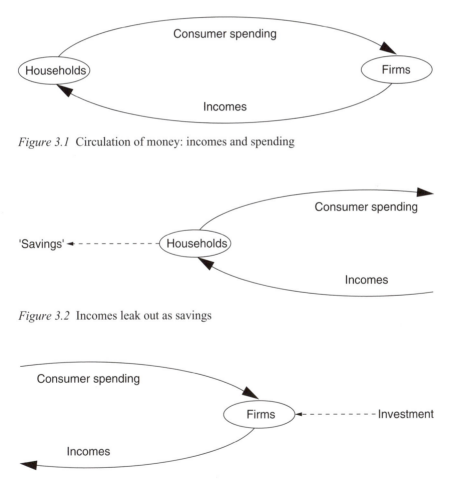

Figure 3.1 Circulation of money: incomes and spending

Figure 3.2 Incomes leak out as savings

Figure 3.3 All spending goes through firms

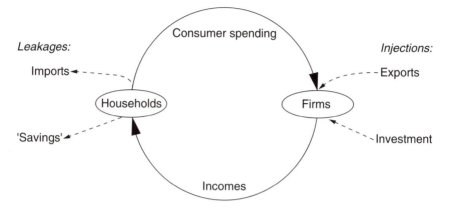

Figure 3.4 The circular flow of incomes and expenditure

the economy is in equilibrium if net additions to money circulation equal net leakages and thus aggregate income equals aggregate expenditure. So long as the injections of export revenues and investment equal the outflows of import spending and savings then the amount of money flowing round the system must remain constant. What happens if this equilibrium is disturbed? If, for some reason, there is a general reduction in wages then clearly incomes would fall, households would be able to spend less and there would be a fall in the circular flow of incomes, consumption and therefore employment.

Key variables here are the propensities of households to save, spend, and spend on imports. The greater the fraction of households' income that is spent on domestic goods and services, the greater the impact any change of income will have on firms' revenues and production plans. An economy-wide wage cut will thus be rapidly transmitted through to increased unemployment. Conversely, any increase in incomes will quickly generate increased production and the creation of new jobs.

Because there is a circular flow involved here, any small change to the system has a cumulative, *multiplier* effect. Suppose, for example, wages are cut first in the construction workers industry. Falling incomes will not only impact on those families directly involved but because their spending represents someone else's income then the recessionary impact spreads further. Local shops, transport firms and other related services will lose custom, and they in turn will pass on less spending and hence revenues to businesses dealing with them. Incomes and, therefore, expenditure fall round all the economy. As the recessionary outlook begins to take hold, the spiral of decline gathers pace. Is there no bottom to the depression?

This was the fear expressed in the 1930s. Indeed, due to the fact that one country's imports represent another country's exports, falling incomes and spending in the USA rapidly impacted on all other trading nations. The Great Depression was transmitted world-wide.

As can be seen in the macroeconomic model above, incomes and spending will fall and keep on falling so long as leakages from the circular flow exceed injections. Stability is only attained when outflows equal inflows, and Keynes' great insight was that there was no inherent necessity for such an equilibrium to exist at full employment within an economy, it could just as easily obtain at lower levels of economic activity – an unemployment equilibrium.

So countries could get stuck with a quarter of their workforce unemployed, and no private businesses still operating would see any reason to expand.

If the private sector sees no future in investment, if no consumers at home or abroad have money to increase their spending, how is the gloom to end?

The answer according to Keynes was that governments could bring about an autonomous increase in injections. The multiplier process outlined above could thus be made to work in a positive fashion: if governments place orders for building, say, more roads and houses (and, in the 1930s, military spending) then 'first round' employment and incomes will rise. Subject to some fraction not being spent, the rest of consumers' incomes will be passed on as 'second round' expenditure, incomes and employment, which in turn stokes up 'third round' and further recovery.

The economy will grow and grow until the cumulative total of leakages just rises to equal the size of the government-induced injections and thus the circular flow re-balances itself: at a higher, aggregate total of national income.

As noted before, it should be seen that the speed and extent of the expansion (or contraction) of the economy depends on people's propensity to spend any slight increase in their incomes. That is, the greater their *marginal propensity to consume*, the greater will be the multiplier effect.

In the 1930s, the pressing economic problem was to devise a new form of analysis and new policy prescriptions for a world wallowing in a deep depression. Note that Keynesian macroeconomics was concerned solely with the general levels of income, output and employment of an economy. Micro-economic discussion about whether or not labour should be deployed here or there, released from industry A in order to transfer to industry B, was outside its concern. Keynesians might well have argued that such debate is irrelevant when millions are out of work and all industry is below capacity.

Such debate is not irrelevant today, however. Neoclassical, 'supply-side' economists have said that too many resources in Europe and North America are tied up in inefficient, declining industries. Unemployment *ought* to rise in such sectors, freeing up workers to move to newer, growth areas. Current unemployment is thus alleged to be a measure necessary to reallocate resources within the economy. Wage rates should fall in mining, steel, etc., tempting workers to leave these uncompetitive, low-skill industries and move into better high-wage, high-skill employment. The problem, therefore, is the classic, microeconomic one of allocative inefficiency. Any government policy to stimulate aggregate demand will only delay the necessary re-deployment of resources within the economy.

Modern Keynesian economists argue, however, that recent (particularly European) unemployment level is excessive and partly due to government

BOX 3.2 MACROECONOMICS AND THE CASE OF JAPAN

Throughout the 1990s, Japan was stuck with a typical Keynesian depression – some have argued that it was the first of its kind since the Great Depression held the USA in its grip. In the year 2000–01, output growth was –0.8 per cent and prices fell by 0.5 per cent. Such deflation is dangerous since people withhold spending if they think prices will sink lower . . . but this only drives down all incomes. (The paradox of thrift again.) So around the turn of the millennium, aggregate demand in Japan was well below that necessary to generate full employment, the rate of inflation was negative and interest rates were close to zero. (US Economist Paul Krugman commented that the 10-year bond rate in 1998 was less than 0.7 per cent; that is, financial markets were then betting that the depression would last for at least ten years.)

Savings ratios in Japan have always been high and well above those in other countries and so a *recent* fall in consumer spending could not be the cause of the deflation. Krugman attributed the problem to low investment and even lower expectations: a typical Keynesian explanation of demand deficiency: things were bad because they had been bad for so long. There was sizeable room for expansion, but how to fill this demand deficiency or output gap?

Fiscal stimulus. The textbook Keynesian remedy is to increase government spending. However, the size of the demand deficiency was so great that such a large increase in budget deficits for so long (ten years?) would be simply politically impossible to achieve, given the highly conservative nature of Japan's ruling elite.

Bank reforms. A corrupt, under-regulated and inefficient banking system needed cleaning up. But bad debts in banks and industry require micro-economic reform of financial practices: more transparency, accountability and the *contraction* of business until traders can be trusted. No quick fix possible here.

Managed inflation. If expected future inflation was to *increase*, people might go out and spend right away rather than wait and suffer the effect of rising prices later. Krugman thus argued for the perverse policy recommendation that the central bank should engineer a credible and sustained rise in money supplies to generate inflation – that way, it might prompt an increase in consumer spending and the recovery of aggregate demand. The key, therefore, was to convince the Japanese public that the inflation would last . . . and this in a country where the central bank has earned a reputation for being ultra-conservative. They should pursue a policy that involved making 'a credible promise to be irresponsible'. Unlike Western economies, it was recommended that Japan give its central bank a minimum inflation target to achieve for a sustained period, over a decade, in order to jump-start consumer spending. Krugman suggested: 'how about a 4 per cent inflation target for fifteen years?'

How has Japan reacted? Since 2001 the Bank of Japan reports that it has kept interest rates down at zero and has pumped up money supplies. The monetary base (see chapter 7) has increased between 4 and 5 per cent per annum. Meanwhile firms, saved by increasing exports to China and the USA, took the opportunity to restructure at home, cut labour costs (ouch!), reduce debts and finally – as of 2004 – secure steady growth in outputs. GDP growth is forecast as 2.5 per cent in 2004 and 1.5 per cent in 2005. Deflation, or falling prices, has at last ceased and although a jump in inflation is not likely, nor any sudden increase in consumer spending, after years of falling household incomes there are now signs of growth and of fragile optimism for the future. The depression has at least bottomed out, if not actually reversed as yet.

policies of restricting money supplies and aggregate demand. If spending in the economy as a whole is made to rise, employment and output in all industry would rise. If private sector demand is depressed then government has the responsibility to increase spending and thus create an upturn in the economy. More demand will cause more entrepreneurs to hire more labour and supply more goods.

'No!' cry the supply-siders. Increased spending will not generate more production, but only trigger off more inflation; it cannot create more jobs if unemployed workers have been thrown out of inefficient businesses and are predominantly equipped with the wrong skills (or are unskilled) to cater for consumer demand. It is not the aggregate level of spending that is wrong in the economy, they argue, but the balance of efficient versus inefficient industry that is at fault.

CONCLUSION

This modern controversy has, in fact, moved macroeconomics forward, past original Keynesian concern with manipulating levels of aggregate demand, to focus policy-makers' attention also on the overall capacity (or incapacity!) of the economy to produce: i.e. the aggregate level of supply.

Such economic thinking has been the reaction to the dominant Western economic problem of the 1980s and 1990s – inflation and slow growth. The notion that increased aggregate demand would pull an economy upward into growth has been shown to be inflationary where economies have experienced bottle-necks in their productive capacity. Where vital labour skills and applied technology have been missing in industry then short-term boosts in consumer spending have not been met with increases in production – but rather the shortfall in supplies has been closed by an increase in general price levels (inflation) and buying more imports (i.e. balance of payments problems).

So we need to get the balance right between aggregate expenditure and aggregate supply. The end result today is that we recognise different types of unemployment and it is important to diagnose each problem separately and apply the appropriate remedial policy according to the situation. Keynesian 'demand-deficient' or *'cyclical' unemployment* requires an injection of increased spending. *'Structural' unemployment* where there is a mis-match between available skills and job opportunities requires education and re-training of the workforce. (*Which* type of training, and *how* it is implemented are important microeconomic questions that depend on the economy in question.) Apply the wrong medicine and, either way above, the result will be continuing unemployment, trade deficits, no or slow growth and a rise in the general level of prices.

Most Western economies have now emerged from the 1990s recession but they are still searching for the Holy Grail of sustainable, non-inflationary growth. Questions that might be asked to help to resolve some of these issues include:

- Have the more efficient, high-tech. businesses in the economy been laying off workers? If so there may well be a deficiency in aggregate demand.
- As the recovery takes place, will there be increased demand for goods and services that the economy has no spare capacity to produce? If so this may prompt an increase in inflation and a rise in imports – symptoms of a supply-side, microeconomic imbalance.

The controversy now is not theoretical but empirical – what does the evidence show? This is a matter for each society to settle for itself.

KEY WORDS

Allocative efficiency   Economics is classically concerned with the efficient allocation of resources. A change in consumer demand away from foods stuffed with additives, colouring and flavouring in favour of environmentally friendly health foods will leave shops, factories and farms with unwanted stocks of some goods and shortages of others. Some productive resources will be made redundant, others will now be in short supply. Similarly, a breakthrough in technology – like in the exploitation and transport of natural gas – can make some productive processes much cheaper, others more wasteful than before. The speed and efficiency with which producers can adjust to changing conditions, the less the amount of waste generated, the more efficient the allocation of society's resources.

Disequilibrium   This is where the forces in the market place are too weak-acting to overcome obstacles and to secure balance or equilibrium.

The fallacy of composition   What works for one individual may not work for all individuals if they act together. An individual can miss the traffic jams and get home quickly if he/she leaves the office half an hour early, but this policy will not work if everyone thinks and acts the same. Similarly, if one person demands and wins a large pay increase – good for him/her. But if all workers succeed in gaining higher wages then industrial costs rise, fuelling inflation and the real value of the wage increase thus falls to zero. Everyone loses.

Human capital   Capital, in economics, is a resource capable of producing goods and services. Human capital is thus gained if people's health, education and vocational training improves such that they become more productive in employment.

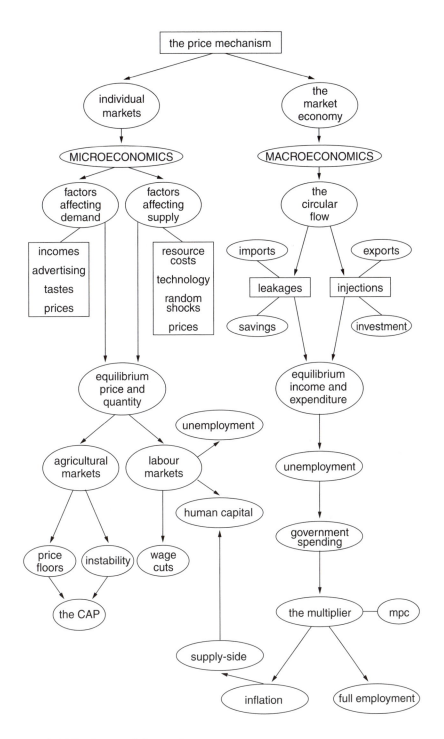

Figure 3.5 The themes of chapter 3

Macroeconomics   The analysis of levels of aggregate demand and supply on a national scale. Rates of inflation, unemployment and economic growth are considered, as are government policies to influence these variables.

The marginal propensity to consume (mpc)   How much a community will spend, rather than save, from a given increase in its income. If you were given $10 and spent $7 then your mpc would equal 70 per cent.

Microeconomics   The study of how resources are employed and goods and services are produced and consumed in an individual market place. The supply, demand and determination of price of one product compared to another is analysed, as is how efficiently, economically, changes from one market are communicated to another.

The multiplier   A Keynesian concept which refers to how much national income is affected by a relatively small change in spending injected into the economy. Any one monetary injection may flow round and round the economy a number of times. For example, if domestic investment rises by $x million and, as a result, national incomes rise by $5x million the *investment multiplier* is 5. Similarly, if there is a rise in $y million in export earnings and incomes rise by $3y million, then the *foreign trade multiplier* equals 3.

Supply-side   Economic theory which emphasises the importance of policies to free up markets from government regulation, thus allegedly stimulating supply.

Unemployment   This can be defined as the amount of people who are actively seeking work but cannot find it. Who is 'active' or not is a matter of contention which leads to changing official statistics and arguments between theoretical economists.

QUESTIONS

1   Examine how prices and the employment of resources would move if there was a sustained increase in the demand for natural gas in the place of coal. What are the implications if either (a) prices or (b) resources do *not* move?
2   What causes price variability in agricultural markets? Should such variability be prevented? Why or why not?
3   Under what circumstances will a cut in wages (a) reduce or (b) increase unemployment?
4   Under what circumstances will an increase in the aggregate level of spending in an economy lead to (a) increasing employment and incomes or (b) inflation?
5   Microeconomics is concerned with efficiency and macroeconomics is about aggregates. Explain and discuss.

FURTHER READING

Almost any introductory text on economics will enlarge upon the theories of price determination and on the macroeconomics of aggregate demand and supply. Particularly recommended are:

Begg, D., Fischer, S. and Dornbusch, R. *Economics*. McGraw-Hill, 2000.
Krugman, P. 'It's Baaaack: Japan's slump and the return of the liquidity trap', *Brookings Papers on Economic Activity*, 2, 1998.
Parkin, M., Powell, M. and Matthews, K. *Economics*. Addison Wesley, 1998.

4   Unemployment and inflation

Topics to be considered in this chapter:

- Creative destruction.
- Keynesian demand-management policies.
- The Phillips curve.
- Supply-side policies.
- The expectations revolution.
- The inflation/unemployment record in selected countries.

INTRODUCTION

Unemployment is not a natural phenomenon. No creatures in the wild are unemployed – you do not see any birds or animals lying idle. Nor are people in tribal or agricultural societies ever unemployed. In the Middle Ages mass unemployment was unheard of. There was simply too much to do: crops to be harvested; cloth to be woven; stone to be quarried, shaped and placed in construction. Today, in poorer parts of the world, in those remote corners untouched by so-called modern civilisation, you will not find anyone unemployed either. No. Unemployment is solely the creation of modern, industrial society. It is not natural. It is not even man-made. Unemployment is rich-man-made.

The world's first industrial revolution took place in Great Britain. People moved from the land into the growing industrial centres. New products, new processes, new sources of power were created and with them revolutionary changes imposed on society. Factories were built requiring modern workforces. Cities grew. Transport and trade links were forged that brought in sources of supply and facilitated the distribution of final products. And the enormous increases in wealth that were accumulated fed increasing populations, trade and investments of global proportions.

From British shores modern industrialisation and urbanisation spread quickly across Europe and thence further overseas. International trade blossomed as change spawned further change, bringing more and more people into the money economy.

The growing sophistication and integration of world trade brought with it increased specialisation, interdependency and thereby fragility. We call this process today *globalisation.*

The very success of trade means individuals specialise in those employments that can earn them most money. Sophisticated products such as a modern motor car are the outcome of millions of specialised tasks and production decisions spread across many different factories, regions, even countries. Every person's job is dependent on someone else's, and all are dependent on the final consumer demanding the finished product.

CREATIVE DESTRUCTION

What happens when new products appear on the market place; when consumer tastes change?

Austrian economist Joseph Schumpeter described modern economic and social evolution as a process of *creative destruction* – new products and processes are created at the expense of old ones. New jobs destroy traditional ones.

But one of the features of modern economic society is that the destruction of the old is frequently far removed from the creation of the new. In medieval village society, for example, specialisation had not progressed to the extreme where single skills were concentrated in whole regions; where buyers in one place did not know the producers in another; where one could not see the consequences of one's decisions of what, and what not, to buy. But in modern trade, economic interdependency links distant communities in ways impossible to see, and of course what the eye does not see, the heart does not grieve over.

Cynics might argue that this was particularly true in the days of the first industrial revolution when the traditional societies destroyed were full of brown-skinned people in far-off lands. What do cotton mill owners and workers in the north of England – and consumers of their products – care about the destruction of traditional Indian industry?

Such beggar-my-neighbour attitudes caught up with the Western world in the 1930s Great Depression. The economic fortunes and destiny of modern trading nations are inevitably interlinked. The attempt by some countries and communities to increase their wealth at the expense of others (in tariff and trade wars) meant that world trade and thereby incomes quickly collapsed. From there, World War II served forcibly to underline the destructive dead-end of blinkered nationalism.

In 1945, the Western nations sought to create a better post-war world. And following the work of John Maynard Keynes, government economic management was thought to be the key to minimising unemployment. If modern market economies are inherently unstable and liable to cause booms and slumps then governments have the duty and ability to intervene and smooth out the path to growth via macroeconomic, *contra-cyclical* fiscal and monetary policies.

It seemed to work at first. But since the 1970s creeping and then galloping *inflation* has appeared as the price to pay.

UNEMPLOYMENT VERSUS INFLATION?

In the last half of the twentieth century, modern Western nations had difficulty escaping from a rising cycle of unemployment. Success at restraining job-lessness was frequently at the expense of releasing increased inflation; and vice versa. Whereas in the 1960s inflation was kept down at the cost of less than 4 per cent unemployment, in the 1990s inflation only just abated in Europe with over 10 per cent of the labour force out of work. To this day, governments are still inhibited in their dash for growth and more jobs by the fear of notching up another ratchet in inflation.

Unemployment today affects an increasingly wide range of industries and individuals. Over 19 million (9.1 per cent) are registered as looking for work in the 25 EU counties and we can assume many more are unregistered. In the USA at the time of going to press it is nearly 8 million unemployed (5 per cent of the workforce). Although traditionally the older mining and manufacturing industries have suffered most, that is no longer the case – the growth in jobless-ness now impacts on professional, white-collar services as well.

The worst affected are typically the young, unskilled, the ethnic minorities, men more than women, and those working in manufacturing and construction. But the forces of globalisation affect employment in all job categories in all regions, and the long-term unemployed are a growing percentage.

Certain microeconomic explanations for unemployment have been held responsible. Powerful trade unions, overgenerous unemployment benefits, inefficient, uncompetitive industry, immobile labour have all been blamed for causing unemployment and, in consequence, a number of critics have empha-sised the importance of hitting these targets. So long as the pattern of world demand continues to change, the argument goes, then the market economy's production of goods and services must keep pace with it. Any cyclical slump in world trade will affect all countries, but those structurally rigid, least-flexible economies will suffer most of all. Japan can hold inflation steady with less than 3 per cent unemployed. Not so in Europe.

A number of issues are raised here. Just what exactly *is* the relationship between unemployment and inflation? Does the one affect the other? If so, is this relationship stable over time, and how does it differ between countries? We need to examine the arguments and the evidence involved.

It has been asserted above that both macro- and microeconomic influences are relevant: the general level of activity within an economy and the flexibility of labour markets both impact on unemployment and carry implications for inflation. But whereas some economic theorists argue that these two phenomena are alternatives, that there is a *trade-off* between unemployment and inflation, others say that no such relationship exists, or – if anything – there is a positive correlation at work.

Keynesian theory puts the case that these two economic evils are opposites – policies to reduce inflation will exaggerate the rate of unemployment. Supply-side theorists – in the ascendant after the oil price shocks to the world economy during the 1970s – have argued that there is *no* long-term conflict between unemployment and inflation. Countries can have less of both if they free up market rigidities and thereby release the forces for economic growth. It is time to turn to an examination of these rival claims.

THE KEYNESIAN ORTHODOXY

Keynesian economists held centre-stage throughout the post-war years up until the end of the 1960s. Government policies, informed by Keynesian emphasis of aggregate *demand management*, were successful in keeping unemployment down to unprecedentedly low levels, albeit at the (relatively minor) cost of creeping inflation (see Figure 4.1).

Textbook Keynesian macroeconomics held that a country is in stable equilibrium where the level of *aggregate demand* flowing round the economy (that is, the combined total of spending decisions of all households, firms and public authorities) just equals *aggregate supply* (total output of all producers). Since the former tends to be more unstable than the latter (Keynes particularly emphasised the volatility of firms' investment plans) then governments must accept the responsibility of spending more in times when private consumers were uncertain and witholding expenditure, and spending less/taxing more when confidence was high and aggregate demand in danger of running out of control. Despite the market economy's tendency for cyclical booms and slumps, therefore, government contra-cyclical demand-management policies could keep the system in stable equilibrium.

Note that unemployment and inflation were characterised as opposites. If aggregate demand exceeded supply then this excess pressure would force up the level of prices: inflation would occur. If aggregate demand was less than supply then unemployment would result. The presence of either symptom in the post-war period was put down to difficulties of 'fine-tuning' the required demand-management policies.

All the evidence of these years reinforced the ascendancy of Keynesian thinking. In contrast to the economic instability of the interwar period when governments were generally non-interventionist, active post-1945 demand-management policies coincided with steady growth and full employment in the Western world. When A. W. Phillips published his famous findings on unemployment and inflation in 1958, the victory of Keynesian theory over classical views on unemployment was complete.

Professor Phillips was concerned about the link between the rate of change in money wages and unemployment. Working at the London School of Economics, he correlated UK inflation and unemployment performance for almost a hundred years from 1862 to 1958 and found that the relationship between the two was remarkably stable. The *Phillips curve* (see Figure 4.2), shows a clear trade-off between unemployment and inflation with the unavoidable policy implication that, in the short run, if a country opts to reduce one it must exacerbate the other – exactly in accordance with orthodox Keynesianism.

The Keynesian 'revolution' of the 1930s had thus become the mainstream orthodoxy of the 1950s and 1960s. As always in economics, there was a continuing academic debate between adherents and critics of these views but this had little impact on the practical policy-makers. Keynesian demand management was predominant in Western governments.

The onset of the 1970s, however, blew all these certainties out of the window. This was the decade when everything seemed to go wrong for most developed and many underdeveloped countries of the world. Unemployment and inflation accelerated together, trade balances went into the red, economic growth slowed down and – for some – went into reverse. No amount of manipulative fine-tuning could fix things. Major structural changes in the world economy were at work and Keynesian orthodox economics which had failed to foresee this and seemingly contained no policy prescription for it was thus discredited.

In evolution, the death of the dinosaurs – due it seems to some external earth-shattering impact for which they were not designed to cope – left the field wide open for other, until then relatively insignificant, mammalian creatures to populate.

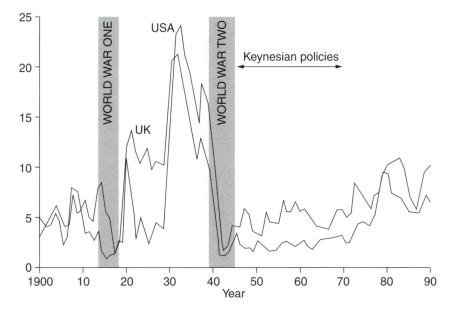

Figure 4.1 % unemployed in the United Kingdom and the United States, 1900–90

Source: Datastream.

So it was that 'supply-siders' – evolutionary heirs to the earlier strain of classical economics but until the 1970s generally populating the fringes of academic debate – were suddenly able to inhabit the centre ground left vacant by floundering Keynesians.

SUPPLY-SIDE ECONOMICS

Two developments are generally held responsible for switching the attention of economic commentators to the importance of aggregate supply in the equation quoted earlier in this chapter. The first of these developments, all would agree, was sudden and thunderingly obvious – the massive oil price shocks of the 1970s which greatly increased energy costs and enforced large transfers of world incomes from Western consuming nations to exporting (particularly Middle Eastern) nations. The second (and more disputable) development was cumulative and imperceptible until too late – the gradual sclerosis of certain microeconomic organs of mature market systems.

The supply-side critique of Keynesianism focused on *government failure* in a mixed economy – specifically, that well-intentioned interventionism impaired the efficient functioning of (especially labour) markets, frustrated economic growth prospects, led to government budgets getting out of control and increased a country's inflationary tendencies.

The capacity of the supply side of the economy to respond to rapidly evolving consumer demand is considered essential to the long-term health of an economy. Governments and public-sector institutions are blundering dinosaurs compared to the fleet-footed market mammals of private enterprise. Economies dominated by the former need to be de-regulated and re-populated by the latter, it is argued.

This requires the unrestricted mobility of labour, capital and enterprise to flow to those employments in an economy that are most popular, productive and profitable, and away from those sectors that suffer declining demand.

Policies to promote such mobility of resources imply: *deregulation* of markets (i.e. removing government controls); adjusting tax and benefits systems; *privatisation* of public enterprise; and the breaking up of private monopolistic and restrictive practices.

By such measures, supply-siders assert, increasing productivity and long-term economic growth can be secured. Unemployment will fall and – since aggregate supply can thus keep up with growing aggregate demand – inflation need not occur.

This supply-side economic philosophy is basically a reassertion of the fertility and efficiency of free markets – a breeding ground of growth allegedly denied sustenance by governments concerned to promote 'welfare capitalism'. That is, critics of liberal Keynesian political economy asserted that by trying to spread the benefits of post-war capitalism more equitably in society, rather than concentrating rewards on the primary wealth-creators, lumbering governments had trampled on the main source of economic growth. It was time to make room

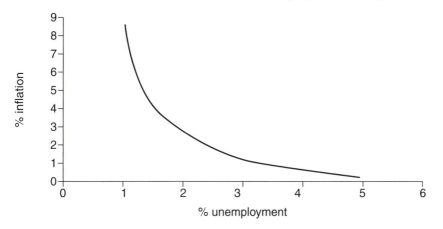

Figure 4.2 UK Phillips curve, 1862–1958. The data support the Keynesian hypothesis that unemployment and inflation are in general inversely related: as inflation falls unemployment rises and vice versa.

for the overtaxed, underfed but still success-hungry enterprise culture. As such, therefore, the key distinction between Keynesian and supply-side economics is not so much about policies but about objectives.

This philosophy was most famously associated with two politicians separated by the Atlantic Ocean: Margaret Thatcher in the UK and Ronald Reagan in the USA. Of these two, the one who was least constrained by any political opposition and was thus most effective in pushing through radical supply-side policies was Britain's Margaret Thatcher and she thus became a key propaganda figure in promoting what became the new economic orthodoxy.

There was a third politician associated during the 1970s and 1980s with this right-wing economic philosophy: President Augusto Pinochet of Chile. The move from state-regulated protectionism and welfare provision to radical, free-market policies was even more extreme in the Chilean case – although the political context of this 'experiment' was not one that many could triumphantly celebrate (see Box 4.1).

BOX 4.1 SUPPLY-SIDE POLICIES IN ACTION (1) CHILE

The right-wing economic revolution in Chile was preceded by policies inspired by an entirely opposite political philosophy: that of the pro-Marxist government of Salvador Allende. In the democratic elections of 1971, Allende won a slender majority and in the attempt to revitalise a stagnating economy and to increase the economic participation and welfare of the poorest, his administration immediately set about pushing the up till then accepted practice of protectionist, interventionist government to an acute extreme. Widespread nationalisations were embarked upon, public spending rose rapidly, wages were increased and prices controlled. Such extreme policies divided the country politically and caused an economic crisis. The country became riven with strikes. Chronic shortages emerged in the supplies of all sorts of goods and services and a rapid exodus of funds took flight to foreign bolt-holes as wealth-holders liquidated their capital in order to avoid nationalisation and seizure. The chaos was ended in 1973 by an infamous and bloody overthrow of the government led by the commander of the armed forces, General Pinochet.

The new military dictatorship pursued a radical transformation of Chile's polity, economy, and society. As was well publicised at the time, political dissent was ruthlessly crushed. Less well known internationally was that, on the economic front, fiscal deficits were cut back, money supplies were reduced and major structural changes were put in place to transform Chile into a privately owned, deregulated and export-oriented economy. Many state-owned enterprises were sold off, tariff protection was swept away, the financial sector was deregulated, labour market controls were removed and much government provision of social security and health services was transferred to the private sector.

Such radical supply-side changes occurred well before the same economic philosophy became the accepted orthodoxy in North America and Europe and, ironically, Chile suffered as a result. Although by the late 1970s Chilean recovery and economic growth seemed well under way, it had in fact been built on a fragile base. Financial deregulation in a small, developing country context meant that a relatively restricted group of families (the *grupos*) gained a controlling interest in banks and businesses and issued too many interlocking loans of dubious character at a time when external events conspired against them. (This chain of events was very similar to what was to happen almost twenty years later in East Asia – see chapter 10.)

The very success of supply-side policies being implemented in the USA and the UK, meanwhile, brought a tightening of world interest rates and the onset of the 1980s international debt crisis (see chapter 10). For Chile, external debts and internal 'cronyism' sparked a currency crisis and, as the peso crashed so too did a number of domestic financial and commercial institutions. In early 1983 the military government had to step back in and re-nationalise the banks in order to rescue the economy.

Better regulation embodied in new banking laws, a more flexible exchange rate and (in 1989) the establishment of an independent Central Bank all helped to build a stronger financial sector. The re-privatisation and capitalisation of those banks and businesses that went under in 1982/3 signalled another, and this time more secure, economic recovery and this continued from 1985, through a return to democracy, to the present day. External shocks (the Mexico crisis of the early 1990s and the Asian crisis of the late 1990s) have had their impact but they have not deflected Chile from its growth path.

Alejandra Cox Edwards and Sebastian Edwards, Latin American economists based in the USA, comment that the supply-side reforms implemented in the period 1975–80, rather than the post-1985 adjustments, formed the foundation for this growth. 'It takes a considerable amount of time – in the order of 8 to 10 years – for an economy to adapt to new rules of the game and new incentive

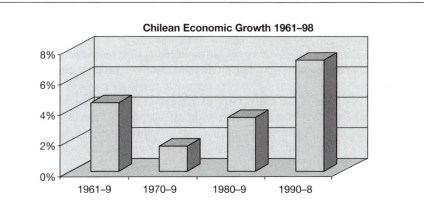

Figure 4.3 Chile: economic growth, 1961–98

Source: Jadresic, E. and Zahler, R., *Chile's Rapid Growth in the 1990s: Good Policies, Good Luck or Political Change?*, IMF Working Paper 153, October 2000.

structures' (Edwards, A. C. and Edwards, S., 'Markets and democracy: lessons from Chile', *World Economy*, 15, 1992).

Notwithstanding the success of this record (see Figure 4.3) – an example that has since seen the spread of similar policies throughout Latin America – it has not been without cost. The initial liberalisation of price controls in an economy characterised by shortage in 1973 led to a massive leap in inflation. Removing worker protection at the same time meant a similar increase in unemployment (see Figure 4.4). Unrestricted capitalism then brought the economic crisis in the early 1980s. As mentioned above, the free-market economy needed a decade to bounce back – but these were years that began with considerable hardship for the poorest sector of the population, which needed a military dictatorship to force the required policies through and, despite eventual growth for the economy as a whole, the benefits have only recently began to trickle down to the lowest levels of Chilean society.

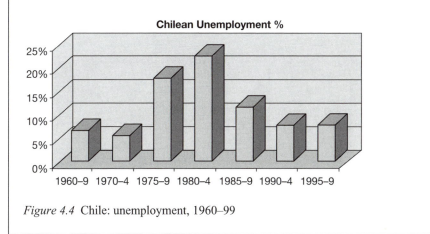

Figure 4.4 Chile: unemployment, 1960–99

THE EXPECTATIONS REVOLUTION

In the late 1960s, at the time when the 'unemployment or inflation' trade-off was widely accepted by government policy-makers in most parts of the world, two US economists were predicting the breakdown in this Phillips curve relationship.

Milton Friedman of the University of Chicago and Edmund Phelps of the University of Pennsylvania both independently argued that the stable function between these two alleged opposites that had lasted for almost a century could not continue. Their reasoning was based on the way that behaviour changes when expectations change.

For most of the time for which Phillips had compiled his data, periods when prices were rising alternated with periods when prices were falling. For any given year prior to the late 1950s, therefore, it was reasonable to expect that inflation would average out at zero. Inflation in the late 1960s, however, was beginning to creep up. It was becoming the norm. Indeed, governments were beginning to use the Phillips relationship as a policy-making guide: opting deliberately for a low rate of price increases as the necessary evil to reduce unemployment. Such a change in economic fundamentals would be bound to affect expectations, Friedman and Phelps argued.

If workers and their union representatives expect that prices would rise in the future then they would build in this factor to their wage demands: asking for higher pay in future to protect their real incomes. If employers then granted such wage increases they would thereafter try to pass on these extra costs by pushing up prices even higher. Inflation begins to accelerate. Workers find prices are higher than expectation so put in for even greater wage increases next time. The end result must be an inflationary wage–price spiral: whatever the level of employment that existed when this process began, it can only be maintained by faster and faster rises in inflation. The original Phillips curve must transform into a vertical line (Figure 4.5).

The implication of Friedman and Phelps theorising is that *any* rate of inflation could occur at a given level of employment or unemployment, it all depended

% inflation

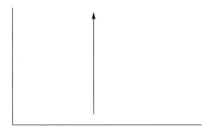

% unemployment

Figure 4.5 The expectations-augmented Phillips curve

on expectations. There was thus no unique rate of inflation that would necessarily obtain once peoples' expectations, and their behaviour, started to
change.

The expectations-augmented Phillips curve, as this became known, was a
theoretical construct, not an observed relationship like the original. However,
events in the 1970s seemed to confirm this prediction: inflation *did* take off in
the USA, Europe and indeed all round the world, following the OPEC oil price
crisis. The stable Phillips curve had broken down and so to did the Keynesian
paradigm that had so dominated post-war policy-making.

'Stagflation' – stagnation plus inflation – seemed to dog the late 1970s and
the old Keynesian remedy of spending your way out of a recession could no
longer be applied. (It would have resulted in greater and greater inflation.) So
what could be done?

Supply-side economics borrowed the theoretical advances of what became
known as 'the expectations revolution' to offer a solution: if governments
and/or central bankers acted with authority to cut back inflation this would
affect expectations and quickly bring wage demands and prices under control.
Cutting back money supplies and government spending might, of course, cause
unemployment but this should only be a short-term phenomenon while
expectations took time to adjust. Theoretically speaking, it should be possible
to go straight *down* the vertical line in Figure 4.3, just as quickly as inflation
went straight up.

Moreover, inflation – according to supply-siders – is public enemy number
one. Unemployment in declining sectors is unavoidable and indeed it is to be
accepted rather than prevented if resources are to transfer their allegiance.
Inflation, however, distorts relative prices and incomes, affects everyone in an
economy and particularly prejudices business confidence in the future. As such,
it inhibits investment and thereby economic growth. The economic priorities
and policies of Western governments such as in the US and UK were quite clear,
therefore: inflation was a more important concern than unemployment.

Restrictive monetary and fiscal policies were recommended to cure inflation.
Growth, meanwhile, could be revived by stimulating the private sector and
reducing the role of the state which, it was alleged, only inhibited enterprise and
crowded out private investment.

Around the world, therefore, the consensus grew that the only route to
escape the twin evils of recession and inflation was to introduce contrac-
tionary monetary measures plus free-market policies in a bid to re-invigorate
supply-side economic growth consistent with stable price levels. The call was
thus to contain government budgets and domestic money supplies, restore
private ownership and competition to industry and commerce, reduce stifling
regulations, cut taxes and remove protection from labour as well as goods
markets.

What has been the impact of these radical policy changes on unemployment, inflation and economic growth during the 1980s and 1990s for those
countries in the forefront of the supply-side revolution? Within this frame of
reference in particular, has the new supply-side orthodoxy been vindicated,

BOX 4.2 SUPPLY-SIDE POLICIES IN ACTION (2) THE UK

In May 1979, the Conservative (Tory) party came into office in the UK, trumpeting the virtues of supply-side policies and, in the case of Margaret Thatcher, her political authority to implement the new right-wing economic doctrine was unchallenged.

Deregulation began in *financial and capital markets* with the abolition of foreign exchange controls (October 1979), and the removal of a variety of restrictions on credit (May 1979, June 1980, August 1981). The division between banks and building societies disappeared (October 1983) and along with it went any rationing of long loans and mortgages.

The notion here was to improve the competitiveness and efficiency of money markets. It should be emphasised that – following the writings of the influential Chicago economist Milton Friedman – government control of the overall money supply was considered essential, although its allocation between competing users was thought rightly a matter for the markets to decide.

This is easier to pronounce in theory, however, than it is to put into practice. Modern money is a very slippery concept (see chapter 7, below) and freeing up competitive forces both within the UK domestic banking sector and on the foreign exchange markets meant that it was impossible in the early 1980s for the government to contain money supplies within the declared target range. (For this reason, by the late 1980s the government had abandoned any attempt at monetary targeting.)

With the reforms introduced, there were no direct controls on funds entering or leaving the country; on the rapid expansion of UK banking activities and on the multiple creation of credit. Nigel Lawson (Chancellor of the Exchequer at the time) wrote after that 'the only checks on excess were the price of credit (i.e. the rate of interest) which the government could control and prudence (on the part of bankers and financiers), which it could not' (*Financial Times,* 27 January 1992).

Since deregulation and the growth of the financial services sector was to be encouraged, yet the amount of inflation was not, then rates of interest had to rise. There was no other way – as the quantity of money could not be influenced, its price had to be.

The consequence was that in the early 1980s, with high interest rates and energy costs, British industry suffered a severe slump. Many manufacturing businesses closed, causing much unemployment, though this was explained away by supply-side advocates as the justifiable extinction of inefficient industrial dinosaurs. (Note that this high interest rate policy of Thatcher/Reaganite supply-siders had international repercussions that spread far beyond the slump in domestic industries alone [see Box 4.1 on Chile and chapter 10 on international debt].)

Deregulation of *labour markets* meant, for the Tories, destroying trade union power to affect wages and inhibit labour mobility. Legislation to curb the unions was enacted in the 1980 and 1982 Employment Acts and in the 1984 Trade Union Act.

In addition to enfeebling the unions, there was a call to restructure welfare provision to labour in order to reduce the financial incentive for (particularly young people) drawing unemployment benefit rather than seeking work. School leavers' entitlement to register for dole money was withdrawn and 'make work'

Youth Opportunity Programmes and Youth Training Schemes were introduced (1983, 1988).

Perhaps the most important policy with regard to labour markets was the government's acceptance of high levels of unemployment. Supply-siders argued that Britain's jobless rate was 'voluntary' in the sense that more and more people were allegedly preferring not to work, rather than accepting whatever they could find at the going wage. That is, the level of *'natural' unemployment* necessary to persuade people to become occupationally mobile had increased. The government's willingness to accept jobless people's pain was necessary, therefore, to force changes through.

Privatisation of Britain's public enterprises was embarked upon to 'roll back the frontiers of the state' and to unleash the supposed forces of the free market throughout the economy. Three purposes were allegedly served by this policy: to increase economic efficiency; to reduce dependency on government finances; and to increase the spread of share ownership (people's capitalism).

From British Aerospace to Rover Cars, British Gas to local water authorities, scores of state-owned corporations and public utilities were sold off, raising around £30,000 billion between 1979 and 1990.

(One theoretical concern about all privatisation programmes is the conversion of state monopolies into private ones. Supply-side reform is best served by *increased market competition*. Economists have argued that selling off giants like British Telecom without breaking them up was premature. Despite the difficulties of dismantling certain natural monopolies (those public utilities that *cannot* operate efficiently on a small scale, e.g. in the distribution of gas, electricity, water, telecoms, etc.) more could have been done to promote dismemberment into competing units.)

In the education and health sectors, where full-scale privatisation was not possible, *quasi-markets* were promoted. That is, changes were introduced to devolve financial management down to the level of each school and hospital; to encourage 'opting out' of local authority control; and to introduce as far as possible the practice of competition between 'consumers' and 'suppliers'. Consumers in this context were school students or hospital patients. For every student/patient on a school's/hospital's list the government allocated state funds. If such consumers transferred their 'custom' from one school/hospital to another, state funds would transfer accordingly.

Tax reform, in addition to all of the above, was part of the doctrine to promote the spirit of free enterprise. Tax cuts give people more freedom to choose what they wish to do with their money, it was argued, and they give greater marginal incentives to work. ('Why work an extra hour's overtime if it only puts you into a higher tax bracket?') The basic rate of income tax was brought down over the 1980s from 33 per cent to 25 per cent and the top rate came down from 83 per cent to 40 per cent. Corporation tax on business profits was similarly reduced from over 50 per cent to less than 40 per cent. (In compensation, VAT rates were raised in stages from 8 per cent up to 15 per cent and the infamous Poll Tax was introduced.) The supposed beneficial impact on incentives, enterprise and thereby economic growth of these tax changes was considered paramount. A steeply *progressive tax* system was thus weakened and made more regressive. *Note*: The distributional effect of *widening the gap between rich and poor* was considered (by the rich!) a price worth paying in order to promote a more dynamic, growthful economy.

or does the Keynesian theory that it supplanted still have relevance for the new millennium?

For the UK, the evidence revealed in Figure 4.6 is mixed. Inflation over the period has fluctuated above the European average, rising again in excess of 10 per cent by the beginning of the 1990s, though it has since fallen. The most significant sustained change was the establishment of high unemployment levels compared to earlier decades: the lowest attainable jobless rate in the 1980s was higher than any unemployment peak since 1945. In the late 1990s, UK unemployment has fallen and prices have stabilised but the supply-side contention that growth can be attained with falling inflation and unemployment cannot be claimed as a great victory. Non-inflationary growth is quite feasible whilst recovering from recession: unutilised resources are simply re-employed, thus contributing to growth at little extra cost. But such a recovery from the early 1990s recession is no great achievement if the recession was induced by supply-side policies in the first place.

Figure 4.6 shows that inflation and unemployment are still opposites. UK supply-side policies seem to have been successful in so far as both are now falling but evidence continues to support a Phillipsian trade-off, albeit at different levels than before. In other words, inflation is *not* unrelated to unemployment as implied in Figure 4.5. (Some have argued, following Friedman, for a set of short-run Phillips curves that have shifted out and back – each short-run curve consistent with a different level of expectations.)

How do other countries' experiences of inflation and unemployment during the 1980s and 1990s compare with that of the UK's (see Figures 4.7 to 4.10)? Have other economies succeeded in bringing down inflation and unemployment together, as was allegedly possible?

There are, of course, a vast number of variables that are at play here in determining the economic fortunes of the countries surveyed below. The pattern which emerges in comparing the UK, the USA, France, Germany and Italy, however, is remarkable for its similarity. Inflation and unemployment swing up and down in opposition to each other almost without exception. The Phillips-type pattern of a short-term trade-off between the two seems remarkably well illustrated in all cases. The precise relationship between inflation and unemployment is now not as stable over time as it was in Phillips' day, but nonetheless these two economic objectives do appear to be alternatives – at least in the evidence featured here.

US economist Alan Blinder uses a very helpful analogy to illustrate how managing a national economy in the stable world environment of the 1950s and 1960s compares to the crisis-ridden 1970s and thereafter. It is like driving a car – there is always a short-term trade-off between speed and safety. The faster you go, the more dangerous it is: speed and safety are alternatives. Now consider what it is like driving in clear weather on a good road, compared with driving in blizzard conditions in unknown country. The same trade-off still exists, but now the relationship shifts to a completely different level. Hazardous external conditions have transformed the way these two alternatives operate on your driving.

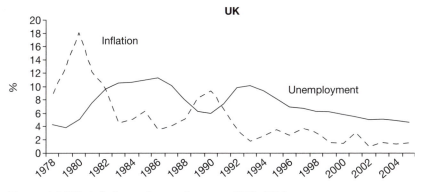

Figure 4.6 UK: inflation and unemployment, 1978–2005
Sources: *World in Figures*; OECD; *The Economist*.

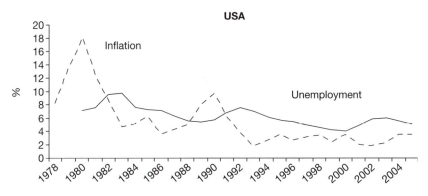

Figure 4.7 USA: inflation and unemployment, 1978–2005
Sources: *World in Figures*; OECD; *The Economist*.

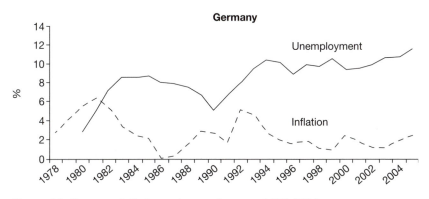

Figure 4.8 Germany: inflation and unemployment, 1978–2005
Sources: *World in Figures*; OECD; *The Economist*.

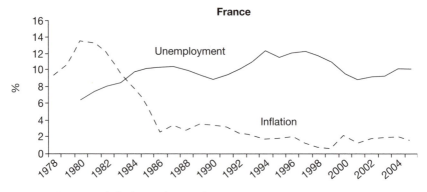

Figure 4.9 France: inflation and unemployment, 1978–2005
Sources: *World in Figures*; OECD; *The Economist*.

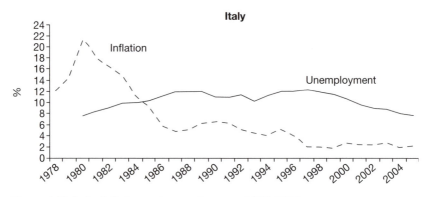

Figure 4.10 Italy: inflation and unemployment, 1978–2005
Sources: *World in Figures*; OECD; *The Economist*.

Look at the inflation/unemployment trade-off in the early 1970s; compare the data for the late 1970s/early 1980s; and consider again the late 1980s/early 1990s. Conditions seem to indicate different levels of trade-off, different Phillips curves, for each of these periods. Compared to the 1950s and 1960s when a stable international environment existed with fixed exchange rates, the oil shocks and financial instability of the 1970s and early 1980s hit the major trading nations like a storm. Inflation then was politically unavoidable and it took all countries a number of years to get it under control – though some succeeded more quickly than did others.

Expectations have played their part here. With soaring prices, it is no surprise that people's wage demands were affected, just as Friedman and Phelps anticipated. But the evidence seems to show that the unemployment/inflation trade-off has not disappeared – when expectations change the Phillips curve merely shifts to a different level.

It is easy to talk with the benefit of hindsight, however. The policy change driven by US/UK governments and promoted elsewhere by the IMF and World Bank (later referred to as the Washington consensus, see chapter 10) at the time was analogous to taking aboard a fanatic supply-side driver who was determined to hammer one side of the trade-off road rather than the other. Management of national economies in unstable times – keeping the car on the road – needs sensitive handling, with regard to a number of policy instruments, and it is not helped by dogmatic reliance on the free-market accelerator only, with a blinkered disregard for bystanders. Yet this was the result of the paradigm shift that occurred when Keynesian thinking was overtaken by the incoming supply-side school.

The evidence surveyed to date – around the world from Chile, via the USA, UK and on to New Zealand – shows that supply-side economics carries great social costs. The theory was that radical anti-inflationary policies must be ruthlessly applied in order to transform expectations and thus bring prices rapidly down at minimum cost to unemployment. Labour markets should be simultaneously 'de-regulated' in order to promote mobility of workers between jobs. This supposedly results in a prompt movement vertically down the expectations-augmented Phillips curve.

The reality was somewhat different. Unemployment rose almost everywhere and stubbornly resisted inducements to quickly decline. People from South America to Europe and the Pacific refused to react like cattle and be led from market to market since (surprisingly?) they remain emotionally committed to their occupations and communities. In consequence, the costs of implementing the prescribed free-market medicine have been measured in terms of long-lasting loss of work and incomes which has given economics a new concept: *hysteresis* – any given situation will be gloomy if the past was gloomy. Or, if you let things get bad now, you'll get stuck that way – maybe not for ever but, according to Edwards and Edwards (Box 4.1), for up to a decade or so. This hurts.

Mainland Europe, it can be argued, is still struggling to bite this bullet. Unemployment remains high and microeconomic, supply-side 'reforms' have not yet been implemented in the face of fierce political opposition due to the fear of hardship they will cause. Inflation and unemployment are still short-run alternatives but the issue is now at what long-run level they operate. Changing expectations and bringing down this level – contrary to supply side theory – takes time and is certainly not costless. It is perhaps the most empirically significant and most poignant legacy of the expectations revolution.

CONCLUSION

It has been argued that unemployment is the creation of modern, Western society. Its causes are manifold: there are both macro- and microeconomic factors at work. It has been mentioned that sophisticated, integrated economies must continually evolve if sufficient new jobs are to be created to replace the old. Macroeconomic, contra-cyclical policies to maintain a consistent, high level of aggregate demand are important, as are microeconomic job information services, re-training packages and the re-targeting of government hand-outs to subsidise labour mobility and redeployment rather than redundancy and welfare dependency. Because there are social and private costs and benefits involved, governments, employers and employees all need to be involved in sharing the responsibility for new training and employment programmes.

In particular, unemployment concerns the nature of the relationship of the individual with the state. The individual cannot say: society owes me a living; nor can society insist that unemployment is always and everywhere the fault of the individual. Coalminers cannot be blamed for the development of undersea oil and gas.

We live in a mobile age. The structural changes required to meet the fickle demands of world markets are great – and the pace of change is likely to quicken, not slow down. Politicians remote from unemployment maybe cannot see or feel sufficiently its ill effects. Arguing that market forces alone will solve the problem with minimal government 'interference' is a declaration of faith unlikely to be shared by those whose jobs are no longer in demand.

This is not to deny that inflation is an important consideration also. Rising prices will reduce the standard of living of all whose incomes cannot similarly increase. As well as effecting a change in the relative distribution of incomes, the functioning of the price mechanism for all goods and services within the economy becomes impaired. Efficient organisation of the entire economy suffers. Inflation, once uncontrollable, can just as surely lead to social and economic misery as increasing unemployment.

The solution of difficult social problems requires a flexibility of approach from us all: individuals must seek perpetually to upgrade their skills; society must subsidise their efforts. Unemployment represents a colossal waste of resources. It is inefficient, uneconomic to have human potential lying idle; deteriorating over time. But this is an issue of normative as well as positive economics: unemployment is the creation of the modern market economy and therefore society needs a moral vision that is as geographically far-reaching as the spread of its trade.

Traditional communities – wherever they live and work in the world – will continue to be overtaken by revolutions in the global market place. Unemployment matters wherever it occurs, and individuals, employers and governments must all assume responsibility for making efforts to overcome it.

KEY WORDS

Deregulation   This usually refers to the removing of government regulations, restrictions and rules on the provision and sale of goods and services.

Globalisation   an imprecise but highly evocative term that motivates all sorts of protests. It simply refers to the increasing spread of world trade, free from government interference. Some fear this allows very large multinational corporations to exert undue influence in dictating prices and exploiting the poorest but the best guard against this

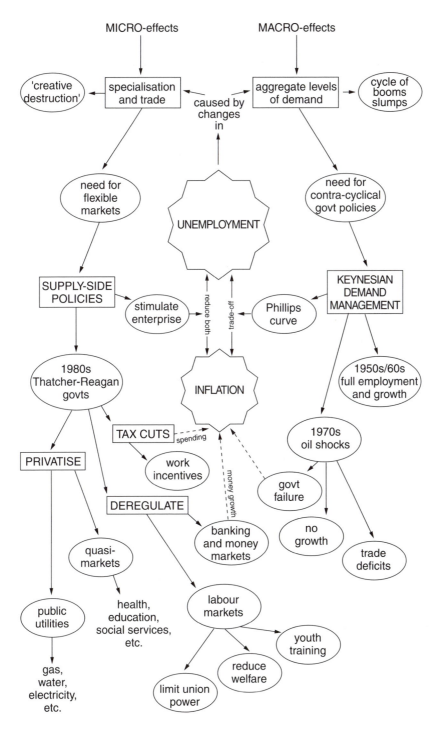

Figure 4.11 The themes of chapter 4

is more competition, more trade, more choice so that no one dealer can dominate any marketplace.

Hysteresis   A term borrowed from physics, where the state of a system is dependent on its past history. In economics, this means that if unemployment is made to rise suddenly (due maybe to the collapse of a key industry) then it may get stuck that way since peoples' skills – their human capital – rapidly depreciate when they are not being used. It is a modern form of that old Keynesian notion of an underemployment equilibrium.

Inflation   The percentage rise in the general level of prices of a country over a year, measured by reference to an officially recognised price index.

Progressive tax   This is a tax which takes a rising fraction of people's income as their incomes increase: for example, an income tax which takes nothing from a poor person; taxes 25 per cent of those earning above $20,000 p.a.; 30 per cent of those earning above $40,000; etc. Such a tax contrasts with a *proportional tax* – which charges the same percentage on incomes on all people, whatever their earnings – and a *regressive tax* which takes a higher percentage of a poor person's income than a rich person's. (A *poll tax* which charges the same *amount* – say $100 – on all people irrespective of their incomes is an example of a regressive tax.)

Trade-off   The economics of a two-good (or two-bad) world. You can only have more (or less) of one thing if you have less (or more) of another. The research conducted by Professor Phillips revealed that if people wanted less unemployment then they had to trade this off for more inflation.

QUESTIONS

1 'Any cyclical slump in world trade will affect all countries, but those structurally rigid, least-flexible countries will suffer most of all.' Explain and discuss.
2 What is meant by Keynesian, 'counter-cyclical' government policies? How could such policies be used to reduce: (a) unemployment; (b) inflation?
3 What are the objectives of 'supply-side' economics? What are the policies involved? Are there any costs in implementing them?
4 What causes inflation? Distinguish between Keynesian and supply-side views.
5 'The Phillips curve trade-off between unemployment and inflation still holds, only it has shifted out.' Is this true? If so, why?

FURTHER READING

Blinder, Alan S. *Hard Heads, Soft Hearts*. Addison Wesley, 1987.
Nell, Edward J. (ed.). *Free Market Conservatism*. Allen & Unwin, 1984.
Snowdon, B., Vane, H. and Wynarczyk, P. *A Modern Guide to Macroeconomics*. Elgar, 1994.

5   Free trade, regional agreements and strategic policies

Topics to be considered in this chapter:

- Protectionism.
- Trade agreements – a range from independence to economic and political union.
- The theory of comparative advantage.
- NAFTA and the challenge for Mexico.
- Strategic trade policies.
- Japanese economic development.

INTRODUCTION

Free trade in world markets randomly visits misery on groups of workers and business people whose products seem suddenly to go out of favour. Most countries can find examples of established industries that – thanks to changing technology and the costs of production, or some fickleness in consumer demand – have lost their markets to new competitors.

- In the early 1980s, Hong Kong, South Korea and Taiwan together accounted for nearly a third of the world's clothing exports. That has now fallen to around 8 per cent as world demand snaps up cheaper produce from China.
- In the late 1980s and early 1990s, as communications and transport costs fell, US carmakers transferred assembly plants to Mexico; Volkswagen invested in the Czech Republic; Philips consumer electronics went further afield to China.
- Outsourcing that first occurred in manufacturing now affects 'white-collar' services: in November 2004, Lloyds TSB – a British bank – said it expected to transfer 2,500 jobs to India by the end of 2005. US researchers predict that over 70,000 jobs in the legal profession will leave their country for other, less costly shores.

The process of creative destruction that causes distress to some brings opportunity to others, of course, but the differential impact on costs and benefits means that the misery can be painfully concentrated in certain regions and countries at certain times. The benefits may seem too often to be more accessible to other people, other places. During periods of instability and wrenching change the political impetus for protectionist policies – to cushion certain communities and industrial sectors from the harsh realities of international competition – may thus prove unstoppable. It often plays on the short-sighted sentiment that a country's wealth and welfare is best ensured by denying foreign advantage.

TRADE PROTECTION

Mercantilism has a long and sorry history. It advocates securing trade gains at the expense of other countries; erecting barriers against imports whilst aggressively promoting exports. At the extreme, it drove eighteenth- and nineteenth-century European empire-building and colonialism – the rush to carve up resource-rich and militarily less-powerful American, African and Asian lands before rivals could do likewise. In the 1930s, mercantilist 'beggar-my-neighbour' policies were pursued in the attempt to escape the Great Depression. The same protectionist, nationalist sentiments emerged across the world during the stagnating 1970s and the recessionary late 1980s.

In the new millennium, myopic attitudes to trade have taken a novel twist. Laudable, but fundamentally uninformed, concern for the welfare of poorer nations has fuelled protests against the international gatherings of trade ministers and government leaders. Diverse meetings in Seattle, Prague, Washington and Gleneagles have witnessed angry demonstrations against the supposed representatives of 'global capitalism' which allegedly set the rules of world trade against the poor. The irony is that if there is to be any golden rule to lift incomes for the whole world – poor as well as rich – then it must be to free up trade for all and not to resort to blinkered protectionism. Both reason and empirical evidence reveal that international trade benefits those that support it – it is not a zero-sum game where if one gains another must lose.

Yet protectionist thinking never goes away. As implied above, it is simply more apparent at some times and places than others. When the world economy is booming it becomes less relevant since all are becoming richer; when world economic growth slows, becomes stagnant or shrinks, however, then one country's economic fortune can be at the expense of another's. The protectionist barriers go up.

At such times it requires considerable diplomatic effort to prevent trade restrictions from spreading. A general collapse in world trade, everyone agrees, is bad for all, but what does it matter if *my* country alone subsidises its exports and protects its vital industries? Such is the argument of the *free-rider* – who benefits most if everyone else agrees to the rules.

The General Agreement on Tariffs and Trade (GATT) was set up in 1948 as part of the attempt to rebuild a positive world order after the disasters of two world wars and an intervening depression. Despite all the difficulties, it has been outstandingly successful and in 1995 it graduated to become the World Trade Organisation (WTO). Originally, 23 countries participated in the first GATT round of discussions in Geneva. At the close of the Uruguay round of trade negotiations, which started in Punta del Este in 1986 and finished in Marrakesh, Morocco, in December 1993, 116 countries signed up and, at the last count in 2005, the WTO claimed 148 members. In the meantime, the average tariff on world trade has come down from around 40 per cent to less than 4 per cent; the global economy has grown sixfold and international trade has shot up almost off the graph (see Figure 5.1).

The correlation between trade and growth is clear to see. The contrast between the interwar years, when international relations were mercantilist and trade growth was negative, and the half-century since 1950 when both functions have grown exponentially is particularly marked. It underscores the importance of continuing efforts to reduce trade restriction.

Negotiating world-wide reductions in trade barriers, although worthwhile, is extremely slow going. The binding principle that drove GATT and now the WTO is the commitment to end discrimination in trade and to generalise 'most-favoured nation' status to all. Thus any advantage granted to one trading partner must be extended to every signatory. This is time-consuming to arrange. The issue that inevitably slows progress the most is the distribution of gains involved in any new round of cuts. Why should one nation agree to reducing *tariffs* and *quotas* if these seem to give greater competitive advantage to another? Poorer countries dependent on the export of a precious few products are wary of the exploitative power of rich nations with highly developed industrial bases; old rivalries amongst mature economies are easily awoken; there is also much disagreement between poor nations themselves. The recent round of talks to free up trade in farm products and services (launched in Doha, in the Gulf state of Qatar in 2001) has been declared on and off several times since due to widespread distrust over the commitment to remove agricultural subsidies. These are all legitimate concerns and require much time and diplomacy to address.

The fewer the parties involved in any negotiations, and the more they have in common, the easier it is to secure agreement. It is for this reason that regional

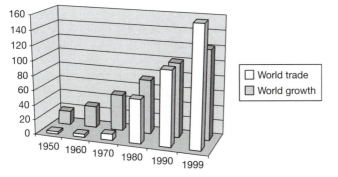

Figure 5.1 Index of world trade and growth, 1950–99 (1990 = 100)
Source: WTO.

trade blocs have grown rapidly, against the background of a WTO-inspired, general expansion of international trade. So long as the regional deals involved do not lead to a raising of barriers to outsiders then, somewhat pragmatically, WTO rules do not prohibit such arrangements. Realistically, the post-war movement towards European Union (EU) in particular – although highly discriminatory with respect to farm trade – has been unstoppable. The very success of the EU has been an added reason for the growth of other regional associations, both in the desire to emulate its success and in the fear of losing out in a world increasingly subdivided into power blocs.

TRADE AGREEMENTS

It would be helpful at this stage to define the different types of trading agreements between nations before going on to discuss in further detail some of the issues involved. There are various levels of relationship possible – from negotiating a limited reciprocal reduction of tariffs on certain goods only, all the way through to the full integration of entire economies. The spectrum of choices involved appears below in order of increasing complexity.

1 *Independence*. A country may opt not to join any regional trade grouping but choose to arrange its own policies on a bilateral, country-by-country basis. This way it is not constrained by any rules set up by prior agreement with others. Minimum levels of commitment, sovereignty loss and gains from trade are involved.
2 *A free trade area*. Here a number of countries may agree to reduce tariffs and quotas on designated items between themselves, but leave each individual country to pursue independent policies with respect to the rest of the world. Intra-area trade may thus be completely free of all restrictions on goods and services; or (more realistically) tariffs may be reduced but not entirely removed on some, not all, items.
3 *A customs union*. In addition to free trade between member countries, a common external tariff may be erected against all outside trade. This barrier will be of different heights for different goods, and erected against some countries and not others, but what makes a customs union different from a free trade area is that it has a common trade policy for all member countries with respect to all external parties.
4 *A common market*. This involves free trade not only in goods and services between member countries, but also in the unrestricted movement and employment of labour and capital. Additionally, a common market usually implies an increasing number of common policies (e.g. in Europe, the Common Agricultural Policy) and – with regard to trade – a progressive reduction in non-tariff barriers also. This implies that all the rules and regulations, different specifications and standards embodied in member countries' goods and services become 'harmonised', or that mutual recognition is accepted.

5 *Economic union.* Many common policies are pursued at this stage, in particular a common currency and monetary policy. This would therefore necessitate a common central bank and other economic institutions, co-ordinated fiscal policies, convergent financial performance, an industrial and competition policy and almost certainly a 'structural fund' or regional policy to address the possible problem of differential growth rates between regions/countries.

6 *One nation.* With an increasingly integrated Union economy, political sovereignty will inevitably be pooled between member countries. Central political institutions tend therefore to parallel the growth of common economic structures. A common parliament and legislature grows up at this stage and, with them, well-defined political and economic relationships are established between member states and the centre. Common social and regional policies will evolve from economic union; a common foreign and defence policy will similarly evolve from a common external trade policy.

(Note that these stages have been delineated as primarily an economic process; the sixth above, however, could be characterised instead as the ultimate stage of a separate political process which examines the degree of integration of political institutions and constitutions.)

It should be emphasised that once started on this process, there is no inevitability in progressing through this sequence of increasing economic integration, nor do these stages themselves represent discrete and well-marked steps along the way. As will be seen, a free trade area may still be rather slow in reducing internal trade barriers yet achieve breakthroughs in other common policies, such as with the mobility of capital, or in exchange rate agreements.

The European Union provides the best example of a regional association of nations that has both deepened and widened its trading relationships through the various stages outlined above. This supra-national development, which first began with the Treaty of Rome in 1957, has provoked different reactions from other countries around the world – from applications to join from near neighbours; to negotiations for concessions from distant partners fearful of being shut out; to the establishment of other regional groupings of countries seeking to rival the EU's growing economic influence.

The most notable recent example of another regional association is the North American Free Trade Agreement (NAFTA), signed between the USA, Mexico and Canada in December 1992. It will be instructive to examine NAFTA first as an illustration of the issues involved in the economics of free trade, and then later to look at the EU in more detail as we go on to consider matters related to closer economic integration.

NAFTA

The background to NAFTA is marked by the changing attitudes and economic policies between the three partner countries during the 1980s. There is a long history of unease on the part of both Canada and Mexico of being swamped by a closer relationship with the very much larger US economy. Nonetheless, the oil crisis of the 1970s (see chapter 9), followed by the recessionary 1980s brought about a gradual change in thinking. As has already been outlined in the previous chapter, a growing shift in world economic opinion towards more free-market policies gathered pace.

For both Canada and the USA, the potential benefits from increasing liberalisation of trade under the last round of GATT talks were eagerly awaited and the longer the Uruguay round dragged on (thanks to European blocking over agriculture) the more a fall-back position of at least free trade throughout North America became attractive. Negotiations for a US–Canada deal began in earnest in 1986 and, despite fierce opposition from some worried Canadians, a free trade agreement was secured between these two countries in 1987, eventually ratified and carried into effect on 1 January 1989.

It can be argued that the difficulties of reaching accord between Canada and the USA are not great, given that culturally and in terms of living standards these two nations are not so very far apart. Although a vociferous (especially Canadian) minority would disagree, certainly the general mistrust of and resistance to closer Mexican–US ties was greater. Mexican economic history reveals foreign, especially US, dominance of much of its industry, including railways, oil, mining, banks and plantation agriculture – particularly through 'el porfiriato': the 1876–1910 rule of General Porfirio Diaz. Since the revolution of 1910 the Mexican economy had been characterised by a fear of dependency on foreigners, a dominant government sector, widespread nationalisations and the promotion of import substitution industries behind a wall of protectionist tariffs. The spiralling debt crisis of the early 1980s, however (see chapter 10), the inefficiencies of much of the domestic economy and the growing need for a vibrant export sector all signalled a sharp about-turn in the Mexican economic strategy. Started in the 1980s by President Miguel de Madrid as a way of negotiating debt relief, the free-market reforms were stepped up by his successor, President Carlos Salinas, who opened the way to NAFTA talks in 1990. The Agreement was finally signed between Presidents Salinas, George Bush of the USA and Prime Minister Brian Mulroney of Canada in December 1992. Newly elected US President Bill Clinton negotiated additional accords on environmental issues and labour laws in 1993 and NAFTA came into effect on 1 January 1994.

NAFTA commits the three participant countries to the elimination of all tariffs and quotas between them within fifteen years. Non-tariff barriers, such as different product safety standards, are subject to decision by a tri-national panel of judges. Trade relations with third parties are not affected, however. North America thus becomes a free trade area, not a customs union.

Cross-border investment between the USA, Canada and Mexico is now much encouraged by NAFTA, so the mobility of capital is allowed for, as in a common market, though this is not extended to labour. (The contentious issue of increasing illegal Mexican migration to the USA has been one of the alleged advantages supporting the NAFTA accord: insofar as free trade facilitates rapid economic growth in Mexico, the flood of illegals moving north looking for work should eventually cease – which will be to the relief of the authorities on both sides of the border.)

THE THEORY OF COMPARATIVE ADVANTAGE

It is time now to examine in more depth the economic argument for free trade that underlies all the developments outlined above. How is it that reducing trade barriers should lead to increasing wealth and welfare for the countries concerned? Will all benefit equally, or will free trade lead to a widening gap between rich and poor?

The economic theory of international trade and *comparative advantage* is at the heart of this debate and we need to understand this analysis more fully if we are to understand the drive behind the WTO, regional associations like the EU and NAFTA and indeed all bilateral and multilateral trade liberalising deals.

We may begin by considering the case of a number of trading countries, each with its own unique endowment of natural resources. It should be seen that instead of each one trying to provide for their domestic needs independently, all countries benefit by specialising in what they are best at and then trading with others in order to purchase, at less cost, what others produce. Free trade thereby enables specialisation, increased production and thus higher standards of living for all participants.

The same principle acts for any individual student: on leaving college a large market society enables the graduate to specialise in his or her chosen employment, selling skills for an income that allows him/her to purchase a far wider range of goods and services than could ever be provided for by the student in isolation.

Although particularly relevant to European nations of similar size and development, it should be emphasised that the theory of free trade as just outlined is also relevant to a small, relatively less-developed country doing business with a larger, wealthier neighbour – say Mexico with the USA.

It might be asked, what has a rich country got to gain in trade with a poorer neighbour when it can produce everything more efficiently itself? Or, conversely, might not a smaller country suffer exploitation from its larger trade partner?

Clearly these arguments are incompatible. They cannot both be true.

The same can be said for the following pair of arguments: producers in high-wage countries can often be heard claiming that they can never hope to compete with cheap labour industries in the developing world and so some government support is thus argued as essential. Equally in poor countries other critics can be heard demanding exactly the same sort of assistance because they cannot compete with Western high technology, i.e. cheap capital.

All these arguments are false. Even where trading partners are completely mismatched, economics can demonstrate that both parties may benefit from free trade. This principle was first established in 1817 by economist David Ricardo: the principle of comparative advantage.

Consider again the case of individuals. Why should a doctor, for example, employ a secretary to type letters which she could do more quickly herself? This is exactly the same question as: why should the USA buy manufactured goods, clothing and foodstuffs from Mexico that it could just as easily produce itself?

I hope you can see the answer. It is a better, more cost-effective use of resources for the doctor to devote her time to medicine than to waste 20 minutes or so typing a letter. Her less-competent secretary may spend half an hour on the same task but then her time is less valuable and the doctor can meanwhile get on with some more beneficial employment. Similarly, US resources could be devoted to self-sufficiency in clothing, but it is more efficient to import much of this and concentrate on higher-tech products. For their part, the (currently) less-efficient Mexican producers can find a market for their produce, will gain better incomes than if they were confined to domestic sales alone and may start the process of improving their skills and development prospects.

In economics, we say the doctor possesses absolute advantages in both medicine and typing, but a comparative advantage in only one: the former. The secretary has absolute disadvantage in both practices but a comparative advantage in typing. Similarly, in trade with the USA, Mexico has a comparative advantage in lower-tech, labour-intensive industries like manufacturing assembly and clothing.

It is this important principle of comparative advantage which determines the direction of trade. Once this is understood, a country is well on its way to concentrating its resources, establishing trade and increasing economic growth.

This point is sufficiently important to warrant further investigation. Consider the case of Japan. There are those who once considered this country was a Far Eastern power-house that could outcompete European and American business in all sorts of world markets. From the analysis just presented you should be able to see that it was impossible for Japan to possess a comparative advantage in all its industries. In practice, the growth of Korean, Taiwanese, Hong Kong, Singaporean, Malaysian and Thai manufacturing industries – Asian dragons that have grown up in Japan's own backyard – prove the point. This leads to an important finding: comparative advantage is a dynamic, not a static, concept. In 1950 Japan had no advantage in producing cars and motorcycles. Nor in 1960 did Mexico possess any advantage in producing consumer durables like cars, computers and other electronic products; nor even in producing sizeable quantities of oil and gas. But in free-market society where: (1) prices are flexible; (2) consumers exercise choice; and (3) resources are free to move their employment, then industries will grow and decline. Comparative advantage will keep changing.

A secretary may not want to be a secretary for ever – she may want to train to be a doctor. Mexico may not want to specialise in cheap-labour industries for ever but may want to secure economic growth and, in time, produce sophisticated high-quality goods and services. Free trade offers a pathway to progress. Countries have to start somewhere. Unless Mexico (and all other countries) can sell its produce in unrestricted markets it cannot begin to reap the benefits of specialisation, trade and growth.

The dynamics of the free market are behind the thrust to implement NAFTA, to enlarge its membership to include others (such as Chile) and in the impetus it has given to other Latin American groupings such as Mercosur (a customs union between Brazil, Argentina, Paraguay and Uruguay) and CARICOM (the Caribbean Community of West Indian states).

THE COSTS OF FREE TRADE

This analysis of free trade does not deny, however, that there are very real costs involved. This chapter started with the assertion that the dynamics of creative destruction impose misery on selected communities in all trading countries. It is for this reason that free-trade agreements are usually phased into operation over a number of years. Additionally, public authorities and vested interests in the negotiation process have an important responsibility to monitor the distribution of costs and benefits involved amongst the people affected.

With respect to NAFTA, disadvantages cited include the alleged increasing polarisation or dualism of economic society throughout all of North America. It is argued, for example, that the multinational, Mexican-based *maquiladoras* or assembly plants set up to serve the US market have bled jobs away from north of the border, have generated increased profits for their owners and managers, yet have built few local linkages through which to contribute much towards the host economy south of the Rio Grande.

There is undoubtedly some painful US labour experience behind these criticisms, but even if there is a limit to low-skilled assembly-line jobs (which there will not be if free trade stimulates economic growth), it can still be argued that it is better in the short run that they be diverted to those parts of the continent where there is a higher concentration of such workers and where educational, re-training and labour-market opportunities are least developed. That is, even in a stagnant market, redundant US workers would be better placed to find new work than Mexican ones since they have better access to supportive welfare and labour-market infrastructure. (It is, of course, not much consolation for unemployed US car workers to learn that Mexico has a comparative advantage in their type of work and that Mexican workers are more needy anyway . . . These sort of movements in world economic forces require sensitive management.) In the longer term, these fears are proving groundless as free trade stimulates more efficient deployment of resources, increased growth and more (though changing) job opportunities for all. For example, US exports to Mexico, and domestic employment therefrom, have risen as tariffs have come down since the mid-1980s.

The assertion that new, export-oriented industrial developments in Mexico build few links with the domestic economy is a more serious criticism and strikes at the heart of the principle of comparative advantage with respect to less-developed countries. This argument deserves close examination.

According to theory, as large and small trading partners reduce barriers, separate markets increasingly become one. There can only be one price for each good or service traded in a single market and inevitably the dominant influence on prices will come from the larger, richer economy. That is, Mexican exports – and Mexican labour services – will thus increasingly sell for higher, US/Canadian prices. The distribution of gains from free trade are thus predicted to be greater for the smaller economy. This is known as 'the importance of being unimportant'.

The macroeconomic impact of increasing export earnings will be magnified thanks to the *foreign trade multiplier* – injections to the domestic economy stimulate a rise in national income commensurate with the marginal propensity to consume (refer back to chapter 3). This may at first be regionally focused where export industries are located in certain development zones (e.g. in the Mexican case, in border towns such as Ciudad Juarez, Tijuana and Nogales) but eventually the beneficial effects must ripple through the entire economy as second- and third-round incomes rise.

The most important gains from trade, however, come from the long-term impact of increasing international competition for local industry. Providing the immediate trauma of adjusting to change is phased in carefully, local businesses learn to adapt to international prices, quality standards, and the demands of consumers. Efficiency gains are high. National resources move to employments that are internationally competitive. *Economies of scale* can be enjoyed in selling to far larger markets than are available within the domestic economy alone. Even where such free-market changes are not phased in but impact with a big bang, the evidence from such countries as far apart as the People's Republic of China, Poland and Chile is that short-term costs are eventually outweighed by long-term recovery.

THE CHALLENGE FOR MEXICO

All such benefits require, however, that the economy involved is responsive to market incentives. If, in the case of Mexico, the *maquiladoras* are, indeed, screwdriver plants where skills transmitted are few; if all inputs are imported, and if there is little involvement of the local economy in producing components and providing services then dualism results. (McKinsey & Co, US consultants, calculate that locally produced intermediate inputs represent less than 2 per cent of the value of *maquiladora* outputs!) Thus a rich, westernised enclave co-exists with a poor hinterland but none of the economic benefits mentioned above are transmitted across the barbed-wire fence which divides them. The gulf between the modern enclave and the surrounding community is culturally and economically as wide as the distance between New York and Mexico City.

'Underdeveloped' countries are defined as such in the Western, economic sense. They may be highly developed with regard to their own cultural identity, which has evolved over centuries. They may, however, be relatively unresponsive to modern market signals. Development, therefore, means building bridges across the divide. The early foreign investments in Mexican assembly plants were not motivated by this ideal, and most are still not. But enlightened self-interest on the part of business management and government officials, at local and national levels, can do much to dismantle barriers and to encourage positive economic interchange.

Many entrepreneurial talents lie dormant in poor communities, and the appropriate skills and opportunities to develop them require nurturing. Cultural differences, values, hierarchical and dependent social relationships that are embodied in traditional patterns of land ownership and the colonial inheritance cannot be simply wished away and rapidly assimilated into modern industrial structures.

NAFTA can bring, and is bringing, the benefits of free trade to Mexico, but the distribution of these benefits is inevitably uneven. It takes time and a determined sense of direction in government to build bridges to all sectors of the community. The fewer restrictions on social and economic mobility, the more the gains from trade will be widespread. Mexico, however, is a profoundly unequal society where the income gap between rich and poor *widened* during the 1980s and 1990s. Increasing free trade, liberalising markets, removing exchange controls and privatising state industries without doing more to reform ownership patterns, regressive tax systems and restricted entitlement to education and health programmes runs the risk of further concentrating wealth in a capitalist elite and alienating the rest. Just as NAFTA has been celebrated in affluent districts of Mexico City and in the development zones along Mexico's northern border region, so Zapatista rebels in the southern state of Chiapas have forcibly reminded their countryfolk that the national economy lacks the flexible political, social and economic framework to engage all its people in the development process.

In purely economic terms, the arguments in favour of free trade are far greater than those against – any elementary textbook will emphasise this. But all the economic benefits which flow from the application of the principle of comparative advantage are based on the assumption that the countries involved possess the preconditions, the infrastructure, the social dynamism and cohesion to make the necessary changes and enjoy the rewards therefrom. Wherever there are market rigidities – for example, entrenched social attitudes and/or political restrictions that inhibit geographical and occupational mobility – then the gains from trade will bid up wages and profits of those with scarce talents and will increase the sense of frustration and loss of those excluded from the wealth-creating process.

Entering the new millennium, NAFTA is driving growth in Mexico. Since 1994, the greater part of $170 billion foreign direct investment into Mexico has thankfully not gone into screwdriver plants producing cheap goods for export but has looked to develop other, higher-value products for home as well as overseas markets. Competition has improved and productivity risen. GDP is surging at 7 per cent p.a. Exports are increasing by over 10 per cent per year. The downside, however, is that inequalities are widening. Average incomes in northern states such as Nuevo Leon are over six times those of Chiapas and Oaxaca in the south. *The Economist* reported (28 October 2000) that infant

DOUGLAS COLLEGE LIBRARY

mortality of the richest 20 per cent of the population was 13 per 1,000 in 1998 but for the poorest 20 per cent it was 52 per 1,000. Children of the richest 10 per cent spend 12.1 years at school; the poorest 10 per cent average only 2.1 per cent. Dualism is endemic and will not go away without radical reform.

As Mexico is finding out, as weary East Europeans have discovered and also as mature industrial economies such as the USA and the UK know to their cost, opening up free trade is not a fully automatic, value-free economic policy that can be implemented by the central government with a hands-off, let-the-markets-decide attitude to the allocation of the country's resources. Microeconomic intervention is necessary to promote higher value added, to facilitate training, dismantle barriers and to provide access to new employment opportunities throughout the economy, wherever rigidities occur. The process may be slow and in many cases governments may be as prone to failure as the markets they are attempting to reform.

There are no easy answers. How are revolutionary Zapatistas who want access to better land, education, jobs and incomes to be persuaded to lay down their arms and return to their peasant holdings? How are richer middle classes who have voted for the economic restructuring and have appropriated its benefits to be persuaded to identify with the poor and indeed to pay for the improved conditions they demand?

Applying the principle of comparative advantage needs careful management, therefore. This is usually recognised in theory in the case of *infant industries*: that is, granting a level of protection to fragile industrial start-ups that are not yet strong enough to withstand the gales of international competition. The protection is supposedly removed when the infant is strong enough to look after itself and thus free trade may return again to rule. In poorer countries where large fragments of the economy may be underdeveloped, the infant industry argument can be used to justify more widespread protection and intervention. If coordinated in a national, integrated manner, rather than in a piecemeal, business-by-business fashion prompted by powerful interest groups, then the overall result can be a *strategic trade policy*, as used with effect by Japan and certain newly industrialised countries such as South Korea, Taiwan or Singapore.

STRATEGIC TRADE POLICIES

The idea of a coherent trade policy is not to obstruct the workings of free trade but to facilitate them – so as to better exploit the opportunities offered by comparative advantage. Government intervention is urged to raise productivity generally and to help make the country's economy more competitive. Where substantial external economies exist in the provision of social infrastructure – educational reform, research and development, transport and communications – where efficiency gains and scale economies require time to learn, and where local capital markets are insufficiently responsive to support developing industry, then properly targeted government subsidies and protection can compensate for the inadequacies of the free market.

DOUGLAS COLLEGE LIBRARY

Countries with low savings and investment, inadequate capital stock, failing educational systems and poor communications and other public utilities prevent their private business sectors from competing on equal terms with other trading nations. Over time, with such impoverished social capital, a country's comparative advantage is bound to trade down to relatively lower-tech., lower income-earning specialisms. (It is precisely this argument that worries many US and European commentators who fear that their mature, rigidified economies are insufficiently equipped to meet the long-term competitive challenge from fast-developing Asian 'dragons'. Brown and Hogendorn (*International Economics*, Addison Wesley, 1994), for example, quote that 1 in 4 students studying for a doctorate in the USA came from Taiwan – a country with a population 8 per cent of that of the US.)

Japan provides the best-known example of a country which used a strategic trade policy. Its relevance today may be questioned – Japan's economic performance through the 1990s has been characterised by recession – but the role of this policy in aiding Japan's development in the past may be instructive for the Mexicos of today.

The typical, developing-country scarcity of entrepreneurial resources and the concentration of economic power in a business elite led in Japan's case to a series of interlocking groups controlling major industrial enterprises, banks, trading companies and government agencies. Rather than promote protection, corruption and the cosy guarantee of personal enrichment, however, the driving ethic of a cohesive and integrated Japanese entrepreneurial class was to set guidelines for national economic development – a combination of free enterprise and government direction that has existed since the Meiji Restoration of 1868.

After World War II, government agencies such as the powerful Ministry of Trade and Industry (MITI) implemented an industrial policy of identifying and supporting winners in international trade: promoting exports, guaranteeing low-cost loans and subsidies, sponsoring research and development and establishing industrial standards which effectively became non-tariff barriers to foreign competitors. During the 1950s, foreign technology was copied systematically in targeted industries. Such technology provided the foundation on which to build successful products. Later high rates of savings, investment and innovation enabled Japanese technology to overtake foreign competitors in an increasing number of industries.

Japan sought first to develop its shipbuilding industry: it had been destroyed in the war, and as an island economy success in trade was dependent on shipping. Rebuilding and modernising the steel industry was also a priority. By 1956 Japan had become the world's biggest shipbuilder and was fast becoming a leading steel exporter as well. The emphasis next turned to developing motorcycles and a car industry. (In 1951 Honda was a small, unheard-of family business. It is not now.) This was followed by consumer electronics which in turn has led to a concentration in computers, artificial intelligence and frontier technologies.

Original protective tariffs on Japanese industry have long since come down. With the exception of agriculture (comparatively inefficient, but protected for social reasons) Japan is now an open economy. Its continuing trade surplus today is a result of a highly efficient manufacturing export sector and it is not the result of restrictions on imports, as some would assert. Despite recent political turmoil, financial mismanagement and a severely depressed home market, the one bright star throughout the slumping 1990s was Japan's ability to export. (Its trade surplus in the 12 months to April 2001 was a staggering US$98.9 billion – the world's largest.)

A less well-known, but equally important component of Japan's post-war strategic trade policy was not only to pick industrial winners, but also to facilitate disinvestment in declining industry. This is because a market economy grows through a process of continuous industrial renewal – creative destruction – which requires *losers* as well as winners. Again, in Japan's case, selected industries were targeted to be run down. Companies involved were encouraged to diversify into more profitable product lines; depreciation allowances to write off old capital and subsidies for new plant and equipment are granted; labour unions are involved from the outset in planning transfers to alternative employments. Much industrial retraining was undertaken by firms in cooperation with local government. As a result, the Japanese shipbuilding industry in the 1990s was less than half the size it was in 1980, steel contracted severely, many coal mines are shut down and capacity in other heavy industries was greatly reduced.

For most of the last half of the twentieth century Japan got it right with respect to its strategic trade policy. So right that its particular partnership of government with industry provided the model for much of East Asia. The fact that the economic performance of countries in this region has been less successful recently (Japan's average economic growth through the 1990s decade was a mere 1 per cent p.a.) does not prove that a 'hands-on' attitude of governments must ultimately fail any more than markets totally free from central command must ultimately succeed. (Banking crises that rocked the region in the 1990s can in part be blamed on financial markets that are too immature and under-regulated.) The fact is that the Japanese model of 'market friendly' policies achieved by consensus-seeking partnerships between political, business and union leaders has transformed East Asia from a relatively poor and introverted region to one of the world's richest and most successful trading zones. The moral is that this market place is not yet fully developed – there is still a lot left to do!

CONCLUSION

The final conclusion offered here is that the principle of comparative advantage provides for substantial benefits in trade, but market economies must be flexible enough to respond to the changing dynamics of international commerce. In less-developed countries in particular, where the geographical spread of the modern market sector may be limited and entrepreneurial resources may be scarce, governments need to work with business to design the appropriate policies in order to establish the institutions, the infrastructure, the preconditions necessary to secure economic development for all.

In the more mature economies of Europe – flexible in some ways, traditionally resistant to change in others – the gains from trade have so overcome the historical rivalry between these countries that further economic integration has been pursued along the spectrum from free trade areas through customs unions to a common market. It is to this analysis we turn in the following chapter.

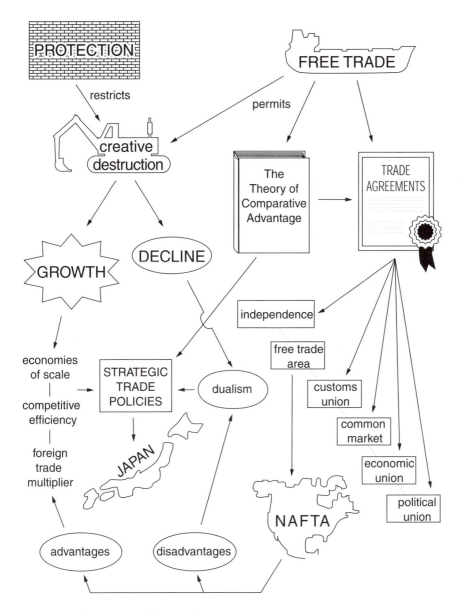

Figure 5.2 The themes of chapter 5

KEY WORDS

The European Union   A common market of (at the time of writing) twenty-five European nations: Belgium, the Netherlands, Luxembourg, Germany, Italy, France, the United Kingdom, Ireland, Denmark, Greece, Spain, Portugal, Austria, Sweden, Finland, Cyprus, the Czech Republic, Estonia, Latvia, Lithuania, Hungary, Malta, Poland, Slovenia and Slovakia. The Union will continue to widen its membership and deepen its integration but how and when is the matter of intense debate.

Free rider   Where sufficient fee-paying customers exist, trains will run to provide them with service – thus allowing the occasional passenger to ride free if he/she can avoid detection. Obviously the business cannot survive if everyone attempts to free ride. The concept has been widened to include anyone who benefits from cheating when everyone else follows the rules.

Mercantilism   A seventeenth-century political philosophy which emphasised the importance of promoting foreign trade surpluses and securing commercial advantage over rival states.

Quota   A quota is a fixed limit placed on the number of imports allowed into a country. Although the volume of imports is limited, their price may be forced upward (due to scarcity) and thus total spending on them may not fall much, if at all.

Tariff   A tariff is a tax on imports. It raises costs to foreign suppliers, reduces their revenues and thereby reduces a country's spending on imports.

QUESTIONS

1 What are the economic benefits to be gained from removing restrictions to international trade? What are the costs involved?
2 Regional trade blocs are becoming increasingly important in world trade. What are the nature of these trade arrangements; what are the reasons for their growth; and are there any economic dangers in the continuance of this trend?
3 Examine the case for: (a) enlarging NAFTA to include other Latin American countries; (b) deepening the economic integration between Canada, the USA and Mexico beyond a free trade area.
4 How can less-developed countries limit the spread of dualism in their economies?
5 Should governments intervene to manage their country's trade or are international markets best left alone?

FURTHER READING

A wealth of information on trading relations and agreements can be found on the World Trade Organisation's website at www.wto.org.
Farrell, M., Puron, A. and Remes, J. 'Beyond cheap labour: lessons for developing countries', *The McKinsey Quarterly*, 1, 2005.
Krugman, P. and Obstfeld, M. *International Economics: Theory and Policy*. Addison Wesley, 2000.

6   Customs unions and common markets

Topics to be considered in this chapter:

- The economic theory of customs unions:

  1 Trade creation.
  2 Trade diversion.

- Criteria for a successful union.
- Common markets and the effect of mobile resources.
- The European experience.
- Non-tariff barriers.

INTRODUCTION

Freeing up trade between partner countries brings increasing economic benefits and such results may thus fuel arguments for even closer integration. In the case of the European Union, this drive for closer relations began on 1 January 1958 with the creation of a customs union between the original six founder members – Belgium, the Netherlands, Luxembourg, Italy, France and West Germany – with the objective to form a common market with overtly political as well as economic aims. The Treaty of Rome, signed on 25 March 1957, committed the participants to the 'promotion of peace', 'increased prosperity' and 'ever closer union among the peoples of Europe'.

Other European countries were not ready at this time to commit themselves to such binding objectives and so the United Kingdom, Norway, Sweden, Denmark, Austria, Portugal and Switzerland preferred instead to establish the European Free Trade Area (EFTA) in 1960. As it turned out, however, the greater economic success of the (then) European Economic Community later drew in the UK, Ireland and Denmark in 1973; Greece became a full member in 1981, and Portugal and Spain joined in 1986. EFTA effectively dismantled itself, with Austria, Finland and Sweden in 1995 all becoming members of the EU. In May, 2004 a historic eastward expansion of the EU took place to admit the most progressive of the transition economies that had formerly been under Soviet influence: Estonia, Latvia, Lithuania, Poland, the Czech Republic,

Slovakia, Hungary, along with Slovenia, plus the two Mediterranean islands of Cyprus and Malta.

Today, the EU member countries number 25 but this very growth has given cause for much concern and prompted calls for reflection on where Europe is headed: should the kaleidoscope of countries involved aim ultimately for a deeper or wider union? A one-size-fits-all template, or a flexi-fit design where individual countries can opt in or out of various components? There are wide differences of opinion at present – both over the shape of economic union desired and also over the nature of political ambitions. The debate has become more urgent due to the disagreements over the constitution for Europe and it has revealed divergent visions of what Europe should be. This has implications particularly for other countries outside the Union and currently queuing up to join, such as Croatia, Romania, Bulgaria and especially Turkey.

As a way into this debate we shall be primarily concerned with the economics of European union. The reader will be left to decide for him or herself what political structure should be constructed upon this foundation.

THE ECONOMIC THEORY OF CUSTOMS UNIONS

The tighter customs union of a group of trading countries all maintaining a *common external tariff* (CET) against outsiders raises important economic issues that are distinct from free trade areas (FTAs) and thus warrant separate analysis.

One of the features of a FTA is that member countries practise independent policies with respect to the rest of the world, and this fact can be exploited by outsiders. There is nothing to stop, say, West Indian cane sugar being imported into one low-tariff country (like the UK when it belonged to EFTA) and then being redirected within the association to a higher-tariff partner (say, Switzerland). Importing countries wishing to frustrate this tariff dodging have to apply costly, complex and (frequently) ineffective ways to identify trade origins. This difficulty of trying to impose rules of origin documentation on EFTA trade actually acted as a form of non-tariff barrier to all commerce between member countries.

A customs union does not have this problem. There is no way into the sheltered market by breaching the external wall at its lowest point, since all member countries have a common tariff. The EC was thus able to enjoy right from its beginnings much freer trade between all its participants.

But such internal freedom comes at the cost of creating a potentially far greater problem – a 'fortress Europe' mentality. Locking-in trade between member countries of a customs union creates a large market place of pooled economies in which all can share, but this is at the expense of denying free access to other countries, and the potential gains from trade that they may bring. How far beneficial trade is created, on the one hand, and blocked, on the other, is difficult to measure in the real world (how can you know what might have been?), but there are a number of guiding principles. The issue to examine here is *trade creation* versus *trade diversion*.

Trade creation

When countries first join a customs union there is an initial impetus to trade due to the removal of barriers between them. If the economies involved are relatively large and diverse then the efficient industries in each will gain from the enlarged market; the less efficient will suffer from the increased competition.

The consumption effect of trade creation will be that each country now benefits from an increased selection of goods and services provided by a wider range of producers, and prices will be driven down in all member countries to the lowest level that prevailed before the union.

The production effect of trade creation is that, as the sales and profits expand in the more efficient producers, so resources from the less-successful businesses will transfer to this better paid employment. (Assuming a customs union, not a common market, the redeployment of resources at this stage takes place within each member country, not between them.) Increased competition within the union promotes the eventual dynamic gains of more efficient industrial practices, plus the economies of scale available in a larger market.

Trade diversion

Trade diversion, on the other hand, occurs when one member country previously imported commodities from a low-cost, more efficient third-party producer, but subsequent to the introduction of the customs union now finds these imports shut out by a high external tariff. Consumption must now turn to the purchase of higher-cost alternatives provided by a less-efficient domestic or partner-country producer.

The production effect of trade diversion is that resources are now kept employed in protected, inefficient industries rather than being made to search out more productive, more competitive destinations.

It should be appreciated from this analysis, therefore, that not all trade that is generated within a customs union is necessarily beneficial. Some or even much of it may be instead of what could be more economic trading relationships elsewhere.

For example, an initiative to produce, say, a new super-jumbo jet in a European-wide joint venture is bound to be trumpeted in the press as a great economic benefit by the politicians and industrialists involved. Whatever the media hype, however, it should not obscure the fact that it all depends on the costs involved – it might be wiser for Europeans to purchase American or Japanese products and devote European resources to other employments where their technological edge (i.e. comparative advantage) is stronger.

If closer European integration is the result of erecting trade barriers against the USA and Japan, rather than the outcome of fundamental economic compatibilities, then such integration will profit no one. A customs union that promotes internal growth only by reducing its trade links with the outside world will not produce an efficient reallocation of shared resources in the long run.

So long as common external tariffs are maintained, then whether the overall impact of economic integration is a valid cause for increased prosperity depends on the balance of the beneficial trade creating effects versus the harmful trade diverting effects of the union.

If growth in European trade and incomes by itself is no indicator of the benefits of economic integration, what is? Under what circumstances is a given customs union on the whole trade creating or trade diverting?

CRITERIA FOR A SUCCESSFUL CUSTOMS UNION

Competing, not complementary economies

If member-country economies prior to union are similar – that is, they tend to be competing in the same markets at home and abroad – then the eventual customs union will most likely be trade creating. If the original economies are complementary – for example, one being a primary producer, the other being a manufacturer – then closer integration may be trade divertingly inefficient.

This at first sight seems confusing. But think of it this way: market *competition always breeds efficiency*, through a process of survival of the fittest. Two competing countries with rival industries, each with slightly different cost structures will cause the relatively less efficient businesses in both countries to decline, with resources thus switching to the more efficient ones. Note that the initial impact is negative – much publicised unemployment – but in the longer term the size of the united market has grown for all, so the potential for redeployment must be good. There is a beneficial trade-creating effect: resources are now more efficiently allocated within each country compared to before.

Now consider the other scenario. A customs union with complementary, non-competitive industries will dovetail neatly together at first – one country perhaps producing the raw materials which supply the other – but neither partner now has any competitive impulse to improve. Both nations are protected by CETs from foreign rivals. Domestic consumers and employers which might have preferred to purchase lower-cost foreign produce/inputs have their trade now diverted to less efficient, more costly domestic goods and services.

Low common external tariffs

Protection promotes inefficiency. Trade diversion will therefore be less the lower the general level of CETs. A customs union is a second-best alternative to all-round free trade. The nearer a CU approaches this free trade ideal, the greater the benefits to incomes and growth for all.

When the United Kingdom joined the EU it had to submit to the community's *Common Agricultural Policy*. The trade diverting effect of this has been to support British and other European farmers at the expense of cheaper foreign producers. The fact that New Zealand can produce better lamb and dairy produce and the West Indies cheaper sugar means that resources are tied up in European agriculture that would be more economically employed elsewhere, and consumers end up paying more. In fact, since at least the 1970s one of the ongoing political struggles within the EU has been to try and reduce the agricultural CET, and, although still discriminatory, trade diversion now is less than it would otherwise have been.

Negotiations within the EU's agricultural commission, and between the EU and the WTO have been lengthy and, at times, bitter. The focus has shifted within the EU away from insisting on protective price supports (which act as trade-excluding tariffs) to providing more income and welfare payments to farmers (which have a somewhat less distortionary effect on trade). As a result, the European CET has come down, but there is still substantial trade diversion. The losers continue to be farmers in North America, Australasia and numerous developing countries; and European consumers.

More members

The larger the union, the more countries that can join the free trade zone, the larger and more widespread will be the benefits. Clearly the economic resources that can be reallocated and the trade-creating benefits that can be generated therefrom depend on the geographical size of the union. The gains from specialisation and economies of scale applicable from the union of the Benelux countries (the forerunner to the EU) were minuscule compared to what is now possible within the European Union. In education, for example, there may not be an enormous demand for specialists in International Economics if the market extends only as far as the borders of the Low Countries. In a unified European market, however, whole university departments are possible as small niche markets become big ones. That is as true in Dresden as it is in Durham; in electronics as well as education. And as the European market widens towards the East so more trade will be created: British manufacturers will be able to sell extra to Hungary; Polish farmers can increase sales to Germany.

Little diversity

In order to best benefit from the economies of large-scale production – where costs and prices can be kept down for all – the market should be homogenous; with little diversity. A large European market is not large if it is fragmented into small product areas where consumer tastes and preferences are diverse and must be separately catered for. The more that participants of a union perceive themselves to be different to other groups, therefore, the less scope there is to profit from a common market.

This important point is very relevant to a continent as culturally varied as Europe. In the Americas, two consumers living 3,000 miles apart speak the same language, live the same lifestyle and respond to the same advertising campaigns. The same is not true in Europe where selling something as mundane as a chocolate bar in northern France requires a totally different psychology to selling it in southern England. Thousands of years of history have bred differences in prejudices that neighbours in the same town in places like the former Yugoslavia, Northern Ireland and Spain still fight, and die over.

The economic benefits from the European Union are limited, therefore, insofar as the market place remains fragmented in many smaller, distinctively different communities.

Flexible technology

The need to cater for local differences in consumer tastes can, however, be responded to using modern, flexible technology allied to an educated and highly skilled workforce. Manufacturing techniques are becoming more and more sophisticated in custom-designing products at relatively low cost. It used to be: 'any colour you want, so long as it's black!' The premium that had to be paid to satisfy individual preference was prohibitively high. This is no longer the case today, thanks originally to pioneering Japanese-style manufacturing innovation. Small runs of production can be as economic as long runs for an increasing array of sophisticated goods and services. Computerised systems can re-tool assembly lines and switch products in minutes today – a process which used to take months and even years in the past.

The difficulties presented by the fragmentation of markets in culturally diverse unions, therefore, can be considerably reduced by modern technology. The gains from trade are enhanced.

A productive labour force

An increasingly competitive world economy requires labour to be increasingly efficient. If the long-term growth of *labour productivity* in Europe fails to keep pace with that of labour elsewhere then keeping business within the EU will ultimately become trade diverting. One inescapable feature of European labour markets is an *ageing population* and, with it, a falling *participation rate*. These are benefits of past economic success and improved welfare provision which have produced falling birth rates, smaller families and increased indulgence in leisure activities. But a smaller and older working population compared to America and Asia does not mean labour will lose its dynamism over time, however, if educational standards rise in compensation. That way, you can teach old dogs new tricks and European labour productivity will thus continue to improve. Crucial, therefore, is the implementation of an efficient education system that raises skill levels and facilitates occupational and geographical mobility of labour. Equally important is the erosion of social prejudices, and official and unofficial regulations that restrict the ability of people to change and improve skills and employments.

Foreign direct investment

High external tariffs – whether erected by individual countries or by customs unions – have prompted in the past much *foreign direct investment*. Japanese and American multinational corporations, fearful of being shut out of a fortress Europe, have set up their own factories in Britain, Germany, Spain, etc. to serve as a base from which to sell to all of Europe, without restriction. Certain European industrialists and politicians have on occasions complained about allowing such foreign rivals inside the protective union, but in fact the result is greater gains in efficiency and a reduction in trade diversion. Insofar as CETs can be by-passed by foreign direct investment then domestic industry cannot be sheltered from international competition. Philips, for example, the giant Dutch consumer electronics producer, has had to drastically shake up its organisation in order to face up to the challenge from Sony and other multinationals in Europe, let alone in the rest of the world; and so long as Europeans continue to buy Nissan cars produced in the northeast of England then all other motor manufacturers must also revolutionise their production facilities and practices in order to match Japanese efficiency. Wherever incompetence has nowhere to hide it must be cut out.

THE ECONOMIC THEORY OF COMMON MARKETS

This last point introduces the notion of moving capital across national frontiers. Just such an issue separates a customs union from a common market – where not only goods and services but also labour and capital are free to move among member countries. The impact of this next phase of increasing economic integration means that now resources may not only be reallocated *within* European nations but also *between* them.

The free flow of people between countries will inevitably be slowed by social factors – even if there is a complete matching of skills. A lawyer in Madrid, for example, may not wish to leave family, friends and business contacts in order to work in Milan. The absence of a homogenous European market makes such mobility even slower: legal systems in both countries are different. Labour movement will still take place, indeed it is in the process of so doing, but it will take time.

With financial markets, however, mobility is already here. Large sums of liquid capital flow all over Europe and around the world to take advantage of marginal differences in rates of profit. With economic and monetary union we can expect more and more investment to flow in and out of partner countries. What are the implications of such increased capital mobility?

It is important to emphasise at this point that we are concerned here with long-term *investment capital* – that is, money that flows into a country in order to set up an increase in productive capital, a new factory, for example – and not speculative flows of funds that are simply taking advantage of differential exchange or interest rates in order to make a financial gain. (This latter issue is touched upon in the chapter on currency union, below.)

There are contrasting views on the issue of mobility of productive capital and a resort to economic theory is necessary to explain them.

Consider two possible locations for capital investment: one in the heart of Europe, the other in the periphery. One, say, in the lower Rhine valley, the other in the upper Douro in Portugal. It may well be that the opportunities for profitable investment in the Rhineland 'core' are many and widespread; those in the periphery in the Douro are more limited in extent. Be that as it may, assume that the rate of return on investment in the two locations is different: what can we predict will happen?

With no restriction on capital mobility, funds will flow out of the less-profitable investment location and into the more-profitable one. This has two effects: one in each centre.

As capital moves out of the less-profitable site the supply of investment funds dries up and as a result their increased scarcity begins to drive up rates of return. Conversely, funds moving into the more-profitable location begin to satiate demand. Profit rates must fall. So long as any difference in rates persists, funds will move between the two locations until any discrepancy is eroded. The conclusion reached, therefore, is that the mobility of capital between different countries will eventually bring about an equilibrium in profit rates between them.

Actually this theoretical conclusion needs to be amended a little because there are reasons why capital may not be quite as internationally mobile as implied; why differential rates of profit may persist in rival centres. For example, the risk of currency fluctuation may be a disincentive to move funds across borders. Lack of information or uncertainty over cultural differences may similarly impede movement. Nonetheless the analysis can be adjusted to conclude that profit rates in both centres will converge to a differential that accounts for the divergence in risk assessment. Oporto, therefore, may evolve a rate of normal profits that is x per cent above that ruling in Frankfurt to compensate for the perceived higher risk factor.

So far this adjusted analysis supports the general contention that countries have nothing to lose from removing all restrictions on the long-term movement of capital. Donor countries and recipient countries alike both benefit from a more efficient, more profitable employment of European resources. Capital moves across frontiers in pursuit of greater profits; capitalists in periphery countries that are exporting their funds stand to earn greater incomes. There may be a fall in labour employment at first in these sites as capital investments such as new manufacturing plant transfer to the core, but total incomes rise in both countries so winners have more than enough to compensate losers, it is alleged.

There is a powerful argument, however, against this conventional view of the positive outcome of free market forces as applied to capital mobility. Criticism focuses particularly on the limited scope of this analysis: it assumes that only one factor (capital) is mobile and that *all other factors remain constant.*

Given this restrictive assumption, the conclusion is valid. But other factors are very likely to change in a Europe of increasing economic integration. In a dynamically changing environment there may be many forces at work that shift the profitability perspective in both capital-donor and capital-recipient countries.

EXTERNAL ECONOMIES AND DISECONOMIES

Consider firstly the implications of inward investment to a vibrant and innovative core region. As more capital accumulates here there are a variety of reasons why profit rates may *not* fall.

Certainly, there will be shortages of land, office space, certain labour skills, etc., which force up prices and act as an *external diseconomy* and disincentive for further capital inflow. Social costs of increased traffic congestion, pollution, possible crime, may also increase.

But these problems may spark off increased efforts to overcome them. There exist many economic benefits to regional concentration: *external economies* of increased competition and efficiency; the establishment of service and supportive industry; research and development; innovative technology; the growth of skills. If these benefits from concentration increase at a faster rate than the costs involved then the profit rate will not fall.

Employment opportunities for capital and labour (especially those with entrepreneurial skills) will not decrease, indeed they may act as a continual beacon to drain these resources away from the periphery.

By the same argument exactly the opposite effects are operating in the periphery (see Figure 6.1).

The most mobile, employable resources are moving out of the country. What gets left behind are those that are increasingly unemployable: an ageing capital stock; decaying infrastructure; inappropriate skills; out-of-date technologies; a market place of falling incomes and influence. Profit rates are shrinking faster than the attractions of return investment in this depopulating region can reverse.

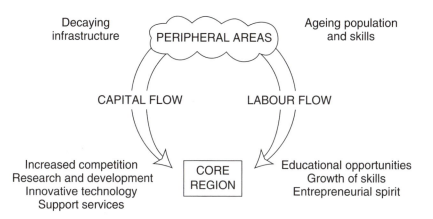

Figure 6.1 The most mobile, employable resources move out of the periphery

As an illustration of these themes, British critics point to the problem of industrial decay in certain regions of the UK. Unemployment rates in Northern Ireland, South Wales and northeast England, for example, remain persistently above the national average. That such a phenomenon has lasted for well over half a century despite repeated central government efforts to reverse the pattern of decline is evidence that the centripetal forces which drain the peripheries of resources are strong and they are not easily reversed.

Some have predicted that just such an outcome awaits Europe: the unbridled effect of free-market forces operating on capital employed in Europe will generate cumulative growth in some countries and cumulative decline in others – but due to the severely proscribed powers of the Brussels bureaucracy, such polarising economic effects will occur without the mitigating effects of sufficient redistributive transfers from a strong central authority. Despite its economic difficulties, Northern Ireland continues to enjoy substantial income support from the UK. The same will not be true for poorer areas in a free-market Europe, it has been alleged (by Wynne Godley, of Cambridge University, amongst others).

Such pessimism may be a little overdone. What future awaits a European Union of mobile resources is impossible to predict with certainty. That incomes as a whole will grow is highly likely, notwithstanding the tendency for periodic slowdowns or recessions. That the distribution of incomes will change is equally likely. But to deduce from this that Europe will polarise into richer and poorer regions, accentuated over time, cannot be safely predicted. The centripetal model – where resources drain into the core region – is one possibility. The alternative scenario is a multipolar Europe, where growth centres arise in a number of regions – each exploiting its own comparative advantage. The immensely rich cultural diversity of Europe might be said to support this argument.

THE EUROPEAN EXPERIENCE

It is time now to look in a little more detail at the patchwork quilt of countries that together make up the European Union and examine how far they can be said to form a truly common market (see Table 6.1).

No map or set of statistics by themselves, however, can completely capture the true nature of the heterogeneity of Europe. Centuries of commerce and conflict, nation-building and empire-building have bred regional differences that are impossible to simply summarise. Some parts of the continent have enjoyed stability, independence and freedom from dictatorship or invasion for nearly a thousand years; others are still at war, trying to define their national frontiers. Certain states have well-established, mature market economic systems with flourishing, outward-looking industrial and financial sectors; others are still struggling to make the transition out of peasant agriculture and centrally planned command systems.

The objective of attempting to generate increased prosperity via increased economic integration through all the stages from loose free trade areas to tighter

Table 6.1 European nations, selected data

Country	Area (000 sq km)	Population millions, 2003	Pop. density per sq km	GDP/head (PPP) 2006*	% growth GDP 05–06*	% GDP invested	Language
Austria	84	8.1	96.2	121.1	2.1	21.1	German
Belgium	31	10.4	339.3	118.2	2.3	19.3	Flemish/French
Cyprus	9.2	0.7	77.4	82.6	4.2	19.2	Greek/Turkish
Czech. Republic	78.9	10.1	129.4	72.6	4.2	28.1	Czech
Denmark	43	5.4	124.9	121.6	2.1	20.1	Danish
Estonia	45.2	1.4	30	55.2	6.2	28.8	Estonian
Finland	305	5.2	17.1	116.3	2.9	19.2	Finnish
France	544	59.6	109.6	109.7	2.2	19.9	French
Germany	357	82.5	231.2	106.9	1.6	17.6	German
Greece	132	11	83.7	82.8	3.1	25.2	Greek
Hungary	93	10.2	109	63.3	3.8	22.7	Hungarian
Ireland	70	4	56.4	142.3	5.1	24.6	English
Italy	301	57.3	190.2	103.1	1.7	19.9	Italian
Latvia	64.6	2.3	36.1	47.7	6.9	29.8	Latvian
Lithuania	65.3	3.5	53	51.9	5.9	24.8	Lithuanian
Luxembourg	3	0.4	173.4	226	4.0	20.2	French/German
Malta	0.3	0.4	1257.3	70.1	1.9	21.8	Maltese/English
The Netherlands	34	16.2	478	117.4	2.0	21.0	Dutch
Poland	312.7	38.2	122.2	49.1	4.5	20.5	Polish
Portugal	92	10.4	113.2	70.8	1.7	22.9	Portuguese
Slovakia	49	5.4	109.7	55.2	5.2	26.6	Slovakian
Slovenia	20.3	2.0	98.4	80.6	4.0	25.8	Slovenian
Spain	505	40.7	80.6	98.1	2.7	29.7	Spanish
Sweden	411	8.9	21.8	116.9	2.8	16.8	Swedish
United Kingdom	244	59.3	243.3	120.2	2.8	17.2	English

Source: Eurostat.   Note: *forecast.

and tighter unions inevitably involves so much more than economic issues. Given the enormous cultural, political and economic diversity of European nations referred to above, it is scarcely surprising that promoting the ever closer union of such disparate and partisan peoples is fraught with difficulty and delay.

DISMANTLING THE BARRIERS

The easy part is always done first. Eliminating tariffs and quotas and constructing the common external tariff for the original six founder countries was achieved within ten years from 1958. The same process has been repeated (more rapidly) with each successive enlargement of the Union and has now begun again with the ten new Eastern European and Mediterranean entrants.

Linking national markets together, however, is not enough. Establishing the four freedoms of unrestricted movement for all goods, services, labour and capital, and creating a level playing field for all competing firms was (and still is) frustrated by national differences embodied in numerous *non-tariff barriers*.

A single market which exhibits different prices for the same model of motor car; which restricts the sale of insurance and financial services in certain regions; where certain governments are allowed to grant hefty subsidies to some airlines but not to others, and grant exclusive public service contracts to domestic suppliers only; where its people still need passports to move around and where differing technical standards, tax regimes and laws all operate together, is quite obviously not a common market in the sense normally understood by the term. And yet all these differences and more are the product of European institutions – despite the fact that eliminating such differences was the original objective of the Treaty of Rome in 1957, and additionally was the specific goal of the Single European Act, agreed in 1985 – that is, to achieve a progressive reduction in all restrictions according to a timetable terminating in 1992.

In truth, even without tariffs and quotas there is an infinite range of other factors that can impact on and distort trade between neighbour countries and thus act as forms of non-tariff barriers.

State aid

Nationhood is still officially protected within Europe. Many governments still protect favoured businesses from going under when they suffer from foreign competition since local vote-winning frequently takes precedence over commitment to European ideals. National interests remain inextricably identified with the economic health of certain domestic companies and with the political complexion of certain governments. Lip service to being 'European' is continually being paid in official circles, but the real losers are European taxpayers and consumers who are required, on the one hand, to subsidise the loss-making businesses and, on the other, to continue to pay higher than free-market prices for their products. However, wherever the costs of failing industry are easily identified in terms of the loss of earnings to well-defined groups of workers and the political outcry of numerous citizens, and the benefits are measured in terms of a fractional reduction in future prices to faceless billions of consumers, then the government decision to subsidise national political interests rather than European economic integration will continue to frustrate progress towards a common market.

Public procurement

National governments are extremely unlikely to award highly visible contracts to non-national firms instead of to a domestic producer. When the German Ministry of Transport purchases Fiat cars and French agricultural officials serve banquets featuring Welsh lamb and Rioja wines then the common market will have truly arrived. The public procurement market in Europe is estimated to be very large (approximately 10 per cent of the combined Union GNP) yet only a tiny fraction of this is genuinely open to competition from non-national suppliers. According to the EC Commission's Cecchini report (1988) 0.14 per cent of this trade was won by foreign firms – hardly an open market place. The 1992 programme introduced by the Single European Act outlawed the more discriminatory practices, so that public authorities are now obliged to advertise contracts widely, and for a sufficient period of time, to allow non-national firms to compete for orders. However welcome, this cannot prevent, of course, the continuation of national preference in public purchasing.

Taxation

Europe's internal frontiers are now more open than ever before to the passage of transport – customs checks on lorry loads of goods have (at long last) all but disappeared – but value added tax differences remain between member countries, as do varying excise duties on such goods as wine, beers and spirits. There therefore continues much costly paperwork to calculate tax charges and refunds and this inevitably inhibits and distorts free trade. (The impact of these formalities is naturally greatest for small- and medium-sized European firms which do not have large outputs over which to spread these fixed costs.)

Technical differences

Rules on the harmonisation of technical standards, or mutual recognition of partner countries' regulations, have been in place since 1992, but there is still a long way to go before all nations accept Community standards for every good and service produced. Many manufacturing businesses across the continent cite differing technical standards between countries as their biggest single impediment to pan-European sales. Consumer electronics products, for example, have to be equipped with a variety of different plugs if they are to be compatible with domestic electricity supplies in every member country. Specific state controls on banking, insurance and finance and restrictions on foreign participation and joint ventures in Spain, Greece and Portugal are another form of non-tariff barrier to free competition in services.

Language

It is impossible to quantify the impact of differing languages as an impediment to trade – obviously they are a major barrier. The lack of a common language is probably the single most important non-tariff barrier to commerce and communication across the entire continent, and yet this is – at the same time – the most important distinguishing characteristic of the European Union. What other part of the world demonstrates such linguistic and cultural diversity? Differing languages *are* Europe. Yet the mobility of resources and the inter-national trade in goods and (especially) services is inevitably greatly slowed by language differences. How can you do business with someone if you do not know what they are saying? Europe now has twenty official languages and many other dialects. Translation and interpreting costs in EU administration are immense and selling products across the union involves communication problems that businesses in North America are blissfully free from. *The Economist*, for example, noted that a US company selling computer software packages has access to a domestic market of 57 million home users prior to 2004. In Germany, the biggest European market, there were only 11 million users and those are in a language that has little further sales potential outside the country. Small wonder, therefore, that international trade in software services is dominated by large US firms which enjoy the advantage of home economies of scale. In Europe, less than a third of this linguistically fragmented market is taken up by European firms. Sixty per cent use American software. (Note: despite examples like these, there has never been any suggestion that Europe should attempt to evolve a common language; unlike the increasing momentum towards harmonisation or convergence on other issues.)

Currency

Different currencies have evolved in Europe for much the same reason as different languages. They are the natural outgrowth of people living in different communities, each trading with each other, but distinct from other societies (see the passage on optimum currency areas, chapter 8, below). Weights, measures, units of exchange and the language of commerce all evolved together. Agreement on standardisation of weights and measures has been achieved and, even if much still remains to be done – as referred to above – progress has still gone a long way. Currency agreement is more problematic, however. That differing currencies are a barrier to trade is evident – though exactly how big a barrier they are is open to controversy. Some would say that sophisticated foreign exchange markets, and particularly the ability to deal in currency futures, eliminates nearly all problems of financing trade. Others would argue exactly the opposite: that such currency markets actually destabilise international trade.

To overcome this non-tariff barrier to trade implies moving towards a single European currency – which represents the next stage in economic integration between countries. There is much controversy involved here and it requires, in addition, greater understanding of the particular economics of money and banking. These topics will be treated in more detail in chapter 7.

CONCLUSION

We can conclude here that promoting the closer economic integration of countries involves numerous and complex economic, political and cultural issues. Increasing economic prosperity in customs unions is not automatically assured – there may be much trade diversion involved as well as trade creation – and additionally some regions will benefit more than others.

The heterogeneity of many different countries and cultures continues to fragment the common market of Europe, but at the same time it is precisely this quality that provides the immense resourcefulness of the Union.

There are problems that are worrying for the future: an ageing population combined with a lower participation rate means in future 75 per cent of the population must be supported by only 25 per cent at work. To carry this weight must mean European labour markets have to become more and not less efficient. The forces of globalisation are unlikely to diminish so we must learn to live in a younger and more competitive world economy. Protectionist sentiments from some political leaders and a refusal to reform and move on do not help.

The *occupational mobility* and adaptability of European lands and peoples will in the long run provide the key to who gains, and by how much, in the process of integration. The more such fractious peoples see their interests in common, the quicker (as well as closer) integration will be achieved and the greater will be the economic benefits enjoyed. But this process cannot be hurried: after thousands of years of separate development, Europe needs time to resolve all its differences. An economic integration of varying speeds for differing countries is both necessary and inevitable.

Finally, let us finish with a global perspective. What is the impact of increasing European economic integration on the rest of the world?

As mentioned in chapter 5 above, one reaction of those left outside a common market is to set up rival trading blocs. A desire to emulate the EU's success and a fear of losing out in competition have fuelled the growth of other regional associations such as NAFTA, the Association of South East Asian Nations (ASEAN) and others. The great danger here, however, is that world trade may become dominated by a few, large, rival groups, and – in an atmosphere of mutual distrust – common external tariffs may be easier to erect than to negotiate a general reduction in protection. If this occurs, then world trade may

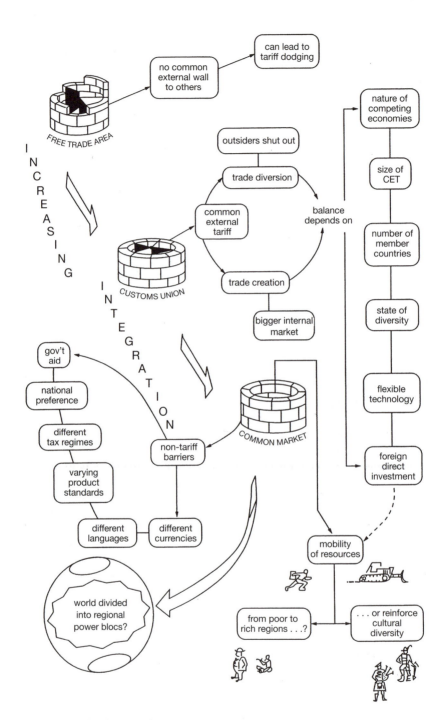

can lead to
tariff dodging

no common
external wall
to others

FREE TRADE AREA

nature of
competing
economies

size of
CET

INCREASING

outsiders shut out

trade diversion

common
external
tariff

balance
depends on

number of
member
countries

CUSTOMS UNION

trade creation

bigger internal
market

state of
diversity

INTEGRATION

flexible
technology

gov't
aid

national
preference

different
tax regimes

varying
product
standards

different
languages

non-tariff
barriers

different
currencies

COMMON MARKET

foreign
direct
investment

mobility
of resources

world divided
into regional
power blocs?

from poor to
rich regions . . .?

. . . or reinforce
cultural
diversity

Figure 6.2 The themes of chapter 6

become greatly distorted over time. The potential for much trade diversion exists, rather than trade creation, but this is an outcome which would benefit no one and is a matter of concern that ought to be in the minds of all governments attempting to set up trade deals. Success in achieving a closer European Union would be a hollow victory if this were to take place in a world divided by mercantilist power blocs.

KEY WORDS

Ageing population   An ageing population occurs when people live longer, have fewer babies and thus pensioners and the elderly begin to outnumber children. The average age of the population of a community rises when both birth rates and death rates decline over time, assuming immigration remains constant.

Common Agricultural Policy   The Common Agricultural Policy was the first and the central economic policy of the EEC, set up at its foundation in 1957. Its aims were to stabilise post-war agricultural prices and incomes, to ensure market supplies and to increase general agricultural productivity. Its main feature has been to guarantee farm prices at what have evolved as higher than market prices, to subsidise agricultural exports and to support the European farm sector in general. Its effects have been to successfully meet all its aims, but at the cost of creating incentives to overproduce, increasing farm sizes, promoting environmentally damaging farm practices, distorting income distribution and causing widespread trade diversion.

External diseconomies   are disadvantages that a business suffers from its locality – such as transport difficulties and high rents in the centre of a busy city which force up costs for shops and offices. (Note the difference of the above to social costs and benefits – these are the effects *imposed by a business on its surroundings*.)

External economies   are advantages conferred on a business from the environment in which it is operating – for example an incoming firm that recruits specialised labour from a region that has built up an expertise in certain skills.

Foreign direct investment   Where a business sets up and directly owns and controls productive capital equipment in another country.

Labour productivity   The average output per person in a business or community. This will rise if people work harder, longer or have more capital equipment/technology/ education to assist them.

Occupational mobility   This refers to how easily resources can change their employment from one industry to another. A coal miner of many years' experience and with highly specialised skills is likely to be occupationally immobile, for example – he may find it very difficult to retrain as a computer programmer. Land on the edge of a city, however, can be switched from farming to a car park to the site for a housing or industrial estate with comparative ease. Note, that land is typically occupationally mobile but geographically immobile – it cannot get up and go elsewhere in search of a job. (Contrast this with a cement truck . . .)

Participation rate   The fraction of people economically active in a given population. The smaller the population of working age compared to pensioners or children, the lower are average wages and greater the attractions of leisure and other non-wage employments (such as child rearing, or being in education) the smaller will be the participation rate. Similarly, in countries where women are expected or compelled to be in the home the participation rate will be lower.

QUESTIONS

1 Distinguish between trade creation and trade diversion. Using these concepts, examine the case for deepening the economic integration between Canada, the USA and Mexico beyond a free trade area.
2 How might the deployment of resources and the distribution of incomes be affected as a customs union becomes a common market? Who are the winners and losers?
3 Does cultural diversity enrich or impede economic integration and growth? If the EU opts to deepen its integration over time what might be the social costs involved?
4 What are tariff and non-tariff barriers to trade? In your view, which specific barriers are most difficult to eliminate between partner countries and why?
5 As more countries show interest in forming and deepening regional trade associations, should the World Trade Organisation become involved in regulating such agreements? Explain how and why.

FURTHER READING

El-Agraa, A. M. *The European Union: Economics and Policies*. Prentice Hall, 2001.
A range of detail can be found on the EU website: http://europa.eu.int/.

7 Money, banking and international finance

Topics to be considered in this chapter:

- The functions, forms and qualities of money.
- Fractional reserve banking and the creation of credit.
- Central bank attempts to control money supplies.
- The globalisation of finance: causes and effects.
- The impact on government policies.

INTRODUCTION

Money is arguably mankind's single most important invention. It has enabled societies all over the world to exchange goods and services, to grow and prosper. Indeed, communities need money in order to function.

Shortly after the dissolution of the Soviet Union, in the winter of 1991–2, many people lost faith in the value of the Russian rouble. As a consequence, the economy disintegrated, living standards collapsed and many people resorted to bartering their belongings in the streets in order to get sufficient food.

The usefulness of money is easily demonstrated, therefore. Without it, people cannot agree to do business and cannot support standards of living much above subsistence level. With money, however, trade can be facilitated and very sophisticated lifestyles may develop. Far from being the root of all evil, money is the foundation stone for trade, economic growth and the development of civilisation. It is certainly worthy of serious study.

THE FUNCTIONS, FORMS AND QUALITIES OF MONEY

The prime **function** of money is to act as a *medium* of exchange, and any commodity which is held for this purpose – rather than for its own intrinsic value – can thus be defined as money. Money in addition acts to place a *price* on all goods and services traded, and this includes putting a value on time – the rate of interest on riskless investment indicates how much people are prepared to accept in future compensation for going without their money now. Money should also function as a *store* of wealth: 'hard' currencies are distinguished from 'soft' ones in that they keep their exchange value for longer – the latter, in other words, are less acceptable as money.

Money at first took many **forms** in the course of its early evolution – salt, corn, sea-shells, etc. – in the many isolated communities where it arose. In all cases, however, in order to function properly as described above any form of money must possess certain **qualities**, such as: portability, divisibility, scarcity, durability and, most of all, *acceptability*.

In the last resort, *anything* which is acceptable in exchange is money. It is this unique characteristic of money that makes it so different from any other commodity in the global economy – it does not matter what is used, so long as it enables exchange to take place. Hence the old saying: 'money is as money does'. And of course it is this property which makes it so difficult to control by any central authority: as soon as one form of money becomes restricted in its use, another form will immediately evolve. We can call this the phenomenon of **endogenous money supply**. That is, the supply of money circulating in an economy cannot be directly controlled by the state for any long periods; it is determined by the popular institutions and practices of the society itself. We shall return to this important principle again and again.

The earliest, most acceptable forms of money that crossed the world were precious metals. Gold, in particular, had all the right qualities except that it was too scarce. As trade grew, the supply of gold could not keep up. The amount of gold thus had an inherently restrictive effect on trade (causing gold prices to rise) which created the demand for substitute metals such as silver and thus the discovery of Gresham's law (named after the Elizabethan financier): that 'bad money drives out good'. (If the official exchange rate between two currencies differs from that which is publicly recognised, traders will hoard the preferred currency and off-load the other in market exchanges. The 'bad' money thus changes hands whilst the 'good' disappears into pockets.) In the case of silver, it wasn't such a bad currency. The development of European empires and the rapid opening up of trade in the Age of Discoveries was financed by increased supplies of South American silver onto markets and, despite periods of excess supply and unstable prices, it eventually superseded gold as an acceptable currency. Hence the evolution of a pound of sterling silver in the UK as the unit of account – the *pound sterling*. Equally, in the Spanish empire, the weight of silver passed into the language of money – as the '*peso*' and '*plata*'.

In time, of course, silver suffered from the same problem as gold and, indeed, all forms of commodity money. Its supply could not perfectly match the rate of growth of world trade. Accordingly a new form of money evolved: paper promises.

A promise to pay – *provided it is believed by the recipient* – is 'as good as gold'. Better, in fact, since promises are far less costly to produce than precious metals, and so the supply of banknotes ('I promise to pay the bearer on demand the sum of . . .') could more closely match the rate of growth of trade.

The catch, of course, is to ensure acceptability. Many banks from the earliest times have therefore had to promote an air of respectability, solidity, stability and all those other adjectives that are embodied in the architecture of banks and the comportment of their managers. How else would they win the confidence of a community and be entrusted with its savings? How else to inspire traders to accept their promises to pay? As Groucho Marx used to say: 'Integrity? If you can fake that you've got it made . . .'

THE MODERN BUSINESS OF BANKING

Modern *fractional reserve banking* demonstrates the importance (and profitability) of generating confidence. So long as confidence holds, banks can issue many more promises to pay (liabilities) than they have liquid funds to cover. It does not matter how little in total a bank holds in its reserves, providing they have just enough to satisfy the next claimant who walks in the door. And, of course, the more respectable the institution, the less likely anyone is to challenge its promises. All the more room, then, for the bank to keep creating loans that it will call in at some future date to be repaid with interest. (It profits the banks to increase the indebtedness of the public.)

The only limit to the money supply now is the bankers' sense of self-discipline. In fact, history shows they have little. Competitive forces drive commercial bankers to create more and more credit in pursuit of more and more profits. But confidence in banks can evaporate as their liabilities expand too fast, outstripping reserve assets. How can so much credit ever be supported? Empires are being built on sand, and a slight shift somewhere in the system can bring everything crashing down. If all claimants simultaneously run to the bank to withdraw their deposits there is little there to pay them. Only promises. And if they are not believed, there is nothing.

The history of money and banking is thus a history of boom and slump – of the over-expansion of credit, of increasing indebtedness and of bank crashes – recent problems being no different from earlier ones, though perhaps they have been bigger and more spectacular of late. Many people around the world, indeed entire nations, have got badly into debt and are now paying the consequences in terms of greatly reduced circumstances. Some lost fortunes in the collapse of savings-and-loans institutions in North America. Similarly, hundreds of millions of innocent Asians suffered in the late 1990s when bad loans and nervous creditors brought down a succession of banks in Japan, Thailand, South Korea and prompted crisis and collapse in Indonesia. All affected have naturally asked: 'Why? What did *I* do wrong?' And: 'Isn't there someone responsible for protecting us?'

TRYING TO CONTROL WHAT GOES ON

In each country it is the role of the state-run *central bank* to control national money supplies, to regulate commercial financial operations and to prevent abuses of the system. It is to the Federal Reserve in the USA, the Bank of England and the European Central Bank that hard-hit people in these countries turn to complain. The problem is that world financial practices have evolved too quickly for nationally confined authorities to keep up with them. And successful government moves to improve competition and efficiency in financial markets – making it easier/less costly for dealers to move money from one world centre to another – have inevitably made it more difficult for central banks to control what goes on.

Recent experience in the USA and Europe in administering monetary policy has demonstrated that it is extremely hard to directly control the quantity of money circulating in an open, rapidly evolving, modern, market economy. This is because any central government attempt to regulate bank activity according to one target or definition of money simply drives the market to use other forms of money (as predicted by the argument of endogenous money supplies, described earlier). In this case, multinational corporations and others expanded their operations in those markets where the big national banks were restricted. Such *disintermediation* is the result of the institutional and technological changes in financial centres: many more foreign banks and domestic near-banks have set up in London and New York in recent years and have participated in new offshore and onshore money markets with sophisticated telecommunications technology linked world-wide.

Faced with embarrassing, partly self-inflicted impotence in controlling their own backyards, monetary authorities in Europe and North America have turned more and more to increases in interest rates (the price of money) in order to rein back consumer demand, thereby indirectly restricting the supply of credit from the banks. This of course means more pain for everyone as borrowing costs more, spending falls, businesses suffer and unemployment rises.

Clobbering the customer in order to get at his supplier seems neither equitable nor efficient. It is, however, the measure mostly commonly resorted to in the attempt to control that most slippery of concepts: modern money.

As different countries lurch from boom to bust there are those who argue that national economies should disconnect themselves from destabilising world developments by unlinking their currency and their monetary affairs from any fixed international exchange rate system. In contrast, there are others who argue for exactly the opposite course of action – that greater monetary discipline is necessary, requiring stable exchange rates, supra-national regulation and, in the extreme, monetary union.

These are issues that are complex and need careful analysis. The economics of banking, recent changes and their impact on money supplies – both nationally and internationally – are continued in more detail below. The particular arguments for and against monetary union in Europe are considered in the next chapter and the issues relating to international financial crises – which seem to erupt with debilitating regularity every few years – follow later on.

THE ECONOMICS OF BANKING: A SIMPLE MODEL

To understand more clearly how the financial world operates, how it is changing and how it affects the lives and livelihood of ordinary people like you and me we need to simplify the analysis of banking with the use of an elementary model, introducing more complex and realistic qualifications later on, once the basics are understood.

Control of the money supply within a country (assuming for the time being the country can be isolated from international events) lies within the relationship which develops between state authorities and private financial markets. This relationship is never stable in any society – it is in a continual state of evolution – but at its simplest level we can begin this analysis by assuming that there are only two forms of money: cash and credit (transferred by cheque).

The institutions of a banking system

Financial market places are where people and institutions buy and sell money – that is, they loan and borrow funds – and in the process determine rates of interest (the price of money) and the money supply (the quantity of funds circulating). Assume that the only traders in this market place are the central bank, several competing commercial banks and numerous private individuals and businesses.

The central bank holds the bank account of the government (it loans and borrows money for the government, amongst others); acts as a banker to all the commercial banks (they all keep their own accounts at the central bank); is responsible for setting the rules and regulations in all financial trade; and is charged with conducting the government's monetary policy within the economy (and internationally).

Commercial banks are *financial intermediaries*, that is they specialise in the business of mediating between those who have surplus money and those who have insufficient. More simply, they accept people's savings and then loan these funds on to others who wish to invest. In the process they make money: creating more or less credit as society demands, subject to the effectiveness of central bank intervention. Theoretically, with open competition and access to all relevant information in the money markets, intermediaries will allocate funds only to the most efficient employments.

Private individuals and businesses of all sizes are customers in these financial markets – they are the many people who save and the not-quite-so-many who invest.

The central bank directly controls the issue of cash (coins and banknotes) within the country. It is held in the hands and homes of private individuals; is deposited in commercial bank reserves and is also kept by these institutions in their cash balances at the central bank.

The creation of money

A country's *cash base* (defined as M0) is at the heart of its money supply. Commercial banks issue more or less credit to customers (as we shall see) as their cash reserves grow or decline. We can consider how this process takes place first of all in the case of a stable, conservative community where people have no reason to doubt the trustworthiness of their bankers. (Such communities cannot be built quickly – they are the product of lifetimes of responsible financial conduct, where people grow to respect those who hold their money.)

All customers who deposit cash in the banks may come to use cheques as a safe and easy substitute to transfer funds – especially for large purchases. Most people will not cash in their cheques in order to withdraw funds and then transfer this money to someone else. Cheques are handed over instead, and the banks involved subtract the cash involved from one person's account and then add it on to another's. The cash, therefore, never sees the light of day: it stays in the hands of bankers.

The more trustworthy the community, the fewer cash transactions will be necessary, the more acceptable will be cheques. Thus *the form of money changes*: commercial bank promises to pay (cheques) take the place of central bank promises (official banknotes).

Suppose that for every $1 transaction that takes place in the form of cash in this community there are ten times this number of cheques accepted. This means that commercial banks can expand the money supply by ten times the value of the cash base. For every $1 cash deposited by a customer in a bank, therefore, credit can be extended by $10 (by issuing cheques to people asking for loans). The banks are confident that at any one time only one in ten customers will ever come in and demand cash in exchange for their cheques – so cash reserves are sufficient if they only back 10 per cent of all loans created.

The size of the *credit multiplier* (ten, in this example) is a function of the stability and spending habits of the community involved. For politically unstable or economically underdeveloped societies the credit multiplier may be as low as one – that is, every $1 loan is backed by $1 cash, ready to be withdrawn at a moment's notice. Highly sophisticated financial communities, on the other hand, may have very little need for cash. Billions and billions of transactions may change hands daily with an infinitesimally small fraction ever being converted into cash. It is in these circumstances that numerous financial intermediaries have grown up borrowing and lending credit over varying time periods, and – quite clearly – the direct influence of the central bank as the controller of the cash base is greatly diminished.

Control of the money supply

Theoretically, the central bank can control money supplies of the commercial banks by varying the economy's cash base through *open market operations*. That is, the central bank borrows money from the public through the means of selling *bonds* and *bills of exchange* in the open market place. This means they sell paper (promises to repay loans at some future date) to private individuals and businesses in exchange for cheques. By cashing in these cheques the central bank reduces the commercial bank cash reserves. For every $1 reduction in cash reserves, banks must call in $10 worth of loans (assuming the economy maintains a stable 10 per cent reserves/assets ratio). Conversely, by buying back bonds and bills the central bank increases the flow of cash into the commercial banks, which then can increase lending tenfold.

There are other means by which central banks can attempt to control money supplies. Different countries can use one method, or a combination of methods, depending on what suits their practices and institutions best. For example, instead of operating indirectly through open market operations, central banks can directly reduce commercial bank reserves by seizing or freezing a fraction of their deposits – such cash cannot therefore be used to support credit and, again, loans must be called in to a multiplied extent.

Alternatively, central banks can demand a certain reserve ratio by law, and then *increase* this ratio at times when they wish to restrict money supplies. Thus if banks maintain a 10 per cent ratio of cash to loans and then the central bank insists on a 12.5 per cent ratio, this implies that instead of every $1 cash supporting $10 loans, now it can only cover $8 worth. Twenty per cent of credit circulating in the economy must now be cut back.

Either by reducing banks' cash reserves or by increasing cash ratios, if central banks are successful in curtailing money supplies then they will drive up interest rates in the open market. They may, in fact, decide to operate the other way round: by charging higher base rates on central bank loans (which underpin the money markets) they may drive all interest rates upward and thus choke off demand (and thereby supply) for credit.

All of these measures have been used to a greater or lesser extent over the years as central banks have struggled to assert their authority and thus regulate monetary policy. (Monetary policy is important because it is one instrument used by governments to manage the macroeconomy. Actually, much controversy has burned between economists as to precisely how important this policy instrument is, relative to other controls. The general consensus now is that money supplies and interest rates *do* affect such phenomena as rates of inflation and investment, but the relationship is not as close or as predictable as some have argued.)

The difficulty, however, is that there has been an accelerating number of changes recently that have impacted upon banking practices and – as indicated in the introduction to this chapter – central bank authority and control have for the most part been overtaken by events. Many of the old certainties in this market place have now disappeared.

THE GLOBALISATION OF FINANCE

Central banks are no longer monopolies of the money supply in their own, isolated economies. Thanks to increasing competition and innovation in the banking industry, the widespread application of telecommunications technology and follow-my-leader deregulation of markets in all the world's major financial centres, enormous sums of money can now flow around the world, in and out of different countries, at the press of a button.

The Bank of England estimated that, in 1992, the world's daily volume of foreign exchange dealing was valued at $1,000,000,000,000 ($1 trillion). That was *each day* in 1992; it is even greater now!

By this estimate, international money flows are *over 100 times greater* than all world movements of real goods and services. The buying and selling that these enormous funds are in exchange for, therefore, is in paper promises: all sorts of bonds, bills, securities and derivative financial instruments that private money-makers have invented. The forms of credit are so numerous today that what counts as money – and what does not – is almost a matter of individual preference.

Causes

What has driven this globalisation of finance and what have been its effects?

Trade

The first major impetus to international banking occurred during the Cold War years of the 1960s when foreign (especially Soviet) trade surpluses denominated in US dollars were looking for a place of deposit, free from restrictions of the US monetary authorities. The *Eurodollar* (later Eurocurrency) *market* grew up, therefore, with banks of varying nationalities operating in London free from reserve asset requirements and interest-rate ceilings demanded either by the Bank of England (because they were not dealing in pounds sterling) or by the Federal Reserve in the USA. Being an 'offshore' market, the banks involved were also outside the exchange controls designed to support the (then) world fixed exchange rate system. Their customers were large, private and public enterprises with international interests and which dealt in large sums of money (e.g. a minimum transaction of US$1 million). By operating wholesale and free from any restrictions, Euromarket banks had lower costs than their US counterparts and so could offer better rates of interest to their clients and could profit on small percentage differences. The first lesson of this new industry was thus well learnt: large turnovers, small margins and fleet-footed avoidance of rigid regulation was the secret of success.

The accelerating internationalisation of finance gained pace in the 1970s when global recycling of petrodollars became the major preoccupation of bankers (see chapters 9 and 10, below). Massive balance of payments deficits of Western, oil-consuming nations had to be matched by opposite movements of large sums of capital financed through the banks. The reverse side of this same coin was that oil-rich OPEC states with small populations and a limited capacity to quickly spend these fortunes needed international banks to place these funds in interest-bearing deposits. Trade imbalances of any kind require financing – these imbalances were the largest the world had ever seen and the opportunities for expansion of international finance were a major boost to the industry.

Deregulation

At the end of the 1970s, the stagflationary effects of the oil shocks on Western economies heralded the ascendancy of conservative economics as espoused by Britain's Margaret Thatcher and Ronald Reagan of the USA. After decades of interventionism, subsidies and controls in all manner of industries, governments in the 1980s seemed to rediscover the dynamism of free markets. Deregulation, privatisation and the liberation of prices became the new orthodoxy. Restrictions on international capital movements were lifted in one country after another.

Note that increasing international competition drove deregulation more than anything else. As 'offshore' and foreign banks in London dealt increasingly profitably with large international accounts free of Bank of England controls then UK domestic banks lobbied the government to allow them unrestricted access to this market also. As the amount of business grew in London so the same political pressures built up in New York, Tokyo and Frankfurt: central authorities must lighten the load of their controls or risk the loss of business avoiding their shores. Deregulation rapidly became the dominant political economy, therefore, even in countries with allegedly socialist, or interventionist administrations such as France and Japan.

Innovation

We have met this notion before: any system of heavy-handed regulation drives private profit-seekers to innovate and avoid paying such costs. In banking, with such a slippery commodity as money, the volume of dealing simply changes its form and keeps on growing. If governments resist the tendency towards deregulatory financial policies then they will attempt to exert more and more restrictions on their particular money markets. This will drive interest rates up and make it even more profitable for international dealers to try and avoid regulations and move money around. The opportunities for financial innovation and profitable *arbitrage* increase. Controls cannot succeed in such an international environment – the political movement towards deregulation becomes unstoppable.

Technology

Advances in computing and telecommunications technology provided the means to accelerate these changes world-wide. Round-the-clock, 24-hour trading in a global financial market place is possible with the three largest financial centres of London, New York and Tokyo all linked together. As Tokyo goes to bed, London is waking up and so New York switches from one set of traders to another. And with computers programmed to gather and analyse masses of business data, the *transaction costs* of seeing and acting upon subtle changes in financial information have become greatly reduced. (This fact alone explains why such a lot of international trading occurs: assume 500 dealers each operating in Japan, the USA and the UK. The cost of contacting each one increasingly diminishes as technology improves – banks thus have no economic incentive to restrict the number of contacts. The addition of *one* extra dealer in this network, therefore, will increase the number of trades possible by *1,500*. That is why daily transactions in international money are measured in trillions of dollars.)

US economist Robert Solomon quotes that the cost of a three-minute transatlantic phone call between New York and London fell by 90 per cent between 1970 and 1990 while the average price of computers fell by 95 per cent. 'Distance has become virtually irrelevant in business and financial decisions', he says. Meanwhile, US international trade in bonds and equities rose from 9 per cent of GDP in 1980 to 89 per cent in 1990 to 164 per cent by 1996.

The significance of information and transaction costs falling is that the *barriers to entry* to this industry have therefore all but disappeared. Specialist knowledge which used to characterise each segment of financial markets is now widely available to any firm that can tap into the relevant global telecommunications network. Highly efficient and accessible technology has brought increased competition from enterprises formerly unrelated to the industry and, as a result, has been responsible for much *dis*intermediation – the direct matching of buyers and sellers outside the money markets by businesses 'doing it themselves' without the brokerage service of official banks or finance houses.

Risk

Each change mentioned above drives others. Anti-inflationary, conservative governments drive up interest rates rather than expand money supplies. With no restrictions on capital movements, 'hot money' flows in to take advantage of higher rates of return. Domestic currency is in demand, therefore, and the exchange rate must rise. This causes businesses to recalculate their costs and profits in international trade: exports become more expensive and imports cheaper as the price of currency appreciates. (All these events occurred in the early 1980s in Europe and the USA. The business recession created was sharp, painful and costly in terms of business failure and unemployment.)

Businesses are at risk in a world of volatile interest and exchange rates, and risk encourages banks to offer innovative financial packages to help such enterprises to weather the storms. The growth of clever ways to hedge against various types of financial risk has therefore led to an explosive increase in options, futures and all sorts of trading in *derivatives* (and, more insultingly, *junk bonds*), each new financial product being rapidly copied by other banks and centres as soon as it hits the market. Thus dealing in three-month Eurodollar futures totalled US$670 billion at the end of 1989, rising to US$1.1 trillion by late 1991.

Diversification

The appropriate response to a world of increasing risk is for businesses to diversify their spread of assets. As currencies, interest rates and commodity prices have become more volatile, so institutional investors whose profits depend on these prices have increasingly widened their portfolios and purchased assets in a number of different centres. Pension funds, insurance companies and unit trusts have taken a more and more active part in international trading, therefore. For example, in the 1980s decade UK pension funds increased their holdings of foreign securities from 7 per cent to 18 per cent of their portfolios; US funds widened their spread from 1 per cent to 4 per cent and the Japanese from 1 per cent to 16 per cent.

Effects

The implication of all these changes for individual countries is that now it is extremely difficult for governments to use monetary policies to control their economies as they so wish. Any changes they may want to introduce can have unpredictable repercussions, thanks to the volatile and interdependent world we all live in, and so the idea of fine-tuning an economy through regulating the quantity of money or the structure of interest rates is hopelessly impractical.

Multiasset markets

How can central banks control the money supply when money itself can no longer be closely defined? In today's financial markets, dealers work with a whole spread of assets of varying liquidity and security from cash through Treasury and commercial bills of exchange, to all manner of different bonds, securities, certificates of deposits, equities, and longer-term advances and mortgages.

Liquidity is the ease with which any of these assets can be converted into cash. Very short-term loans are highly liquid since they will be repaid quickly. Reliable long-term assets can be very liquid also since they may have a high resale value or *secondary market*. (Government securities of, say, one year to run can be re-sold immediately to any one of a number of interested buyers.) Less reputable commercial bonds and longer-term assets may be more difficult to place a present value upon – they are less liquid – but they carry a higher rate of interest as a result.

With so many different financial institutions holding varied portfolios of income-earning financial assets, which particular ones do you include in the money supply? If the central bank restricts the circulation of those assets it has directly under its own control it will simply prompt the expansion of other financial instruments to take their place. If interest rates on government bills and bonds rise then a whole chain of substitutions may take place as dealers adjust their holdings of these as opposed to other assets. Prices and interest rates on a host of near and distant alternatives will all shuffle up or down accordingly.

As a result of such diversity, central banks have identified an ever-increasing array of monetary aggregates as the money supply: M1, M2, M3, M3c, M4, etc. – each in turn being used for control purposes, only to be just as quickly abandoned as the authorities found that each did not behave quite as it should have done. Experience has produced *Goodhart's law*: whichever measure seems best to represent the money supply will cease to function as such as soon as the central bank tries to regulate it.

Institutional changes

In addition to the vast, innovative spread of assets held by banks, what actually constitutes a bank now is becoming irrelevant. Once upon a time, financial markets were segmented and specialised: commercial or retail banks offered deposit and (relatively short-term) loan facilities to the public; merchant banks, acceptance houses or investment banks underwrote share issues for businesses; building societies and mortgage institutions funnelled many small savings into long-term house loans; discount houses and money market brokers bought and sold very short-term government and commercial debt. All these and more traded in specialised financial products and set their own prices in their own secure worlds.

Now domestic and international competition is rife. The barriers between different financial sectors have come down – so that retail banks have become building societies and similarly they offer wholesale banking services to big business. With cross-border restrictions falling, subsidiaries of foreign, international banks have meanwhile poured into every small financial centre around the world; and, most important of all, many large, national and multi-national companies have now entered into the competition as well. As late as the 1970s, US banks controlled about half of the long-term loans made to business in that country. By the mid-1990s, that figure was down to around 20 per cent as other institutions entered the market and, especially, firms sold their own commercial paper.

Dozens of international mergers and acquisitions have occurred since the 1970s between banks, securities firms and brokerage houses in Europe, the USA and Japan. As a result, which finance house is operating where, dealing in what business is no longer the cosy, predictable affair it used to be. In the 1990s, the international reach of the world's 100 largest banks amounted to over 4,600 offices in different locations – it is certainly far greater today. This remarkable globalisation and opening-up of the banking industry is important because it has made the rapid mobilisation of funds from one centre to another all the more easy and, by the same token, has made the monitoring and control of domestic financial operations by national authorities virtually impossible.

Exchange rate effects

With financial sectors operating increasingly beyond the reach of central banks, government attempts to change money supplies and interest rates within the domestic economy may have little short-term effect on real economic variables such as consumption, investment and employment, but it may have an unpredictable and immediate impact on the exchange rate.

Suppose, for example, that the central bank intends to restrict the money supply, push up interest rates and restrain inflationary expenditure. These efforts may have little impact on the real economy if business activity and expectations are operating in a contrary direction. If official bank lending is tight then, as already explained, large corporations can raise funds by borrowing internationally through a process of issuing their own bonds or securities (though they have to take on the risk of unanticipated exchange rate movements).

High domestic interest rates will anyway attract foreign savers to move their funds into the country, so through a combination of this effect, plus local businesses pulling in cheaper foreign loans, there will be a flow of funds on to the foreign exchange markets and therefore an increased demand for the domestic currency.

Given that the central bank is consistent in wishing to curtail the money supply, the only outcome of increased foreign demand for the currency must be a rise in the exchange rate. Thus the effect of the authorities attempting a credit squeeze is not necessarily to dampen aggregate investment and consumption spending, but to drive up the price of exports and to reduce the price of imports. The country's trade balance will worsen, and industries producing exports and import substitutes will suffer.

All countries have therefore found out that they can have either an exchange rate policy, or a monetary policy, but not both. The domestic interest rate appropriate for one cannot be simultaneously used to control the other. If governments are unhappy that their exchange rate is too high, making exports too expensive and uncompetitive in world markets, then they must reduce interest rates and/or sell more currency to bring its price down. Either way they lose control of the money supply. Alternatively, if they stick rigidly to a monetarist prescription of expanding money supplies according to a prearranged target, they cannot then control interest rates and exchange rates as they so wish, but must leave them to be determined by the free market.

CONCLUSION

In a multiasset financial world the clear-cut distinction between a community's base of cash reserves and its total money supply disappears. There is no simple 1:10 credit multiplier relationship; reserve assets are not easily identifiable nor are they completely within the control of the authorities; and – thanks to institutional changes – official banks subject to central bank regulation now represent a diminishing fraction of financial operators.

All the measures referred to above by which central authorities are supposed to influence monetary aggregates – increasing or decreasing commercial bank reserves through open market operations, direct intervention or changing minimum asset requirements – are now only to be found in outdated economics textbooks. These measures cannot work in open, deregulated markets since other highly liquid assets can be quickly substituted for those reserves the central bank calls in, and many non-bank financial operators are out of reach anyway.

In effect, most developed countries since the mid-1980s have opted to pursue an exchange rate policy rather than take any overt monetary stance apart from deregulation. For all the reasons given above, monetary policy is too blunt and unpredictable an instrument to serve the needs of governments.

The impact of all these changes on the world economy cannot be easily summarised – we are still in the process of living with them. What is clear is that international financial markets react faster today than ever before and can move such volumes of money that even those central banks with the deepest pockets cannot buy them off. Governments in Mexico and East Asia recently found this out to their cost.

At such times, when private markets force changes upon public authorities, criticisms typically surface alleging that democratically elected administrations are being held hostage by faceless speculators, profit-hungry conspirators or 'global capital'. (For example, Malaysian Prime Minister Mahathir Mohamed blamed Westerners in general when the ringgit depreciated by 35 per cent in the latter half of December 1997.) Beware of such politically loaded complaints!

It is true that in interdependent and volatile financial markets, if government policies in one country are not considered trustworthy then both national and international wealthholders will quickly desert those shores and look for safer havens. In these circumstances it is probable that local capitalists, and not faceless international speculators, will be the quickest to move – they are likely to know local conditions best and have most to lose. For example, domestic and not US and other foreign investors were the first to jump ship in the 1994–5 Mexican crisis. (The same was true in the economic turmoil that accompanied the end of the Allende government and preceded the Pinochet dictatorship in Chile in 1973. Although international monetary movements were much more restricted then, that did not prevent much of the blame being heaped on foreign – and especially US – interests.)

This does not mean that governments have much less power these days – it is just that they cannot fool people for so long any more. The penalty for implementing unsustainable economic policies is now a financial crisis sooner rather than later. One implication here is wholly positive: governments cannot pull the wool over the eyes of their electorates and so they must make a better job of communicating what it is they want to do and how they intend to pay for it. Any attempt to fudge the issues will be penalised.

The better the quality of information fed to financial markets the more efficiently – and less harmfully – they will react. The problem is that we live in a media age now where we are almost drowned in information and it is not always easy to discriminate objective quality from conjecture. There is no doubt that – in times of global crises – reputable (as well as disreputable) enterprises and practices have suffered from the sudden withdrawal of funds. Disentangling cause and effect, apportioning blame and reforming faulty market structures is not easy.

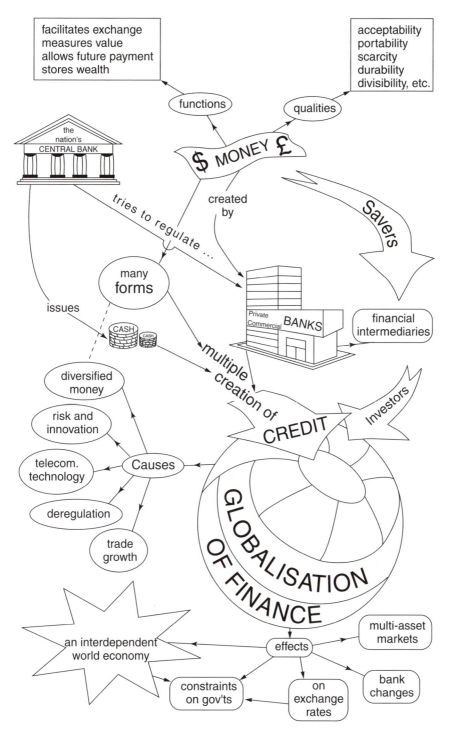

Figure 7.1 The themes of chapter 7

And one major worry still remains. Are the interests of money market dealers the same as those of the people in whose country they operate? Are their priorities shared by simple farmers, industrial labourers and the average person in the street? Maybe elected governments with a social conscience (especially left-wing ones) that want to build more public hospitals/housing and implement more redistributive incomes policies will be subject to far more demanding financial terms by distrustful, right-wing capitalists?

This is an understandable and recurrent concern. The answer is twofold. Firstly, the large sums of money that move across international markets are not in the main those of individual speculators, they more often feature pension and savings funds that are protecting the interests of millions of ordinary workers and people in the street. And, secondly, professional fund managers are less interested in the politics of governments than in their financial credibility. No matter if socialist administrations want to build public hospitals and tax the rich – if they borrow the hard-earned pennies of countless ordinary citizens, will they pay back on time?

Financial markets, therefore, operate similarly to all others. The more competition and the more quality information they act with the better they will function. But they *are* subject to collective failure – as is examined in more detail in chapter 10 – because their limitations are no more nor less than those of the market economic system in general. And the more globalised they become, the more markets will link the fortunes on one side of the world to those on the other. They are just one dimension of our interdependent, international economy.

KEY WORDS

Arbitrage   This refers to the exploitation of marginal differences in prices of financial assets between different markets. If the price of a given currency, commodity or bond in Frankfurt or New York is higher than in London then it pays to buy in the cheaper market and sell in the other. The smallest price differentials can yield significant profits if large volumes are traded. Risks are low since arbitrage implies simultaneous transactions at known prices. Its economic effect is to secure price equivalence between rival centres.

Barriers to entry   These are the restrictions imposed on any new enterprise wishing to start up business in a given field. Such barriers may be legal, bureaucratic, financial or economic. Governments may restrict foreign firms from buying domestic industrial assets by law; the process of acquiring all the necessary licences may be exhausting; the costs of insurance or borrowing local funds may be excessive, or the capital equipment necessary to start business may be highly expensive.

Bills of exchange   These originated centuries ago as three-month trade deals. You give me capital on the understanding that it takes me three months to equip a ship, sail out to the South Seas, buy lots of exotic goodies, come back and sell them off at a profit and then pay you back the agreed amount. A bill of exchange is now a promise to pay a given sum in three months' time. The cheaper you buy this bill, therefore, the more you stand to gain. Note that if a private bill, or bond, is guaranteed by a reputable third party (e.g. a well-known bank or business) then you have little risk of loss – the price of this paper is likely to be higher. Such is the case also with Treasury Bills, which are issued by the government.

The riskier the dealer, however, the cheaper he will have to sell his paper – the more profit he has to offer to attract a buyer. (See junk bonds.)

Bond   Old English for promise. A bond is a written promise, a legal contract – usually a promise to pay a fixed rate of interest on a given loan. For example: you pay me $1 million and I will promise to pay you 10 per cent for as long as you have my 'bond'. My bond may be returned to me and cashed in at an agreed date; or you may decide to sell it to someone else (at whatever price you can get) in a 'secondary market'.

Central bank   The government's bank, charged with the responsibility to run monetary policy, which includes making loans to and accepting deposits from private, commercial banks and thereby determining the rate of interest on government debt. *Open market operations* is the term used to refer to the central bank's dealings with free-market banks and credit institutions – especially when it attempts to influence the quantity of money they hold.

Credit multiplier   Most private, commercial banks will hold a given proportion of their total assets in the form of a reserve – liquid funds that they can use to meet customer demands. A 10 per cent reserve implies that for every $1 in the till they have $10 in longer-term loans circulating. A given increase, say $100, in the reserve base of such a financial community can thus lead to a tenfold increase in longer-term loans – up to $1,000 in this case. Total credit is thus a multiple (e.g. ten times) of bank reserves.

Derivatives   Any tradable paper which derives its market value from that of some underlying asset is a derivative. This would include a promise to buy a certain security at an agreed price at a given date in the future ('futures'); or the option to buy certain shares at a given price within a certain time period ('options'). The enterprise which buys a derivative from a financial institution is in effect paying the seller to take on the risk of a change in economic conditions and prices over the lifetime of the business. For example, a plantation company may be unsure of the income it will earn from sales of a future harvest and thus be unable to make required investments today. An astute bank will offer to sell derivatives on the company's behalf, guaranteeing capital to the plantation, taking on the risk of a commodity price collapse but making a nice profit if it calculates correctly.

Disintermediation   Commercial banks act as intermediaries between savers and investors. Increasingly, however, buyers and sellers of money have met each other outside banks' doors. Big businesses can sell their own paper promises in financial market places to whoever is willing to accept them. This is *dis*intermediation: the matching up of funds that does not feature on the balance sheets of recognised financial institutions.

Endogenous money supply   This is where the supply of money in a country is not created and directly controlled by the central authorities but is determined by the actions of private individuals, businesses and banks. The form of money and the nature of credit-creating institutions can change where state attempts to restrict commercial banking activities bite hard – thus leading to an endogenous money supply.

Fractional reserve banking   Commercial banks traditionally keep a relatively small sum of liquid funds in reserve in order to meet customer demands for withdrawals. That is, if a bank possesses $5 million in cash deposits from savers it may decide to create $50 million in credit to loan out to needy investors. The bank's reserve: assets ratio is thus 1:10. That is, it figures that out of the $50 million of its cheques circulating no more than one tenth will be cashed in.

Goodhart's law   Charles Goodhart, who went from the Bank of England to the London School of Economics, claimed that any observed statistical correlation between two variables would break down as soon as public authorities attempted to use it for policy-making purposes. This comment is as relevant for central bank attempts to control the money supply by restricting trade in certain reserve assets, as it is for relying on a Phillips curve relationship to control unemployment by opting for a bit more inflation. Goodhart's law recognises the fundamental uncertainty of social science.

Junk bonds   These are commercial bonds *not* guaranteed by first class banks or acceptance houses and they thus carry a lower price and higher risk factor than other market instruments – though they may turn out to be perfectly reputable, despite their name.

Liquidity   Forms of wealth that can be quickly turned into cash without loss of value. Banknotes and coins are 100 per cent liquid. Some bonds and short-term loans can quickly be sold off in the markets and thus converted into cash without much loss of face value. If you own a vintage car, some old paintings, certain shares and longer-term commercial loans, however, you may have difficulty in finding buyers unless you sell at a discount – these are illiquid assets.

Secondary markets   No one would buy a very long-term promise to pay if it meant that they could not get their money back in emergencies. Ploughing millions into buying shares, bills or bonds would not occur if there were no market place where you could sell them off second-hand to other willing customers.

Transactions costs   This is how much it costs to make a certain trade. If it requires time and effort to find out about asset prices in a neighbouring market; if governments restrict access to foreign currencies or charge a tax on the value of trades, then the cost of doing business may be prohibitively high. Why invest in Country X if the transactions cost involved is higher than in Country Y?

QUESTIONS

1 How and why have the forms of money changed through history? What difficulties has this presented to central authorities trying to control the money supply?
2 Commercial banks hold only a fraction of their assets in reserve. Explain the reasons for this and its relevance to their ability to create money. How has financial innovation affected this ability?
3 How can central banks attempt to control the money supply in their domestic economies? What are the costs involved in so doing?
4 Why does so much money move around the world?
5 'The more globalised they become, the more markets will link the fortunes on one side of the world to those of the other.' Consider the implications of this statement.

FURTHER READING

Hallwood, C. Paul and MacDonald, Ronald. *International Money and Finance*. 3rd edn. Blackwell, 2000.
Solomon, R. *Money on the Move: The Revolution in International Finance Since 1980*. Princeton University Press, 1999.

8 Exchange rates and currency union

Topics to be considered in this chapter:

- Separate currencies.
- Fixed and floating exchange rate regimes.
- Costs and benefits of a currency union.
- An optimal currency area.
- A European future.

INTRODUCTION

Money – at its most perfect extreme – is invisible, costless to produce, environmentally neutral, has no intrinsic value but is exchangeable for anything. It allows the construction and trade of productive assets and the creation of great art, science and civilisation.

In less-than-perfect everyday practice, however, money occurs in a variety of different forms in a number of different market places and is only imperfectly exchangeable. Some currencies are a significantly better store of wealth than others, and a certain price must be paid to persuade people to transfer their holdings from one form of money to another. At worst, *hyperinflation* can occur – destroying the credibility of a currency – and when this happens the domestic economy breaks down, as has happened a number of times to different countries in Europe in the twentieth century.

In one part of Europe a currency union recently broke down. The economy of the old Soviet Union was bound together by the Russian rouble which formed the common medium of exchange for a currency area that stretched from Tallinn to Tashkent, Kiev to Vladivostok. Now the Union has dissolved under the pressures of separatist and independence movements; and the hyperinflation of the rouble has spawned a number of breakaway currencies, some successfully (as in the Baltic States), others with more difficulty (in the Ukraine).

Meanwhile, in another part of Europe currency unions are in the ascendant. Belgium and Luxembourg have had a common currency for years; on 1 July 1990, the unification of East and West Germany brought about the integration of the Ostmark and the Deutschmark, with the latter replacing the former; and, despite all the difficulties with the European Exchange Rate Mechanism (ERM) during the early 1990s, there are now twelve members of the European Community which have tied their currencies into the *euro* in the new millennium.

What is the rationale behind currency areas? Why do some parts of the world use one distinctive form of money and other parts use others? What are the stages involved in enlarging a currency zone and what are the costs and benefits for those communities entering a union that previously used their own, separate means of exchange? Let us consider each of these questions in turn below.

DIFFERENT COMMUNITIES: DIFFERENT CURRENCIES

Look quickly at the variety of forms of money that have existed through history: commodities, for example, such as salt, goats, corn, precious metals and even cigarettes. The fact that some societies traded with sacks of corn or livestock and others with a variety of different metals seems bizarre to us today, but perhaps this sentiment will be no different to some future European observer who looks back to the twentieth century and sees some communities trading in pounds, others in francs and others in pesetas. Why cannot Europe bring together its fragmented national markets to form one continent-wide currency bloc for the increased wealth and welfare of all?

Currency areas, like linguistic zones, evolve principally for social, and not economic reasons, and – like languages – the lack of a common currency in a large, populated land mass isolates individual communities and ties them into their own social confines. A currency becomes, therefore, the economic boundary to a social grouping. It is like saying: 'We only trade with these people, not those . . .'

Of course, with improved political and social relations between countries, increased economic growth and steady progress in telecommunications and transport technology there has been rapid expansion in international trade since the mid-twentieth century.

The economic benefits realisable from international trade are in fact driving the move towards European currency union. After two 'hot' world wars and one cold one, political relations between (most) European neighbours are now more harmonious; incomes and consumers' buying power have increased steadily and, thanks to the falling cost of transport and telecommunications exchange, people know of goods and services produced elsewhere, can gain access to them at reasonable prices and – with the globalisation of banking services – can get the foreign exchange necessary to make their purchases.

Barriers to international trade have always existed and, at first, it was the natural barriers of mountains, seas, rivers and geographical remoteness that were the most difficult to overcome. It is still costly to transport Mediterranean fruit and vegetables long distances to northern Europe, for example, and Welsh lamb back in return, but continuous transport innovation since the Middle Ages (culminating in the Channel Tunnel and the integrated network of high-speed road and rail links today) has been devoted to overcoming this problem.

The greatest obstacles to trade now are the man-made, nationalist barriers. The intervention of governments has never failed to create more and more complex tariff and non-tariff barriers to reinforce political and social prejudices. It has therefore taken immense efforts on the part of individual political idealists and institutions like the WTO and, within Europe, the EC Commission to counter these mercantilist, isolationist tendencies.

Thanks to the EC's success in reducing intra-European restrictions on trade (see chapter 6), the single, most important economic barrier to trade within the common market that remained was the lack of a common currency. The Maastricht treaty, signed in 1991 by all member countries, was centrally concerned with this issue and it laid down strict criteria that European currencies/economies were supposed to fulfil in order to bring about currency union.

Twelve countries in Europe now have full economic and monetary union (EMU). The pathway to this destination was steep and set about with pitfalls; some European partners stumbled on occasions and in consequence went along it more slowly than others; some complained loudly about where the road led and decided not to take it. Many critics, both inside and outside Europe, argue that a 'one size fits all' monetary union is entirely inappropriate. Nevertheless, twelve European nations now share a single currency at present and debate continues with regard to the wisdom of this move and the prospects for enlarging this eurozone.

STAGES TOWARDS CURRENCY UNION

What are the stages involved in this journey? The route to increasing monetary integration has travelled through many twists and turns since the end of World War II.

1 European nations, like all others, firstly pursued *independent monetary policies*. Governments were free to control their own money supplies; to borrow and lend as much as they wished; to run budget deficits and charge whatever interest rates they could get away with internally.

From 1944 to 1971 such independence was subject to the international system of *fixed exchange rates* agreed at Bretton Woods, USA, in 1944. This was effectively a dollar standard system where all world currencies were tied to a dollar price with very little room for movement (maximum fluctuations were to be contained within 1 per cent either up or down). A balance of payments deficit incurred by any trading country was cancelled by a payment of dollars. If the dollars required were greater than existing reserves, then the deficit country in these circumstances was forced to sell its own currency to buy the necessary foreign exchange, thus automatically deflating domestic money supplies, incomes and spending. If such deficits were recurring and the country concerned wished to escape from a continuous cycle of deflation then realignment was possible by refixing the relevant currency's dollar price at a lower value. (This was described as *'the adjustable peg'*.) With this system, certainty and stability of trading rules was thus established after the chaos of the 1930s and the 1940s and individual countries were free to conduct their own policies within this disciplined framework.

The slowly increasing economic strength of Germany and Japan since World War II, and the sudden leap in economic importance of the Organisation of Petroleum Exporting Countries (OPEC) in the 1970s, could not be contained within a fixed rate system frozen since 1944. International exchange rates were therefore floated free throughout the 1970s, although – in order to moderate some of the wilder fluctuations involved – most countries attempted a form of *managed floating*. This involved national authorities intervening in foreign exchange markets, buying and selling their own currencies in the attempt to limit the extremes of price movements. The US Federal Reserve would, for example, start selling part of its foreign reserves and buying overseas-held dollars in order to defend a target floor in the price of its own currency. Conversely, if it thought that the price of dollars to yen was increasing too much – putting US exports at risk compared to cheaper Japanese goods, for example – then the Fed would start selling dollars and buying yen on the international money markets.

2   An additional or alternative means of managing exchange rates is to institute some form of direct control: traders cannot bid down the price of a particular currency if the authorities concerned restrict their access to it. With *exchange restrictions* imposed, importers, for example, would have to apply to their central bank for the purchase of the foreign money required to buy the goods they desire. The bank can thus ration out foreign currency slowly, to preferred customers and at the official price, as a means of delaying import penetration and protecting the exchange rate.

Removing exchange restrictions allows a free market in a country's currency and thereby makes that nation vulnerable to any changes in international trade. This measure may be introduced, however, to signal to the international financial community that the government has instituted a fundamental shift in its policies – as in the case of the incoming Thatcher government of the UK in October 1979 – and it can also be used, as in a widening group of EU countries during the 1980s, to promote the tighter integration of a number of economies together.

3   Closer integration is secured by *tied floating*. The countries concerned agree to fix their respective exchange rates to each other within a confined range of values and allow them to float up and down more or less as a whole – or rather as a flexible 'snake' – against all other world currencies.

In March 1979 the European exchange rate mechanism was set up to overcome the problems encountered with the floating international exchange rate system of that time. For European countries that conducted a lot of trade with one another, the short-term speculative fluctuations in exchange rates that were possible under the floating regime of the 1970s were a destabilising disincentive to trade. (For Europeans with a population similar to the USA, this is rather like businesses and consumers in New York trying to trade with others in Washington and Los Angeles yet having to cope with forever fluctuating currencies and price levels in both cities.) Agreement was thus secured between contributory partners to fix exchange rates within bands of movement of 2.25 per cent (6 per cent for Italy, Spain and the UK when they first joined). To keep currencies tied to this restricted range of movement, all members of the ERM had to commit themselves to follow broadly *similar monetary policies* and to secure, therefore, convergence in economic performance.

The system instituted was similar, on a regional scale, to the Bretton Woods 'adjustable peg' system of fixed exchange rates. The anchor currency, however, which evolved was the Deutschmark (DM) rather than the US dollar and the system could be characterised as a *'crawling peg'* – the wider bands of currency movement and, smaller, more frequent realignments made for a more flexible regime (during the 1980s) that was less liable to the sudden shocks experienced when currency devaluations occurred (see Figure 8.1).

4   The ERM was part of the European Monetary System that also included the European Currency Unit – the Ecu – *a parallel currency*. This is the next stage in increasing monetary integration since once currencies have been fixed in price in relation to one another then they can clearly be valued in terms of a common unit of exchange.

The Ecu was a 'basket' of European currencies, each weighted in accordance to their importance in intra-union trade. It was introduced as the official unit of account for EU finances, for intergovernmental exchange of debt, and with the hope that it would become an increasingly important denomination in the international bond markets and eventually the currency for Europe. It didn't – less than 1 per cent of EU trade was quoted in Ecus since, like that other pure fabrication the 'international language' Esperanto, the Ecu had no natural constituency – but it nonetheless played its part in signalling the way forward on the road to a single currency for Europe.

5   To consolidate the next step towards currency union it is important to move towards *irrevocably fixed exchange rates*, assuring financial markets that there can be no further realignments within the system. This is a difficult feat to achieve. Money markets in an increasingly volatile world must be convinced that participating countries are not only politically committed to the union but also that their economies are not all pulling in different directions. Otherwise, if – for example – economy A is stronger than economy B then the exchange rate of currency A compared to B will rise as dealers trade more in one than the other.

The transition period from declaring fixed exchange rates between partners to actually introducing the new common currency is fraught with difficulty for particularly these reasons, as European experience in the early 1990s proved. Despite well-publicised claims of unshakeable faith in their currencies by various political leaders in Europe, they were unable to prevent the major speculative attacks on the ERM in 1992 and again in 1993 (see later).

6   A single currency is the final stage in monetary union. This simply confirms that a group of currencies with irrevocably fixed rates are as good as one. (It is argued that there is no theoretical difference, for example, between the existence of two separate units of exchange circulating at a fixed price – say one Deutschmark equalling one guilder – and the introduction of a common currency, the euro, which represents the same thing. While this statement is absolutely correct, it is another thing, however, to convince the money markets of this equivalence. As mentioned above, so long as two currencies are representative of two different communities, two different political and economic realities, then money markets are unlikely to accept that any exchange rate between the two is irrevocable.) Major institutional changes are required to dissolve the reality of separate currencies and to create the enlarged, common currency area. Specifically, a new central bank is required to control the new currency and administer the one, unified monetary policy for all the participating countries. The European Central Bank (ECB) was established on 1 June 1998 in Frankfurt, Germany and it now serves as the guiding monetary authority throughout continental Europe for the euro – which came into being on 1 January 1999.

A single currency, then, is the ultimate expression of an integrated, common market.

CONTROL OF THE MONEY SUPPLY

Money's value and usefulness is derived from its liquidity or flexibility: it can be turned into almost anything. (Who, after all, would place any value on money that cannot be quickly exchanged for anything else?) The more easily it can be used, however, the more easily it can be abused: money loses its value if too much of it is created. It is for this reason that, in all communities

---

BOX 8.1 CURRENCY BOARDS

A unique way of fixing an exchange rate in an irrevocable union with another currency is by means of a *currency board*. This is typically the last resort of a country with a currency that nobody trusts. Maybe it has recently been subject to rapid inflation and/or its international value has varied unpredictably. Or the central bank – which should be the hub of the country's financial system – is either underdeveloped or else it is hopelessly unreliable. A currency board basically abdicates responsibility for controlling the country's money supply in favour of tying it into someone else's currency.

In 1991, Argentina ditched its old currency and introduced a new one – the peso – which was convertible into US dollars on a one-to-one basis. This was made possible only by insisting, in law, that every peso the country issued had to be backed by a dollar in reserve. Thus the country's central bank became a currency board. The money supply could only increase if dollar reserves grew; if dollars were lost the money supply had to contract. Pesos were thus as good as US dollars and, indeed, they became interchangeable in every street and in every store across the land.

After years of soaring prices, inflation in Argentina was suddenly tamed; confidence in the currency was restored and the reputation of the government, and particularly that of the finance minister Domingo Cavallo, was made.

Ten years later, however, the absence of an independent monetary policy began to hurt. The strength of the US economy during the 1990s caused the dollar to rise and so, along with it, the Argentine peso had to rise also. But Brazil – the major trading partner of Argentina in Mercosur (the common market which also includes Uruguay and Paraguay) – meanwhile experienced domestic financial difficulties. The Brazilean *real* was devalued by 40 per cent in 1999. This left Argentina very vulnerable. How could it sell its exports which were now priced so highly compared to its neighbours? In any other currency system the Argentine peso might be expected to come down in value to help promote export sales and safeguard jobs. Not so in a currency board which insists on a fixed exchange rate. (So many Argentine loans were based on the one-for-one rate with the dollar that if the peso devalued the country would be bankrupt. Debtors would have to pay back many more pesos to reach the same dollar value.)

Unfortunately, with a currency board, there is little room for manoeuvre. Either you stay with a high dollar/peso price and endure the sluggish economic performance, not to mention the inequities and social unrest that goes with it; or the peso is devalued, exporters are relieved but financial and political chaos ensues.

In December 2001, it all ended in chaos. The economy was in deep recession, tax evasion was rife, public finances were heavily in debt and those quickest to see the end began withdrawing dollar bank deposits as fast as they could. With a billion dollars a day leaking out of the financial system the government was forced to close everything down and announce the end of convertibility. Within minutes, black market prices of the peso dropped by 25 per cent in Buenos Aires and later, across the River Plate in Montevideo, by 50 per cent. With banks locked and peoples' savings now depreciating rapidly inside, riots took place. Stores were looted, some bank branches were ransacked. The police were called out and at least thirty people died in the shooting.

The moral of the story is that the 'irrevocable' fixing of one currency price to another will never last if markets are not convinced there is the political will for the communities so married to stay together through better or worse.

and throughout history, there have been continuing efforts to control the supply of money.

The relationship between state authorities and private financial markets is the key to understanding how money supplies are determined. This relationship is never stable in any society – it is in a continual state of evolution. On some occasions, for example, private commercial banks have created too much money in order to fund their own ventures or lend to their preferred clients and when carried to excess this led to a collapse in credibility with markets refusing to accept that bank's money. (Innocent bank customers who thus lose all their deposits can criticise central authorities for failing to regulate bank activities here.)

In other cases, governments have created money in order to pay for their own spending (on wars, massive public works, to repay debts, etc.). This leads to debasement of the legal tender, economic dislocation and, in the extreme, markets will again turn to another form of money.

Germany, which experienced two destructive hyperinflations in the twentieth century, learned the hard way that social cohesion is dependent on monetary discipline. Bitter experience has shown that government budgets must not be spendthrift and public sector borrowing should not be excessive. (This is because government credits – bonds and bills – quickly become accepted in the markets as a form of money; thus lending can get out of control and only after the crash do societies realise their mistake. It is not just one bank's customers but everyone who loses money in these circumstances.)

A history of political division and economic fluctuation in Europe resulted in the late twentieth- century desire to surmount all differences and to secure a common currency. But, however noble these political ambitions, we have seen that a currency union requires close harmony in the participating economies and a disciplined central control of the money supply if the common unit of exchange is to work to the advantage of all concerned. What are the economic risks and rewards involved in forming a currency union? And why should any separate country not yet included join the euro?

BENEFITS AND COSTS OF A SINGLE CURRENCY

- One direct benefit of a common currency easiest to appreciate is in *the elimination of transactions costs.* Previously, any trade between euro partners involved paying the cost of exchanging one currency for another. All tourists know this problem – travelling from the north of Italy through Austria and into Germany and in half a day you used to lose a considerable sum of money in commission charges changing cash from lire to schillings and then into Deutschmarks. Monetary union has eliminated this deadweight loss: that is, the significant cost that consumers have to pay and for which they receive nothing.
- The indirect benefit of removing transactions costs and *increasing the transparency of European prices* is more difficult to calculate. European

consumers are now able to compare prices of the same goods on one side of the continent to the other and make their purchases accordingly. Note that price discrimination between different countries is easier to conceal when people use different currencies – it was calculated that during the 1980s, buying the same Ford car in the UK was up to 30 per cent more expensive than in Belgium, for example. Hiding such differentials is impossible with a common currency. There are still price differences but these are now only due to differences in real costs, (e.g. transport) not profiteering. There is an undeniable gain in removing the cloak of exchange rates behind which much price discrimination could previously be hidden, though quantifying the stimulus this is now giving to freer European trade and increased consumer welfare is difficult to predict.

- A common currency *removes any uncertainty over future exchange rate movements*. Cross-frontier investment is impeded by the risk of a change in currency prices. Estimated profits from an investment in another country can be reduced or even wiped out if the currency in which those profits occur unexpectedly devalues. Such exchange rate uncertainty can be partly reduced by hedging in currency futures – paying others to take on this risk – but, again, this cost is another deadweight loss which businesses can well do without. A single currency thus leads to an increase in cross-border investments.

These three benefits are all related: they result from the increased workings of a pan-European price mechanism. Wider, freer trade across the whole continent, it is alleged, will secure a more efficient allocation of combined resources.

- The dominant cost that is raised over currency union is the considerable *loss of economic and political sovereignty* involved. With only one pan-European currency, there can be only one monetary policy. National governments opting for the euro have now ceded this instrument of their control, therefore, to the European Central Bank. No member country of the union is free to increase or decrease their money supply, devalue or raise the price of their currency, and adjust the level of interest rates to suit their own particular circumstances. Thus if one European nation grows faster or experiences less inflation than another, and as a consequence is able to sell a surplus of exports to its neighbour, then before EMU the deficit country could correct the trade balance by choosing either to devalue its currency or it can deflate (i.e. reduce) its national income. Both ways restrict a country's ability to purchase foreign goods, but most would agree that the latter option is the more painful. With monetary union, of course, this policy choice is now not available: only deflation is possible.

    Further, national governments find that under a common currency they lose *fiscal* as well as monetary independence. If one government spends more than it raises in taxes *and* it can no longer print its own money to cover the difference, then that government must borrow more from the ECB. But no one nation in the union is likely to remain silent if it sees another in its midst splashing out more than its share of the common currency. The ECB must therefore constrain *all* governments from running excessive deficits. (What is excessive? That is now something that is supposed to be decided by the union, *not* by individual governments.)

Loss of sovereignty: only one cost of currency union has been mentioned here, but this is the big one. What is the solution to this problem now there is a single European currency? What policy options do national governments have if they feel that their country is losing out in competition with other European states?

The answer at the national, macroeconomic level is: not a lot! If monetary policy is designed to suit a common European market then differences between member nations obviously cannot be accommodated. That was why the transition period between announcing the intention of forming the euro in Maastricht 1991 to its eventual introduction in 1999 was so painful. Asymmetries between the different European economies in the 1990s were too obvious to ignore by financial markets – despite pretences to the contrary by political leaders. When forced to choose between national interests and a fixed European Exchange Rate Mechanism, therefore, speculators bet that individual governments would put national interests before European ones. They were not wrong. Centuries of cultural differences could not be assumed away by Euro-enthusiasts. The speculative attacks of 1992 and 1993 cost certain European governments, treasuries and economies dearly and economists still quarrel over the implications. Similarly, the growth of the euro area since 1999 has not been plain sailing, and stresses and strains within the union are an ongoing concern and source of controversy, as we shall see.

THE PATHOLOGY OF A CURRENCY CRISIS: EUROPE IN 1992–3

The problem of any intended currency union is ensuring economic convergence between participating countries. Political idealism should not run ahead of economic realities. Just as it had brought down the Bretton Woods system before, so political inflexibility and the pegging of government reputations to currency prices caused the ERM to blow apart in the early 1990s. The build up of international speculative forces against the fixed European exchange rates simply became too great to withstand.

By 1991 the ERM had evolved to become a truly fixed rate system. The Maastricht treaty had emphasised the importance of currency convergence for all members of the intended union and it therefore became a sort of virility symbol of governments to achieve this harmony as early as possible. Five criteria were required to be met by countries wishing to enter the select monetary integration club: price stability; budget balance; low levels of national debt; equivalent interest rates and fixed exchange rates.

Why were these criteria imposed? Imagine what would happen if one country was borrowing more or deflating more than another. Interest rates in one country would be higher than another. With unrestricted financial markets, currencies would flow out of one country and into the other and exchange rates would diverge. How can anyone be convinced that convergence to a single, common currency is achievable?

But with five, well-published criteria to fulfil, it obviously became easy to compare the success of each European nation in reaching these goals. Newspapers in all member countries published charts grouping those nations closest to meeting these essential targets – the pressure was on all governments to improve their position in the rank-order. A currency that devalued in this rarefied atmosphere would indicate an apparent economic weakness and thus lack of political influence for the nation concerned in the councils of Europe.

Unfortunately, at the same time as this convergence in performance of different member countries was becoming an inescapable political straitjacket, the external economic forces defining Europe were undergoing radical change.

It has been mentioned that countries forming a currency union should not be subject to differential economic experiences. An external and asymmetric shock which impacts on partner countries to contrary effect cannot be accommodated by a common monetary policy. For countries in transition, straining to present a harmonious appearance to financial markets prior to currency union, this is the worst scenario to confront.

Yet this is precisely what happened. The collapse of communism and the unification of East and West Germany in 1990 happened astonishingly quickly – too quickly for the previously divided economies to adjust. East German industry could not compete in the modern Western market place. Factories closed and unemployment increased. It says much about their sense of shared political and social identity that West Germans were prepared to pay the increased taxes that were required to support their neighbours. Taxation alone, however, could not pay for all this – government borrowing had to rise. With the Bundesbank unwilling to increase money supplies (it would have been inflationary) increased government borrowing meant that German interest rates rose.

High interest rates were not an appropriate policy, however, for other countries of Europe at this time which were struggling with recession. The spending boom at the end of the 1980s decade (prompted by supply-side tax cuts, amongst others – see chapters 3 and 4 above) had led to inflation, increased indebtedness and, consequently, the imposition of deflationary cut-backs. Falling incomes and rising unemployment were the inevitable inheritance at the beginning of the 1990s.

All the elements necessary for a European currency crisis were, by 1992, now in place:

- The ERM had become a rigidly fixed exchange rate system.
- EU governments were anxious to prove their anti-inflationary, convergence credentials.
- Due to the shock of unification, the Bundesbank had independently set its interest rate at a relatively high level within Germany.
- Deflation and unemployment were becoming increasing problems for a number of Germany's partners.

• Popular support for currency union and the stringent convergence conditions was by no means overwhelming.

It is not difficult to see the incompatibility of these features. In order to ease the widespread recession (which affected the USA, Japan and many other countries too) there was much talk of the need to reduce interest rates. With German intransigence, however, this was impossible without undermining progress to European currency union. Critics, nevertheless, were not slow to point out that US interest rates were far lower than European ones and this country had entered a period of booming growth.

Pressure to devalue was greatest on those European states who had most to gain from so doing and where internal political criticism of currency union was known to be strong.

Given fixed exchange rates plus the prediction that they may not stay fixed for very long, you have the perfect scenario for heavy speculation. Sterling fund-holders, for example, have little to lose if they convert all their money into Deutschmark: if there is no change of currency prices then they can simply buy back later when all the fuss has died down; but if sterling is devalued then they can repurchase far more than they had before. This is not just greedy speculation against a particular country's interests: no responsible manager of insurance or pension funds, for example, can sit idly by if those funds are about to be devalued.

In 1992, the Italian lira was thought to be inflation-prone. In contrast, inflation in the UK was no different (if not lower) than in Germany, but it was suffering from the recession and political support for the pound's membership of the ERM was questionable. Heavy selling of both currencies took place in September of that year and, with the Bundesbank unwilling to supply Deutschmarks, devaluations were inevitable. Additionally, the UK left the exchange rate mechanism entirely (rather than just realign the pound's price at a lower level) and brought its interest rates down.

A year later, it all happened again when the French franc came under attack. Similar to the UK, France's inflation record was not in dispute – it satisfied more of the Maastricht convergence criteria than Germany – but now it was deep in painful recession and speculators were betting that the country could not go on any longer without taking the medicine of reducing interest rates. This time, speculation embraced not only the French franc but also the Belgian franc, Spanish peseta and the Danish krona. The ERM could not continue in its present form. The 2.25 per cent narrow band of movement allowed between currency prices was widened to 15 per cent – as good as returning the currencies of Europe to independent, managed floating.

A COMMON EUROPEAN CURRENCY

All these events appear to be very persuasive evidence that squeezing very disparate economies into one currency and one common monetary policy is impossible. The early experience of the European Central Bank cements this impression.

The original central banks of the member countries of the euro now transmit their own, national economic information to the ECB. The Governing Council of the ECB – made up of all the governors of each national central bank plus members of the executive board of the ECB – take this information into account when deciding the appropriate monetary policy for Euroland as a whole. In circumstances when external events impact on euro nations asymmetrically, the ECB can do little. If Ireland is suffering from inflation and Germany, in direct contrast, is enduring deflation then to act in favour of one country (or countries) in the union risks aggravating problems in others. For this reason, in the early years of its existence, the ECB earned a reputation for impotence. But this is not quite the whole story – there is a growing appreciation that it is not at the level of macroeconomic monetary policy where the all-important flexibility is required. Microeconomic occupational and geographical mobility of resources is more necessary, and thus it may be that responsive supply-side policies can compensate for macro-money rigidity – if not straight away, than certainly over time with increasing economic integration.

Consider an external shock to Europe which impacts on euro nations in the same way (e.g. a North American recession) – but to different degrees of distress. All European exporters may lose sales and jobs, but the country with the more flexible markets will suffer less than others. The ECB will act to try and minimise the pain (say, reducing the eurozone interest rate) in this case but the remedy will be more beneficial for some rather than others. In such a scenario, the governor of the ECB can be expected to recommend to euro political leaders that they take more action to liberalise and harmonise their economies.

In its 'Economic Survey of the Euro Area', published July 2005, the Organisation of Economic Cooperation and Development (OECD) notes that progress on integration has been disappointing, growth has been sluggish, inflation has not eased sufficiently and it thus recommends certain key reforms to improve prospects. Tellingly, these are to make labour markets more flexible, to improve competition particularly in the services sector where protectionism is still excessive, and to restrain government spending where budget deficits continue to threaten euro stability.

The costs of any monetary union will be lessened, therefore, and the benefits maximised, the more integrated and flexible the contributing national economies become. The OECD reports, however, that thanks to its sclerosis, the economic performance of the euro area has been lagging behind that of other OECD countries (Australia, Canada, Denmark, New Zealand, Sweden, the UK and the USA) since the mid-1990s and the forecast – if reforms are not implemented – is that it will fall even further behind.

This argument leads directly to the question: how flexible and internationally integrated must a group of economies become before a common currency brings more benefits than costs? What is an optimal currency area?

THE ECONOMICS OF AN OPTIMAL CURRENCY AREA

Consider the situation, referred to earlier, where one country (country A) experiences an increasing deficit in its trade with another (country B). Over time, if the unequal demand for these countries' products persists, country A will move into deepening recession, while B's economy will boom. How can this disequilibrium situation be resolved in a single currency area where realigning exchange rates is not an available policy option?

1 Microeconomic, 'supply-side' *flexibility of labour markets is required.* Where wages are flexible and/or labour is geographically and occupationally mobile in and between the two countries concerned then there is no need for separate currency price movements.

    A slump in demand for A's goods will produce a fall in demand for A's labour. Where wages are flexible (downward) then, it is argued, there will be no unemployment since labour is retained at lower cost. The cost and thus price of A's exports will fall, winning back an increase in demand. The opposite effect operates in the case of Country B. Booming demand bids up the wages of B's labour. As costs and prices rise so B is not likely to sell as many exports. The trade imbalance between A and B rights itself.

    If wages in both countries are 'sticky' and do not move smoothly in response to changing conditions of demand (they tend not to) then unemployment will result in A, overfull employment and perhaps inflation might occur in B. Where labour is mobile, however, A's unemployed workers simply migrate to B, thus removing unemployment in one country and reducing the inflationary pressure in the other.

    If neither conditions hold, if wages are sticky and labour is immobile, then differential economic conditions in both countries cannot be alleviated without exchange rate movements. An optimal currency area is thus one which enjoys flexible labour markets.

2 The problem of deficits and surpluses is hardly a matter for concern between large, mostly self-sufficient countries where only a small fraction of goods and services are internationally traded. In contrast, where a group of countries exchange a high fraction of their produce then they have much to gain from a single currency. Frequent changes in exchange rates between them would trigger far-reaching shocks throughout their economies. Open economies with a high *proportion of tradable goods and services* exchanged between them, therefore, benefit more and suffer less in a currency union (Figure 8.1). It makes less sense to include those neighbours who are less integrated within the group or have stronger trade links with countries outside the region.

3 Disequilibrium between states involved in a monetary union is less likely to be extreme the more that *economic structures are similar.* World economic events are never stable and who knows what the next shock will be – after recession in the USA, financial crisis in East Asia, the collapse of

communism – will it be another war, revolution or oil shock? Whatever the crisis, it is less likely to put a strain upon a currency union if the impact has a similar, and not an asymmetric, effect on the countries involved.

THE CASE OF EUROPE

If we apply this analysis to Europe now we can see how far these countries concerned make up an optimum currency area.

With regard to labour markets there has been growing concern that European labour is far less mobile than in North America. This is true geographically – it is more difficult for labour to move around Europe where different cultures, languages and laws act as a disincentive, compared to the homogeneity of North America, for example – and also occupationally, where social welfare legislation and government minimum wage laws (such as embodied in the 'social chapter' to the Maastricht agreement) are argued to reduce labour mobility. Workers are less keen to change jobs if they have accumulated many non-wage benefits in their present occupation; employees are less willing to take on extra labour if it will be difficult and expensive to sack them. Such market 'distortions' have been blamed for a European average unemployment of persistently over 10 per cent in the early 1990s: almost double that of the USA which has far less protective labour legislation.

The argument that social welfare legislation distorts labour markets and is responsible for unemployment is by no means accepted by all. But for whatever reason, wages and labour do appear to be generally less flexible in Europe than in the USA.

Consider the accompanying graphs on rates of unemployment and real wage movements for selected European countries and the USA (see Figures 8.2–8.5). The latter has had consistently lower rates of unemployment than in Europe and its rate of growth of real wages has been lowest when unemployment is higher. The two graphs move up and down in opposition to each other. Compare this with the European countries. With the exception of the Netherlands and the UK, others seem unable to show that their higher unemployment levels have had much effect on containing wage rises. Clearly, on this evidence, labour markets in Europe appear to be far less flexible and responsive to economic realities than those in the USA.

Insofar as integration within a European common market is concerned, some countries are much more tied into the economic fate of their neighbours than others (see Figure 8.1).

For the Netherlands and Belgium large fractions of their exports are sold to their European partners, so clearly any change in exchange rates between them would significantly affect their export revenues – with knock-on effects for the domestic economy. (This is the *foreign trade multiplier*: any change in export demand has a multiplied effect on domestic incomes.) A common currency suits these nations, therefore. (Ireland trades more with the UK which is outside the euro, so it has less to gain than this data seems to imply.)

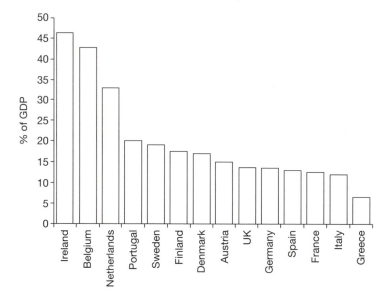

Figure 8.1 Exports to the European Union as a percentage of GDP, 1996
Source: OECD.

For countries such as Italy and Greece however, a far lower proportion of their exports are sold in Europe and so they will feel the constraints of a common currency more than others. Monetary union for these countries remains a risk and it is important to work at loosening internal markets, eliminating structural unemployment until their trade patterns are more tied into the rest of Europe and the balance of costs and benefits shifts more emphatically in their favour.

The economic structure of union countries should not be so dissimilar that external shocks have an asymmetric impact on the countries concerned. German unification was a one-off event but it perfectly illustrated the perils of how unforeseen circumstances can pull European countries in opposite directions – are there any other such shocks out there waiting to happen? Unfortunately yes!

Firstly, in the case of the UK, its industrial structure is strong in energy and financial services and its housing market is dependent on variable-rate mortgages. This is not the case for much of Euroland. Changes in oil prices will have a differential impact on UK industry; changes in mortgage interest rates will have a distinctly different effect on UK borrowing and spending than in the rest of Europe. (The argument about oil prices is even more relevant for Norway – a major oil producer that has decided to stay out of the EC.) This makes joining the euro a worrying prospect for the UK.

Secondly, a bigger problem faces Europe regarding their Eastern members who are still waiting for equal treatment in farm policy. Agriculture is a major employer in Poland, Hungary and the Czech Republic. (It is not unimportant for euro countries like Greece, Portugal and Spain!) Strains apparent in Europe's

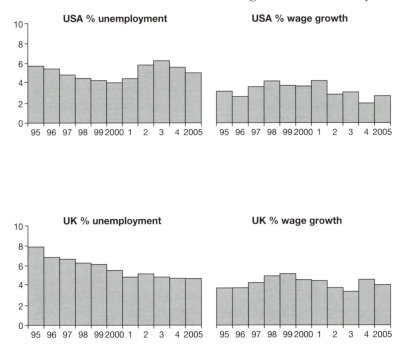

Figure 8.2 US and UK: unemployment and wage growth, 1995–2005. In any market place, excess supply should lead to falling prices; as unemployment rises, wage growth should fall and vice versa. Contrast US and European labour markets here and overleaf. While there is evidence for this in the case of the USA, in The Netherlands and to a lesser extent in the UK, for Spain, Italy, Belgium, Germany and France, real wages grew even where unemployment was much higher – a clear indication of inflexible, unresponsive markets.

Source: *The Economist.*

Common Agricultural Policy have not been resolved; they are increasing now that a common currency exists and EC enlargement has only been possible by limiting the access of the new entrants to the CAP, which still awaits major revision.

A CONCLUSION FOR EUROPE

The conclusion offered here, therefore, is that the European Union as a whole is not an optimum currency area. The striking economic diversity of European nations indicates that, already for some members of the euro, the costs of joining the union are much greater than for others. For these countries, improving microeconomic flexibility is an urgent priority.

In 1999, twelve countries of Europe took the plunge to link their currencies together but three that did not have since grown faster. It may be that the strains of monetary and economic integration have inhibited the advance of the brave

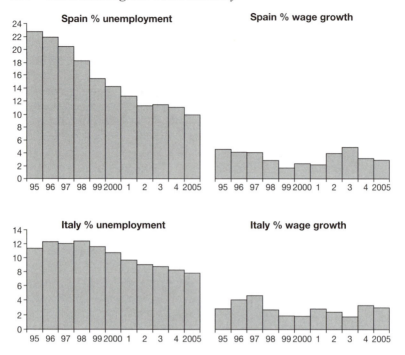

Figure 8.3 Spain and Italy: unemployment and wage growth, 1995–2005

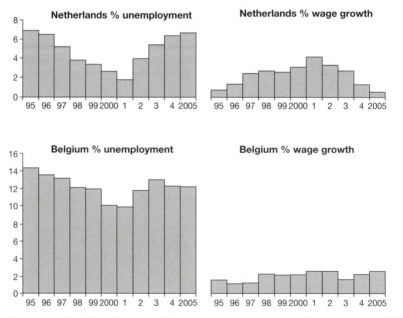

Figure 8.4 The Netherlands and Belgium: unemployment and wage growth, 1995–2005

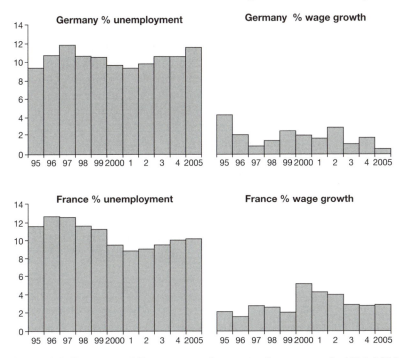

Figure 8.5 Germany and France: unemployment and wage growth, 1995–2005

twelve and in the future they will grow all the faster as they reap the rewards of this sacrifice . . . but at the time of going to press there is clearly no persuasive evidence to support this idealistic view.

Instead, in 2003 the EU took the momentous step of opting for greater breadth rather than depth. If the original 15 showed great diversity then within the 25 countries that now make up the Union there is even less of an economic case for a common currency.

The existing euro members clearly thought it imperative to swap monetary independence for a single unit of exchange in the new millennium but, whatever the historical, political and social arguments involved, there are quite clearly economic costs – expressed in terms of recession and slower growth for those countries that have had greater difficulty in squeezing their economies into the 'one-size-fits-all' shape. Since monetary policy cannot be adjusted to fit all former independent economies then alternative policy instruments must be fashioned to help. Unfortunately, so long as European resources are reluctant to move with market demand and change employments, and so long as national governments lack the political will to make needed reforms, then the pessimistic OECD forecast referred to above is likely to prevail. Certainly, there is no central 'structural fund' large enough to make redistribution between rich and poor regions effective nor provide sufficient incentives to ignite microeconomic dynamism.

A currency union is no easy economic option, therefore. The cultural richness of Europe brings with it a similar patchwork of economic variety and the central institutions of the EU – the Commission, the Council of Ministers, the Parliament and the ECB – must somehow evolve the structures and policies to serve the disparate needs of the continent's people. A common currency underlines the communality of Europe but it similarly reduces the number of policy instruments at macroeconomic level. Microeconomic instruments must, in consequence, be found to take their place.

It was stated at the beginning that currency areas were the economic expression of social groupings, and so the argument for currency union, in the end, stretches beyond economics. The experience of German unification is instructive in this regard. Only when the peoples of Europe (or any other combination of countries contemplating monetary integration) see their economies and thus their destinies inextricably entwined, such that even the most myopic nationalists are willing to find the ways and pay the costs involved to secure the common good, will a single currency be an unmitigated success.

KEY WORDS

Adjustable peg   Where a currency's exchange rate is fixed, or pegged, in terms of another and then it is decided to re-fix or adjust the price to another level. The fixed exchange rate system continues but with a different central rate. A *crawling peg* implies a system where the prices are adjusted in small steps on a monthly basis over a longer period of time, rather than a big, once-and-for-all readjustment.

The euro   is the new, common currency for 'euroland' – twelve of the fifteen EC members who have agreed to enter monetary union. The name of the currency was adopted by the European Council in December 1995; the money itself was introduced – in non-cash transactions – on world markets on 1 January 1999 as the fixed-rate currency for Austria, Belgium, Finland, France, Germany, Ireland, Italy, Luxembourg, the Netherlands, Portugal and Spain. Greece has since joined (2001) and on 1 January 2002 euro banknotes and coins entered into circulation.

The Exchange Rate Mechanism   was set up as one component (along with the European currency unit, the Ecu) of the European Monetary System in 1979. The ERM tied the (then) European Community currencies together at fixed rates within agreed tolerances for movement (2.25 per cent, except Italy: 6.0 per cent. The UK opted not to join). Realignments of the currencies' central fixed rates were allowed for through negotiation with other partners, and indeed were a common feature through the early part of the 1980s – the French franc was devalued three times and the Deutschmark upvalued seven times from 1979 to 1987.

Exchange restrictions   Any attempt by governments to restrict free trade in a country's currency.

Fiscal transfers   The transfer of tax revenues from – in this case – West German taxpayers to East German development funds.

Fixed exchange rates   This is where a currency fixes its price in terms of another within strictly defined limits, e.g. 1 per cent movement up or down. To fix a price in a free market means the supplier must buy back any quantity surplus to requirements, or increase the quantity if there is a shortage. That is, if the price is fixed, supplies must adjust to secure equilibrium.

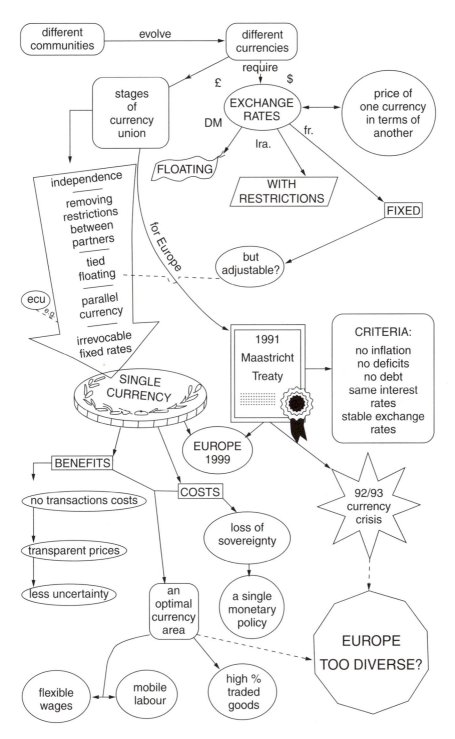

Figure 8.6 The themes of chapter 8

Foreign trade multiplier   An injection of increased spending in an economy will lead to a multiplied growth in the circular flow of income (see chapter 3). Increased spending, for example, can come from foreign customers buying more of a country's exports. Any given impulse of spending raises incomes many times since increased first-round earnings for exporters are then passed on in the form of more spending on business supplies; this increases second-round incomes for a whole range of producers, who then spend this, and so on. The larger the fraction of exports to total production in an economy, the more important the foreign trade multiplier, i.e. the impact of export demand.

Hyperinflation   This is where the rate of growth of prices increases so rapidly that people lose confidence in the value of money. The local currency then ceases to become acceptable as a medium of exchange and traders either turn to another form of money, if available (e.g. foreign currencies), or they resort to barter.

Managed floating   Exchange rates, like any prices, can be left free to let the markets decide what they should be. Governments may wish, however, to limit any excessive swings in their currency's price by entering the market to buy it when they think the exchange rate is too low or sell it if it is considered too high. They thus attempt to 'manage' or control the floating price at an acceptable level.

An optimal currency area   Some relatively small communities have their own currency and set themselves apart from larger neighbours (e.g. Bahrain Dinar – population 0.4 million); whereas, in contrast, some extremely large populations share a single unit of exchange (the Chinese Yuan – population 1,134 million). The economics of optimal currency areas considers what size of trading community is best to have a common currency.

QUESTIONS

1 Explain how the Bretton Woods fixed exchange rate system operated. What are the advantages of fixed rate regimes and why did this one break down?
2 In 1991, European governments agreed to move towards a common currency and they committed their economies to satisfy certain convergence criteria. What are the economic reasons for these Maastricht conditions?
3 What policy options do national governments have if they feel that their country is losing out in contrast to other partners in a currency union?
4 What caused the break-up of the European Exchange Rate mechanism in 1992–3? How can different countries' currencies move closer to a union without suffering speculative attack?
5 Where would you draw the line for countries in Europe to join the euro? Can you argue the case for any group of countries outside Europe to adopt a single currency?

FURTHER READING

De Grauwe, Paul. *The Economics of Monetary Union*. Oxford University Press, 2003.
Economic Survey of the Euro Area 2005, published on the website: www.oecd.org.

9 The economics of oil

Topics to be considered in this chapter:

- Factors influencing oil demand:

  1 Derived demand.
  2 Incomes and income-elasticity.
  3 Complements, substitutes and cross-elasticity.

- The oil industry: competition, monopoly and oligopoly.
- Exploration; production; transportation; refining; and distribution.
- The costs of production; diminishing returns; economies of scale; vertical integration.
- The major oil companies, OPEC and the struggle for ownership of supplies.
- The history of oil prices.

INTRODUCTION

Oil is a very important twenty-first-century product. It is a vital source of energy, an irreplaceable transport fuel, and an essential raw material in many manufacturing processes.

Crude oil is a source of great economic power. Since its production cost in many places is far below its selling price in world markets, so the ownership and control of oil reserves has been a means by which great wealth has been earned and lost.

The countries that export and import oil are – for the most part – geographically, economically and culturally separate. Oil has thus become the world's most important internationally traded item – both in volume and value terms – and changes in this trade have had enormous financial, political and socio-cultural repercussions on the parties involved. (Wars, revolutions and mass migrations are only perhaps the most visible manifestation of these.)

Understanding oil prices proves the key to understanding these issues. As oil prices change, so this impacts on consumer desires to use one form of energy or another; what sort of car to buy, or whether to use a different mode of transport altogether. The implications of changing consumer demand spread throughout the industrialised world causing classic microeconomic reallocation of resources. Oil prices affect decisions to invest billions of dollars in different industrial projects: whether to build major highways or rail networks; high-speed trains or electric cars; offshore drilling platforms or nuclear power stations. Industries grow and decline; workers get laid off and seek employment elsewhere; certain regions and countries earn more, others less.

Oil prices also affect macroeconomic variables such as the levels of national incomes, aggregate spending and the balance of payments of different countries. The enormous sums involved affect countries' rates of economic growth, levels of international debt and the overall functioning of the world's financial system.

Finally, oil prices affect how quickly the various forms of energy are exploited – whether we use nuclear power, renewable sources of energy, or whether oil, gas, coal or forests are burnt – and how, therefore, global environmental degradation will be affected.

All these decisions are influenced, one way or the other, by whether the price of oil moves significantly up or down.

OIL DEMAND AND SUPPLY

A study of oil prices involves examination of three major areas of interest – the consuming countries, the producer countries and the international oil industry which mediates between them. This relationship has been described as a *trilateral oligopoly* (Roncaglia, 1985); that is, each of the three parties referred to above is dominated by an important core or oligopolist element: the wealthy OECD countries amongst the world's consumers, OPEC amongst the producer countries and the major international oil companies in the industry. How the nature of oligopoly relationships within each power group has changed and how this has affected the interaction of the three parties together leads to a greater understanding of the determination of oil prices and the myriad of other issues that spill out from this.

Consumption

The biggest consumers in 2004 were: the USA (20.5 million barrels per day [mbd]); the European Community (14.6 mbd); China (6.7 mbd) and Japan (5.3 mbd). As a group, the OECD countries – which include North America, Western Europe, Japan, Australia and New Zealand – exert most pressure on world markets at present since they have the highest incomes yet produce insufficient oil to satisfy their own needs. OECD countries consume 60 per cent of the world's oil, yet produce only 25 per cent. Total world demand for oil has increased steadily since the 1990s from 65.5 mbd (1990) to 80.8 mbd (2004). This average hides wide disparities, however. The unprecedented collapse in incomes, industrial output and energy demands of the former Soviet Union, for example, meant demand for oil fell every year throughout the 1990s from 8.4mbd in 1990 to 3.4mbd in 2000, only recovering to 3.7 mbd in 2004. In contrast, the Asia/Pacific region – which includes huge populations in nations such as China, India, and Indonesia as well as the developed countries of Japan, Australia and New Zealand – has exhibited strong growth: a 50 per cent increase through the 1990s, despite the Asian currency crisis of 1997–8, and – in particular – China's annual growth in demand (2004) is a staggering 16 per cent.

The industrialised world has grown through the twentieth century dependent on cheap oil (see Figure 9.1). Note that consumption of this fundamental raw material is a *derived demand*, that is, it is derived from people's demand for such essential, everyday products as electricity and transport services. As world incomes, trade and travel have increased at an accelerating pace this century, so has consumption of all energy supplies – from 7.7 billion barrels of oil equivalent (bboe) in 1925 to around 72.3 bboe in 2004. Of this, the actual *growth* of the world economy has been fuelled mostly by oil (and recently, by natural gas – a related energy source); demand for other forms of energy has changed, by comparison, relatively slowly.

Revealed by these figures is the finding that demand for oil is *income elastic*, that is, as incomes rise so consumption of oil increases at a faster pace. While this has been true of general world demand during the first half of the twentieth century, because of the enormous changes in oil markets since the 1970s this is no longer the case today for the richest countries (for example OECD annual oil consumption growth was only 1.3 per cent in 2004, compared to GDP growth of 3.3 per cent. The West has tried hard to reduce its dependence on OPEC oil). Income elasticity of oil demand can still be high, however, for developing countries where in the early stages of growth, human and animal effort and primitive energy supplies (like burning wood fuel and animal dung) are replaced by more efficient oil-driven machinery. (As mentioned above, China's oil consumption grew by 16 per cent in 2004 whereas its GDP grew by 9 per cent.)

Quite apart from this structural change in energy demand for countries in the early stages of development, the sheer force of numbers involved in

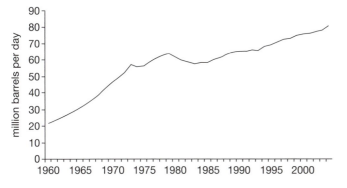

Figure 9.1 World oil consumption, 1960–2004. Note the rising rate of consumption until the oil price hikes of 1973 and 1979, after which demand slumped and then recovered but at a slower rate of increase.

Source: BP Statistical Review of World Energy, 2005.

population growth drives the accelerating demand for oil in countries like India and China. There is a huge potential demand building up in these countries where, at present, energy consumption per head is a tiny fraction of that in the developed world. With increasing populations, increasing industrialisation and increasing incomes we can predict that the less-developed world will compete strongly to command a greater and greater share of the world's oil. (One feature of note here is the difficulty in making accurate forecasts for some parts of the developing world. With poor data collection from some countries and increased oil smuggling in others there has been an increase in discrepancy between oil production, consumption and inventory figures over the last few years!)

At the time of writing, rates of growth of industrial production in China (population 1,268 million), India (population 1,064 million), Indonesia (population 215 million) and Brazil (population 177 million) were 16.8 per cent, 10.8 per cent, 10.1 per cent and 5.5 per cent, respectively. (This compares to USA industrial growth of 3.9 per cent and Japan, 0.1 per cent.) Growing industry needs energy. Workforces need transport to and from work; raw materials need to be brought into factories, transformed into finished products and then distributed throughout the country and abroad. As cities and industrial areas grow, more roads need to be built, more houses and factories go up, more lighting, heating and transport is demanded. At present, energy consumption per capita of poor Asians and Latin Americans is less than an eighth of rich North Americans, but this only goes to show what growth potential there is locked up in continents with the fastest growing incomes and most of the world's population.

As well as income, an important determinant of oil demand is the price (and thus availability) of *complementary goods*. In particular, so long as humankind's love affair with the motor car continues, so will its dependency on oil. There is no sign yet that there is a limit to this particular market. As technology improves, and increasing world competition between motor manufacturers stimulates efficiency, the relative price of cars is falling. In the 1970s, the cost of buying a standard family car in Western Europe was equivalent to the average annual real wage. It is half that now. Car ownership per head is thus increasing everywhere.

The most saturated market is the USA, which has more cars than drivers, but even here – although sales growth has slowed and environmental concerns are becoming ever-louder – vehicle numbers and miles travelled are still both increasing. If this is true of North America, small wonder that the big, multinational producers are competing strongly to get a foothold in the potentially huge markets of Asia. Vehicle sales in East Asia (excluding India and Japan) were predicted to double between 2000 and 2005, based on the assumption that these will be principally lorries, vans, buses and pick-ups, and the dynamic growth sector of private car consumption is expected to double these numbers again in less than another five years.

Based on the evidence so far, the demand for oil thus looks like being buoyant well into the future, given the assumption that no catastrophic slump in world incomes or vehicle consumption occurs. This is not yet a complete picture, however, since there is still a third influence to consider: the price of *substitute fuels*.

Substitutes for oil

The lower the relative price of substitute energy sources like coal, natural gas, nuclear power, etc., the more competitive they become as alternatives to oil. The future demand for oil therefore must take into account what is likely to happen to prices of these competing fuels.

Gas

The change in consumption of one good in response to the change in price of another is measured by the *cross-elasticity of demand*. In transport, for example, the cross-elasticity of demand for alternatives, compared to oil, has been close to zero up until just recently. The only near substitute is liquefied petroleum gas (LPG) though the cost of converting cars *and* setting up distribution networks for this fuel greatly restricts its take-up. There are no closely priced alternative fuels in sight as yet for the vast majority of users of road and air transport, therefore. Fuel cells can produce electric cars but, at present, technology is increasing the efficiency of the internal combustion engine more quickly than that of fuel cells. In power generation, however, long-term cross-elasticities are high between oil and gas, wherever supplies of the latter are relatively easily attainable (i.e. at low cost). The technical difficulties of transporting gas nonetheless mean that it is still not a competitive substitute fuel for *all* oil-fired generators, though clearly as gas technology improves it is pricing itself into more markets.

Consumption of gas is growing fast – driven by demand for its use in power stations and by the increasing investment in gas supply infrastructure in a number of developing and developed countries alike. In the past, the ease of use of gas in substitution for other fuels has been held up more by political and social considerations than by economic factors. In a number of European countries, for example, there has been a comparative lack of government interest in gas, despite discoveries of large reserves. Where power generation has been under public ownership there has been a tendency to support traditional, labour-intensive, coal mining rather than the more economically efficient (but less employment-creating) gas industry. With increasing deregulation, however, this public sector restraint has diminished.

The long-term demand for oil in power generation will therefore be subject to competition from gas, wherever low-cost supplies are available. It is almost certain that natural gas will continue to steal the market share from oil in OECD power markets but this is likely to be a slow and steady erosion. Substantial declines in oil use for this purpose are highly unlikely. (Note that the cross-elasticity of demand for gas as opposed to oil-powered energy *in the short run* is low – since it takes an enormous amount of capital to switch distribution networks and electricity generating capacity from one power source to another.)

Nuclear

The power supply for the future was once popularly considered to be *nuclear energy*. During the 1970s when oil prices were rising sharply and there was a general fear that the world was running out of fossil fuels, nuclear power was held up to be the saviour of the modern Western economy. Cheap electricity produced by the alleged non-polluting, peaceful use of nuclear technology was seen as the only viable means of getting the OECD countries off the hook of OPEC dependency. The strategic incentive to invest in large programmes of nuclear power expansion was thus all-persuasive. Given the one-sided political debate of the times, the purely *economic* arguments for such actions were never properly evaluated.

Privately owned, profit-seeking nuclear power stations that must sell their electricity at competitive rates or go bust are a rarity. Few countries that have invested massively in nuclear power have put their decision to the test in a free market place. West and East European nuclear industries which produce significant fractions of their countries' total energy needs are all in public hands (39 per cent of France's energy is nuclear powered; although the figure for the 25 nations of the EU is 13 per cent).

During the 1980s decade, however, after the oil shortage panics of the 1970s and the rush to find alternatives, a number of private electricity generators in the USA had a good, hard look at the economics of nuclear power stations. They did not like what they saw: it was not so much the cost of generating energy – it was the escalating expense of safely disposing of nuclear waste that really hurt. With low oil prices then asserting themselves in the market place there was no economic case for expensive nuclear energy. Contracts for building new nuclear facilities were cancelled.

Into the new millennium now, despite continuing scares and public anxiety over safety precautions, the world consumption of nuclear energy supplies has nonetheless increased – from 504.0 million tons of oil equivalent in 1994 to 624.3 million tons in 2004. This still represents only a fraction (6.1 per cent) of total world energy supplies, however – a percentage that has actually decreased from a decade earlier.

With rising oil prices (again) at the time of writing, people are looking afresh at nuclear power as the only long-term feasible alternative to oil. For strategic reasons, a number of countries are likely to increase (public) investment in nuclear power but costs remain high and lead times are long. The world's growing energy demands cannot be quickly and economically supplied through nuclear power.

Coal

Total world consumption of *coal* fell intermittently through the 1990s, due to slumping demand in the countries of the former Soviet Union and Europe, but is growing again now thanks to booming growth from the Asia/Pacific region. The political and social arguments to support coal have been strong in this traditional, high-employment sector, but as government subsidies continue to lose out to market forces in Europe and further east in Poland, Ukraine and Russia, the demand for coal will be constrained by its rising real price, even as these economies recover their growth.

One surprise has been the continuing growth in coal consumption in both the USA and Japan (in the latter case, faster than the growth of GDP) due possibly to concerns over an increasing reliance on oil and – in the US case – the fact that domestic coal reserves are still plentiful.

In the developing countries, where labour is cheaper and strikes less likely, coal industries remain economic where reserves have not already been over-exploited. Coal consumption figures for India, Indonesia, Brazil and for selected countries in Africa have thus been slowly rising through the 1990s. If growth in LDC and particularly Asian incomes continues apace into the twenty-first century, however, it is unlikely that coal supplies will be able to keep up with demand. China's output, although steadily increasing (by 60 per cent, 1994 to 2004), has not grown as fast as its GDP (100 per cent over the same period) nor as fast as its consumption of oil (106 per cent) and gas (135 per cent). Oil is thus most likely to remain *the* marginal energy source that will be required to fuel growth for the foreseeable future.

Renewables

Conservationists argue that *renewable energies* must eventually replace fossil fuels if the world economy is to have a sustainable future. This is an important argument that deserves fuller coverage below (see chapter 13). The demand for oil as compared to alternative, renewable energy, however, will depend on at what price these fuels are delivered to the market place.

There is no doubt that demand for renewable energies is growing strongly, but it comes from a very low base (e.g. hydro-electricity, the only economically significant renewable energy source, satisfied only 6.2 per cent per cent of world demand in 2004). For the immediate future, there is no low-cost, environmentally friendly supply that can come anywhere near to meeting total world consumption needs – and no renewable energy is environmentally costless anyway (huge dams and reservoirs required to supply industrial amounts of hydro-electricity are notoriously damaging to local ecologies).

We can conclude, then, that the cross-elasticities of demand for renewable energies in comparison to oil will be close to zero for the time being.

To summarise, consumption of oil is greatest in the world's developed, market economies – though growth here was slow through the 1990s. In contrast, demand in less-developed countries has been accelerating and Asia in particular will play an increasing role in determining the future price of oil.

Demand for oil in transport looks unshakeable; in power generation oil faces increasing competition from gas in a number of OECD countries and, to a lesser extent, from coal.

There are a number of unknowns facing future oil demand. This section will finish with questions involving three different parts of the world, starting with the biggest.

The role of Russia is unpredictable. Production at the time of writing is now outpacing consumption but given its tortuous history and the current uncertainty over the role of government versus domestic and international investment, future changes in outputs or incomes are difficult to guess. Demand for oil will most probably rise in line with the rate of growth of industrial output but where will this lead? Russia never loses its capacity to surprise.

China is the world's most populous state and its economy has recently been booming with market reforms. The 1990s saw China become a net oil importer; the new millennium has seen accelerating growth in consumption. As a result, China has been in the vanguard of the first real demand-led shock to oil prices, but how long will this continue?

Growth in the developing world as a whole can never be taken for granted. International debt crises seem to recur with disturbing regularity, but assuming these do not erupt into world-wide panic, and assuming that governments do not turn the clock back on the successes in economic policy that they have enjoyed recently, it is the argument here that consumers in the less-developed countries will play an increasing part in determining the future movement of oil prices. But just how fast will LDC incomes and consumption continue to grow?

THE OIL INDUSTRY

There has been a shake-up in the world's largest industry recently with the biggest oil companies getting even bigger. Mega-mergers have taken place with Exxon buying Mobil (for US$82 billion!); BP taking over Amoco (US$54 billion) and Arco; Total swallowing up Elf and Petrofina and Chevron digesting Texaco. These major players still leave a number of middle-sized 'independents' (e.g. Phillips, Marathon, etc.) at the table plus various state-owned enterprises (e.g. ENI) and many relatively small, specialist, contract companies (e.g. in prospecting, engineering, undersea diving, transport, etc.). *The Economist* magazine reports, however, that in terms of ownership of reserves, the biggest private oil companies (known as 'majors') are nonetheless relatively tiny beside OPEC state giants such as Saudi Aramco (Aramco owned 259,000 million barrels in 2003. Exxon/Mobil owned the largest reserves of any major: a mere 12,900 million barrels).

All these businesses operate at various stages along the production line of a liquid – from 'upstream' exploration and discovery, through production and transportation, to 'downstream' refining and distribution. In the industry, only the majors have traditionally been heavily involved all round the world in all stages of this production process.

An examination of the constraints that define business practice at every stage in the oil industry provides a fascinating series of examples of microeconomic principles at work, and they eventually build up to determine the nature of the relationship that has evolved between industry practitioners and the producer countries that are host to much of their operations.

Exploration

Oil exploration started in the USA in the hands of the independent, speculative 'wildcatter' where test drilling on land was not technologically difficult, where capital threshold costs were comparatively cheap, where chances of discovery were entirely random, where competition was rampant, and where US property law emphasised the 'rule of capture'. These conditions in effect programmed the sort of oil industry that was to emerge in the USA and they still have an important influence today.

Oil exploration is now technologically complex, expensive, but still a random, financially risky business. Seismological search techniques and computer data gathering and interpretation are infinitely more skilful and sophisticated compared to past methods of finding the appropriate geological structures below ground, but ultimately, whether a given rock formation bears oil or not can only be determined by digging for it, and the likelihood that one test bore will strike it rich are as good as any other. A cheap, independent wildcatter who sets up his rig one day, drills quickly, then cuts his losses, up-roots and moves elsewhere tomorrow is being very economically efficient. A multi-million mega-buck operator who invests a fortune in investigating all the possibilities of one specific location is employing a far less productive exploration strategy.

US oil exploration at the turn of the twentieth century illustrated the *'tragedy of the commons'*. Where an underground oil reservoir was common to a number of different properties, US law held that the oil belonged to whoever could get it out. Each individual landowner, therefore, had an economic incentive to drill holes all over his property in a mad rush to extract as much oil as possible before anyone else could do the same. The more holes are drilled, the more rapidly the oil could be depleted, the more the landowner could capture at the expense of his neighbour. As all tried to do the same, of course, the landscape was desecrated, the common resource exhausted and there was an inevitable excess supply of oil, falling prices and thus falling profits. Success or failure in such a competitive environment depended in the end on the number and cost of test drills, the percentage success rate and the market price at which the oil could be sold off. For many operators, profits were negative.

The economics of exploration today still illustrate many of these fundamentals, though the rush to capture a common resource is no longer applicable in most areas. Instead, risks are compounded by political factors – in many parts of the world, the search for oil goes on in disputed territory. Probabilities of a change in governments, taxes, exchange controls, policies regarding nationalisation of foreign assets, and – worse – guerrilla action, wars, etc., must all be calculated. The total cost of drilling activity must be compared to projected yields and the price of oil. The lower the oil price, the less exploration will take place in risky, marginal areas. It is not worth the expense of looking for future supplies if the rewards involved in present exploration are less than can be earned by placing those same funds in non-risk-bearing bank accounts.

Note the converse implication of this principle: oil reserves are a direct outcome of exploration activity, and the higher the price of oil, the more supplies will be looked for and brought on-stream. The world's oil is thus not fixed in supply (as so many conservationists insist) – it increases with its price.

This principle is true even for one given reservoir: how much oil is there, in economic terms, depends on how far it pays to extract the oil from all the other junk that surrounds it: water, mud, gas, etc. If it is too fragmented, too messy a cocktail, then it does not pay to pump up much other than the purest, most accessible deposit. But if the price of oil increases, then it becomes worthwhile to extract more from this same source. What counts as the total of commercially viable reserves in the world (see Figure 9.2), therefore, *immediately* increases as oil prices increase – the economic boundary of all existing reservoirs shifts out (and this does not include all the other unknown reservoirs that now become worth looking for).

Production

Once a test drill has struck oil, immediate clues are given with respect to the quality of the deposit and the pressure it is under. Further wells give information on the geological spread and characteristics of the underground structures, indicating the optimum location for a production platform.

The nature of oil in the ground varies immensely. Some reservoirs may contain many unstable gases which are best flared-off at the well-head; others may be highly polluting – rich in sulphur, heavy with tar, etc. Deposits can be very fractured and technologically complex to exploit. Pressure and depth vary. Each complication adds to the costs of production.

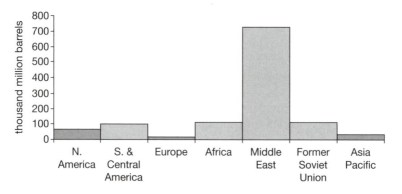

Figure 9.2 World oil reserves, 2004

Source: BP Statistical Review of World Energy, 2005.

For certain sites the geographical, technical and political environment may be relatively uncomplicated and small operators may be just as cost-effective as bigger ones. With other sites, however, where the natural environment is difficult, where distances are long and supporting infrastructure absent (e.g. in the North Sea and Alaska) then investment requirements are much greater. Add to this the hostility or unpredictability of the political scene (e.g. in Azerbaijan, Nigeria, Colombia, etc.) and here oil production is subject to substantial economies of scale. Only the large, multinational oil companies have the resources to manage the risks involved. Small companies cannot afford to compete.

Once all investment is in place for the production of crude oil – once government approval has been negotiated; percentages agreed; contracts signed; production platforms installed; pipelines and storage facilities constructed, then finally the taps can be turned on. The economics of production are then characterised by the following:

- The *marginal cost* of producing one more barrel of oil is very small compared to the fixed cost of negotiating the way in and installing all the necessary production capacity.
- Production is subject to the *law of diminishing returns*. The more the taps are opened, the faster oil is depleted, the quicker pressure drops and the more investment is necessary (in pumping, water drives, etc.) to secure each additional barrel. This production decline curve ensures that returns diminish: the rate of increase of marginal costs depends on the speed of the depletion of the oil reservoir.
- The production rate will depend on the market price of oil. If current oil prices are higher than bank interest rates, then it pays producers to sell oil rather than leave it in the ground. If, however, oil prices and thus rates of return fall *below* market rates of interest, producers are better off withholding investment, depositing these funds in a bank and waiting for prices to recover before they produce more.

Transport

This involves transporting crude from well-head to storage facility, from here to a refinery, and finally taking petroleum products to retail outlets. The location of production sites and markets for consumption determine the pattern of transportation needs. Generally the transportation of oil is highly specialised and this thus falls within the domain of the oil industry rather than becoming a sub-division of the transport industry.

The most efficient way to transport a liquid is via pipelines, rather than in discrete units by sea, road or rail containers. Pipelines, however, represent a huge investment in occupationally and geographically immobile capital and this can only be commercially profitable if a regular flow between producer input and market output can be assured. This way, if dealers both ends of the pipeline keep to the bargain, average and marginal costs of production can be minimised.

Pipelines are a form of *natural monopoly*. That is, it is quite clearly most economic to have one large supply line leading from oil fields to market, rather than have different oil companies construct a number of smaller ones. Such economics supports the creation of a monopoly, or a *cartel* of a group of producers where agreement between them over use of a common pipeline can be negotiated. In the ocean-going tanker market, however, competition is the natural outcome where *barriers to entry* to the world's seas are few and a large number of rival carriers can thus compete over any designated tanker route.

Note, lastly, that the transport of crude oil out from a production region is necessarily more cost-effective than the distribution of petroleum products from a refinery. There are hundreds of different products, all requiring specialised treatment, and with dispersed markets there is thus no potential to exploit economies of scale.

Refining

Oil refineries are the factories of the oil industry – manufacturing finished products for the consumer. They thus have to be responsive to changing consumer demand on the one side and match this up with appropriate inputs on the other. As with all manufacturing industry, however, capital equipment is highly specific. Once built, refineries are tied in to a particular composition of crude, and to the production of petroleum products in a relatively restricted range. There is limited tolerance for changes: costly investment is necessary for any up-grading of product or process (e.g. to build in cleaner, more environmentally friendly technology). Fixed costs, as elsewhere in the industry, are very high and profits are maximised when the plant is operating at capacity with a regular through-put at very low marginal costs.

Individual refineries tend to have a degree of market power according to the geographical region in which they are located. This is determined by the costs of distributing products – often in comparatively small road or rail tankers. Some oil companies dominate in some world markets, others in others. Profit margins vary according to the degree of competition versus market power that reigns. In all cases, guaranteeing secure inputs of crude is essential, hence the importance of *vertical integration* (extending the business upstream and downstream), and/or signing long-term contracts or agreeing to joint ventures with low-cost suppliers.

Distribution

There are numerous petroleum products derived from crude oil, including gases (such as butane, acetylene); light oils (gasoline, aviation fuels, paraffin); fuel oils (for heavy goods vehicles, heating, ships); heavy lubricating oils; residuals (asphalt, bitumen, wax), and waste products (e.g. sulphuric acid). Although the fractions concerned will differ according to the particular crude being refined, they are all in *joint supply*.

Maximising profits in conditions of joint supply is complicated since, although the demand for the lighter oils may be high, for example, there may be little interest in consuming any of the heavier fractions that are produced with it. Prices and profit margins may be slimmed right down on these other products in order to gain sales. Additionally, the state of competition in some product markets may be greater than others, which is another reason for weak margins on some jointly supplied products.

In the market for petrol/gasoline and diesel fuels there are extensive distribution networks where the majors have a strong presence. Some regional markets are more competitive with independents and local state companies represented. Advertising, branding and all forms of *non-price competition* are important.

Gas and oil distribution for power generation is frequently highly competitive with direct contracts being secured between large *monopsony* buyers, on the one hand – electricity generating companies (often publicly owned) and big sellers, on the other – the major oil oligopolies.

In other product markets, like for domestic and commercial heating oils, bitumens, etc., a local refinery may serve a territory where transport costs confer upon it a *local monopoly*.

Considering all the above stages of the production process of oil, we can now conclude the following:

- It is an industry characterised by massive *economies of scale*. As we have seen, huge investment in fixed capital is necessary even before production can take place. With highly capital-intensive production techniques at all stages, the average and marginal costs of production can only be brought down to acceptable levels if overheads can be spread over a very large output.
- Since oil is a liquid, production through all stages is most economic if *a regular flow* of inputs matched to outputs can be assured. Variable flow and fluctuating levels of capacity mean fixed costs have to be paid over smaller ranges of output – profit margins are immediately eroded.
- The need to maintain a regular flow means the industry has a tendency to produce *excess supplies*. With huge fixed costs, a continual need to increase outputs and the marginal cost of producing just one more barrel being relatively low, it will always be tempting to try and sell more than the market can take.
- Reconciling the need for a regular flow with an unstable, unpredictable world means access to crude supplies is essential, as is safeguarding outlets. Vertical integration is one way of minimising uncertainty, since a business can thus bring all stages of the production process under its own control. Securing long-term contracts, combining in joint ventures and entering into a cartel with rivals are all other means of managing a risky business environment, *eliminating competition* and ensuring regular throughputs of oil are achieved.
- Putting all these features together it is not difficult to see why the international oil industry has been dominated by *oligopoly*. With massive

capital entry/threshold costs and the desire to exercise control over an unstable but potentially highly profitable industry, the actions of the majors have demonstrated classic oligopolistic behaviour: long periods of comparative market stability interspersed with fierce price wars; cycles of managed oil supplies and then gluts or shortages, booms and recessions.

PRODUCER COUNTRIES

Trying to give a picture of the world's most important oil-producing countries is like taking a snapshot of traffic in a busy street. There have been so many changes in the rank ordering of the top oil producers that it all depends on when you choose to view the picture.

Russia was the world's largest producer during the 1980s, but economic and political upheaval has caused great swings in ownership, investment and production since then. It still retains important reserves, and although uncertainty continues around which businesses will be allowed to exploit them, in 2004 it produced 9.3 million barrels per day – 11.9 per cent of the world's production, a very recent rapid expansion in output which it is unlikely to be able to maintain for very long.

The USA has always been an important producer but its mature oil fields have been in slow, steady decline since the mid-1980s. Nonetheless, it was the third biggest producer with 7.2 mbd, 8.5 per cent of the world's total, in 2004 (see Figure 9.3).

Middle Eastern countries are big producers and, more importantly, major exporters (see Figure 9.4) – since, unlike the USA and the former Soviet Union, their consumption needs have been comparatively slight. The wars, revolutions and political changes in the region have, over the years, greatly affected the relative standing of differing Middle Eastern states, but generally Saudi Arabia has always been the dominant partner. In 2004 it was the world's number one

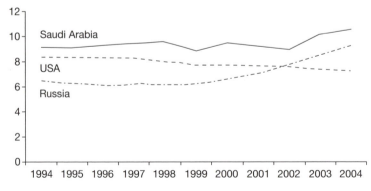

Figure 9.3 Oil production (mbd), 1994–2004.

Source: *BP Statistical Review of World Energy*, 2005.

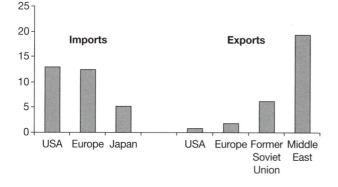

Figure 9.4 2004 trade in oil (mbd)

Source: BP Statistical Review of World Energy, 2005.

producer with 10.5 mbd, 13.1 per cent of the overall total, but perhaps of greater significance is that it holds by far and away the greatest volume of the world's reserves (over 22 per cent, compared to Russia's 6.1 per cent and the USA's 2.5 per cent) and, in addition, its oil is *cheap to produce*. In 1985, Saudi oil was estimated to cost less than US$1 a barrel to extract, compared to $7–8 for Alaska and the North Sea.

Other Middle Eastern states such as Iran and Iraq have large reserves and are potentially big producers but political instability currently restricts investment and therefore production. With booming demand recently, even Saudi Arabia has been caught short with insufficient investment. Large reserves imply huge potential capacity . . . but it requires substantial ongoing investment in fixed capital to bring such reserves onstream.

Perspectives on the changing pattern of oil production from 1994 to 2004 are given in Figures 9.3 and 9.4 but a much longer view is necessary to pick up just how the role of the Middle East has changed to become the world's most important exporting region and thus the most important influence on the international trade in oil.

In 1920 the Middle East provided approximately 12 per cent of the world's oil needs. By 1973 this proportion had grown to 50 per cent. In between these two dates, however, the control of Middle Eastern production and prices passed out of the hands of the major oil companies and into those of the host country governments. The history of the power struggle involved and its impact on the rest of the world is fascinating – only a very brief account is possible here.

THE STRUGGLE FOR CONTROL OF SUPPLIES

In the first decades of the twentieth century, as the use of the motor car was growing and the world's navies were switching from coal to fuel oil propulsion, the Middle East was dependent on the international oil industry for the exploration, discovery and development of its oil resources. Only the majors possessed the necessary capital and expertise to carry out this work. Additionally, the nature of the political relationship between the fledgeling states of the Middle East and the Allied Powers was one still locked into colonial protectorates. Long-term concessions were thus granted by host governments to the majors to produce oil for a fixed royalty: the first big concession was made in 1901 by Iran to the Anglo Persian Oil Co. (later BP). Similarly, Iraq in 1925 awarded its oil rights to the Iraq Petroleum Company – a consortium of BP, Shell, CFP, Exxon and Mobil. In the 1930s the big Arabian Gulf fields were discovered and concessions were given to the Kuwait Oil Company (jointly owned by BP and Gulf) and in Saudi Arabia to Aramco (Exxon, Socal, Texaco and Mobil).

The world's oil supply was thus effectively controlled by the oligopolistic majors. Classic cutthroat competition between them ended in 1928 in a cartel agreement to supervise joint production and to apportion downstream market shares. (Note that cartels work best where there are few parties involved, each one's actions are observable to all and penalties for cheating hurt. These three conditions were all met in the joint concessions on production: any one major trying to take off more oil from a joint source could not hope to go undetected and unpunished by its partners.) Prices were stabilised by a unique agreement where oil sold anywhere in the world was priced equal to that of Gulf of Mexico oil plus transport costs – irrespective if it had come from the Middle East at half that figure. (Such outrageous exploitation was amended slightly by 1945 at the insistence of UK and US navies which were fuelling up in the Arab Gulf yet paying as if the oil had been shipped across the Atlantic!)

The 1930s up to the 1960s, therefore, saw an unparalleled control of the world's oil market where stability of flow, market shares and *joint profit maximisation* were all secured by the majors. With the main producer countries' sources of supply at their disposal and with vertically integrated business empires stretching forward to every market place there was, in effect, no free international trade in oil. Majors that were 'crude long', i.e. with a supply of crude oil greater than their market outlets (such as BP), were tied in to 'crude short' companies (such as Shell) by long-term contracts and so the scope for competition from any other suppliers was strictly limited.

Producer countries were increasingly unhappy with this arrangement. Western businesses were seen as being rich and powerful thanks to poor countries' oil. In 1951 Iran unilaterally nationalised its oil fields, but such was the power of the majors' cartel at this time that they could close down all Iranian production and compensate for this loss by producing more from other sources. Iran was thus forced into signing a humiliating, 25-year further concession in order to start up producing again.

Such a victory for the majors, however, proved to be their last. Iraq in 1961 similarly nationalised 99 per cent of foreign oil capital and subsequently got involved in a long drawn-out series of negotiations with the oil companies which were never concluded to the satisfaction of the latter. Meanwhile, Libya had shown the way by excluding all majors from tendering for concessions in its newly developed oil fields. In limiting the bidding only to the less-powerful independent oil companies, Libya had wrung from them a higher share of the profits and, simultaneously, had increased the downstream competition for the majors.

On 14 September 1960, OPEC was born. Iran, Iraq, Kuwait, Saudi Arabia and Venezuela were the pioneering members of this organisation which was formed in reaction to the oil majors deciding to reduce prices and with them producer countries' revenues. Although its initial impact was limited, OPEC became the forum through which producer countries could exercise increasing bargaining power, where follow-my-leader nationalisations could catch on and where eventual control of oil supplies could be wrested from the grip of the majors and passed into the hands of host country governments.

As well as increasing success in gaining ownership and control of their own oil supplies and in weakening the competitive strength of the majors vis-à-vis the independents, two other events strengthened the producer countries' resolve to become more active players in the world oil market. The first was the floating of the dollar in 1971, which effectively devalued OPEC revenues since oil has always been denominated in dollars. The second highly significant development was the shift of the USA in 1972 from being a net oil exporter to a net importer. Low prices relative to other fuels had stimulated post-war Western dependence on oil and now tight world demand coincided with OPEC being, at last, in control of its own supplies.

The political trigger was the 1973 October War between Israel and its Arab neighbours. OPEC shut off all oil supplies to the USA and the Netherlands (Rotterdam was Europe's major oil port) in retaliation for the West's alleged support of Israel. In three months the price of oil shot up 400 per cent and the shock waves reverberated around the world.

Western oil demand was *price inelastic* – there were no short-run alternatives to buying OPEC oil if modern industry and trade were to continue functioning – and as a result the OPEC economies quickly accumulated enormous wealth at the expense of the OECD consumer countries.

In 1979, the Iranian revolution which deposed the (pro-Western) Shah and ushered in the rule of fundamentalist Ayatollahs caused the second oil cut-back and shock to oil prices. Again OPEC incomes leapt upwards, while the consumer countries were faced with *stagflation* – a slump in growth, large trade deficits and double-digit inflation.

This time OPEC was in danger of killing the golden OECD goose which was laying the golden eggs. Whereas the 1973 price shock did not choke off world demand, by 1979 its effect had brought onstream North Sea and Alaskan oil fields, and simultaneously stimulated Western industry to invest in smaller cars, more fuel-efficient technology plus research into alternative energy supplies. The 1979 shock provoked a further slide into world recession so that now, after decades of a relentless rise in oil consumption, Western demand went into decline.

Oil prices fell in the 1980s. OPEC thus attempted to exercise the same control over supply as the majors' cartel had done before so successfully for all the time up to the 1970s. They failed. The three criteria for a successful cartel mentioned earlier did not apply: the producer countries are greater in number, have widely diverging interests and their actions are less open to observation and joint control than was the case for the majors. The temptation to sell the marginal barrel remains as ever, and for those OPEC countries with pressing development needs and smaller reserves there is always a strong case for trying to maximise revenues now, rather than later.

OPEC has therefore never succeeded as a cartel. Quotas to restrict oil production have been set regularly for member countries and just as regularly-broken. In the early 1980s, Saudi Arabia was willing to act as OPEC's controlling safety valve – always cutting back on its own output as others cheated on theirs – but in 1985 it refused to keep sacrificing its own income for others. It opened up production again and the world oil price collapsed (see Figure 9.5).

CONCLUSION: OIL IN THE TWENTY-FIRST CENTURY

Producer countries

The economics of oil keep changing. Oil production in the new millennium is affected by international political instability in the Middle East and internal political instability in Russia. For decades, spare capacity in Saudi Arabia has enabled this country to act as the central bank of oil – opening or closing the

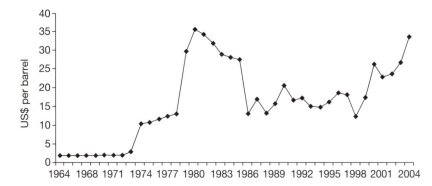

Figure 9.5 The spot price of oil (Dubai light), 1964 to 2004, *given in current dollars.* (Note that in real terms, the high price of 1980 is really twice as high as it is in 2004 since present-day dollars are worth less.) Oil prices are determined by the tightness of world demand compared to supply, and political events are important only insofar as they affect this market balance. The Arab–Israeli War of 1973 pushed up prices drastically, as did the Iranian Revolution in 1979. The Gulf War of 1990, however, had little impact on prices, though Saudi Arabia's decision in 1985 to increase production was a major economic change. Instability in Iraq has *not* been the cause of the latest high prices recorded here (there is more Iraqi oil being supplied than ever before) – booming Asian demand is more responsible.

Source: BP Statistical Reviews.

taps to match supplies to changing world demand – but the stereotypical condition of oversupply had led to underinvestment such that in 2005 most producers were pumping furiously in order to keep up with surging oil demand. Prices are likely to stay high until more capacity eventually comes onstream and then (again, typically) there may be another price slump.

Fundamentals amongst the oil producing countries have *not* changed, however. The southern Gulf states are relatively oil rich, underpopulated and wary of their northern neighbours. Their need to maximise current revenues is not so great as northern states like Iraq which have large populations, are torn apart by conflict and have urgent development demands. Saudi Arabia, in particular, has reserves which will last over eighty more years at current rates of exploitation and it has no interest in restricting production, driving up prices and stimulating Western consumers to conserve demand, develop alternatives and to reduce their dependency on Saudi oil.

In the Russian Federation and neighbouring states such as Azerbaijan, Kazakhstan and others there are large known reserves that are waiting to be got out, but the *political risk* is high, much capital needs to replaced and upgraded and the distances to Western markets are great. Much production potential is here – but the unpredictable arm of government dictates how this potential is to be exploited, deters the application of Western technology and contributes to the uncertainty regarding the future.

No other place on the globe looks, at the time of writing, to have sufficient reserves and production potential to impact on oil markets. Exploration activity is busy and simultaneously new technologies are being developed to tap into unconventional oil sources such as oil shales and tar sands . . . but no sudden windfalls are anywhere in sight.

The oil industry

A number of factors have been re-shaping the oil industry. Firstly, the majors have lost access to cheap crude and have consequently been tireless in their *search for downstream efficiency,* cost savings and protection of market share. More oil is now traded than ever before as oil companies buy and sell between them, wherever a margin can be made. The majors can no longer behave as oil production lines, running their own crude through to their distribution networks and denying all others access. They buy in the cheapest oil at whatever the production stage, from wherever its source (BP calculated in 1991 that confining its refineries to its own supplies of crude could cost up to 25 cents per barrel in some places – a recipe for inefficiency and uncompetitiveness). Also inventories will be kept down as companies attempt to make savings in delivering supplies 'just in time'. As a result the industry is now *de-integrating* downstream – each business unit must act as an independent profit centre if it is to survive – and there has been a steady rise in the prominence of energy-trading companies.

Thanks to the rise in natural gas, big oil companies have got involved in oil, gas, electricity generation and services. The majors are becoming *energy companies*. BP, traditionally strong in upstream production, is expanding its base in gas; Shell, stronger downstream, is looking into power generation and serving customer energy needs.

A significant cause of concern is with *future sources of supply*. At present, with the last big oil discoveries now 30 to 40 years behind them and most fields under their control maturing rapidly (e.g. in the North Sea and Alaska), the majors are anxious to develop other resources. Despite vast potential believed to exist in many parts of the unmapped world, there are enormous difficulties in getting unrestricted access to it and then moving supplies to market.

Allied to political risk, there is always – waiting in the shadows – the risk of *technological innovation* that can turn an industry on its head. Increasing pressure from environmentalists are promoting investment in cleaner fuels, restricting expansion of messier oil and coal processing plants and driving forward research in electric cars and more energy-efficient factories and homes. It may not happen yet, but it must one day: revolution is coming. The reason we don't use horse-drawn transport and steam power today is not due to a lack of horses or coal but thanks to revolutionary advances in technology. Oil may similarly become redundant if some relatively small, quick-off-the-mark energy company can perfect the technique of deriving energy from hydrogen gas. That is the direction that industry pundits and energy gurus are pointing towards for the longer term.

In the near future, however, the most likely outcome is growing *market competition* in oil and gas – particularly from OPEC state companies. They are the ones now with the access to cheap Middle East crude and, just as it was for the majors before them, the incentive is to vertically integrate forward into the market place. A case in point is the merger in 1993 of Saudi Arabia's two state oil companies – Aramco and Samarec – which brought together the world's largest producer with a big refiner. Although this giant has yet to make its move overseas, Gulf producers have been looking for some time to gain refining footholds in Europe and Japan. Kuwait had already begun this process in Europe (with Q8) just before it was invaded. The situation today is different from the growth of the industry in the past, however, in that Western multinational oil companies are now well established in all world markets so any growing competition will be bloody.

Consumption

We have demonstrated that the world demand for oil will continue to increase in the twenty-first century, accompanied also by increasing demand for natural gas. As incomes rise, particularly in the poorer countries, energy consumption is likely to surge, though along with it there will be a transfer to more efficient power generation and fuel production.

As incomes rise, also, consumers are becoming more and more environmentally conscious and are demanding cleaner products and processes. This can bring short-run problems in some places (e.g. local political resistance to building large power plants, as in California) if supply is unable to meet demand.

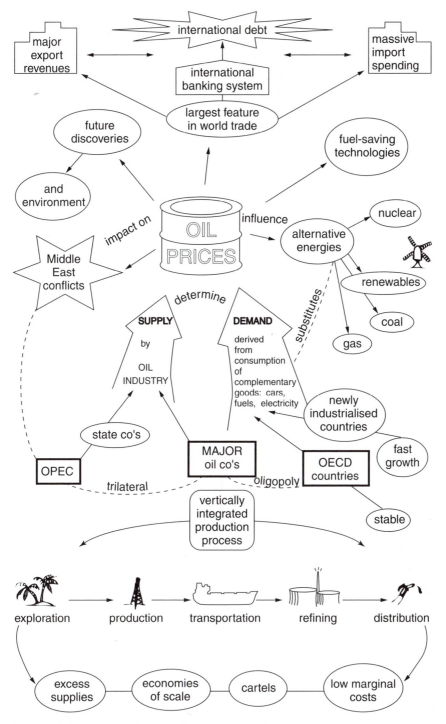

Figure 9.6 The themes of chapter 9

The growth of market trading as the industry de-integrates; the fall in inventories as companies seek savings, and the increasing role of developing countries where demand is less transparent/more uncertain in the short run all contribute to short-run price volatility. Prices may shoot up one month only to collapse later. Over the medium to long term, however, oil prices are not likely to remain high *so long as market forces are allowed to bring existing reserves – which are easily sufficient – onstream* in time to meet the growth in demand. Producer countries would be foolish to try and hold back supplies to force up the oil price since sooner or later technological innovation must one day make cheap, sustainable and clean energy more widely available to us all.

Having said this, however, in the short run – so long as oil supplies remain irreplaceable and their location geographically restricted in politically volatile regions – there will always remain a risk of another energy crisis that may yet rock the world. The economics of oil continue to be a fascinating, controversial and immensely important centre of academic, political and military conflict!

KEY WORDS

Cartel   A cartel is a small group of rival producers that decide to act together, formally or informally, legally or illegally, as if they were a monopoly or single seller. In the case of oligopoly, price competition can be unpredictable, costly, even fatal to the interests of one or more of the rival producers. In such situations, **non-price competition** may be safer: rivalry in advertising, packaging, special gift promotions and other marketing gimmicks. Cutting prices to win sales can always be matched by a rival. A really clever advertising campaign and slogan, however, can be unanswerable in the short run.

Complementary goods   are those in joint demand – for example an increase in demand for cars will lead directly to an increase in the demand for petrol. **Substitute goods**, in contrast, are in competitive demand – an increase in the demand for natural gas is likely to lead to a decrease in the demand for oil.

Joint profit maximisation   Where oligopolists agree they can increase prices together, or at least refrain from price cutting, such that revenues and thus profits are maximised for the group as a whole. The temptation always exists, however, for one producer to break ranks, cut prices and win a larger market share at the expense of its rivals. Hence the typical oligopolistic outcome is long periods of price stability and joint profit maximisation where competition takes place in the realm of advertising and marketing interspersed with shorter, violent price wars where the relative standing of the rivals is reassessed.

Local monopoly   A local monopoly can increase prices up to the point where it pays consumers to travel elsewhere to buy from an alternative supplier. The greater the travel costs involved, the greater the power of the local monopoly.

Monopsony   A monopsony is a large, single buyer. A big business which buys its inputs from any one of a number of small, competitive suppliers can drive the price down since it can choose to award its custom to whosoever it wants. Rival suppliers, on the other hand, have to sell to the monopsonist or not at all. In an industrial situation where a monopsonist is buying from a monopolist then the outcome is unpredictable – a balance of countervailing power prevails (as first described by US economist J. K. Galbraith).

Natural monopoly   A natural monopoly occurs where the most economically efficient form of business organisation is for one, large, sole producer to provide all of the industry's supply. The economies of large-scale production are such that it pays one large enterprise to dominate the industry, rather than have several competing firms try to operate where none can reduce costs sufficiently. This is typically the case in the distribution of water, gas, electricity and (sometimes) rail services where one pipe/rail/transmission line can link major towns rather than the wasteful competition of many competing lines.

The Organisation of Economic Cooperation and Development   This was set up to promote economic growth and financial stability amongst countries of the developed world. Its members include: Australia; Austria; Belgium; Canada; Denmark; Finland; France; Germany; Greece; Iceland; Ireland; Italy; Japan; Luxembourg; the Netherlands; New Zealand; Norway; Portugal; Spain; Sweden; Switzerland; Turkey; UK; USA. The OECD is therefore a club of rich countries.

Price-inelastic demand   This is where the price of a product changes greatly yet its demand changes proportionally less. If consumers are dependent on oil, for example, then producers can hoist up its price, sell not much less than before and thus enjoy much greater revenue.

Vertical integration   A company which owns a pipeline and buys an oil field concession in order to safeguard supplies is vertically integrating backwards (to its sources). If it constructs a chain of filling stations to sell its products it is vertically integrating forwards (to the market). Vertical integration can be contrasted with **horizontal integration** – where one firm attempts to dominate one process only (e.g. a pipeline owner which takes over all others in the region) – or **lateral integration** – where the firm moves out of the industry altogether (e.g. a refinery business which combines with a petrochemical plant, a producer of fertilisers and a coal mine). The major, multinational oil companies have practised all of these business strategies at one time or other in their history.

QUESTIONS

1   Why is the price of oil important? Explain the consequences of a significant rise in the price of oil at the beginning of the twenty-first century.
2   What factors influence the demand for oil? How are these factors likely to change over the next decade?
3   What determines the level of investment in the exploration, production and development of new oil reserves?
4   Explain how and why the competitive structure of the oil industry has changed over its history.
5. What makes for a successful cartel? Compare the fortunes of the majors' cartel with that of OPEC.

FURTHER READING

BP Statistical Review of World Energy, 2005.
Roncaglia, Alessandro. *The International Oil Market*. Macmillan, 1985.
Stevens, Paul. 'Oil prices: an economic framework for analysis', in G. Bird and H. Bird (eds), *Contemporary Issues in Applied Economics*. Edward Elgar, 1991.
http://economist.com/surveys/energy/sources.html

10 Foreign debt, financial crises and international policemen

Topics to be considered in this chapter:

- Causes of the 1980s debt crisis.
- The International Monetary Fund.
- The Mexican peso crisis.
- The East Asian crisis.
- Argentina's final crash.
- Reforming the financial architecture.

INTERNATIONAL DEBT AND GLOBAL CONTAGION

The first, major international debt crisis occurred during the 1980s when a number of developing countries were close to defaulting on the loans they owed to Western banks. These banks were so overextended at this time that there was a real danger that a major default would spark a crisis in confidence. If a sufficient quantity of worried depositors had then tried to grab their money and run for cover, any one of a number of banks might have been forced to close, thus triggering a chain reaction of other bank collapses that would have led to a full-blown international financial crisis and quite possibly a 1930s-like world-wide depression.

Fortunately, despite a lot of nervous nail-biting in Western financial centres, things never got that bad and certain commentators could look back with satisfaction on those times as a crisis that passed, as a 'battle that was won' (William Cline, *The Economist*, 18 February 1995).

It was not won for long, however. In 1994, what started as the Mexican peso crisis quickly rebounded world-wide as nervous international investors tried to liquidate their assets in a number of emerging markets. Then again, in 1997, beginning with the devaluation of the Thai baht, the Asian currency crisis erupted in some of the young and high-performing economies of East Asia – previously thought to be models of successful development – and its effects contributed eventually to the Russian debt debacle in the following year. From this, speculative *hedge funds* failed on Wall Street, and thus the spectre arose again of the possibility of debt default, world-wide contagion and a catastrophic crash of international finance which would hurt the rich as well as the poor.

Financial crises tend to be ranked in importance according to the threat they pose to the developed world and the banking systems that underpin it. The end of the twentieth century saw a return to battle against global financial crisis, therefore – and so the big guns of the US Federal Reserve were brought out at the end of 1998 to fight systemic financial collapse yet again. Billions of dollars were secured to bail out fragile Wall Street institutions that, had they folded, would have brought about economic chaos.

The contrast with the first financial crash of the new millennium, in Argentina in 2001 is quite instructive. This problem could be seen coming by many large depositors who had time to take evasive action and the eventual crunch thus did not present such a great shock to the international community. The fact that banks in Buenos Aires closed their doors against smaller domestic customers whilst their savings were being devalued inside caused riots on the streets of the Argentine capital – but not in the boardrooms of financial institutions across the world.

Whilst success can today be celebrated in having stabilised the foundations of Western banks through a number of different crises, severe indebtedness of developing countries meanwhile continues apace and – although it does not attract the same spotlight of media attention – struggling with this burden continues to be a major problem for many of the world's poor. This is a battle that continues to be fought.

The mountain of money owed by developing nations at the beginning of the twenty-first century currently exceeds the debt that was accumulated by these countries during the worst years of the 1980s. In 1982, total external debt owed by low and middle income countries totalled US$630.2 billion. In 1990 this figure had risen to US$1,460 billion; by 1999 it totalled US$2,573 billion. Such large sums boggle the imagination. What do they mean? How can countries run up such debts? Who owes what to whom and what are the causes and consequences of such financial extremes?

THE 1980s DEBT CRISIS

The story begins with the oil price shock of 1973 when the price of crude oil shot up 400 per cent between October 1973 and January 1974. With the Western developed world unable to cut back on consumption in the short term this meant massive money flows changed hands from oil consumers to producers. Such a quick fall in incomes and consumption could not be countenanced in the West so money supplies were expanded and double-digit inflation ensued. The money inflows to OPEC, on the other hand, could not be spent quickly enough – so they were deposited in offshore, international banks.

With the Western world experiencing recession and inflation (stagflation) and money balances in offshore banks meanwhile rapidly accumulating, the *real interest rates* on loans sank to negative levels. The price of Western

BOX 10.1 LONG-TERM CAPITAL MANAGEMENT: A HEDGE FUND THAT GOT CLIPPED

Stock markets have a legitimate economic function. They allow investors to pull out their capital from declining enterprises and reallocate it to growing ones. Buying and selling company shares, therefore, is an essential attribute of a healthy market economy – and share prices must inevitably rise and fall in response to such trading.

But such behaviour also allows stock markets to act as casinos. Some of the world's best brains are devoted (wasted?) to figuring out when to buy certain stocks and when to sell them and thus how to make a fortune out of speculating. Two financial gurus, Robert Merton and Myron Scholes, shared a Nobel prize in Economics in 1997 for their work on stock market prices. They produced a sure-fire statistical model that demonstrated how to pick winners. This was not just an academic tour de force – it was incorporated in Long Term Capital Management (LTCM), the hedge fund they helped to found.

Merton and Scholes had found the Holy Grail of finance. Their model told them when to buy into stocks that had hit rock-bottom and how to ride them high and sell when they hit a peak. When every one else was selling and prices were plummeting, if you could read the right financial indicators, you could pick up hot growth prospects at a bargain when no one else could see it. LTCM were so successful that they had made billions for their partners in a year or so – and, of course, with their first class reputation (other LTCM founders included legendary Wall Street names) more institutions quickly got into the act. Big banks and brokers from all over the US and Europe were anxious to pile money into LTCM – Chase Manhattan, Merrill Lynch, Union Bank of Switzerland and many more.

The beauty of their model was that it accepted the volatility of human nature and seemed unerringly successful in picking the right moments to buck stock market trends. The key to making money was *not* in following the herd but knowing when to do the exact opposite. All things that go up must come down, and vice versa, and based on precedent and statistical probability, the Merton and Scholes model could spot when.

The problem came when the unprecedented happened. A chain of events which began with the East Asian crisis ended with the Russian debt default of August 1998. The market movements this caused for LTCM were bigger and more long lasting than anything that could have been forecast or imagined. The hedge fund's model told them to keep buying when everyone else was selling but the predicted recovery never came. LTCM's losses were as spectacular as their previous winnings – only quicker. They lost US$4 billion in five weeks. Worse, they held positions worth US$200 billion in big-named institutions all over the world. As *The Economist* mentioned at the time, if LTCM had been allowed to go bust the world's markets 'would have gone frantic'.

As it was, Alan Greenspan, chairman of the US Federal Reserve, called a meeting of top New York banks in September 1998 and brokered a deal worth US$3.65 billion to keep LTCM afloat. The hedge fund *just* survived and, along with it, so did the world's financial infrastructure.

currencies also sank (the US dollar, in addition, was low due to large military spending and excessive US budgets).

With the rich-world recession came the drying up of aid, so poor countries were suffering both from the loss of export markets plus the loss of inter-governmental assistance.

Poor countries are, in general, underdeveloped but capital scarce and thus good candidates for investment. With negative interest rates, there are good economic grounds to increase borrowing – even if they are taken on in dollar-denominated loans and at variable rates of interest. Borrowed capital wisely invested can increase a poor country's productive potential and thus generate the future returns to pay off the loan.

But – there are two buts – it requires that the funds be used to support productive investment (not increased consumption) and it requires that market rates of interest do not rise in the future faster than rates of return on investment. Was anyone watching out for this?

A fundamental weakness in the global market place is that there is no overall regulatory agency responsible for recording and approving international affairs. There is no world central bank or government that has the right or opportunity – not then, nor today – to see all that is going on with multinational money flows. Neither the United Nations, nor the *International Monetary Fund* nor the *World Bank* possess any such authority. The global economy is thus a truly 'free' market with no all-powerful central administration. Banks and businesses operating across frontiers enjoy all the advantages of freedom from restriction, therefore, but at the cost of having no international policeman to turn to if things go wrong.

In 1979 the second oil price rise came and with it came changes of governments and economic policies in the USA and the UK. Inflation surged again at first but was met with stringent monetarist policies, on the demand side, and increasing flows of North Sea and Alaskan oil on the supply side.

In the early 1980s in Europe and North America, recession and unemployment were preferred to inflation and thus, with tight money, interest rates surged, the dollar and the pound rose and – while aggregate demand continued to be sluggish – eventually commodity prices started to fall.

Some developing country debtors like South Korea had invested successfully and could pay the rising interest payments. Others in Latin America and Africa could not. From negative interest rates in cheap dollars at the end of the 1970s, less developed countries (LDCs) were now required to pay real rates which had soared to 16 per cent by 1981 in rapidly appreciating foreign currencies. With aid cut off, with export markets closed, with – in some, though not all – domestic investments performing poorly, certain countries declared they could not pay even their interest payments, let alone the capital on the sums they had borrowed earlier. Mexico in August 1982 was the first to publicly admit that anticipated oil revenues would not cover their debts. For a country expected to have benefited greatly from the oil bonanza this sent the international banking world into shock and there was thus real fear that other, less oil-rich countries, would similarly default, promoting a global financial meltdown. The financial position of other big debtors like Argentina and Brazil soon confirmed these worst fears. Big US and European banks were scared they would go bust and the domino effect would drag the whole world down into a 1930s-type crash.

With the world holding its breath, the IMF and international bankers attempted to solve the problem. In the post-inflationary 1980s world where the dominant economic paradigm was now free-market economics, the IMF remedy was to introduce *stabilisation policies* designed to force debtor countries to pay up, though admittedly over rescheduled time scales.

The traditional rescue package involved:

- Cutting LDC government spending (seen as inflationary).
- Raising taxes.
- Privatising and reducing government intervention.
- Deregulating and liberalising markets.
- Devaluing domestic currencies.
- Reducing tariffs and protectionist policies.
- Promoting exports and opening economies to free trade and foreign investment.

With export markets still sluggish, however, the only way that debtor countries could pay (admittedly rescheduled) bills was by cutting domestic consumption and investment. For most of the 1980s, therefore, for Latin America and sub-Saharan Africa, this was known as 'the lost decade'. The return to conservative, free-market policies meant for the poorest in particular no growth in living standards.

It is not hard to see who were the immediate winners and losers with such a 'rescue package'. The IMF was repeatedly criticised for imposing the greatest pain on the poorest income groups and on defenceless small traders, and for prising open the LDCs for greater exploitation by the rich capitalist classes. The unpopularity of the heartless deflationary measures recommended made them impossible to implement in some countries, which subsequently led to political as well as economic chaos. Equally, it did not go unnoticed that the IMF was profoundly silent in the face of the massive budget deficits, excessive borrowing and punishing interest rates of the world's greatest debtor – the USA.

To be generous, the IMF did not act in any conscious way as the instrument for the industrialised nations to prolong LDC debt dependency and to maintain the existing world order of power relations between rich and poor. It was simply acting in accordance with the orthodox financial criteria by which it was originally set up. It was concerned with countries' short-term monetary stability and an 'orderly' world trade system. Where enacted, its policies certainly improved debtor countries' inflation and balance of payments records. The fact that the burden of LDC debt has continued to increase and for many their development has stalled, and that it helped generate greater overseas earnings for richer countries is the unintentional but inevitable result of its narrow role and blinkered vision.

WHERE WAS THE POLICEMAN?

Why was the focus of 'rescue packages' on rescheduling and on inventing novel ways of shuffling commitments around, instead of actually forgiving substantial fractions of the debt? Why were LDCs forced to open up their domestic economies to greater foreign penetration rather than Western markets being made more accessible to LDC exports? Why could not any one of the international players in this drama have taken a more active lead in promoting the long-term development needs of debtor nations instead of emphasising the primacy of short-term monetary balance?

The answers to these questions are both economic and historical. The main economic difficulty is concerned with the notion of market failure in unregulated world trade. Free markets 'fail' where individual decision-makers, acting independently, bring about outcomes that are socially inefficient/sub-optimal. Hence the need for regulation or intervention by central authority. Take the example of an individual, profit-seeking bank: what incentive does it have to forgive a particular debt if the LDC concerned uses the money it saves to pay off other banks' interest charges? The forgiving bank loses out to its main business competitors. Another example: what incentive does any welfare-maximising country have to put into effect painful, import-reducing/export-promoting remedies if the main beneficiaries of any dollars earned will be foreign creditors?

Economic philosophies move in historical cycles and, as has already been explained, the 1980s debt crisis was played out in a period when free-market, neoclassical economics was in the ascendancy. The conventional wisdom that dismantling restrictions to trade was the right policy for all countries gained evidence to support it all the way around the world from the USA to China. But freeing-up global markets can only benefit LDCs if their productive resources can respond rapidly enough to the price signals that the markets send them. It does not help if international resources are quicker to seize the business opportunities that are presented than LDC industries, and if richer, creditor countries are not pressured as much as debtors to reduce their tariffs.

The outcome of these inconsistencies in the 1980s was that, on the one hand, creditor nations continued to demand more sacrifices from LDC debtors than they were prepared to make themselves; on the other hand, a number of poor countries found it politically impossible to put into effect those policies asked of them; and there was no international arbitrator to bring both sides together to negotiate a more balanced and practicable solution.

By the 1990s the fear of a global financial crash had receded and, although developing countries still remained in debt (some of them heavily), rescheduled loan agreements were thought for most to be sustainable. However painful, it was believed that the recommended, pro-market economic policies were superior to the protectionist and interventionist government policies that had preceded them and which were blamed for most poor countries' long-term sluggish performance.

World Bank chief economist for Latin America, Sebastian Edwards, writing in the mid-1990s, noted that reforms to free up markets, liberalise and increase competition and international openness were never seriously questioned – not by the political elites, at least. With increasing popular unrest, however, it was conceded that social programs must be improved to reduce poverty and to provide a social safety net for the disadvantaged. But with this proviso, the pro-market paradigm went unchallenged. Such a major change in government policies in Latin America, despite the pain of the lost decade, must be considered a remarkable success for the pro-market school.

For a group of forty or so severely indebted countries, however, their situation was getting no better. The debt stock to GDP ratio for much of these (particularly African) nations was still over 120 per cent in 1996 and complaints about the inappropriateness of the free-market *Washington consensus* were persistent.

It took over a decade but such criticisms eventually had some impact. The United Nations, the IMF and the World Bank were all aware that more had to be done to stop the relentless rise in international debt for the most direly troubled. Rich world leaders therefore met in 1996 and signed the Heavily Indebted Poor Countries (HIPC) initiative. It was the first attempt to commit all creditors to multilateral debt reduction for the worst cases. The idea was that low income countries with unsustainable debt burdens could apply for HIPC eligibility and, if approved, this would open the door to them receiving much more financial assistance.

The aims were laudable. At last all creditors had agreed to some debt forgiveness. The problem was that the eligibility procedures were long and complex, the assistance offered was very limited and – first in 1994 and then, more spectacularly, in 1997 – the world's financial institutions became more preoccupied with another group of nations. It was not so much the poorest countries that became the cause of concern – it was the fate of some of the star performers in the developing world.

THE MEXICAN PESO CRISIS

Mexico's response to the 1980s debt crisis in swallowing the bitter pill of traditional deflationary policies had been widely applauded by international financiers. Indeed, Mexican decision-makers advocated this medicine as a means of ensuring access to NAFTA and the huge export market that they hoped would lead them into a golden age of growth. In this respect they were successful: in December 1992, and again with additional agreements on 1 January 1994, Mexico duly signed up to NAFTA.

But Mexico was maintaining a fixed dollar/peso exchange rate as part of the stabilisation package to promote increased trade, even though exports were not growing as fast as imports. Short-term capital inflows since 1992 caused by increased international interest in Mexico were masking a growing deficit on the current trade account. At the same time, there was little growth in productivity in export industries and little restraint on excessive consumer spending/ low domestic savings. Presidential elections in Mexico in 1994 limited economic policy options – there was no political support for restrictive fiscal and monetary policies.

Then rebellion by the Zapatistas in the poor southern region of Chiapas, along with other political assassinations and kidnappings, began to frighten off foreign inflows of capital. Despite attempts to play down the problems, by mid-December 1994 word was out that Mexico's financial position was unsustainable. Devaluation of the peso took place on 20 December.

This was a major shock to international financiers who had not seen it coming. Worse was the realisation that the Bank of Mexico had been dragging its feet in publishing official statistics and still there was no indication that the new government was going to do anything to institute corrective fiscal and monetary policies.

A full-blown crisis in confidence in the Mexican peso occurred. But what was different in the 1990s, compared to all other crises that had come earlier, was that now the crash was communicated instantly world-wide through inter-connected, globalised capital markets. With the spreading panic, similar flights of capital took place with frightening speed from other developing countries in the Americas, Africa and Asia. The US government first arranged a US$18 billion rescue loan on 2 January 1995 to reassure the markets. It didn't work. Investors were still panicking and fleeing for cover. This was systemic market failure, bringing a global impact that was later described by Michel Camdessus, the head of the IMF, as the first evidence of the beginnings of the new millen-nium. Only after Mexico announced *another* bitter adjustment programme on 9 March 1995 plus a massive US/IMF loan promoted by Bill Clinton (of US$51.8 billion!) did world financial markets begin to calm down.

The Mexican peso crisis was a traditional *balance of payments deficit* made calamitous by international finance markets transmitting the panic world-wide. It rang alarm bells in showing that, in the global economy, short-term speculative flows of money can reverse direction overnight and plunge countries and their governments into crisis very quickly. In the event, Mexico was fortunate to have a large neighbour that could not afford to let it crash, but even so the country was plunged into a severe economic contraction (minus 6 per cent growth in 1995) and its external debt in 1999 totalled US$167 billion (albeit 'sustainable').

THE EAST ASIAN CRISIS

Mexico 1994 proved to be merely a curtain-raiser, however, for the even more volcanic financial eruption that hit East Asia and shook developed and emerging markets all round the globe. It struck first in Thailand in 1997 but quickly spread to bury the economies of South Korea, the Philippines, Malaysia and Indonesia.

Explanations for the crunch range from those who insist the cause was major structural weaknesses in the Asian economies to those who say it was just a speculative financial bubble that burst. There is a wide literature on this event and it is still being written but most would agree that the following factors were all involved:

Structural weakness

Despite being lauded as models of free-market economics, East Asian economies had in fact developed with much government intervention. Financial markets, in particular, had been subordinate to government controls: interest rates were fixed at low levels, loans were directed to approved customers and it was 'understood' that such deals would not be allowed to fail. Central bank monitoring and regulation of bank practices was underdeveloped in these circumstances. However, liberalising immature financial markets which still retain a culture of implicit government guarantees brings considerable danger. Serious *moral hazard* existed. Yet whereas this structural weakness had led to banking crashes in Latin America (see chapter 4) it had been avoided in East Asia. (South Korea and Indonesia, for example, had maintained debt levels to manageable proportions throughout the 1980s and, unlike many other LDCs, had secured impressive growth.) Not having made mistakes earlier, therefore, there had been no incentive to change this structure of Asian *crony capitalism*.

Vulnerability to global money

Coming into the 1990s still with undeveloped stock markets, many Asian businesses were built not on share capital (as in the West) but on loan capital from domestic banks. Now, with 1990s liberalised money markets, that loan capital could come not only from domestic banks but also from overseas – in foreign currencies. Foreign institutions, in addition, were impressed with the growth record of the successful Asian economies. There was no shortage of foreign loans. What was not so noticeable, however, was that in many of these countries, from Japan to Korea to Thailand, incoming funds were funnelled through domestic financial institutions not so much into productive investments (there is some evidence that rates of return were falling in industry due to diminishing returns) but into booming property markets, inflated by what US economist Paul Krugman called *Pangloss values* (i.e. over-optimistic forecasts).

Fixed exchange rates

Fixed exchange rates are conducive to increased trade, though – as has been demonstrated in Europe, Mexico and others – exchange rates can only remain fixed if the countries concerned experience similar economic fortunes and they react the same way. Thailand had fixed the baht/dollar rate but the US economy was booming whereas Thailand was not. Its main export was electronic goods and its principal market was Japan – which languished in recession. Meanwhile the competition from China was hotting up and the world market in electronics was becoming saturated.

Macroeconomic incompatibilities

Government attempts to raise Thai interest rates and restrict money supplies to protect the exchange rate did not work – with liberalised markets and overoptimistic domestic rates of return, financial institutions simply borrowed abroad to fund their spending. This revealed the impossible triangle: open capital markets, fixed exchange rates and domestic control of money are together incompatible.

Negative shocks

The baht/dollar exchange rate couldn't be maintained. Thailand devalued in the summer of 1997 and this was the trigger for a financial collapse that spread around the region and then eventually the world.

Loans raised in foreign currencies now became very expensive. A property market collapse meant over-extended banks had insufficient assets. Implicit government guarantees to bail out banks are only believed if it is thought that the government has enough funds – but the fear that they might not have enough causes *everyone* to panic. Fear in Thailand was mirrored by exactly the same fears in Korea, Malaysia, and Indonesia. The fragility of financial sectors and economies built on crony capitalism were exposed. Foreign money that had been so eager to flood in to these countries now got out at frightening speed. Currencies, stock markets and real economies tumbled. The extent of the economic contraction for the following countries is illustrated in Table 10.1.

These are extreme movements. The IMF was quickly called upon to help out but no quick fix could be offered. Rescue programmes were designed to stabilise these economies (providing bail-out loans on condition of cutting back public spending, closing profligate banks, restructuring debts, devaluing the currency and charging penal interest rates) but – as the figures show – severe hardship could not be avoided.

Meanwhile, in Russia, with no solution to its ongoing internal chaos (see chapter 2), the collapse in Asian demand did nothing to help its sliding oil and commodity prices. The country was broke and would quite probably have been unable to meet its commitments even without external shocks brought on

Table 10.1 South East Asian economies in trouble

Country		1997	1998
Thailand	GDP in US$ (bn):	149.1	111.3
	% growth of GNP per capita:		−8.5%
	% growth of investment		−32%
South Korea	GDP in US$ (bn):	476.5	320.7
	% growth of GNP per capita:		−7.4%
	% growth of investment		−38.6%
Malaysia	GDP in US$ (bn):	100.2	72.5
	% growth of GNP per capita:		−9.6%
	% growth of investment		−42.9%
Indonesia	GDP in US$ (bn):	215.7	94.2
	% growth of GNP per capita:		−18%
	% growth of investment		−44.8%

Source: World Bank.

by its neighbours. Russia's problems were difficult to overstate. Hugely in debt to the West, unable to raise tax revenues and now with insufficient export earnings, as real interest rates rose Russia became unable to pay the interest charges on what it had borrowed. It announced it couldn't pay back its debts to the West.

The world's banking system was staring global meltdown in the face yet again. The virulence of the contagion which swept through financial markets now broke businesses in Wall Street as well as Moscow, Seoul and Jakarta.

As had been first identified in Mexico, the speed at which capital inflows could reverse and become outflows shook the most secure of financial foundations (let alone the distinctly shaky ones!) and this has now become the defining characteristic of the global economy in the new millennium.

ARGENTINA

Argentina's recent financial history has been tumultuous. It did not immediately embrace the Washington consensus reforms in the 1980s, described earlier. It had other problems to concentrate on – the debacle of the Falklands War, deposing the brutal military government and restoring justice and democracy. But under pressure to right all the wrongs inflicted on the nation by the generals, the incoming Alfonsin government could not meet all the conflicting demands placed upon it and so finished with the hyperinflation of 1989/90 that eroded public support and brought in a new administration headed by Carlos Menem.

With this change of government came a determination to restructure the economy. Following the, by now widely accepted, orthodox policies of financial conservatism, Menem brought in reforms to increase privatisations, increase public sector revenues, end subsidies and protection to industry and to reform the Central Bank. The economy minister, Domingo Cavallo introduced a new currency with the 1991 Convertibility Plan that pegged the peso to the dollar and, in one fell swoop, this eliminated inflation. From 4000 per cent (!) in 1989 the rate of increase in prices came down to single digits by 1992. Domestic money supplies could now only be increased if US dollar reserves increased. In other words, the Argentine Central Bank was converted into a currency board.

With confidence returning, the economy achieved a remarkable rebound – growing by 28 per cent between 1990 and 1993. From being an economic basket case, in a space of just a few years Argentina had turned round and was being lauded in financial markets as a paragon of virtue. The crucial test came with the Mexico devaluation crisis of December 1994 but, after a brief slowdown, growth resumed strongly in late 1995 and with it came increased world approval. In the international financial community, especially the IMF, many of Argentina's economic policies were now being widely applauded and the country was offered as a model for other developing countries to emulate.

And then it all went wrong. At the heart of the matter was Argentine's love affair with the dollar. By pegging the peso at a one-for-one exchange rate it had brought much needed confidence and stability to the domestic currency – very popular with people on the streets – but this could only last so long as the USA and Argentina formed an optimal currency area. Unfortunately, these two countries, economic realities were poles apart (review the economics of optimal currency areas mentioned in chapter 8). First was an asymmetric shock to trade: as the US economy boomed in the late 1990s and the dollar strengthened on world currency markets, so too did the peso that was pegged to it. But the US made up only 14 per cent of Argentina's export markets. It's main customer was Brazil which in 1999 devalued its own currency, the *Real*. Argentina now had difficulty in selling its goods abroad since they were priced in expensive dollars. Additionally, international borrowing and speculative investments of capital that had increased in the confidence-inspiring 1990s had built up external debts that totalled 50 per cent of GDP by 2001. Entering the new millennium, export revenues were falling rapidly yet dollar denominated liabilities were rising.

Now the old structural weaknesses of the country raised their head. Contrary to optimal currency requirements, labour markets were far from flexible: they were instead demanding increased wages and employments as Argentine growth slowed. No salvation there. And as recession deepened from 1999 on, so tax revenues on incomes and spending slowed even faster. An all-to-familiar hole in the government's budget opened up. On top of that, tax avoidance – an old vice – became rampant and with little room to reduce public spending, the finance minister resorted to more and more borrowing. The IMF tried to bridge the widening gap in Argentina's fiscal affairs and thus restore weakening international confidence but it was a losing battle. By November 2001, bank withdrawals started to accelerate as people feared the worst – and this only hastened the inevitable collapse. Banks shut their doors; riots erupted and at least thirty people died as the authorities tried to restore order. Within hours, the peso started trading on the black market at a 50% discount. All those whose income was measured in pesos but whose costs, or debts, were measured in dollars faced financial ruin. The government resigned. A succession of presidents followed but none could honour Argentina's financial commitments in full and to this day creditors are still waiting to be paid.

The question to ask at the end is this: are developing countries best advised to open up their economies, to liberalise markets and to promote free trade – especially free mobility of capital – if the result is to bring financial crisis, economic collapse and increased international indebtedness and dependency? And if middle-income countries and large, resource-rich transition economies can so quickly be plunged into economic ruin, what future is there for poorer LDCs? Isn't there some way that the key global institutions of the UN, IMF and World Bank can do a better job?

REFORMING THE INTERNATIONAL FINANCIAL ARCHITECTURE

There is general agreement that the IMF and the World Bank face today a distinctly different world to that which they were originally designed to manage. International capital speeds across the globe without any international control.

The result is that managing LDC economies in today's volatile environment is like walking blindfold along a tightrope in a storm – buffeted on all sides, unable to see what is front and yet with a yawning chasm below as the penalty for failure.

But although the economic realities of the new millennium are different from those in 1944, there is one basic similarity. The original rationale for the Bretton Woods institutions was to bring about international collective action in situations where markets did not work and where there was a role for intervention for the public good. This vision is just as necessary now as it was in the past. Unfortunately the political leadership needed to reform and update the key global authorities is absent. So, despite general agreement about the problem, there is precious little accord about implementing solutions.

Various ideas have been floated. They include:

Improved transparency

Better and more rapid disclosure of financial information by governments, banks and the IMF should allegedly make markets work better. However, in some circumstances this may enhance instability, not diminish it. Also, it is not always clear what information is most relevant to declare and nowadays, with the increased speed of transactions, balance sheets can anyway be out of date almost as soon as they have been compiled. Furthermore, with regard to the IMF, there are difficulties in revealing confidential information submitted by governments.

Regulation and supervision

Common rules on banking practice and tighter surveillance should expose cronyism and high risk and bring about more developed and safer financial markets in the long run. But despite the Basle Accord on financial standards which has been part of international practice since the 1990s this has not prevented reputable institutions from coming unstuck in the past. Also, the notion of objectively assessing a country's risk is contentious. Who is doing the risk assessment? Is this just another mechanism for making LDCs dependent on the rich world?

Capital controls

If hot money flows are destabilising to so many low and middle income countries then an obvious policy measure would be to restrict them. Malaysia has instituted temporary crisis controls on outflows – hardly popular with foreign creditors – while Chile has used more acceptable taxes and reserve requirement restrictions on inflows. Note however that any LDC acting unilateraly in this fashion runs the risk of undermining international confidence and thereby reducing its access to global capital. It therefore requires multilateral agreement secured through the IMF to control hot money flows – it is just that there has been no progress achieved on this. Rich countries prefer case-by-case bilateral deals since this gives them more discretionary power.

Exchange rate regimes

The immediate postwar world was more stable due to the fixed exchange rate regime that operated – albeit to the cost of slow growth for the UK and the USA that provided the key currencies. It is argued that emerging markets today will remain vulnerable to crisis so long as the major reserve currencies, the dollar, the euro and the yen, remain unstable. There is no doubt that in all of the financial crises mentioned so far, misalignments between domestic currencies and international ones have sparked the ensuing crashes. But various proposals for exchange rate coordination between the big three have nonetheless proved fruitless. No one wants to provide the stable peg around which to anchor the global architecture.

The lender of last resort

In national banking systems where all follow the regulations laid down by the central bank, if financial markets fail then approved private traders are assured of last resort loans in order to prevent a crisis. Why can't the same provision be made internationally? If loans coordinated by the IMF can be put together to respond to crises after they have occurred, cannot they be made available *before*? It would be less expensive that way – as the saying goes: 'a stitch in time saves nine'. This is another good idea in theory – but so far too difficult to organise supranationally. And while automatic access to a financial safety net sounds good it also creates moral hazard and the risk that irresponsible bank behaviour would never be reined in.

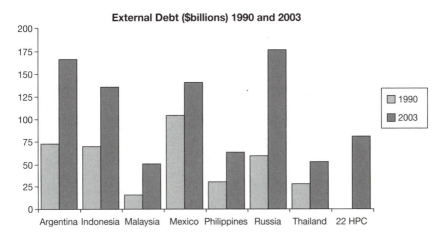

Figure 10.1 Total external debt for selected countries affected over the 1990s decade – the absolute increase is greatest for Russia, then Argentina. Note that the *combined debt* for 22 poor and highly indebted (mostly African) countries in 2003 is contrasted with middle-income countries affected by financial contagion. Although these countries' individual debts were not so great in absolute terms, poverty meant they were more disabling.

Source: World Bank.

CONCLUSION

The Bretton Woods accord which set up the IMF and the World Bank was prompted by the Great Depression and World War II. Although Professor Deepak Nayyar of Delhi University says the world need not wait for another crisis of such proportions to introduce much needed reform of the global financial system, the political will is still not there yet.

Meanwhile, in addition to the vulnerability of crisis-torn middle income countries, the debt dependency of the world's poorest continues. What sort of future awaits both groups of countries in the new millenium?

Despite all that has been mentioned about the volatility of the world economic environment this does not mean that national governments are completely powerless. Wise domestic policies and sound internal investment are still the best bet for development. There is no external force that requires LDCs to open up their financial markets to inflows of hot money. Foreign direct investment in essential capital goods can be welcomed on the one hand yet resistance or greater caution can be exercised over short-term loans and speculative portfolio purchases. In the last resort, if international policing fails and if rich country governments exercise no control over what flows of money leave their shores that is no excuse for LDC governments not to exercise discretion over how business is conducted at home and what money is welcomed into their own countries. Both Taiwan and Singapore possess efficient financial and industrial markets and if they can avoid the worst excesses of global systemic banking failure so can others. There remains much that can be done here (see next chapter).

For the heavily indebted poor countries, international assistance is still needed. The story here is a little better now – international campaigns such as Jubilee 2000 aimed at promoting debt forgiveness have had some effect. Reacting to all the publicity, debt relief has been expanded and speeded up, more countries have been admitted and more finance arranged. Debt ratios for some of the most needy have improved over the decade since 1996 (see table 10.2). In June 2005, leaders of the group of eight (G8) major industrial powers proposed cancellation of 100% of the debt of eighteen of the poorest countries eligible under the HIPC initiative. At the time of writing, the IMF, the World Bank and the African Development Fund have pledged to take this recommendation forward for implementation.

Despite such claims of support, however, there is no doubt that more can be done to facilitate growth and help the development of LDCs. Western policy makers that promote outward looking, trade-friendly policies on the one hand and openness to capital on the other cannot continue to place barriers to the commodity exports and cheap labour goods that are the stock in trade of the developing world. Equally the growth in net private capital flows around the world still continues to destabilise emerging markets and, despite encouraging signs that it has reduced of late (international speculators have had their fingers burnt and are a little more cautious now!), history shows that financiers have short memories. Those in debt need access to export markets and safeguards on global capital. Yet the world economy continues to be one where the trading rules – in both goods and financial markets – are determined mostly by the richest players with an eye to their own interest. The IMF, the World Bank, the World Trade Organisation and the United Nations have all attracted criticisms for the international order which they govern. Cries for their reform are not going to go away!

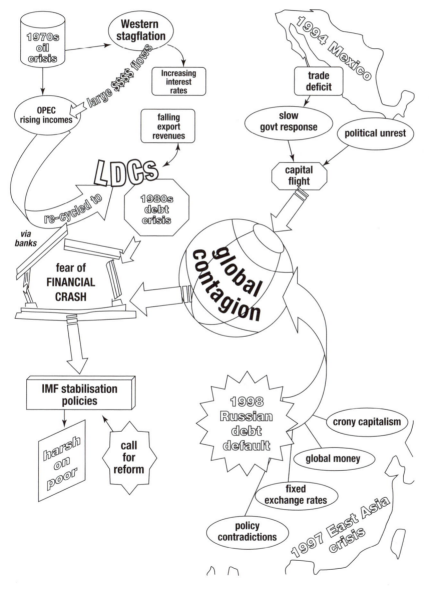

Figure 10.2 The themes of chapter 10

Table 10.2 Debt indicators for heavily indebted poor countries compared to other less developed countries (%)

	28 HIPCs before relief, 1999	28 HIPCs after relief, 2003	Other LDCs 2003 average
Total net present value			
– of debt to exports ratio	293	150	149
– of debt to GDP ratio	62	31	50
Ratio of debt service to exports	17	7	11

Source: World Bank, 2005.

KEY WORDS

A balance of payments deficit   occurs when a country's total earnings on foreign trade fall short of its total spending.

Capital flight   is where worried private investors liquidate whatever capital they can and spirit it out of the country into safer havens where there is less risk of loss. Thus in addition to whatever official loans or payments are entering or leaving the country private capitalists may be flying out funds as fast as they can. Note that large private sales of domestic currency in the attempt to buy foreign monies may precipitate a collapse of the domestic exchange rate.

Crony capitalism   where businesses raise capital not in the open market place – which requires revealing balance sheets to public scrutiny – but from private contacts and associates, some of whom may be open to corruption.

Debt-service ratio   Debt service is the payment of capital plus interest charges necessary to pay off a loan over an agreed period of time. This sum can be expressed as a percentage of the debtor country's earnings on export sales: the debt service as a ratio of its income from trade.

Hedge funds   These are also known as highly leveraged institutions (HLIs) and attract short term deposits in order to place them in (hopefully) high yielding, though volatile, stocks. You hedge your bets if you spread your placements around a number of HLIs. By their nature, however, speculative flows move in and out of these hedge funds very quickly and, additionally, there is the fallacy of composition: sitting in London or New York and switching funds from Hong Kong to Buenos Aires to Kuala Lumpur may make perfect sense to you but it can provoke a panicky and contagious chain reaction. Huge inflows and outflows of such capital have thus proved to be very destabilising for immature stock markets and hedge funds have been accused of being at the root of recent financial crises.

The International Monetary Fund   was set up in 1944 to underpin the fixed exchange rate system agreed in Bretton Woods (see last chapter). The IMF would supply short-term loans of foreign exchange to central banks of the developed world if this was required to protect them from a currency crisis. (Speculators might sell a country's currency if they feared a devaluation, but heavy selling would thus bring about the consequence that was feared. IMF funds could increase a central bank's financial power to resist such a move and successfully defend its fixed rate.) The IMF was established at the same time as its sister organisation, the **World Bank** – which was charged with providing long-term loans to developing countries. The IMF, however, has been drawn more and more into administering help to LDCs since defending fixed rates has been unnecessary after the collapse of the original Bretton Woods system in 1971 and it has been the poorer countries in the world economy that have lately been in greatest need of short-term loans and financial crisis management.

Moral hazard   If central authorities guarantee to support your business even if investments you make turn out to lose money then there is no incentive for you to make wise decisions. The authorities are encouraging a morally hazardous, economically inefficient business environment.

The real rate of interest   equals the money (or nominal) rate of interest minus inflation. If you borrow $100 and pay back this sum plus 10 per cent interest next year then you must pay $110. But if inflation rises by over 10 per cent, then – in real terms – if you pay $110 next year you will be paying back less than you borrowed. The real rate of interest is negative.

Stabilisation policies   are those measures recommended by the IMF to restore confidence and stability in a country's financial affairs. They have been variously described as orthodox, conservative, right-wing and austere in that they usually recommend cutting money supplies, increasing interest rates, floating or refixing exchange rates, balancing government budgets, freeing-up markets and reassuring creditors that they *will* be repaid.

Washington consensus   The pro-market, financially orthodox and conservative economic paradigm that ruled the globally important, Washington-based institutions such as the IMF, the World Bank and the US government in the 1980s and 1990s, and which I have elsewhere referred to as Thatcherism and Reaganism.

QUESTIONS

1   What were the causes of the 1980s debt crisis? Examine the role of international bankers and governments in both debtor and creditor nations. How might this crisis have been prevented?
2   Is it sound economic policy to rely on foreign capital for development assistance? Under what circumstances is it wise for a LDC to incur increasing debt; when is it unwise?
3   Consider the role of the IMF in rescheduling the debts of Latin American and African countries affected by the 1980s crisis. What were the various mechanisms used to help them out? What were the criticisms of these deals?
4   In what ways did the East Asian financial crisis of the 1990s differ from that of the 1980s?
5   What are the changes required to reform the global financial infrastructure? What are the difficulties involved in implementing these reforms?

FURTHER READING

Akyuz, Y. 'The debate on the international financial architecture: reforming the reformers', *UNCTAD Discussion Paper*, 148, April 2000.

Edwards, S. *Crisis and Reform in Latin America: From Despair to Hope*. Oxford University Press, 1995.

Krugman, P. *What Happened to Asia?* (January 1998): http://web.mit.edu/krugman/ www/DISINTER.html.

Nayyar, D. *New Roles and Functions for the UN and the Bretton Woods Institutions*, World Institute for Development Economics Research, 2001.

11 Development, growth and Asian dragons

Topics to be considered in this chapter:

- Definition and measurement of development.
- Strategies for development:
  1 Primary product exploitation.
  2 Import substitution.
  3 Export promotion.
- Theories of growth:
  1 Rostow's stages of growth.
  2 Harrod–Domar growth model.
  3 Neoclassical and endogenous growth models.
- Experience of South Korea, Taiwan, Hong Kong and Singapore.

INTRODUCTION

Wide disparities of income in the world have been a reason to turn to economics right from this subject's very beginnings – see Adam Smith, *An Inquiry into the Nature and Causes of the Wealth of Nations*, 1776.

Over two centuries later, however, modern economics still cannot make up its mind about the answers to this 'inquiry'. Surprisingly, there is not even agreement about how important the study of poverty and wealth is – are the problems of development and growth central to economics, or are they a specific branch or application of the subject?

A quick look at any introductory textbook seems to indicate that development economics is nowadays a somewhat low priority, end-of-book sort of topic. Since 'Development and Growth' is the title of this chapter also, maybe that is the impression given here as well. If so, take another look at the preceding pages. The philosophy running through this book is that national and international differences in poverty and wealth, rival theories and systems of economic organisation, are absolutely central to the subject. Moreover, no matter how extreme these differences appear to be, it is the contention here that the same economic forces are at work in all countries. Policy questions of demand-side and supply-side economics, budgetary and monetary control, free trade and regulation are debated in and out of governments all round the world. As we have seen, decisions taken in some countries can impact on others in sudden and unpredictable ways. We all live on the same planet and if in the end different countries come up with radically different forms of economic organisation, the same principles of economics can nonetheless be seen to play out in each, albeit dissimilar, context.

Not all critics will necessarily agree with this claim. It can be argued that less-developed countries are structurally different from their richer neighbours and thus a different analytical approach is necessary to understand them adequately. For example – growth theories that are appropriate to model the behaviour of rich, market systems may well be insufficient to satisfactorily encompass and explain the barriers to development encountered in many poor countries. Thus the notion of dualism – a formal, high-wage market sector coexisting but separate from the informal, poorer, traditional sector in LDCs – has been analysed via two-sector growth models (earning the pioneering economist W. Arthur Lewis a Nobel prize). But more radical, Marxist-inspired theories dispense with either interpretation above and simply insist that the poor are the inevitable residual left over after the rich have gained most of the spoils. Starting with such an assertion, however, no matter how attractive it might be to some, is hardly consistent with the practice of objective social science.

That the world can be divided into rich and poor nations which enjoy markedly different standards of living is indisputable (see Tables 11.1 and 11.2). That such a division of wealth and poverty exists *within* countries is similarly evident. What is debatable is the nature of the interaction between these two sectors. Is there any evidence that wealth is trickling down from rich to poor? Or perhaps there is no appreciable economic interaction? Or maybe that the exchange is reversed – the rich are getting richer by exploiting the poor? These are just three possible interpretations of the nature of world economic relationships and evidence must be sought before jumping to any conclusions.

Table 11.1 GNP *per capita*, selected countries, 2003 (US$)

Country	Current	PPP adjusted
USA	37,870	37,750
Japan	34,180	28,450
United Kingdom	28,320	27,690
Germany	25,270	27,610
France	24,730	27,640
Canada	24,470	30,040
Italy	21,570	26,830
Korea	12,030	18,000
Mexico	6,230	8,980
Brazil	2,720	7,510
China	1,100	4,980
India	540	2,880

Source: World Bank.

Table 11.2 Development indicators, selected countries, 2003

HDI rank	Country	Real GDP per capita (US$ PPP)	Life expectancy (years)	Adult literacy (%)	HDI 0–1
1	Norway	37,670	79.4	99	0.963
4	Luxembourg	62,298	78.5	99	0.949
5	Canada	30,677	80	99	0.949
6	Sweden	26,750	80.2	99	0.949
10	USA	37,562	77.4	99	0.944
11	Japan	27,967	82	99	0.943
15	UK	27,147	78.4	99	0.939
20	Germany	27,756	78.7	99	0.93
25	Singapore	24,481	78.7	92.5	0.907
34	Argentina	12,106	74.5	97.2	0.863
37	Chile	10,274	77.9	95.7	0.854
46	Uruguay	8,280	75.4	97.7	0.84
61	Malaysia	9,512	73.2	88.7	0.796
62	Russian Federation	9,230	65.3	99.4	0.795
77	Saudi Arabia	13,226	71.8	79.4	0.772
85	China	5,003	71.6	90.9	0.755
93	Sri Lanka	3,778	74	90.4	0.751
120	South Africa	10,346	48.4	82.4	0.658
127	India	2,892	63.3	61	0.602
135	Pakistan	2,097	63	48.7	0.527
177	Niger	835	44.4	14.4	0.281

Source: UNDP, *Human Development Report 2005.*

Note: GNP and GDP are both measures of national income, but GNP differs from GDP in that the latter does not include a country's net income from abroad (a significant difference for relatively small countries which have a high proportion of investments overseas, or have large foreign debt-service payments).

A little in the evolution of these themes will be discussed below. As before, the different theories and predictions derived are not just of academic interest – they have had and are having an enormous impact on government policy formulations and thus the livelihoods of billions. The most influential school of thought at present emphasises the relevance of mainstream, neoclassical economic theory – both in explaining the world economy's past performance and also in offering all countries practicable policies to enhance their future growth prospects. There is nothing like evidence, however, drawn particularly from poorer parts of the world where markets do not function perfectly, to slay the most beautiful edifice of modern theory with ugly facts!

MEASUREMENT

Any inquiry into the nature of development, however, needs first to identify what is meant by the term development, and how can progress in this domain be measured?

The first and most obvious criterion to consider is the real income enjoyed by the countries studied. The most frequently used measure in this regard is the gross national product per head of population. It is a crude but fundamental reference point that is relatively easy to obtain and is readily understood. The World Bank, for example, classifies low-income economies as those with a GNP per capita of less than US$765; middle-income economies are those with a GNP per capita between US$765 and US$9,386; and high-income economies with a GNP per head of US$9,386 or above per year. (Confusingly, in all its publications now, The World Bank has renamed GNP as GNI – gross national income – though its method of calculation is the same. GNP is retained here, however.)

In this example, all incomes are measured in 1999 US dollars – different world currencies being converted into dollars at the ruling market exchange rates. One difficulty with this yardstick is that current exchange rates are not a reliable means to convert dollars into all other monies – according to the imperfections of the exchange markets they may overvalue some currencies and undervalue others. US$100 can often buy more goods and services in (typically) a poor country than in its richer neighbour. If this is so, then the local currency is undervalued at current exchange rates. GNP figures are thus made more accurate if dollars are converted into other countries' money via exchange rates calculated on a *purchasing power parity* (PPP) basis. That is, exchange rates need to be adjusted such that an identical sample of basic goods and services costs the same in one country as another. (*The Economist* magazine has used a 'hamburger standard' as a quick approximation of this principle – if five dollars when converted into pesos buys a bigger hamburger in Mexico than in the USA, then the peso is undervalued, Mexico's GNP as measured in US dollars is undervalued, and these figures must be readjusted accordingly.)

Compare the figures in Table 11.1 of GNP *per capita*, measured in current US dollars, with GNP *per capita* adjusted to purchasing power parity. Although there are still wide differences between rich and poor nations, the use of PPP figures reduces the gap somewhat. The relative position of economies in this rank-ordering may also be affected (consider Canada in the list above if you compare incomes per head measured in current prices to purchasing power parities).

Even if adjusted to show national incomes on a purchasing power basis, however, there still remain a number of other criticisms of using GNP per capita to measure development. Many poor peoples may not be in close contact with the money economy – they may neither sell the product of their work, nor buy many goods or services. Much of what they consume might be provided by themselves or bartered for in unrecorded trade. Subsistence farmers fall into this category. Similarly, many participants in the informal sector – such as numerous street sellers, stall holders and those employed in small workshops – may be more integrated into the modern market economy but will rarely disclose their output or incomes. Calculating their economic contribution can be estimated via comparing the shortfall between the community's recorded incomes and recorded expenditures, but nonetheless considerable scope for underestimating the true national income of developing countries remains.

The methods used to compile GNP statistics in some countries can be very questionable. If output, expenditure and income data are surveyed with no great professional commitment to the exercise (e.g. by untrained assistants, part-timers, students, etc.) then many inaccuracies will be included due to errors and guesswork on the part of investigators, evasion and fabrication on the part of those surveyed. There may also be deliberate falsification of the results for political purposes.

But even if a country's GNP per capita data were 100 per cent accurate and included all economic activity without exception, it would still not necessarily be the best indicator of development. This is because it shows only a mathematical average income, and averages may conceal very wide income disparities between rich and poor. Plus the whole notion of development implies something more for a country than just a crude measure of monetary wealth. If a nation plunders its stock of mineral resources, desecrates its landscape, pollutes its air, exploits its uneducated workforce and mounts up enormous incomes for a corrupt few, it would 'enjoy' a relatively high GNP per head of population, but would it be developed? For this reason there have been many attempts over the years to define and measure development using a wider range of criteria than just income statistics alone.

A reporter once asked Mahatma Gandhi what he thought of Western civilisation; he replied: 'I think it would be a good idea . . .' The notion that material wealth equates with civilisation was challenged.

Development implies that a country's living standards are improving for all; that there is a reduction in poverty, in inequality, an improvement in general standards of housing, diet, health and education. Apart from such socio-economic indicators, development can also be interpreted as including freedom from oppression and servitude, and freedom to create a greater cultural identity and sense of self-esteem. It implies that the majority of a country's peoples are actively participating in the development process and that no minority is being persecuted as a means to this end.

Defining development so widely leads to problems of measurement. The United Nations, for example, publishes a political freedom index that would rank some countries relatively lower in development terms than if purely economic criteria were used – e.g. China, Chile (under Pinochet), Indonesia, Saudi Arabia, etc. Concepts such as democracy, freedom of expression, the rule of law, etc. are embodied here.

Confining this study to economics, it can be said that rising average incomes are a necessary but not sufficient condition for development. Increased economic power may not lead to greater civilisation (consider Hitler's Germany), but no sustained development is possible without it. Economic wealth is power, and such power is necessary for the creation of good *or* ill.

The United Nations Development Programme uses GNP per capita data calculated on a purchasing power parity basis as a measure of incomes; life expectancy at birth as an indicator of health; and the percentage of adult literacy plus data on educational enrolments as an indicator of education. By weighting these measures together, it comes up with a *Human Development Index* (HDI) on a scale from zero to one.

The nations shown in Table 11.2 are ranked according to their income per head measured in 2003 US dollars at PPP rates (column 3). Referring to the Human Development Index (column 6), however, the ordering of this selection of countries changes considerably. Contrast the rankings of Uruguay with Saudi Arabia, for example, or Sri Lanka with South Africa. In these cases, a higher quality of life is better captured by indicators other than crude measures of *per capita* incomes.

The HDI is not entirely free from criticism, however, because depending on how you weight the three indicators (featured in columns 3, 4 and 5) together you can come up with different results. Compare the findings on the Sweden and Japan, for example: Japan is a country which is richer and with a population of slightly longer life expectancy than Sweden but it is ranked lower on the HDI. There are grounds to question the methodology used here!

There have been many more attempts than those surveyed here to capture the notion of development in measurable statistics, but there is clearly no single, objective indicator of such a value-loaded concept that is without its faults. Since it is differences in incomes that excite most commentators, however, and – as mentioned earlier – it is a popular and frequently published statistic, GNP (or where unavailable, GDP) *per capita* is used most often in this book as *the* yardstick of development (though its weaknesses mentioned above must always be borne in mind).

THEORIES AND POLICIES OF DEVELOPMENT

What are the economic strategies that a less-developed country can pursue to best secure its development? This is a concern that has only received serious attention since the 1950s. There was little interest in analysing the economics of LDCs in the nineteenth and early twentieth centuries – this was the colonial era when Europeans were more interested in action rather than reflection.

International trade in the nineteenth century was relatively simple. Finance was regulated by *the gold standard* and administered by what was in effect the world's central bank – the Bank of England. Thanks to continually improving transport technology, the world economy witnessed a gradual extension of markets that grew wider and wider around their basic centre in Europe. As was entirely consistent with classical economic thinking, colonies and ex-colonies had a comparative advantage in exporting primary produce, so Western capital was poured into plantations and mines, railways and shipping all round the world from Argentina to Indonesia, Kenya to the West Indies.

The LDCs thus entered the world economy as exporters of primary produce to serve Western manufacturers and consumers. Gains from this trade were enjoyed by both parties – the economies of poorer countries were transformed by Western capital and they could thus earn growing export revenues; meanwhile Europeans enjoyed cheap oil, copper, phosphates, rubber, sugar, tobacco, coffee, tea, etc. The distribution of these benefits – how much the colonies and ex-colonies gained in contrast to Europeans – depended on the terms of trade; that is, whether North American wheat, West Indian sugar and Malaysian rubber and tin could be sold in European markets for a high price or a low one. Some countries earned more and thus grew faster than others under this regime: Argentina, for example, was ranked as the eleventh richest country in the world in 1870.

The colonial era obviously brought economic benefits, but not to all people equally. Native populations of the LDCs had little choice in determining their destiny and many had not experienced the growth in incomes that they could see were enjoyed by a privileged elite. Analysis of the role of primary production as a strategy for development is inevitably coloured by this colonial experience, nonetheless underdeveloped countries of the world still today retain a comparative advantage in mineral extraction and agricultural exploitation and it is thus important to consider how far specialisation in primary production is a useful strategy for development.

Strategy 1. Exploitation and export of primary produce

There is no doubt that one of the earliest and seemingly easiest ways discovered to get rich quick is to go and find some source of great natural wealth and exploit it. Over the centuries, gold and silver from South America; spices from the East Indies; gold and diamonds from South Africa; cereals, cotton and tobacco from North America; and oil from the Middle East have all provided the means for some (not necessarily indigenous) people to accumulate wealth. Towns, cities and empires have flourished and declined according to the availability of such valued natural resources. Whether or not such resource exploitation leads to sustainable economic (and environmental) development, however, depends on the extent to which: (1) large surpluses can be generated; and (2) these surpluses can be productively invested in value-adding technologies in new industry. Re-investment is essential – clearly countries cannot go on enriching themselves forever simply by extracting more and more non-renewable natural resources (see chapter 13).

In fact, even if nations could go on and on plundering their natural riches, economic theory and history teaches us that the prices of these resources tend to be high for only relatively short time periods. Except in the extremely rare case of a natural monopoly, competition from alternative suppliers plus the price effect driving consumers to economise on demand tends to quickly bring down the revenues to be earned from the export and sale of scarce natural assets. (Having said that, however, the rents to be earned in the short-lived period when world markets are hurriedly trying to adjust can be substantial: for example, between 1963 and 1973 Saudi Arabian petrol prices averaged US$4.6 per barrel and Saudi oil revenues averaged US$1.39 billion. Between 1974 and 1984 prices leapt to an average of US$27.6 per barrel and average annual revenues soared to US$53.05 billion.)

Prices of primary produce can be volatile. Scarcity and inelasticity in supply means large incomes or *quasi-rents* can be earned for a short while but these surpluses inevitably drive the search for alternatives. Thus the competition between rival countries and mining companies eventually forces profits and prices down. Wars, panic buying or the introduction of mineral-specific new technologies (e.g. cars for oil; nuclear power for uranium) can bump up demand and thus prices for a while, only for the long-term downward price pressure to reassert itself afterwards. Less-developed countries that are *monocultures* – particularly if they are mineral resource dependent – can thus earn very unstable incomes (see chapter 10 on OPEC incomes, for example).

Who benefits from short-term bonanzas? It can be a local business community, multinational corporations or governments, depending on the structure of the industry employed in the exploitation of the natural resource, and the energy and efficiency with which the government can capture any of the rents earned. (Since the 1970s governments have become more adept at taxing and in other ways capturing a rising share of these rents without scaring away the business goose that lays the golden egg. This is true of all types of natural resource exploitation, but has been particularly noticeable in the case of oil.)

But whichever the institution that accumulates the wealth involved, it is the *proportion* of those surpluses earned that is invested in the economy and the *efficiency* with which they are employed in the promotion of diversification and growth that is the key to long-term economic development. Note, such inflows can come in the form of private investment or public investment; from local capitalists or from foreign direct involvement.

A problematic feature of mineral exploitation in particular is that such activity is often carried out on a huge, capital-intensive scale using expensive, imported technology and skills, with relatively little local labour absorption. Whether practised by foreign multinationals, by local private industry or state enterprise, the integration of these businesses into the local economy can be very limited. Dualism results – characterised by palaces in the desert, fortresses in the jungle, tower blocks above the ghetto, etc.

The stereotypical dualistic development pattern is of a small, modern, capital-intensive and innovative business sector which possesses good trade links with the developed world but which grows up as an enclave within a larger, relatively backward, labour-intensive and traditional peasant-worker economy. The level of communication and economic interchange between these two sectors is underdeveloped – indeed the gulf between the rich and poor communities within a LDC can be as great as the gulf between rich and poor countries as a whole.

The benefits of natural resource exploitation may thus not spread very far. This is not just the simplistic case of foreigners coming in like Pizarro to a poor country to plunder its riches and make off with them. (Though this has undeniably happened in the past.) Nor is it a case of corrupt governments and/or local capitalists expropriating riches and wasting them on conspicuous consumption and capital flight into foreign bank accounts. (This too has occurred.) It is just that it is the natural tendency of entrepreneurs anywhere and especially in developing countries to work hard to lift themselves out of poverty, to accumulate wealth and then to strive to protect it.

Lobbying governments to stabilise exchange rates at a high level can be instrumental in this process: it ensures high prices and profits for the export of the natural resource; it means the importation of foreign capital equipment and technology is cheap; so is the consumption of foreign luxuries like cars, fashion-wear, holidays, etc.; and domestic savings can be similarly cheaply converted into safe, hard-currency deposits. Unfortunately, traditional-sector industry and agriculture can be destroyed by high exchange rates: cheap imports compete away their domestic market and high export prices for their products mean they cannot find sales abroad.

An ailment known as *Dutch Disease* is a modern demonstration of this phenomenon. Exports of natural gas found in the 1960s caused the Dutch exchange rate to appreciate. Large revenues were devoted to improving social welfare, but with money supplies outrunning domestic production inflation began to increase. Meanwhile, traditional export industries were suffering from lost markets. Unemployment increased and growth rates declined. The gas bonanza benefited one industry, therefore, at the expense of all others.

The oil bonanza has had a similar effect on countries such as Nigeria, Mexico and Venezuela. In extreme cases there is even what can be called the Kuwait effect – i.e. where oil riches and exchange rates rise so high that almost nothing else in the economy can be produced and profitably exported. Labour forces may be made up entirely of foreigners and there is no incentive for the small, indigenous population to perform any work and develop any skills at all.

These are examples where national incomes are rising by depreciating the country's stock of natural capital. No or low re-investment is taking place. 'Development' is clearly unsustainable.

We can conclude this section by stating that relatively rich natural resource endowments are by no means a guarantee of economic development. Some countries can exploit and retain them productively (e.g. Canada, Australia); others may lose out (see Table 11.3).

Table 11.3 Natural resources and the environment

Country	Natural resource	Minerals as % of exports, 1990	% growth of GNP per capita, 1965–90
Zaire	Cobalt, copper	56	–2.2
Mauritania	Iron ore	81	–0.6
Bolivia	Silver, tin	69	–0.7

Source: World Bank.

Gillis et al. (*Economics of Development*, Norton, 2001) cites Bolivia as an example of a mining country *par excellence*. After three centuries of plundering its mineral wealth it is still one of the poorest countries in South America.

This mixed development record of primary produce specialisation, the drive towards independence on the part of those colonised and the desire of many poor to emulate the economic success of the great powers were all themes that were current in the period after World War II when a new international order was being constructed. Academic thinking was inevitably affected. The economics of development thus evolved as a separate specialism at this time as interest grew in the theories and policies appropriate for LDC growth.

One of the most famous theories to emerge in this era was *The Stages of Economic Growth*, by Walt Rostow (Cambridge, 1960). Rostow identified five key steps or stages that all countries must go through to attain development:

1 *The traditional society*, where nearly all employment is in subsistence agriculture and low living standards prevent much saving and investment.
2 *Establishing preconditions*, where agricultural productivity rises and an entrepreneurial merchant class emerges.
3 *The take-off*, where increasing investment and growth in a leading sector in the country generates enough momentum to lift the whole economy towards:
4 *The drive to maturity*, where success is broadened to include other sectors such that the increased pace of investment and growth becomes self-sustaining.
5 *The age of high mass consumption* is finally achieved where living standards are increased for all.

Rostow's book contains a simple explanation for continuing poverty (see stage 1, above) – a vicious circle where low incomes prevent savings; no savings means no domestic investment; and no investment means no growth of incomes. In addition, it also provides a formula for success: establishing the preconditions in stage 2 leads on to stage 3, to stage 4 and thus 5.

The Stages of Economic Growth was descriptive rather than prescriptive, however. It gave no clear indication of the mechanism of growth and could not predict how such growth would proceed. The different stages involved seemed to follow one another automatically.

A theory of *economic dynamics* was necessary to explain more thoroughly how key variables such as the ratio of savings and investment should interact to produce growth. This was provided in the late 1940s by two economists working independently – Roy Harrod and Evsey Domar – in what has been called the *Harrod–Domar growth model*. Their work, along with Rostow's, inherited the dominant economic philosophy of Keynesianism (see chapter 3) with its focus on macroeconomic aggregates plus it was also witness to the economic power of Stalin's Soviet Union which had been built by massive increases in capital investment (see chapter 2).

The key to growth in the Harrod–Domar model lay in a country's savings ratio (*s*) and in its *incremental capital–output ratio* (ICOR, or more simply *k*). That is, the proportion of national income saved determines a country's flow of funds into investment, and the incremental capital–output ratio determines how much output will grow from this given increase in capital stock (i.e. investment). A country that saves 12 per cent of its income and has a capital-output ratio of 3 can thus have a rate of economic growth equal to $s/k = 12/3 = 4$ per cent.

Post-war development thinking was dominated by these ideas. Both Rostow's work and the Harrod–Domar model emphasised the importance of macro-economic savings and investment ratios. Rostow's book was subtitled: *A Non-Communist Manifesto*, and this indicates its genesis in the Cold War era, where the alternative model for developing countries was the evidently successful (at this time) system of massive, state-directed investment under communist central planning.

The appeal of political independence and, with it, more central government involvement in the management of economic growth was inevitable in this climate. Specialisation in primary product exports was associated with the colonial era and for LDCs emerging from the old European empires, farming and mining were therefore equated with backwardness and neocolonial dependence. Independence for many brought with it the insistence that it should be accompanied by industrialisation and economic self-reliance.

Strategy 2. Import-substituting industrialisation

The workings of an international market system dominated by the big Western nations were distrusted. Governments from Egypt to India, Argentina to Taiwan (then) were empowered to erect barriers against foreign imports, to channel funds into public and private enterprise and generally to promote the rise of domestic industry and skills (ignoring traditional agriculture). Foreign capital was still welcomed in many cases, but restrictions on its use were widespread. Charismatic, popular leaders like Nasser in Egypt, Nehru in India, Peron in Argentina, Sukarno in Indonesia and Mao Tse-tung in China came in on this wave of emerging nationalism.

The economic effects of this change in development strategy were beneficial at first. In addition to large public investments (in heavy industry such as iron and steel works, engineering, construction, railways, etc.), with restrictions on imports there is an immediate incentive for local entrepreneurs to provide all manner of goods and services to the domestic market. The 1950s and 1960s was thus an era of industrialisation, urbanisation, diversifying economies and generally rising incomes for the LDCs.

With internal markets protected, emerging infant industries are guaranteed sales. Employment is thus generated in an expanding range of domestic enterprises which fill the vacuum left by the absence of overseas competitors. The development impact can be very positive: there is much *learning-by-doing* as new skills, new resources and new products to the country are encouraged.

Where foreign capital is employed this may be in the form of joint ventures of local firms with multinational corporations (MNCs). Both benefit: MNCs gain access to a protected market place; local businesses acquire foreign technology and modern managerial techniques.

There is theoretical support for import substitution stategies, too. Almost by definition, the typical less-developed country does not possess perfectly functioning markets that reach across the entire economy. Such market imperfections therefore imply that ruling prices cannot send correct signals to firms and consumers. There may be much latent potential in a LDC's capacity to supply relatively simple manufactured goods (such as basic clothing, food processing, low-tech. machines), for example, but such a comparative advantage may never be developed if LDC prices, market rates of interest and expected rates of return on investment do not reflect this. In particular, there are underdeveloped or missing markets for factors of production. Information for the efficient allocation of capital is lacking; land may be locked up in familial, feudal patterns of ownership; the emergence of entrepreneurs may be obstructed by traditional cultures resistant to change. Limited markets in which an unrepresentative sample of buyers and sellers come together cannot determine prices that allocate society's resources optimally. Profitable investment opportunities may go unrecognised; potentially productive resources may remain undeveloped – especially where substantial external economies exist. (No one manufacturing enterprise will set up in a poor area if local incomes are insufficient to promise many sales, but should a number of different businesses set up together they would generate rising incomes and sufficient trade for all – the employees of one firm becoming the customers of others.)

Price signals from international markets in these circumstances will override national ones. Without protection, with unrestricted access to highly lucrative overseas destinations, a poor country may lose to foreign employments those few resources that are emerging into the money economy. Valued personnel join the 'brain drain'; productive mineral rights are bought up cheaply by MNCs; accumulated savings go in capital flight to offshore financial centres.

The argument for protection, government intervention and regulation of the domestic economy is therefore justified. The conventional 'infant industry' argument (see chapter 5) can be generalised to the whole economy of a LDC. With astute government management a network of young industries can grow; management and labour skills can develop; home-grown technology can evolve until the industrial sector is strong and diversified enough to compete with MDC industry on its own terms – such that continued protection and government allocation of domestic resources becomes redundant.

Government intervention can secure such results, but it need not. Sensitively handled strategic trade policies have been productive in some cases (see chapter 5) but government failure in this regard is, unfortunately, far more common. Import barriers, protective legislation, hand-outs to local firms and direct public ownership and control of domestic industry have more often promoted not the growth of infant industries but their increasing *dependence*.

The absence of foreign competition ensures local businesses can make profits without being strenuously efficient. Worse, entrepreneurs learn that profits are made quickest not by raising quality standards to win sales in competitive markets but by lobbying public officials to get exclusive government contracts; to gain sole rights to import and distribute valued foreign manufactures; and to secure laws that increase protection and confer local monopoly power.

The domestic economy will thus grow and diversify under protection, but – as incomes increase – amongst the business class that benefits most there rises a powerful vested interest in the continuation of these detrimental (to the larger economy) policies. Infant industries therefore never grow up.

Where large state-owned industries make up the manufacturing sector, the pressure to maintain import restrictions and centrally allocated investment comes from within the public sector itself (e.g. in Egypt). Where private industry predominates there may be widespread bribery and corruption of government officials. More subtly, government ministers and top industrialists may graduate from the same restricted elite in society, do business regularly with one another and thus come to grant each other 'favours' on a reciprocal basis (e.g. in India).

The price structure of the domestic economy becomes distorted when government intervention is pervasive. Rather than improving the signalling mechanism, it becomes disabling. Tariffs, quotas and foreign exchange restrictions that are designed to shut out imports can lead to an overvalued currency. Governments subsequently come under pressure from the business class to formally fix the exchange rate at a higher than free-market level – this enables entrepreneurs to purchase cheap foreign capital inputs, yet their sales remain protected from imported consumer goods. Cheap foreign technology, however, means industry now has an incentive to employ more capital than labour. Capital-intensive industrial techniques are unhelpful in LDCs with labour surplus: it reinforces divergent dualism.

In India, for example, growth of industrial output between 1950 and 1970 far outstripped the rate of growth of job creation – the overall capital–labour ratio increased threefold. The efficiency of Indian industry did not similarly improve, however. With the allocation of investment directed by government planning and not via financial markets, industrial growth was the outcome of more and more capital inputs rather than the increasing efficiency of each unit. This Indian experience clearly parallels the dismal performance of Soviet capital as described earlier in chapter 2. Thus India's incremental capital–output ratio rose from around 4 in the early 1960s to 10.5 in 1975 – a damning indictment of its import substitution strategy.

Strategy 3. Free markets and export promotion

Precisely because it was a path-breaking theoretical work, the Harrod–Domar growth model was inevitably a simplification. In particular, reliance on the crude percentage of national income invested as the key to growth placed too

BOX 11.1 TURNING ROUND THE 'PERMIT RAJ'

For over forty years from independence in 1947, the Indian economy followed the Soviet example of excessive government regulation, planning and autarky. For perhaps the best of motives – to limit the polarisation of wealth and poverty – foreign trade and investment was strictly controlled and domestic entrepreneurs were required to gain government permits to invest in any given industry or region, hire and fire any workforce, agree to any price of labour or capital. After years of British colonial administration, the Indians had turned instead to being ruled by the 'permit raj'. As a result, growth stagnated (see Figure 11.1). With snail's pace economic progress almost overtaken by population growth, with the government on the verge of bankruptcy and with the glaringly obvious success stories further east in Asia, the subcontinent embarked in a much-belated change of direction in 1991.

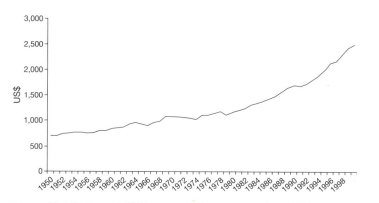

Figure 11.1 India: real GDP per capita in constant prices, 1950–2000. Note partial reforms had increased incomes in the 1980s, only to run out of steam by the end of the decade. The major break with the past was brought in by the government of Prime Minister Rao in June 1991.

With an almost audible sigh of relief pervading the country, regulations were eased, private and foreign investment encouraged, competition fostered, international trade made freer. Economic growth surged through the 1990s and continues to this day. *The McKinsey Quarterly*, a US business journal, reported in June 2005 that annual growth rates 'of 8 to 10 per cent are within reach'. As examples of success, it quotes the Indian airline industry which, from just one state-owned carrier in 1991, now has eight competing airlines and is the world's second-biggest commercial aircraft market; also the car industry which has seen annual domestic sales increase from 150,000 in 1991 to more than a million in 2005. With regard to the service sector, the situation has turned to such an extent that now Western developed nations are becoming increasingly worried by 'outsourcing' – losing domestic business and employment to enterprising Indian competitors who can sell to North American, European and

Australasian markets via efficient telecom links from lower-cost bases within the subcontinent.

To be sure, India is still a relatively low-income country with many problems, but it has many diverse talents also which are at last being released to pursue export markets, trade and growth.

much emphasis on the quantity of capital accumulation rather than its quality. As is evidenced above, after initial successes those nations that had barricaded themselves against world trade and resorted to substantial (and especially centrally directed) investment found their capital productivity falling and thus long-term growth more difficult to achieve.

Import substitution as a development strategy has another weakness too. It distorts internal markets in favour of industrialisation – suppressing farm prices in order to guarantee cheap food for urban labour forces and to divert investment away from agriculture and into industry. When the bulk of LDC populations work and live on the land, however, such policies seem distinctly perverse. Promoting urban industrialisation at the expense of holding down farm incomes is bound to cause dislocation and strife. Rural peoples are forced into the cities in search of better wages, only to end up in ghettos and shanty towns excluded from formal sector employment and straining urban public services beyond their limits.

The industrialisation bias in many LDCs is born of a pessimistic belief that traditional agriculture is inherently backward and has little attraction for modern investment. On closer examination, a number of studies have shown this not to be true. Under the right circumstances, traditional agriculture responds well to market incentives and opportunities for profitable investment are not lacking.

Results from South East Asia and Latin America have shown that in applying new technologies such as high-yield varieties of staple crops, fertilisers and irrigation – all capital-saving rather than labour-saving techniques – agricultural productivity can be rapidly increased. Where peasant farmers are not discriminated against by government policy-makers and where food prices reflect the real costs involved in their production, then the agricultural sector can become an integrated part of the growing LDC economy rather than a forgotten backwater in increasingly dualistic development.

The *neoclassical growth model*, first developed by Robert Solow in 1956, employs these principles mentioned above. The role of flexible market prices, free from any government intervention, is stressed as the prime allocative mechanism. Growth in production is considered as a function of both capital and labour inputs, though each in isolation is characterised by diminishing returns.

The production function illustrated in Figure 11.2 relates the amount of output per person in an economy to the amount of capital employed per person. As capital per head increases at a constant rate: 0, 10, 20, 30, etc. output increases rapidly at first but then progressively slows down: 0, 20, 35, 40, 43,

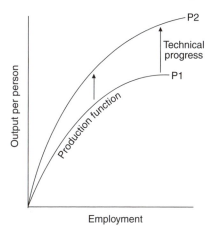

Figure 11.2 Neoclassical growth theory. The diminishing returns on capital employed per head of labour can be shifted by technical progress

etc. This is the principle of diminishing returns – the accumulation of capital becomes less and less productive.

Per capita output can only be improved in the long run by a shift upward in the production function. How is this possible? – by the invention and application of entirely new productive processes: technical change. Thus the production function shifts from P1 to P2. Since increasing capital inputs secures steadily decreasing additional outputs, the neoclassical model therefore identifies technical progress as the only means to shift the production function over time. In addition, it should be noted that this model does not discriminate between agriculture and industry in their respective capacities to generate growth through the application of new technology. Both sectors are assumed capable of responding to new products and processes.

Solow's model was an important contribution to the understanding of the processes of economic growth – but its most annoying conclusion was that growth was mostly secured by a factor, technical progress, which was assumed exogenous and unexplained. Growth was explained by the unexplainable! Where does technical progress come from?

It took another thirty years for Paul Romer to make the next breakthrough in 1986 and devise the *endogenous growth model*. One reason it took so long was Romer had to dispense with one of the basic tenets of economics – that of the principle of diminishing returns – in order to explain growth paths that would not slow down.

'Endogenous' growth demonstrates that success breeds success. If a country can get the conditions right it will find that the only factor of production that is *not* in short supply is creative enterprise. In fact, although the effort and investment required to make one technological advance may be considerable (say, to build an electronic calculator) the investment required to copy it and apply its use elsewhere is very little. By the same token, once creative imagination is engendered in society its rewards can be unlimited.

Note, the returns derived by a given company from its investment in one specific innovation may diminish over time – but they can be almost limitless to a wider world which learns to use the idea. Individual companies that developed ballpoint pens, hovercraft, computers, mobile phones may go broke – but the economic growth these ideas liberate for other companies and countries may have no limit.

The reason technical progress occurs and why it is more productive in some countries than others has led to a number of hypotheses. Recent thinking emphasises the need for investment in *human* capital – especially promoting education and the unrestricted competition in ideas and their application to industry. But this is not enough. The structure of social relations and the institutions upon which markets are based are found to be of crucial importance – no creativity will be released unless individuals can be assured they can organise production, increase trade and enjoy its rewards free from arbitrary appropriation by princes or pirates. Laws of contract, secure property rights and low transactions costs are essential to facilitate trade and to build an entrepreneurial culture that is willing to undertake the risks involved in technological research.

This is problematic for a developing county point of view. How can countries emulate innovative cultures such as are found in dynamic science and technology parks, 'silicon glens' and certain private–public partnerships? The fact is that that some countries have succeeded at some times in this respect – but others not. More research is needed on the delicate and fugitive nature of how to institute entrepreneurial and technological success.

BOX 11.2 THE INFORMAL SECTOR AND PROPERTY RIGHTS

In most Latin American cities a large informal sector can be observed that coexists alongside the modern market economy. Small-scale, informal business activity such as street vending, the production of clothing, fast food, handicrafts and the provision of a multitude of ingenious services all take place outside the reach of the law. It is a trade that goes officially unrecognised, untaxed, unregulated and unprotected.

It is none the less enterprising. For example, Pepe was the smiling, helpful owner of a small kiosk in Santiago. He sold food and drink – some of which he made himself, some of which he traded for elsewhere. He could turn his hand to almost any task you requested and that which he could not fix himself he always knew another who could.

Pepe lived in a place mostly built by his own hand. This is hardly unusual. Informal-sector properties – self-made, semi-permanent residences – have grown up to house small traders and their businesses and they dot most urban landscapes in all less developed countries. You can find them on almost any plot of unclaimed land – under motorway bridges, alongside rivers and railway lines, behind formal-sector factories and shopping centres and particularly clustered together in well-recognised suburbs or shanty towns from Mexico City to Buenos Aires, from Recife to Managua.

The output of such informal-sector enterprise can form a large part of a country's gross domestic product and can gainfully employ millions of otherwise destitute people. For example, data from Central America in the mid-1990s showed that the informal sector accounted for between 40 per cent and 60 per cent of total urban employment. Additionally, skills and business acumen are passed on which not only provide the economy with an important resource base but at almost no cost to the public purse.

Regrettably, however, the informal sector is no springboard for economic development. Shanty towns have been more or less permanent features of too many LDC townscapes for too long. Businesses remain small, vulnerable and technologically primitive and their owners and employees have *not* experienced rising *per capita* incomes over time. So why cannot such a dynamic, enterprising and efficient employer of resources (scarce capital is typically recycled and nothing is wasted in these businesses) act as a spur to the development and growth of the domestic economy as a whole?

The reason why industrial and commercial development seems to get stuck at this low level is tied up with the reason why the informal sector exists in the first place. People have to build their own informal homes and businesses if they cannot get legal title to them. In Lima, for example, a research team headed by economist Hernando de Soto estimated that it cost over US$1,200 and took ten months to start up a legally recognised small clothing factory. Government officials requested bribes four times to expedite the process. Other researchers found that the bureaucracy required to register a business which took only three and a half hours in Florida, varied from a month in some places (Chile, Brazil and Bolivia) to two years in others (Guatemala).

In addition to start-up costs, formal-sector enterprise is costly to run. In poor countries with a limited tax base, government revenues are particularly dependent on direct and indirect business taxes (i.e. high rates of corporation tax and VAT). State regulation and bureaucracy are also particularly punitive – minimum wage legislation, social security laws and controls over the hiring and firing of personnel increase labour costs on average by 20 per cent over the cost of informal labour. Where is the incentive, therefore, for the individual entrepreneur to enter the formal sector?

But though it is easy to enter, the informal sector may be a developmental dead end. Where central government cannot provide a stable institutional environment to establish and protect property rights, enforce compliance with contracts and fairly administer the law in civil disputes the risk of investing in business becomes prohibitive. In modern capitalist market economies, for example, an entrepreneur can raise a mortgage on his property, invest the capital so gained, conduct his business and then pocket the profit left over from paying off his creditors. As an informal, legally unrecognised occupier of property in a Latin American city, however, this process cannot even begin. No bank or private creditor will loan money without collateral. And if – at a high price – capital could be found to invest in the first place, who would then guarantee that any business deal agreed outside the law would be fulfilled?

Pepe's enterprise in Santiago came to an abrupt end. After a while the small stock of resources he built up for his kiosk became the target of others envious of his success. With no protection in law he took up arms to defend it himself but someone got killed in the fight, Pepe was imprisoned and his business collapsed. The moral of the story is that modern economies are built on legally recognised and enforceable property rights and no informal sector will develop very far without them.

It should be noted that neither the endogenous growth model, nor the earlier neoclassical growth model upon which it was based were formulated with LDCs specifically in mind. These theories assume the existence of fully functioning markets already.

With undeveloped resources and limited native enterprise and experience in the immediate post-war period, such growth models are not appropriate for newly independent countries starting out from low levels of income and development. As mentioned above, these nations inevitably chose to eschew relying on private markets and instead followed a government-led, import substitution strategy. Very few LDCs opted to go a different path – to promote a private-enterprise driven, export-oriented economy with internal markets open to international prices. Nonetheless, neoclassical economists have claimed that those few nations that have embraced these policies have earned the greater rewards.

THE ASIAN DRAGONS

It is argued that the remarkable economic successes of certain newly industrialising countries (NICS), and particularly the 'Asian dragons' or 'tigers' of South Korea, Taiwan, Hong Kong and Singapore, illustrate the potency and relevance of free-market economics. There is no doubt that these four countries had an impressive growth record prior to 1997 (see Figure 11.3) – how far this

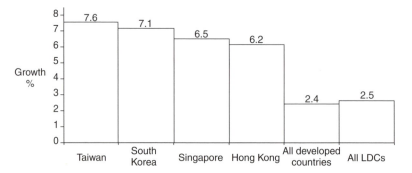

Figure 11.3 Average growth in GNP per capita, 1965–90 (except Taiwan, 1965–88)
Source: World Bank.

can be attributed to the pursuit of neoclassical economic policies, however, needs to be examined. The average growth rates in per capita incomes in these four countries is given below for the period 1965–90. The figures show that these countries outperformed any other nation or group of nations on the globe for well over a quarter of a century.

These four 'dragons' have all since the 1960s followed a strategy of export promotion – actively seeking to exploit their comparative advantage in international trade in order to gain foreign sales for their expanding range of manufactures. Beginning with specialising in labour-intensive, relatively low-tech products, all four sought to gain increasing investment in higher value-added production processes: exporting more and more sophisticated, greater income-earning goods and services.

Although the broad outlines of this growth strategy are the same for all four countries, the details differ. Consider firstly the characteristics shown in Table 11.4.

Hong Kong and Singapore are both city states that act as offshore entrepôts and commercial centres for their surrounding regions. South Korea and Taiwan, in contrast, are altogether bigger countries with significant agricultural sectors. The development process in these two nations had therefore to take rural interests into account – and as a result they are more instructive exemplars for other LDCs.

An agricultural transformation took place throughout East Asia after World War II with the implementation of various *land reforms*. Note that in all pre-industrial societies land is the major form of wealth and source of political power and prestige. Land tenure systems institutionalise the political, economic and sociological character of a country – determining the individual's rights, duties, liberties, the parameters of family life, the class system and the role of the state. Undertaking land reform, therefore, means changing all this.

Land reforms generally take place for political rather than economic reasons – in China it took place with a bloody communist revolution. In Japan, South Korea and Taiwan it followed American occupation as a means of dispossessing the Japanese ruling class which had supported the imperial war against the USA. In the cases of the former Japanese colonies of South Korea and Taiwan, therefore, it brought about a major transformation from cultivation by poor

Table 11.4 The Asian 'dragons', selected data

	South Korea	*Taiwan*	*Hong Kong*	*Singapore*
Population (1999) (m)	43.7	20.8	5.8	2.8
Geographical area (000 sq km)	99	36	1	1
GDP (1999) US$ bn PPP	693.6	446.7	144	81
Real GDP per person (1999)	10,451	12,845	17,844	18,400
Foreign trade* as % of GDP (1999)	77	93	261	358 (1995)

Sources: World Bank, Economist Intelligence Unit.

Note: *Includes re-exports.

tenants on large, Japanese-owned land holdings to a system of owner occupation on smaller-scale indigenous farms. Agricultural surpluses were now not transferred abroad to Japanese overlords but were available for domestic incomes, consumption and investment.

In *Korea* during the 1930s, two-thirds of all rice production was expropriated by Japan. This was indicative of the colonial structure of the economy up until the outbreak of World War II. Following the cessation of hostilities and the division of the country in 1945 into rival Soviet and American-supported zones, the southern half found itself with over 60 per cent of the population, 70 per cent of the rice-growing lands, much of the (then) light industry, but almost none of the heavy industry and power generation capacity. The one notable achievement in the politically turbulent period immediately following the war was the US administered land reform which redistributed cultivable land from large foreign and domestic owners to small (maximum 3 hectares) holdings. Scarcely had the US handed over control to a South Korean administration, however, when a new war erupted.

The Korean War lasted from 1950 to 1953, was fought mainly on southern territory and consequently left the south economically devastated. Half of the country's manufacturing infrastructure was destroyed. The country survived at first on US aid whilst it set about rebuilding. Imports were restricted in this period, exports were insignificant and confined mostly to primary products. Trade deficits were baled out by US aid but the currency became over valued and shortages of essential consumer and capital goods became more and more apparent. Agricultural output, however – based on the successful land reform – recovered rapidly to achieve historically record growth rates of 3.5 per cent p.a. from 1952 on.

The major change to an outward-looking, export-promoting economy took root with the incoming military administration of General Park Chung Hee in 1961. The Korean currency, the won, was devalued in order to cheapen the price of exports; interest rates rose (to encourage savings and limit inflation); and although a battery of import controls was maintained, exporters were given tax-free access to required foreign inputs.

South Korea grew up with a substantial defence force – essential for its security but a significant financial burden – and a military government that took an active part in all economic decision-making. It was thus by government decision – not free-market forces – that Korea sought to promote a variety of export industries. Textiles, clothing and the assembly of electronic equipment can be argued as obvious candidates to exploit the country's comparative advantage in relatively cheap, skilled labour industries. Shipbuilding, steel and high-volume car production, however, are heavy, capital-intensive processes that all grew from infant industries to become world beaters due to government planning and massive and continuing financial support.

Korea's rate of growth of income and rate of growth of manufacturing exports from the 1960s right through the oil price-induced recessions of the late 1970s and the debt-stricken 1980s is truly remarkable. It owed much to the country's ability to sniff out foreign markets and its flexibility to change products and destinations as world consumer demand shifted. Despite occasional mistakes, this ability was not found only amongst private entrepreneurs but also in government planners. The partnership between public and private sectors was very successful in the South Korean case – right up until the late 1990s . . .

One particular feature of Korea's emerging economy was to prove poisonous, however. Industrial conglomerates, or *chaebol*, evolved to dominate the manufacturing sector – business empires that produced everything from initial inputs to a wide variety of goods and services; from steel and gas to cars and electronic products. Key to the growth of these enterprises were private banks and financial houses that could secure the loan capital which funded their expansion. Unfortunately, the cosy relationships these banks enjoyed with their oligopolistic rivals and with the central authorities meant that the financial markets did not operate with the competition and scrupulous efficiency that characterised individual production lines of the manufacturing units.

The Asian financial crisis (see chapter 10) hit Korea far harder than the other four 'dragons' – which did not possess the same industrial and financial market structure. Although Korea is in the process of bouncing back strongly from its 1997 crash, the deep-rooted reform of its economy is still incomplete. Korean 'miracle growth' will not return on a secure footing until this is accomplished.

Taiwan's economic development was even more solidly based in agriculture than South Korea's. This was begun during Japanese rule in the 1930s when, with the purpose of feeding the imperial homeland, much technical progress was achieved in agriculture – irrigated farmlands were extended; application of fertiliser became widespread and high-yield strains of rice and sugar cane were introduced.

The Japanese administration ended in 1945 and in the post-war period Taiwan received over a million refugees from the communist revolution in China. A sweeping land reform – as in South Korea – and the determined efforts of the new government to raise food production to feed the increasing population led to another leap in agricultural productivity. Annual growth rates reached 9 per cent in the early 1950s.

As a result of increasing agricultural output, rural wages rose faster than urban wages at this time. Industry specialised in dispersed, relatively small-scale labour-intensive enterprises. A growing agricultural surplus meant a healthy rural market expanded for industrial goods, meanwhile allowing labour and capital to increasingly transfer from the farms to the cities.

A cautious, protectionist regime dependent on foreign aid and traditional agricultural exports thus gradually came round to support a strategy of promoting manufacturing exports: the Taiwanese dollar was heavily devalued and foreign exchange restrictions eased.

Throughout the 1960s exports increased dramatically as manufactures were kept internationally competitive by the low cost of Taiwanese labour. This was ensured, however, less by the operation of flexible labour markets than by a dominant government determined to ban strikes and minimise protective labour legislation. The expansion of trade continued through the 1970s and showed – as in the case of South Korea – the country's ability to react quickly to changing world markets. As incomes rose, and richer countries protested about Taiwanese continued protectionism, the government instituted liberalising reforms – cutting back on tariffs and quotas – and encouraged more value-added, higher-skill products. The economy remains diverse, integrated, internally and internationally competitive and responsive both to changing government and consumer demands. It is one of the few East Asian nations not to have suffered greatly from the region's financial contagion that soured the end of the twentieth century.

Hong Kong and *Singapore*, while both island city-states which function as offshore industrial and financial centres serving regional and world markets, have a widely contrasting political economy. One is the product of an almost archetypal laissez-faire society – chaotic, vibrant and ever-changing – but with a future now tied into the destiny of the communist-ruled Chinese mainland. The other is a very closely managed economy where the government intervenes in almost all aspects of social behaviour from the length of hair to the size of families and the freedom of foreign press. Both countries have little in the way of natural resources but have successfully exploited their geographical position and their native enterprise to achieve sustained economic growth based on manufacturing exports and re-exports and, increasingly now, financial services. Despite the financial storms that have buffeted the region – and inevitably affected their balance sheets – these two trading economies have the wit and wisdom to endure the worst and recover quickly afterwards.

CONCLUSION

Was the success of these Asian dragons due to neoclassical economic policies, therefore? Not entirely. It is too simplistic to argue that growth is the natural result of liberalising markets. The unregulated price mechanism takes the underlying institutional structure of an economy as given, and in the circumstances of underdeveloped or missing markets, inadequate infrastructure and a grossly unequal distribution of wealth then implementing neoclassical policies can create more problems than they solve.

Free markets in LDCs can be characterised by *positive feedback*: the rich are able to reinvest their surplus income and thereby become richer; while poorer peoples are locked into a vicious cycle of poverty, insufficient savings and no growth. Only by direct intervention to remodel the economy's institutional foundations can the preconditions for free-market growth be established.

Putting productive resources at the disposal of local entrepreneurs who have a direct interest in raising outputs and efficiency will not happen through laissez-faire – it requires central command. This same principle applies to South Korean and Taiwanese land reforms as it does now to widening the access to share capital and reforming the cronyism of many LDC financial markets. There is no ducking government responsibilities here – if the institutional transformation is botched, then the benefits will not accrue to the wider economy but to a privileged few who may have little incentive to spread the rewards any wider.

The provision of essential public infrastructure is something the free market cannot produce. Road, rail and air transport networks must be provided by governments, as well as education and health services which all confer extensive external benefits.

Secure property rights and laws of contract to protect trade, to allow the orderly closure of failing business and the transfer of capital to growing ones are essential. Legal institutions are the means to build honesty and trust which are in turn essential business virtues that facilitate long-term investment in the future.

Where the supply of educated entrepreneurs is limited (especially in the earlier stages of development) then co-opting them to the service of the state in ministerial planning commissions can prove successful in Japan, South Korea and Singapore – though whether this is a recipe that will work over long periods of time or outside of East Asia is uncertain.

On closer examination, therefore, the Asian dragons do not provide unqualified support for neoclassical economics. The direction of strong government has been much in evidence. But, having said this, *the direction in which all have moved has been increasingly to liberalise markets once the foundations for growth have been laid.* Ensuring realistic prices operate throughout the economy is the first important policy common to these countries. Four prices in particular deserve mention: the price of agricultural products, the price of labour, the external exchange rate – these are essential to ensure the integration and not the dislocation of the farm sector, the application of appropriate capital-saving and not labour-saving technologies, and the international competitiveness of exports – and interest rates must be correctly priced too: to attract savings, discourage capital flight and to inhibit inflationary expansion of money supplies.

Economic development is not something that can then be left to laissez-faire, therefore. Sensitive management of a growing economy is something that will always be necessary – firstly, in parenting infant industries; secondly, in providing effective public infrastructure; and, thirdly, in policing fair and competitive goods and financial markets. Resources are allocated between various employments and between a country's present and future needs according to the prices which rule. It is on this issue ultimately that a successful and flexible market economy is built.

It may be that in LDCs, markets are insufficiently, imperfectly developed. They thus send the wrong signals and, without corrective management, will promote sub-optimal, distortionary results. Monopolistic vested interests, a polarised society and a crippled economy can be the outcome. The solution here, however, is not to suspend the market system but to improve and develop it. The experience of the Asian dragons – both through their long period of growth and their (shorter) time of crisis – teaches us is that in the developing world we need more, not less, market enterprise . . . and that its supervision can never be relaxed.

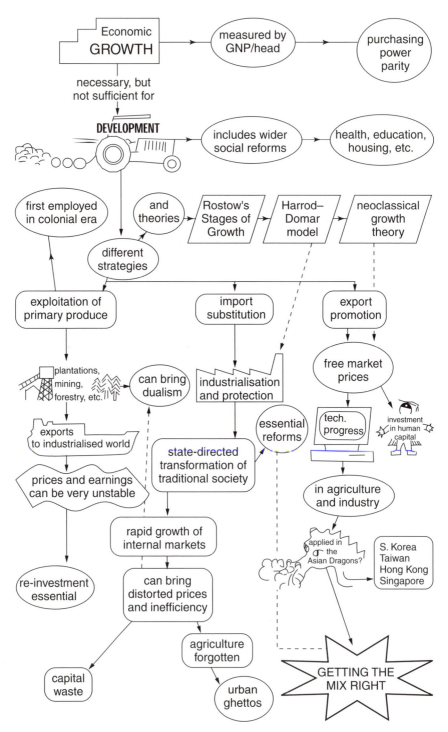

Figure 11.4 The themes of chapter 11

KEY WORDS

Economic dynamics studies the behaviour of variables through time – especially whether they move towards or away from a state of equilibrium. Dynamics can be contrasted with **comparative statics** which considers the balance of variables at a given time period, changes one key variable and then compares the result.

The gold standard operated successfully before World War I when trading countries fixed their currencies to a given weight of gold. Any country's citizen could thus convert their banknotes into gold on demand. In international trade, if a country suffered a balance of payments deficit it would pay what it owed in gold. The subsequent loss of gold reserves meant domestic money supplies would have to contract, otherwise the central bank would have insufficient to maintain convertibility and meet customers' demand. The automatic deflation of the economy this caused could be relied upon to cure the trade deficit. The volume and pattern of world trade in these days was relatively small and uncomplicated; supplies of gold were sufficient to clear the required sums of international indebtedness; and defending fixed exchange rates by forced deflation was not politically costly.

Harrod–Domar growth model An early theory of economic growth derived from Keynesian analysis. It emphasised the importance of entrepreneurs' investment plans: if they guessed right it would result in a balanced rate of growth for the economy; if they guessed wrong it could lead to either spiralling inflation or deepening unemployment. There was no inherent tendency in an economy to attain balanced growth. Key variables in this theory were the *savings ratio* – which determined the flow of funds available for investment – and the *incremental capital–output ratio* which measured the increase in a country's output secured by a given increase in its investment. Both variables were assumed given by the nature of the economy.

Monocultures describes economies that are dependent on the production and export of one principal good.

The neoclassical growth model differed from the above in assuming flexible savings and capital-output ratios, like all prices, according to the markets concerned. Economic growth is characterised by stable equilibrium, therefore, unlike the unstable knife-edge that predicts accelerating inflation or unemployment as in the Harrod–Domar model. A key finding is that the neoclassical equilibrium growth path can be shifted by technical progress. **Endogenous growth theory** developed this line further by explaining how technology could be stimulated and how, in turn, this promoted further growth in a virtuous circle.

Positive feedback A term borrowed from physics where an increase in output reinforces the increase in input. For example, the richer you get, the more you can invest and the richer you get. This contrasts with *negative feedback* which would apply if governments could impose (successfully) steeply progressive income taxes – then the richer you get, the more you have to pay in tax and thus the growth in incomes of the richest slows. (If governments can redistribute tax incomes to the poor, the gap between rich and poor should narrow – and not widen – over time.)

Purchasing power parity A way to measure the value of currencies that takes into account their real worth in the countries concerned – that is, in terms of what money can buy. For example, if one dollar can buy the same sample of goods and services in country X as 100 pesos in country Y then the exchange rate is $1 = 100 pesos measured on a purchasing power parity basis. The actual rate ruling in foreign exchange markets may vary a long way from this, according to the demand and supply of the two currencies concerned.

Quasi-rents   are rents that are comparatively short-lived, due to the rise – after a time lag – of other competing suppliers who bid prices/earnings down in their desire to get into the market and make the same surplus as the original seller.

Rent   is the income received by the unique owner of resources that are fixed in supply but much in demand. Although the term is commonly applied to payments made by tenants to landlords for the use of their property, in economics it is defined more narrowly as the surplus enjoyed above costs by the monopoly owner of any resource.

QUESTIONS

1   What is meant by 'development'? What may developing countries: (a) gain; (b) lose in promoting rapid economic growth in pursuit of modern, Western standards of living?
2   What policies would you recommend to secure the development of a relatively poor but unexplored region, rich in timber and mineral resources and populated only by indigenous peoples?
3   Compare, contrast and evaluate the Harrod–Domar and neoclassical growth theories in terms of: (a) what causes economic growth; and (b) what government policies they recommend.
4   What are the similarities and differencies between the 'Asian Dragons' in the strategies they employed to achieve steady economic growth? Have they anything to teach any other countries?
5   Contrast the role of central government and free markets in promoting economic development. Which is more prone to failure?

FURTHER READING

North, D. 'Economic performance through time', *American Economic Review*, 84, June 1994, pp. 359–68.
Olson, M. 'Big bills left on the sidewalk: why some nations are rich and others poor', *Journal of Economic Perspectives*, 10 (2), 1996, pp. 3–24.

12 Environmental economics: sustaining spaceship earth

Topics to be considered in this chapter:

- Economic growth and sustainable development.
- Readjusting the price mechanism.
- Optimal depletion rates of exhaustible and renewable resources.
- Government policies to safeguard the environment.
- Measuring the value of environmental resources.

INTRODUCTION

If you listen to some people, in the future we are all destined to gloom and doom:

- Way back in 1798, Thomas Malthus predicted – on the observation of incompatible trends in population and food growth in the new American colonies – that humankind could not escape everlasting poverty.
- Some hundred years later, at the beginning of the twentieth century, it was predicted that at existing growth rates of horse-drawn traffic, central London within thirty years would be knee-high in manure and all transport would come sliding (ugh!) to a halt.
- In 1972, D. H. Meadows and others published *The Limits to Growth* in which it was claimed that at existing rates of exploitation the world would run out of oil, other essential minerals and thus the basis for continuing growth by the year 2000.

All these predictions were based on observable growth trends of their time and all have been proved wrong. Why? Because extrapolating existing trends always assumes that things do not change . . . and of course they always do. Like the wedding speeches of Hollywood film stars, economists should bear in mind Sam Goldwyn's maxim: 'Never prophesy; especially about the future . . .'

Experience shows that the price mechanism can provide an effective means to protect the environment. Take the issue of allegedly finite oil reserves. As was shown in chapter 9, when economies grow the demand for energy and oil-based products (such as plastics) will grow with them. Increasing demand for scarce supplies will force up prices – at an accelerating rate as stocks are depleted. This will cause consumers to modify their demands and simultaneously make it profitable for producers to seek out alternative energy supplies. The history of oil prices and outputs shows that, despite the imperfections of this particular market place, increases in prices do call forth greater efforts to search out new oil fields; more efficient and less wasteful technologies to produce oil; increased consumer concern to economise on fuel use; and increased research and development of alternative energy supplies, battery-powered cars, solar-heating panels, etc. Oil prices at the end of the 1990s were lower in real terms than they were twenty years earlier, indicating less relative scarcity, and they can be expected to rise again and fall again in the new millennium as cyclical shortages and surpluses respond to these signals. Although a potentially exhaustible natural asset, oil will continue to be an important energy source long into the twenty-first century.

The most important single reason why certain doom and gloom predictions about the environment have therefore failed to be realised is that the market system employs a remarkably sophisticated and flexible control mechanism – prices – that urges people to change their (environmentally damaging) practices.

The most important single reason, however, that there is a growing environmental crisis is that not all natural resources have a market price. Many environmental goods essential for a decent quality of life have no price – they are *free goods* – and are thus being used to excess. There is no market incentive to economise on their use. In the absence of any other regulation, we can predict that those natural assets which have no price (e.g. clean air, including the ozone layer) will be used up and/or polluted the fastest. Other resources (e.g. fossil fuels, whales, hardwoods) possess positive market prices which are too low, reflecting only private costs of production and not their full environmental and social costs (such as the need to clean up oil spillage, conserve rare species, protect unique and fast-disappearing habitats). In these cases, rates of exploitation will be greater than the environment can sustain.

This point needs emphasising. Provision of most goods and services involves costs to the producer which are internalised in the prices they charge in the market place, and costs to the society at large which are external to this process. For example, in an unregulated market system car users will only pay directly for those internal costs such as fuel, depreciation and the loss of time and energy involved in driving. They will not pay for most of the damage inflicted on others by increased pollution, traffic jams, road accidents and the replacement of rural areas by the ugliness of motorised landscapes. These are the external costs imposed on society. And they will continue to rise so long as market prices fail to reflect this important component of real costs.

ADJUSTING THE MARKET MECHANISM

It is because in the past market systems have failed to value natural resources adequately to include all external, environmental costs that economic growth – especially of the most developed nations – has been seen as at the expense of the long-term health of the planet. Some critics have argued, therefore, that growth and the capitalist market system that drives it are to blame. But, on the contrary, if we are underpricing our valuable natural assets then this is an argument for more market operation, not less. (There is plenty of evidence from Eastern Europe and the old Soviet Union that the opposite extreme from the free-market economy – command systems – are far less environmentally friendly. The nuclear catastrophe that was Chernobyl, for example, polluted half a continent. See chapter 2.)

Economic growth need not impoverish the planet. Increased awareness of the interdependence of all living things and the fragility of this relationship is urging the pursuit of *sustainable development* – where we pass on to future generations at least as much environmental wealth as we inherited ourselves.

The analysis of sustainable development requires us to widen and to redefine our understanding of the economic process. For example, in neoclassical theory, economic efficiency is at the heart of the subject. This can be defined in terms of maximising profitability in the production process and maximising utility in consumption; subject in both cases to budget constraints. Thus efficiency is gained in the market economy if producers switch to processes that yield more per dollar spent on inputs and if households switch purchases to commodities yielding more per dollar spent on consumption. That is, if you have only a fixed amount of money at your disposal, spending any of this scarce resource on items that yield less rewards than others is uneconomic. It is through the measuring-rod of prices that you can determine more efficient, less wasteful allocations of your resources. Producers will decide which are the most cost-effective raw materials and technologies to employ; consumers will decide which combination of goods and services yields most satisfaction.

The problem with the traditional, neoclassical outlook is that it takes no account of the long-term sustainability of this economic process. US economist Kenneth Boulding wrote a path-breaking essay in 1966 in which he argued that the West should stop acting as if it were in a cowboy economy with limitless frontiers and start behaving as if we were all passengers on spaceship earth where maintaining its life-support system is of paramount importance.

The signalling price mechanism needs to embrace not only private profit- and utility-maximisation but also environmental sustainability. Standards of living can only be guaranteed in the future if rates of growth of production and consumption do not exceed the environment's capacity to support them.

Readjusting the price mechanism to reflect humankind's multi-dimensional relationship with the environment is a complex business. Consider the following model:

1 Economic activity begins with primary industry and the creation of resources direct from the environment – mineral extraction, farming and fishing.
2 These resources are processed in secondary or manufacturing industry and converted into finished goods and services which are then distributed to the market place for final consumption.
3 Consumption of goods and services provides utility, which leads to increasing standards of living.

1 Resources → 2 Production → 3 Consumption → Utility

At all stages through this process there is the creation of waste. This occurs in many forms: 1a in primary production with oil spillages; slag heaps; the burning of agricultural stubble, and the discarding of non-commercial animal and fish products; 2a in manufacturing and distribution with spent materials, exhaust gases and depreciated capital; 3a in consumption with the disposal of rubbish and the generation of litter.

1 Resources → 2 Production → 3 Consumption → Utility
        ↓   ↓   ↓

        1a   2a   3a

As final products yield their utility over time they are all eventually wasted – some more quickly than others. A newspaper becomes waste paper after a day or so; a car passes more slowly over the years into burnt rubber, scrap metal and carbon monoxide. Thanks to the first law of thermodynamics we can say that the sum of waste products at each stage of the production/consumption process above precisely equals the total value of the original resources:

$$\text{Resources} = \text{Waste} = 1a + 2a + 3a$$

What happens to the waste? Some of it is recycled. This depends on technological abilities and thus the commercial viabliity of recycling. We can predict that if resources become scarcer and more expensive and technology cheaper then the percentage of waste that is recycled back into production will increase. But according to the second law of thermodynamics we can never approach 100 per cent recyclability since a fraction of energy and matter will always be dissipated in any production process.

Much waste is destined to be dumped back into the environment, therefore. Crucial here is the environment's capacity to assimilate that waste. If waste accumulation exceeds this *assimilative capacity* then we shall damage the environment. Rivers will become polluted, the air foul and the landscape littered.

This decreases our utility directly since people derive pleasure from the natural world – in leisure pursuits, sightseeing, just sitting in front of the television or reading books about it – and it also further impairs the environment's productivity in generating future resources.

We can thus devise a closed, interactive environmental model (see Figure 12.1) to replace the neoclassical view of economic activity. According to this model, the environment is linked to the economic system in three ways:

- as a supplier of resources;
- as an assimilator of waste;
- and as a provider of aesthetic utility.

Economic growth needs the environment and can only be sustainable in the long run if mechanisms exist to restrict economic activity that is harmful to it and promote such activity that is beneficial. Before looking more closely at policies to adjust the relevant mechanisms, however, we need firstly to consider what we are trying to achieve: which activities are environmentally acceptable and which are not? How exactly do we define sustainable development?

SUSTAINABLE DEVELOPMENT – HOW MUCH CAN THE EARTH TAKE?

The Brundtland Report for the World Commission on Environment and Development (1987) defined this as 'development that meets the needs of the present without compromising the ability of future generations to meet their own needs'.

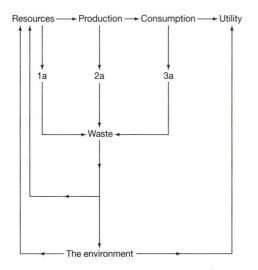

Figure 12.1 The relationship between economic activity and the environment

A number of implications follow from this statement. Firstly, waste generated from the production/consumption process must be kept at a level equal or below the assimilative capacity of the environment. Secondly, the rate of use or harvest of renewable natural resources such as forest hardwoods, fishing stocks, etc. must be equal to or below the *natural regeneration rate*.

It should be emphasised that these assimilative and regenerative rates are not constant. Atmospheres, seas, rivers and landscapes have a tolerance threshold which can lower over time. Alternatively, such capacities can be augmented by the application of man-made capital: fertilisers improve land productivity; air and water can be cleaned. In any equilibrium between economic activity and the environment, therefore, constant monitoring of rates of assimilation and regeneration is necessary and waste disposal and harvesting rates should be adjusted accordingly. Analysis of what constitutes an acceptable harvest rate of renewable resources is explored in more detail further below.

A third consideration is exhaustible resources. Differentiating between these and renewable resources is easy enough in theory but in practice the margin between them is blurred. Mineral resources such as oil and coal are the product of geological processes over millions of years and are clearly exhaustible and non-regenerative in human time-horizons. But what about native habitats like wetlands or tropical rainforests? Forests can be harvested and are renewable, but to what extent is the extraction of hardwoods, even at tolerably slow rates, destructive of a unique natural habitat? A precious ecological balance can easily be disturbed and thus permanently impaired. There are grounds for treating certain such habitats as exhaustible resources.

It is important to emphasise, however, that *all economic activity is to some extent dependent on the use of exhaustible resources.* The evolution of humankind and civilisation has been fuelled by them. If sustainable development is defined as maintaining the same physical stock of earth's resources into the future it therefore means exploiting no further non-renewable assets. But this means no more economic development is possible today, nor – by the same argument – will it be possible tomorrow.

Clearly this is too excessive a requirement. It is hardly consistent with 'meeting the needs of the present'. Exhaustible resources are indeed environmentally irreplaceable, but they are irreplaceable also as supporters of *human* environments. Coal and oil provide essential energy; land is used for housing; forests are cleared for agriculture. Each economic act destructive of the environment yields benefits as well as costs.

Insisting on maintaining a constant natural capital stock into the future ignores, furthermore, the possibility of substituting renewable for exhaustible resources; man-made capital for natural capital.

Consider an example: I am reminded that Roman roads through the English Lake District follow the mountain ridges. Why is this? Why do they not follow the valley bottoms like modern roads? The Romans built their routes on the mountain tops – at considerable expense we can only guess – because it was even more difficult to navigate the valley bottoms which were then carpeted with thick forests. (Exactly the same economic practices were followed over a thousand years later by the early settlers in New England, USA.) Native forests are an exhaustible resource.They have been replaced in their entirety in the UK by town and village, farmland and open moor. The former are undoubtedly an irretrievable loss, but the latter are not without attraction, as any visitor to the Lake District will confirm. In the meantime, the exploitation of native forests throughout the UK helped transform the country into the world's first modern, industrial economy.

The important conclusion from this example is that as exhaustible resources are depleted their reduced stock can to a considerable extent be compensated for by increases in renewable resources and man-made capital.

Finally, technological progress is directly concerned with getting more from less – on economising on the use of our natural inheritance. Engines are more and more fuel-efficient in our cars, homes and power stations. Energy can be generated far more cheaply from clean gas than coal and far more efficiently than from burning the wood and charcoal that led to much of Britain's deforestation in the past. Today, countries use far fewer exhaustible resources to produce one unit of GNP than they did a century ago and they will no doubt use far less in the future than they do now.

All these considerations indicate that preserving the existing physical stock of natural resources for future generations is neither practicable nor appropriate. Sustainable development must always involve some consumption of exhaustible resources alongside continuing technical progress and increasing substitution of other assets.

The relevant questions to ask are, therefore, what rates of exploitation of natural resources are acceptable? How much do we want to raise GNP now as compared to the future? At what environmental cost? Or conversely, how much do we want to conserve the planet? At what cost to our current versus future needs?

Before analysing these issues related to the rates of exploitation of renewable and non-renewable resources, there are a number of reasons for proceeding with extreme caution when attempting to value natural assets:

- *Irreversibility*. There is the possibility of doing irreversible damage to the planet – for example the destruction of habitat; extinction of species; desertification and climate change. If we make a mistake, very often we do not know how to reverse it. The costs involved here are large and stretch over all time. They involve not only what is lost but also the forgone opportunity of what might have been.
- *Uncertainty*. The distinctive feature of natural environments is the wealth of interconnected detail – such that a small change in a fragile ecological equilibrium can have a myriad of unpredictable outcomes over space and time. Our scientific knowledge is limited and the natural world reminds us that it will ever be so. We are uncertain as to the role of the ocean currents in climate determination; we cannot safely predict all the environmental effects of constructing dams and redirecting waterways; it is impossible to

trace the final destinations of all waste materials disposed. The borderline between sustainable economic practices and tipping the balance over into cumulative environmental degradation can in practice be difficult to detect until too late. And note that the unpredictability of outcomes can impact on areas far removed from the scene of the original activity: smoke from British chimneys kills fish in Scandinavian lakes; Syrian dams deplete Iraqi waterways; northern hemisphere pollution holes Antarctic ozone layers.

• *Increasing public concern.* Over time, as nations develop and incomes, education and public consciousness improve, so demands for environmental protection and conservation increase. The controversial fact here is that environmental degradation is only a cost if people care about it. And wealthier nations care more in the sense that they are willing to pay more for conservation. (See later on evaluation techniques.) The costs of exploiting natural assets are greater in rich countries than poor ones (cutting down the forests may be a matter of survival in Brazil today as it was in Britain of yesteryear), and, with increasing economic growth, will be greater for future generations than for those today.

Summing up, the combination of irreversibility and uncertainty, with effects spilling out locally, globally and intergenerationally, all urge us to err on the side of caution when calculating the costs of environmental exploitation.

DEPLETION OF EXHAUSTIBLE RESOURCES

Supplies of exhaustible resources such as mineral deposits are not fixed, they become available to the market as a result of a three-stage commercial process:

1 *Exploration and discovery.* Considerable effort and investment are devoted to the search for and identification of profitably recoverable deposits. Despite enormous technological advances, there is an irreducible element of chance here.
2 *Development.* This is the thorough investigation and preparation for extraction of an identified source. Once the relevant capital equipment is in place, there then remains:
3 *Production and distribution.* The exploitation of reserves involves ongoing investment in extraction and transport techniques in order to guarantee the required depletion rate to satisfy market demand.

The speed at which such reserves can be made ready for market and the speed at which they are then consumed by society are both related to the price of the natural resource in question. These rates of depletion/consumption are of paramount importance – too quick and future generations will inherit less and less; too slow and current generations may be paying too high a cost of sacrifice. (If the price of energy is too high, many people may be denied heating and transport. In the extreme, some may die of hypothermia, or inability to reach emergency services in time. These are clear examples of where current generations and thus unborn future generations are paying too high a price.) The issues involved here are thus of *intergenerational equity* and an *optimal depletion rate* – that is the rate of resource extraction that is 'best' for society.

Economic theory has much to offer on these points. In a perfect market the price of an exhaustible resource indicates its relative scarcity and its environmental importance. Moreover, the optimal depletion rate for any such resource is that where its price is induced to rise at a rate of growth equal to the rate of growth of all prices, i.e. the market rate of interest.

Consider the following example: a community which owns certain reserves of, say, crude oil, is sitting on a valuable capital asset. Should it extract and sell this resource now, or wait and sell it at some time in the future? If oil prices are appreciating rapidly this implies the market views future scarcity as the more serious. The community now has an incentive to delay drilling while their asset is steadily increasing in value. If current oil supplies are plentiful and prices are flat, however, then rates of return on alternative investments in the market place will offer a better reward. The community maximises benefits by selling now and thus investing their oil revenues elsewhere.

We can conclude that if prices of and revenues from natural assets are projected to grow less fast than the market rate of interest then resource exploitation should increase. Current generations are sacrificing more than future ones will. Conversely, if future revenues are likely to be greater than interest rates then current extraction is too greedy and should cease.

If current resource exploitation increases, then that which remains for the future is depleted – sooner or later prices will be forced to rise; conversely, if exploitation ceases and supplies are conserved for future generations then prices will at some time come down and thus prompt renewed extraction.

The optimum rate of depletion for any exhaustible natural asset thus evolves as that where the rate of growth of prices and revenues just equals the market rate of interest.

HARVEST OF RENEWABLE RESOURCES

Farming, fishing and forestry represent use of renewable resources. Sustainable harvesting of the land and seas can thus be determined in relation to the rates of regeneration involved. If the seas are fished, for example, at a catch rate equal to the rate of growth of the existing fish stocks then clearly this resource can be left at a constant size for the future.

Growth rates for renewable resources differ for each one involved. Cattle reproduce faster than blue whales; pine forests faster than tropical hardwoods. Growth rates for a given resource also differ according to its stock size or population density.

This latter point needs further elaboration. Take the case of elephant herds in certain parts of Africa – there is a *critical minimum size* (cms) below which reproduction rates are insufficient to guarantee survival. Above this, however, the herd grows first at an increasing rate – where the natural habitat is under-populated and can thus support higher densities – then the growth rate slows, declines and finally reaches zero where the environment supports the *maximum carrying capacity* (mcc). The herd cannot grow beyond this size because death rates rise above birth rates as food supplies become insufficient.

The graph below plots the stock size of a given renewable resource against its natural regeneration rate. Given no interference from humankind, the natural equilibrium population is at the maximum carrying capacity. If for some short-lived reason (say, a year of good climate and improved food supplies) stocks should grow beyond this point then deaths will eventually exceed births and the stock must shrink. Conversely, if the population is reduced, births would outnumber deaths and growth would resume (see Figure 12.2). The regeneration rate of the resource is the key concept since this indicates the environmentally sustainable harvest rate. As illustrated, the rate of growth of any renewable resource varies with its stock size, the maximum sustainable yield possible being indicated at msy.

The actual harvest rate that will be practised by those exploiting this resource depends on the costs and revenues involved. Generally speaking, the cost of exploiting a renewable resource will rise as the stock size shrinks. In fishing the open seas, for example, harvesting costs may rise prohibitively for some species as their numbers are reduced, the possible locations which they might inhabit are diverse and their market price is relatively low. For large, easy to hunt species such as African rhino and elephant, however, costs of poaching may be low, the gain from sales of rhino horn or ivory may be high and thus stock sizes in these cases may be driven below their critical minimum size (cms) where extinction becomes a real threat.

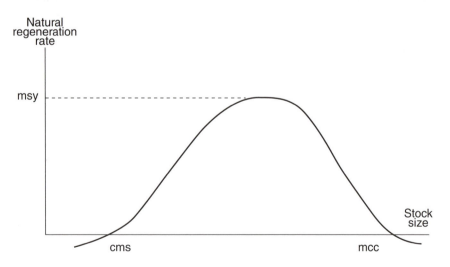

Figure 12.2 How the rate of regeneration of a species varies with its population/stock size

To conclude the analysis of renewable resources, we return to a consideration of interest rates. How much foresters want to fell virgin hardwoods and hunters prefer to exploit scarce species such as whales, rhino or tigers now rather than at some time in the future depends on their *rate of time preference*, or discount rate. The greater the preference for present rather than future consumption, the higher their discount rate – that is, we say that their future benefits are heavily discounted. For peoples and societies with uncertain futures – for example very poor peoples or tribes in less-developed countries; criminals and poachers – and for peoples living in fast-growing economies where alternative investment opportunities offer high rates of return, then there is likely to be a high premium placed on present rather than future benefits.

This means, therefore, that where access to the resource in question is open (like virgin forests, or the high seas) or impossible to police (like some very large African game parks), where harvesters' discount rates are high and where the costs of depletion are relatively low, then species extinction is at serious risk. Harvesting will inevitably take place at a rate faster than the environment can sustain.

PUBLIC POLICY

Confining economic activity to the sustainable limits we have now identified must be the goal of all those interested in conserving the environment. The market economy must be adjusted such that all commodities and economic practices are priced in accordance to the full (i.e. external + internal) costs incurred in their production.

If those overexploiting exhaustible and renewable resources had to pay the price of the damage they inflicted on the environment they would conserve more. If polluters had to pay for their thoughtless disregard of others they would think more and pollute less. Inevitably, as industry's costs rise they would pass on some fraction of this to consumers in the form of higher prices, but this is how it should be: more environmentally damaging produce would be more expensive and consumers would thus buy less of them.

What are the ways that can be used to internalise in market prices all external, environmental costs that societies suffer? Firstly, it can be demonstrated that a free-market society based on *private property rights* can for many natural assets achieve sustainable development. Property holders have a vested interest in protecting their resource and they can force polluters, poachers and all violators to pay through the courts of law for any encroachment they cause.

The classic case was given by Ronald Coase ('The problem of social cost', *Journal of Law and Economics*, 3, 1960) in which he described sparks from a passing steam train setting fire to a farmer's field. The farmer can sue for compensation and in so doing external costs (to the farmer) are internalised to the producer (the railway company). Profits of the enterprise hence fall and this will prompt a cutback in economic activity and/or more careful conservationist practice. Alternatively, instead of cleaning up its act the railway producer can opt to purchase the property rights of all offended parties. Either way, costs and benefits are adjusted through the free market to internalise the externalities involved. Equilibrium is secured in this case without recourse to government intervention, other than in the institution of property rights in the first place.

This equilibrium, however, is subject to two conditions: (1) it requires that the resource in question is capable of exclusive private ownership; and (2) it assumes that transactions costs are not prohibitive.

1 As has already been observed, many vital resources have *open access* (e.g. whales, clean air) so no proprietor can prevent others' exploitation. True, for some common properties, e.g. fishing in a remote beauty spot, negotiated agreement between self-enlightened users can be possible, but there is always the temptation for one party to cheat (the *free-rider* problem). The larger the resource, however – such as a national park – the less exclusive it can be and the huge number of users precludes any effective free-market agreement. Government controls become necessary.
2 Even where property rights are enshrined and enforceable in law, the *transaction cost* of suing for damages (especially where the transgressor is a big, powerful enterprise and the transgressed are many, small, non-organised property holders) may simply be too great an obstacle to overcome. An unscrupulous profit-maximiser may exploit its power, pay minimal lip-service to environmental causes and get away with it. Multinational mining companies working in LDCs have at times been accused of such practice.

Despite this, environmental pressure groups such as Friends of the Earth, Greenpeace, etc., are effective in the unregulated free market. Well-publicised campaigns against environmentally damaging operators, be they private or public enterprises, do succeed at times (e.g. against Exxon corporation in the *Exxon Valdez* disaster of Prince Edward Sound, Alaska). There is evidence, therefore, that sustainable economic activity can be controlled through the free market.

One-off successes are not enough, however, to permanently safeguard the environment from exploitation and degradation. Comprehensive adjustment of the price mechanism is not attainable by such an ad hoc approach. Government regulation of the market system is, in the end, indispensable.

There are a number of public policy instruments that can be employed; one extreme is to dispense with any adjustment of market prices and go straight for *direct controls*. Legislation can be passed to outlaw certain environmentally harmful practices. This can certainly be effective, and for some situations it may be the most efficient means of government intervention – for example, where clearly identifiable behaviour is considered harmful and must be totally prohibited, not just reduced, and where prompt and substantial changes are called for. This might include banning all construction in an area of outstanding natural beauty, or to outlaw hunting/fishing of a threatened species. In neoclassical terminology, such government action may be justified where the value of the resource is deemed to be so great that its 'price' must deter all consumption.

Direct controls, nonetheless, are too inefficient a mechanism to employ in many cases. Public regulatory agencies must firstly set up laws that are responsive to changing environmental circumstances; must catch private operators who break these laws; compile evidence to prosecute them, bring cases to court and then succeed in gaining effective penalties. The transaction costs of devoting resources to this end may be more wasteful than allowing the accused to get away with it in the first place!

Taxation can do the same job of environmental control, in most cases more dependably, effectively and economically than legislation. A carbon tax levied on the emission of exhaust gases, for example, will limit over-rapid exploitation of fossil fuels and, by the argument given at the beginning of this chapter, thus promote research and development of alternatives. Although not costless – it requires a technology applicable to energy-consuming equipment from car engines to thermal power stations, as well as a bureaucracy of tax inspectors – it is an automatic system that penalises carbon-users on a rising scale appropriate to their environmental impact.

Subsidies are appropriate to encourage conservation and recycling activities that have environmental and social benefits not recorded in unregulated market prices. If it is justifiable to tax the production of socially costly practices, by the same argument subsidies should be awarded to bring down the market prices of those products and processes with a high net social benefit and which deserve patronage. Note that subsidies alone are insufficient in themselves to deter environmental degradation – they are relevant to encourage good practice but cannot prevent that which is harmful.

Pollution permits are a novel way of internalising external costs and making the polluter pay. The regulatory agency decides on the acceptable level of

---

BOX 12.1 POLLUTION PERMITS AND GLOBAL WARMING

The debate over global warming is highly politicised and it is not easy to retain a clear view of the scientific and economic realities given all the high emotion this issue excites in the world's media and in demonstrations outside the meeting halls of world leaders.

The first important question to ask is just how serious a threat to the planet is posed by the alleged rise in global temperatures?

The second question is: what are the costs and benefits involved in doing something, or nothing, about this issue?

Some argue that the increase in global warming over the last century is no more than 'normal climate variation', that 98 per cent of greenhouse gas emissions are natural and that mankind has had only a 'minuscule' impact on climate change. (Quoted by the Washington-based Cooler Heads Coalition on www.globalwarming.org.)

Others say that the world is now 'warming faster than at any time in the last 10,000 years', that glaciers are shrinking, the incidence of devastating hurricanes, floods and droughts has increased, that many species have already been driven below their critical minimum population size and that humankind is itself also at threat. (The World Wildlife Fund onwww.panda.org.)

In between these two extremes, USA's National Research Council makes the prediction that the next 100 years should see an increase in global temperatures in the range between 1.5 and 6 per cent and that man-made greenhouse gases (GHGs) will be mostly responsible for this increase.

Given the range of scientific opinion, it is probably safest to assume that economic activity *does* have an impact on the climate and that the world's nations do therefore have a collective vested interest in safeguarding the planet's future. Doing nothing, therefore represents a risk which should be insured against. (Costs could be severe and most probably unevenly distributed – a projected increase in sea levels, for example, would be bad for New York but not Moscow; catastrophic for Bangladesh but not Bolivia.)

Global agreement to reduce GHGs is the best way forward but setting appropriate targets is essential. The original Kyoto treaty signed in 1997 locked the USA into targets that are unattainable without enormous cost (a 30 per cent reduction in US emissions between 2000 and 2010, with all the cutbacks in living standards that implies) and yet these goals give no safeguards over the longer term.

No global agreement will be workable if the costs of securing environmental gains are excessively large, uneven in their distribution and are telescoped to impact more in the short term than in the future. Economic theory suggests an alternative strategy.

The costs and benefits of reducing GHG emissions obviously differ from country to country but it does not matter too much to the planet where the cutbacks occur – so long as the global total does not suffer. It makes sense, therefore, to use a market mechanism such as pollution permits to trade emission controls between one country and another and between the present and the future. The optimum distribution of cutbacks can thus be achieved over space and time.

If it is too costly for some nations (the US?) to make drastic cutbacks today then it will be cheaper for them to pay others for the inconvenience. Meanwhile for other countries (like Russia?) which have suffered from recession and thus have had no difficulty in meeting emission targets, they gain much needed development income from selling their permits. Similarly, if today's technology cannot yet produce economic fuel-cell engines then it pays to invest more in the future. Over time the pattern of costs will change and polluting nations will find it cheaper to clean up their own act rather than pay for permits. New technologies, and polluting practices, will adjust to the flexible price signals of the market place.

(Note that exactly the same market mechanisms can be employed to pay for and allocate the distribution of 'carbon sinks' – that is the reforestation of areas on the world's surface that can act as global lungs to exhale cleaner air. It might be prohibitively expensive to plant forests in the heart of mainland Europe, but it might pay the EC to promote such practice in less densely populated lands elsewhere.)

pollution (or, say, access to a specific natural resource) to be allowed. A batch of permits is issued authorising just that given amount and these permits are then offered for sale in the open market. Prices are determined by demand and supply. The more cars that want to pollute a certain commuter route, the more factories which wish to belch out smoke, the more walkers who want to tramp over a certain mountain, the more they have to pay. Higher prices will shift demand to lower-use days and locations.

WHAT PRICE THE PLANET?

Each of the policy instruments above has its advantages and disadvantages; some are suited to some applications, others to others. All, however, share the need to evaluate environmental resources accurately and to adjust market prices accordingly.

The whole notion of calculating just how much certain resources are worth, and the extent of any damage that might be done to them, however, is fraught with difficulty. How can you measure the costs involved when they are controversial, uncertain and in some cases irreversible? How much is a beautiful view worth? What price clean air, or peace and quiet? What is the environmental cost of burying nuclear waste? But however difficult such questions may be to answer, something must be done. This issue is just too important to leave to uneducated guesswork or to the influence of powerful vested interests. Some rational, scientific means of measuring the impact of humankind's activity on the planet is essential if we are to amend the price mechanism, reduce environmental degradation and promote sustainable development.

Two basic techniques can be identified in assigning monetary values to environmental resources. One involves measuring various costs as indirectly recorded through existing market places; the other involves questionnaires asking respondents what values they assign to, or are willing to pay for, specific resources.

Market surveys

Private property has a market value related to the benefits enjoyed from its use. A significant part of the utility derived from any piece of land is directly related to environmental quality. Thus degradation of a certain locality will result in a measurable fall in property values.

Statistical surveys of a large cross-section of diverse properties at any one time can help isolate the change in valuation attributable to specific environmental degradation. Properties, of course, vary in price for a variety of reasons: the size and state of repair of the property itself; closeness to facilities, etc. After taking into account all these variables, however, the impact of, say, noise and air pollution is calculable. We can relatively accurately approximate the value of clean air, and of peace and quiet, therefore.

By the same process, reductions in farming, forestry and fishing yields can be traceable to the impact of pollutants; the social costs of traffic congestion can be measured in terms of the loss of time and thus outputs of city dwellers; injuries and deaths can similarly be costed (note that insurance companies put a price on people's health and life all the time).

There is an important distinction here, however. There is a difference between someone's or something's exchange value and their/its intrinsic worth. In a market society some people/items have a greater exchange value than others – the death or injury of an average managing director represents a greater loss to the market place than that of the average student. (Terrorists know this they can demand higher ransom demands if they capture top oil company executives. That is why businesses employ bodyguards in Bogota . . .)

The notion of intrinsic value is nonetheless important. The fact that the market places a high value on some businessperson but a much lower one on the salmon he is trying to kill or the stream that he may be dirtying is at the heart of the environmental movement's criticism of the market system. Some fanatical 'Greens' have even argued that businesspeople should hunt each other rather than wild geese, deer or fish, since there is nowhere a shortage of the former, whereas the latter cannot defend themselves and are in danger of dying out in some places! This is a rejection of the market values placed on the resources in question. Some natural assets have a higher intrinsic worth than is recognised by the money economy, it is argued. Market survey procedures as outlined above are thus insufficient to capture how far an increasing number of people value the environment. Other techniques are necessary.

Questionnaires

Economics now recognises that the value of a specific resource includes:

- that which is revealed through existing markets by those directly or indirectly involved (e.g. the value of clean rivers to anglers, walkers and research biologists who splash in them);
- the value placed on the asset by those who might one day be involved and who thus wish to retain the option of using it untainted at some time in the future;
- the value placed on a resource by people who never intend to use it directly but appreciate it for its own intrinsic worth, or existence. (You may live in the centre of Africa, the USA or India and never intend to sail the oceans, but you might nonetheless insist that whales have a right to swim in them undisturbed.)

The total economic value (TEV) of a resource therefore equals:

$$TEV = \text{Actual use value} + \text{Option value} + \text{Existence value}$$

It is possible to gain empirical estimates of these values by using questionnaires asking people to record their willingness to pay for environmental conservation and/or their willingness to accept compensation for its loss.

Construction of the relevant questionnaires is inevitably difficult. They contain biases for a number of reasons: firstly, respondents may conceal their true preferences (this is the free-rider problem met elsewhere); secondly, they may be influenced in their willingness to pay by the surveyor/nature of the questions asked; respondents may be willing to pay more in one form (e.g. taxes) than others (e.g. entry fees); and they may value gains and losses asymmetrically. That is, people may be prepared to pay more to prevent further degradation than to secure environmental gains. For all these reasons, therefore, studies come up with different evaluations for the same resource, depending on how the questionnaire is designed.

Research in this area is still relatively new but, despite the difficulties involved, this questionnaire technique – the contingent valuation method (CVM) – remains an important and in many cases the only method of estimating important but elusive *option and existence values*.

Examples of CVM studies reveal interesting valuations. For the Grand Canyon, USA – quoted by Pearce and Turner – existence values were measured as 66 times more important than user values. People valued this resource highly for its own intrinsic worth, not because they wanted direct access to it for themselves. (This is undoubtedly because of this resource's uniqueness as a national asset.) In Norway, respondents were asked how much they were prepared to pay to stop acid rain. The study came up with 400 krona per person, or 2.5 billion krona in total. This was broken down into 1 billion user value and 1.5 billion existence value; although the willingness-to-pay technique here is almost certainly an underestimate. This is because most Norwegians view acid rain as a problem of imported pollution (from British and German sources, at least) and thus presumably would argue that other nations apart from themselves should pay to clear it up.

CONCLUSION

Economics sometimes gets a bad name from environmentalists who do not understand the subject. They believe that economists are only interested in calculating profits and promoting economic growth at the expense of the environment. This chapter hopefully demonstrates that economics is concerned with calculating *all* the costs and benefits involved in human activity. What price do you put upon a threatened species? a beautiful landscape? the inconvenience of photo-chemical smog? Economics attempts to quantify these issues; make clear what assumptions are being made; minimise subjectivity and increase objectivity in the analysis of the balance of gains and losses. The market system can be made more responsive to these concerns and the discussion on sustainable development and policy instruments above shows what targets can be aimed at and how they can be hit. It has been noted that the possibility of doing irreversible environmental damage, the uncertainty of our impact on complex ecologies we imperfectly understand, and the rising value that societies ascribe to the environment as incomes rise, all indicate the need for extreme caution. The premium for external costs that needs to be appended to many market prices may well be high.

The biggest practical problem this raises is finding the political will to implement these costs in the market prices we must all pay. If this is difficult enough in one country, the problem is far greater where environmental costs are spread across many nations – in the case of global climate change, for example. Voluntary international cooperation is necessary – here with the signing of a treaty on limiting greenhouse gas emissions. But even if vastly different countries' evaluations of the situation could be brought into agreement there is always the temptation for an individual nation to free-ride. Without a supranational government, how do you stop one state from muddying a common pool? International condemnation? Trade sanctions, maybe?

Malthus's predictions of population growth in 1798 were wrong. Planet Earth has supported a much greater increase in our numbers at a higher standard of living than he thought possible. Whether the planet can continue to sustain our continuing economic growth and exploitation of the environment depends on whether or not we can continue to adjust and adapt the market economic system we have devised to provide for us.

Whatever the eventual mechanisms, a political way forward should be found to confront the economics of the environment. For what is certain is that if we do not pay the full price of plundering our natural inheritance today then our inheritors will bear the brunt of these costs in their future.

KEY WORDS

Free goods   Those goods provided to us that involve no economic sacrifice in their production and consumption – sunlight, the air we breathe, a sparkling mountain stream. Free goods have no market price; in contrast, **economic goods** and services are all those that are the product of scarce resources and, even if they are subsidised or given away free, they are costly to supply.

Intergenerational equity   Exhaustible resources can be used today or in the future: by ourselves or by our children. If we choose to consume them now we raise our standard of living, which our children will benefit from, but they will be denied future supplies of natural capital. Conversely, if we choose not to consume known supplies of exhaustible resources today there will be undoubtedly more available for future generations although they will not inherit such a high standard of material wealth. The issue of whether to have jam today or jam tomorrow thus depends on how we value present versus future costs and benefits, and how we wish to spread them between ourselves and our heirs. An equitable decision distributes the costs and benefits 'fairly' between the generations.

Natural regeneration rate   The rate at which a renewable resource regenerates itself in its undisturbed state. This will depend on the size of the resource in question in relation to its environment: a given animal population, for example, will have a *critical minimal size* – below which its reproduction rate falls lower than its death rate and thus it will eventually die out – and at the opposite extreme a *maximum carrying capacity* where (typically) food supplies cease to be sufficient and thus death rates again rise above birth rates and the stock size falls again.

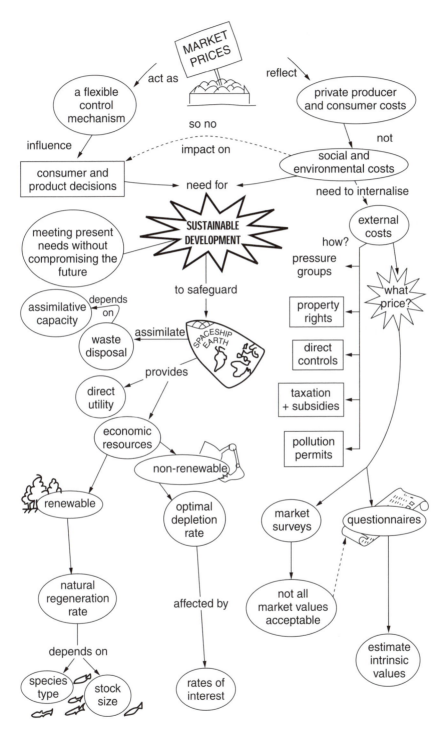

Figure 12.3 The themes of chapter 12

Sustainable development Economic development that ensures that we pass on to our children the same quantity of environmental wealth that we inherited ourselves. Any depletion of exhaustible stocks should thus be compensated for by increases in renewable resources and man-made capital.

QUESTIONS

1 What is the relationship between economic growth and the environment? What are the consequences if we value: (a) growth more than the environment; and (b) the environment more than growth?
2 What is meant by sustainable development? Can any depletion of non-renewable resources be sustainable?
3 How can economics predict which species are likely to be threatened with extinction?
4 What policies could be appropriate to preserve Brazilian rain forests? What are their costs and benefits?
5 How could you measure the value of clean air in the town where you live? Is it worth preserving?

FURTHER READING

The key analysis above is based on:
Pearce, D. W. and Turner, R. K. *Economics of Natural Resources and the Environment.* Harvester Wheatsheaf, 1990.

An easier treatment is found in:
Turner, R. K., Pearce, D. and Bateman, I. *Environmental Economics.* Harvester Wheatsheaf, 1994.

13 Conclusion: into the twenty-first century

Having entered the new millennium, what are the themes of most importance that we take into the future?

Firstly, I hope it has been sufficiently demonstrated that the global economy *is* a global economy. The fortunes of all the passengers on spaceship earth are interlinked. Changes in the welfare of some citizens on one side of the world have their impact, sooner rather than later, on their distant neighbours a hemisphere away. Numerous examples have been illustrated and the reasons for increasing international interdependence have been analysed.

Trade joins all our destinies. Since 1945 there has been steady growth in world commerce and a progressive reduction in all sorts tariff and non-tariff barriers. The private, material benefits from free trade have been sufficiently persuasive to draw in increasing numbers of isolated and economically under-developed communities into international market places. From smallholders in Taiwan to dockworkers in Poland and urban squatters in Latin America, all individuals have something to gain in joining the money economy, selling their skills and buying new products. Similarly, the fall of autarkic command economies was in part due to the pulling power of consumerist lifestyles embodied in a wide range of inexpensive foods, fashion-wear and popular music available in all countries outside the iron curtain. (Coke, Levi jeans and The Beatles were perhaps more influential than all the nuclear hardwear that threatened the communist regimes!)

More importantly, increasing economic growth of all countries, and especially that of the wealthy market economies, has required the unrestricted purchase of energy supplies and raw material inputs from all around the globe plus the simultaneous development of widespread export markets. The gains from free trade have also driven the creation of economic associations such as the European Union and NAFTA and, barring the resurgence of mercantilist rivalry, over time such groupings should deepen their integration, widen their membership and reduce their barriers to external parties. Other trading blocs can also be expected to follow these initiatives.

Growth in export sales has spurred the development of less-developed and newly industrialised countries and this process will no doubt continue – if it slows for some as they increasingly mature so it is likely that others will start along the same road. Increasing world competition, especially in the sale of manufactures, is not likely to abate, therefore, and the forces of creative destruction will become more widespread, impacting on all countries. As a result of all these pressures on resources, world energy prices must inevitably rise and this will set off another round of exploration and technological innovation.

Increasing competition in export markets is not constrained by a fixed limit to world incomes, as some have feared. Trade has brought rising incomes to all in the past, and if some countries persistently run export surpluses this is still feasible if, like Japan recently, they experience outflows of capital – that is they recycle their export earnings abroad.

This leads us to the theme of the globalisation of finance. Commensurate with the steady growth of world commodity trade has been the recently accelerating movement in international money markets. Competition between rival financial centres has brought deregulated, liberalised capital markets in one country after another, such that funds can move across the globe out of one pocket into another in minutes and outside the reach of governments and their central banks. The telecommunications revolution has helped facilitate this international mobility of capital, plus it continues to broadcast all manner of financial information that communicates market worries from one side of the globe to the other. As a result we all now live in a world of fragile interdependency, uncertainty and risk where individual countries no longer have the luxury of being in control of the most important economic variables which influence their, and our, destinies.

With all our destinies so obviously interlinked now, we can expect increasing conflicts to arise over the distribution of global spoils. Poor people do not starve quietly when they see others enjoying lifestyles they are denied. Realisation that we are all passengers together brings with it economic responsibilities. Those that gain in the process of creative destruction should not and cannot now be uninformed of the social costs born by those that lose out. But apart from ethical considerations are there any economic, free-market reasons why winners should be concerned with the fate of losers? What does it cost to the inhabitants of Software Valley, Computerville if thousands are made redundant in Metal Basherstown, Labourersland?

So long as those whose incomes are growing rapidly possess short time horizons and are predominantly self-interested then any costs imposed on others will be heavily discounted. As is evident in free-market environments from Mexico City to New York, Rio to Rotterdam, wealth can live next door to poverty with negligible (or at best very slow-moving) mechanisms to bridge the divide and promote convergent growth. It has been mentioned before that winners have a natural incentive in market societies to identify with others of the same fortune elsewhere in the world and to lock their doors against losers in their own neighbourhood.

John Kenneth Galbraith warned as long ago as 1958 of the dangers of a world moving inexorably towards a destiny of private wealth and public squalor (*The Affluent Society*, London: Hamilton). Some fifty years later the same tendencies still exist, though the pace of change has accelerated and, if today the telecommunications revolution does not allow us to be ignorant any longer and brings the social costs of creative destruction into our living-rooms, so it also promotes everything else from mind-numbing game-shows to orgies of violence. Retaining sovereignty over our destiny remains as difficult as ever. The weaknesses of the market economic system (referred to in chapter 1) show no sign of diminishing.

Perhaps the most important development that takes us into the twenty-first century, therefore, has been the marked change in economic philosophy which now informs public policy-makers. Keynes wrote that the ideas of economists and political philosphers are more powerful than commonly understood. As has been noted, since the 1980s the world seems to have rediscovered the vibrancy and relevance of free markets but with it has come an extreme ideological variant which – unlike in Keynes's time – now challenges the worth of government intervention in the economy. The ascendancy of neoclassical ideas is born of oil shocks, stagflation and the collapse of the command economic model. The economic consequences of the world supremacy of these ideas affect us all today and will continue to do so tomorrow.

It is with this issue – an examination of the appropriate role of governments in economic organisation – that this book started and will ultimately finish. If relationships between individuals, markets and governments are badly bungled then the future will bring hardship for billions. The network of interchanges between these three parties, however, is so complex and the wealth of options in building a mixed economy is so great that, I believe, there are no simple formulas, no one right answer (like: 'take government off the backs of the people') that is appropriate for all countries, for all times.

The political imperative of our times, however, emphasises the need to reduce government expenditure, to reduce tax burdens, to accelerate the spread of privatisation and the deregulation of all existing markets. The danger is in going too far in reducing the role of government, of failing to accept sufficient responsibility for countering unemployment, for improving public services and for rectifying market failure. Faith in government as an active and effective partner in the economy is thereby undermined and instead there is the insistence that the welfare state breeds a parasitic entitlement mentality, a 'nanny' state.

This ideology has been articulated by the world financial community and promoted in the actions of numerous European, North/South American and Asian/Pacific governments. Its socio-economic costs, however, have not been insignificant and indeed the polarisation of incomes, the environmental damage and breakdown of community and family life that have been accompanying features of 'freer', more mobile, markets are building up severe problems for future generations.

There is no denying the power of self-interest in fuelling the free-market engine, but equally there is no excuse for the pilots to abdicate responsibility for where this motor is projecting our spaceship.

There is much that governments can, and must, do. If private markets display high discount rates and blinkered vision then no one else other than public servants can moderate recurring cyclical instability and promote the long-run development of human resources, conservation strategies and community support.

All the undoubted, and accelerating, scientific progress achieved over the last hundred years and the sophisticated technological wizardry which this has brought us only serves to emphasise how limited is humankind's understanding of our own nature. 'Animal spirits' still seem to drive us from boom into bust. Human memories remain as short as ever, and our ability to hang together as a community – to make individual sacrifice for the common good – seems more elusive now than ever before. There is therefore no evidence to suggest that world markets can escape periodic cycles of growth and recession in incomes, expenditure and employment without the influence of government.

Unemployed people on their own are limited in their ability to move with the market. They cannot acquire new skills without help and there will be few private businesses that will take on this long-term investment since they cannot guarantee the workers so trained will stay with them long enough to pay back a market rate of return. Additionally, highly productive human resources are far more complicated and costly to identify and develop than undersea oil reserves. How do you spot a potential genius amongst the children of Calcutta's teeming millions or in the unemployed of Moscow? Yet we all benefit if our neighbours are educated. This must remain a responsibility of public authority since no profit maximiser will undertake it.

The private market imposes no prohibitive costs on chopping down trees to provide wood fuel, on dumping toxic wastes in the seas or on the killing of rhinoceros to smuggle out their profitable horns. The fallacy of composition ensures, however, that our spaceship will become impoverished – if not poisoned – unless we are persuaded to change our individually destructive habits. It would be monumentally myopic of the dominant species on this transport between the stars if we greedily exhausted all our supplies in the mere minute or two of the geological timescale we have been aboard.

By exactly the same argument, lack of awareness or concern about what we are doing to *human* environments can even more quickly bring about cumulative and irreversible decline. I refer here not so much to obvious communal insanities like drug wars, arms races and nuclear sabre-rattling which are fed by unscrupulous sellers of cocaine and military hardware, but to the far more subtle, free-market necessity for mobile labour that rewards private interest but places a negligible, if not negative return earned on constructing family and community stability.

Stability is important in all human affairs. Humans are social animals and economic philosophies must recognise this. For example, the development of human relationships in business can bring long-term profit. The decision whether to cut one's losses and sell out in a failing business project, or to put more money, time and effort into turning it around is extremely difficult but building up trust between management and workforces and promoting goodwill with customers has proven to be a sound investment particularly when the external economic environment turns nasty. (This is particularly true of businesses engaged in higher-quality goods and services.) Wherever private rates of return fail to recognise this, however, then the market will opt to maximise short-term gain by selling out, liquidating capital and moving resources elsewhere.

The success of promoting trust and goodwill in business relationships is causing management in both manufacturing and financial enterprises to take aboard these ideas, but where is the private profit in promoting stable family life, deepening friendships and supportive communities? The emphasis on individual mobility and reward leads indirectly to the weakening of social ties, and with it increasing social costs such as a growing sense of isolation; rising stress and mental illness; more crime; increasing divorces; neglect of the weak, unfortunate and elderly. There are enormous external benefits to be earned in societies that are stable and healthy but the hand of government is necessary to guide markets to this end. A publicly funded welfare state is needed to cope with the problems of social breakdown and to identify policies to avoid them.

Finally, it is the greatest injustice that we carry on into the new millennium with passengers on our starship that experience vastly different standards of living. Those in the first-class cabins enjoy a society that promotes growth and development and seem to be totally unaware of the deprivation that exists for three-quarters of the passengers locked away down below. Simple rules of conduct separate the two communities. In the rich world, people have evolved sophisticated rules that reinforce property rights and commitment to contracts – such that consumers can pick up a phone or computer, order what they want and pay for it all in the safe knowledge that their transaction will be honoured. But in the poor world you can't trust anyone outside of your immediate friends and family. How can the market place expand and the specialisation of skills and technologies develop if there is no central authority that can be trusted to uphold the law and insist that promises must be kept?

The conventional wisdom that government is the enemy of the market is a false dichotomy. Markets assume underlying social and power relationships as given and so, with free rein, they may do little to help the disadvantaged. The Zapatistas of Chiapas have spoken for many inside and outside their country. Liberating the supply-side resources of a country requires microeconomic intervention to dismantle barriers, provide opportunities, promote enterprise and penalise those who would subvert trade. Markets *need* government.

The future therefore requires a new political economy which is devoted to examining the relationship between individuals, markets and the state and to intervening where necessary to remove rigidities and to empower all to participate to the fullest. It should be operative at three levels: supranationally, nationally and locally.

International debt crises are a product of an unregulated world market system. Supranational guidance is required to push wealthy, creditor nations to open up their markets, to limit their financial demands and to lead the poorest debtors out of a spiral of decline.

The major trading nations should be entreated to follow economic policies that, collectively, do not lead to overexpansionary growth or to beggar-my-neighbour protectionism. Global macroeconomic demand management is called for.

Similarly the environmental impact on the planet of localised consumption and production decisions – such as to cut down forests, or to pump out toxic exhaust gases – not to mention the global reach of multinational corporations and certain politically ambitious governments, requires a world forum for discussion, regulation and enforcement.

Wherever the single nation-state is too small to tackle problems on its own then international agencies such as the IMF and the World Trade Organisation need to be strengthened and constitutionally charged to take the long view and safeguard world interests.

At a national level, the policing of competition, privatisation schemes, land reforms and the restructuring of taxes are necessary to engage *all* in the ownership and control of resources. A commitment to reduce unemployment and inflation requires analysis of their respective causes plus demand and supply-side intervention where appropriate.

Some nations have made a notable success of the strategic direction of their economies. This requires, however, a social structure that recognises the importance of state/industry partnerships, open government, rule-abiding businessmen and civil servants and a general willingness of all to contribute to the proper functioning of the market place.

The effective operation of essential public services such as the police, health, education, and the caring professions is best managed at local levels where providers are in direct contact with their customers. Supply-side investment in human capital operates at this level. Identifying education and training needs, providing job information, promotion of native enterprise all start with the individual – so too does the analysis of community and family dynamics, offering counselling services and recommending action to stabilise relationships, enrich lives and deepen human resources.

Over two hundred years ago Adam Smith wrote approvingly of the social benefits of the free-market system where, by an 'invisible hand', self-interested agents brought about the greater good for all. This was in a tightly homogenous culture where all shared the same value system and the state operated effectively to protect individual rights. In a fast-changing, chronically uncertain world where our economic and technological power to create or destroy embraces vastly disparate peoples and indeed the entire planet then it must be concluded that some rather more visible hands would be very welcome to guide the wealth of nations throughout the twenty-first century and beyond.

Index

Note: page numbers in **bold** denote refences to figures and tables.

acid rain 249
adjustable pegs 146, 162
Africa 191, 192
Aganbegyan, Abel 36
ageing population 112, 121, 123
aggregate demand 24, 62, 65–7, 68, 74, 76, 88
aggregate supply 67, 74, 76
agriculture 32, 34, 220; China 40, 44, 53, 54; Common Agricultural Policy 59–60, 110–11, 123, 159; East Asian land reforms 225, 226, 227; Eastern Europe 158–9; market instability 58–9; prices 229; Soviet Union 37
Allende, Salvador 77, 138
allocative efficiency 60, 65, 68
Amazon rainforest 27
Aramco 172, 180, 184
arbitrage 133, 140
Argentina: colonial trade 212; currency board 149; debt 192, 199, **201**; development indicators **208**; financial crisis 149, 189, 198–9; Mercosur 99; nationalism 216
Armenia 43
ASEAN *see* Association of South East Asian Nations
Asian 'dragons' ('tigers') 224–8, 229; comparative advantage 98, 103; GDP growth **46**; income per head **46**
Asian financial crisis 13, 24, 127, 188, 190, 195–8, 227
assets 16–17, 134–5
assimilative capacity 236, 238
Association of South East Asian Nations (ASEAN) 121
asymmetric information 40, 53, 54
Australia 166, 167
Austria 107, **117**, **158**

balance of payments deficits 132, 145, 195, 204, 231
Baltic countries 42, **48**
Bank of England 128, 132, 133, 211
banking 127–40, 191, 200; Asian financial crisis 196; Chile 78; fractional reserve 127, 141; globalisation of finance 131–7; Japan 66; lender of last resort 201–2; money creation 129–30, 150; Russia 48, 49; United Kingdom 82
barriers to entry 134, 140, 176
Belgium: currency union 143; European Union 107; exports 157, **158**; GDP **117**; population **117**; unemployment **160**; wage growth **160**
bills of exchange 130–1, 140–1
Blinder, Alan 84
Bolivia **214**, 215
bonds 130–1, 134, 135, 137, 141
Boulding, Kenneth 235
BP 172, 180, 183, 184
Brazil: coal consumption 171; currency board 149; debt 192; deforestation 240; forest management 27; GNP **207**; industrial growth 168; investment **49**; Mercosur 99
Brundtland Report (1987) 237
budget deficit 48–9, 53, 145
Bulgaria 108
Bundesbank 153
Bush, George 96

Camdessus, Michel 195
Canada 96–7, **207**, **208**
CAP *see* Common Agricultural Policy
capital: common markets 113; competition 19; controls 200–1; flows 48, **48**, 198, 204; joint stock companies 34; loan 196; mobility 24–5, 41, 76,

96, 113–14, 133, 254; natural 238, 250; neoclassical growth model 220; privatisation 40; *see also* human capital
capital flight 195, 197, 204, 214, 229
capital-labour ratio 218
capitalism 26, 76, 92
car ownership 168
CARICOM (Caribbean Community of West Indian states) 99
cartels 176, 177, 180, 181–2, 186
cash 129, 130, 135
Cavallo, Domingo 198
Cecchini report (1988) 119
central banks 127–8, 129, 137–8, 141; currency boards 148, 149; money supply 130–1, 135–6
centralisation 9, 10, 14, 21, 51
CET *see* common external tariff
chaebol 227
cheques 129, 130
Chernobyl disaster 38, 235
Chevron 172
Chile 77–9, 100, 138, 200, **208**
China: agriculture 40, 44, 53, 54; central planning 17, 26, 35, 36; coal 171; development indicators **208**; electronic goods 196; exports **45**, 50, 91; foreign investors 48; free-market changes 100; GDP **45**, **46**; GNP **207**; income per head **46**; industrial growth 168; industrial output **45**; investment **49**; land reforms 225; nationalism 216; oil 167, 168, 172; transition 35, 42, 43–6, 47, 51
cigarette prices 61
classical economics 57, 60, 76, 211; *see also* neoclassical economics
Clinton, Bill 96, 195
cms *see* critical minimum size
coal 170–1, 238
Coase, Ronald 243
collectivisation 17, 51
collusion 19, 20, 23, 30, 61
colonialism 92, 211–12, 216
Columbus, Christopher 33
COMECON 39, 53
command systems 9, 26, 28, 253; central control 10, 14–15; economic philosophy 12; environmental issues 24; feudal society 33; industry 19; inefficiencies 35–6; resource ownership 17; system failure 21; transition process 35, 39–40

Common Agricultural Policy (CAP) 59–60, 110–11, 123, 159
common external tariff (CET) 94, 108, 110–11, 113, 118, 123
common markets 94, 113–15
communalism 12, 18
communism 17, 50
community breakdown 255, 257
comparative advantage 41, 97–9, 102, 103, 104; Asian 'dragons' 224; colonies 211; primary production 212
comparative statics 231
competition 19, 23, 253–4; customs unions 109, 110; financial markets 129, 133, 134, 136, 140; free trade 100; globalisation 88–90; LDC development 218; market entry 41; non-price 177, 186; oil industry 177, 184; perfect 11, 22; supply-side economics 83; transition economies 51
complementary goods 168, 186
conservation 240, 245
consumer sovereignty 11, 21, 22, 27
consumption 235, 236; mass 215; oil 166–9, **167**, 184–6, 189
contagion 188–9, 198
contingent valuation method (CVM) 249
contracts 13, 34–5, 222, 229, 257
convergence 152–3
convertible currency 41, 53
corruption 34, 35, 48, 49, 53, 218
costs: environmental 234, 240, 245, 246, 247–9, 250; harvest of renewable resources 242; marginal 175, 176, 177; opportunity 1, 8; social 243–4, 247–8, 255, 257
crawling pegs 147, 162
creative destruction 72, 91, 99, 104, 254, 255
credit 127, 128, 129, 131
credit multipliers 130, 141
crime 25, 53, 257
critical minimum size (cms) 241, **242**, 250
Croatia 108
crony capitalism 196, 197, 204
cronyism 13, 51, 53, 78, 228
cross-elasticity of demand 169–70
currency: appreciation 134; barriers to trade 120–1; common 95; convertible 41, 53; European crisis 152–4; foreign demand 137; optimal currency areas 156–7, 164, 199; speculation 138, 154; trade 144–5; *see also* devaluation; exchange rates
currency boards 148–9, 198

currency union 95, 128, 143–4, 157–62;
benefits 150–1; costs 151–2, 161; ECB
experience 154–5; European currency
crisis 152–4; stages 145–8
customs unions 94, 108–13, 121
CVM *see* contingent valuation method
Cyprus 108, **117**
Czech Republic 42, 91, 108, **117**, 158,
158

debt 39, 49, 188–205, **201**; debt crisis
189–94, 257–8; debt-service ratio 204;
financial crises 188–9, 194–9;
forgiveness 202; Mexico 96; Russia
198
decentralisation 26, 42
deflation 66, 67, 145–6, 151, 153, 194,
231
deforestation 27, 239, 240
demand: aggregate 24, 62, 65–7, 68, 74,
76, 88; cross-elasticity of 169–70;
global macroeconomic management
258; income-elastic 167; labour market
60, 156; market systems 22, 29;
microeconomics 57–8, 59, 60; oil
165–6, 166–9, 171–2, 181, 184–6;
price mechanism 15–16; price-inelastic
181, 187
Deng Xiaoping 43
Denmark 107, **158**
deregulation 76, 87, 88, 255; Chile 78;
financial 131, 133, 138, 254;
stabilisation policies 192; United
Kingdom 82; *see also* liberalisation;
privatisation
derivatives 134, 141
devaluation: Argentina 149; European
monetary union 147, 151, 153, 154;
Indonesia 23; Mexico 195; Russian
rouble 49, 125, 143; Thailand 188, 197
developing countries: communal
ownership 18; debt crisis 189, 191–4,
199–200, 202–3, **204**; entrepreneurial
culture 222; extended family ethic 13;
informal sector 20; liberalisation 199;
oil demand 167, 172, 186; resource
flows 25; tradition 16; *see also* less
developed countries
development 210, 211–24; free markets
and export promotion 218–24; import-
substitution 216–18; indicators **208**;
primary production 212–16;
sustainable 24, 212, 235, 237–40, 252
diminishing returns 38, 53, 175, 220, 221
discount rate 243, 255

disequilibrium 57, 68, 156
disintermediation 128, 134, 141
diversification 134–5, 213
Domar, Evsey 215
dual track pricing 44, 46, 53
dualism 11–12, 28, 102, 207, 213; *see
also* inequalities
Dutch Disease 214

East Asia: financial crisis 13, 24, 127,
188, 190, 195–8, 227; Japan's
influence 104; *see also* Asian
'dragons'
East Germany 50–1, 153
Eastern Europe 21, 35, 36, 39, 42;
agriculture 158–9; capital flows **48**;
command economy 9; environmental
degradation 235; EU enlargement 118;
free trade 102; GDP growth **46**;
income per head **46**; market reform 50,
51
ECB *see* European Central Bank
economic dynamics 215–16, 231
economic goods 250
economic growth 21, 253; Argentina 198;
Asian 'dragons' 224–8; Chile 78, **79**;
China 43, 46; endogenous growth
model 221–2, 224, 231; environmental
issues 235, 237, 240, 250;
Harrod-Domar model 215–16, 218–20,
231; India 219; neoclassical growth
model 220–1, **221**, 224, 228, 231;
South Korea 226–7; Soviet Union
36–8, **37**; Stages of Economic Growth
model 215; supply-side economics 76,
78; Taiwan 227–8; traditional societies
32
economic integration 104–6, 109, 110,
114, 116–18, 121; *see also* common
markets; customs unions
economic and monetary union (EMU)
145; *see also* currency union
economic systems 10–26; allocative
mechanism 14–16; decision-making
10–12; economic philosophy 12–14,
255; industry 18–20; resource
ownership 16–18; system failure 20–5
economics 1–8, 206, 249; *see also*
classical economics; Keynesian
economics; neoclassical economics
economies of scale 18, 19, 29, 34, 100;
customs unions 109, 111; oil industry
175, 177; US software firms 120
Ecu *see* European Currency Unit
education 112, 256, 258

Edwards, Alejandra Cox 78, 87
Edwards, Sebastian 78, 87, 193–4
efficiency: allocative 60, 65, 68; equity
    trade-off 25; market competition 110;
    neoclassical theory 235; primary
    production 213
EFTA *see* European Free Trade Area
Egypt **49**, 216
employment: corporate 14; full 17, 65;
    import-substitution 216; informal
    sector 20, 29, 222–3; Soviet Union
    37–8; *see also* labour
EMU *see* economic and monetary union
endogenous growth model 221–2, 224,
    231
endogenous money supply 126, 141
energy resources 169–72, 239
entrepreneurs 17, 33, 57, 214; China 44;
    less developed countries 217, 218, 228,
    229; macroeconomic theory 67;
    transition economies 50, 51; *see also*
    private enterprise
environmental issues 9, 233–52, 256, 258;
    deforestation 27; exhaustible resources
    240–1; harvest of renewable resources
    241–3; market failure 24; market
    mechanism adjustment 235–7; oil
    prices 166; public policy 243–7;
    renewable energy 171; valuing
    resources 247–9
equilibrium: labour market 60, 61;
    macroeconomics 64, 65, 74;
    microeconomics 58, 59, 60;
    neoclassical growth model 231; social
    cost 244
equity: intergenerational 241, 250; market
    failure 22, 25
ERM *see* Exchange Rate Mechanism
Estonia 107, **117**
EU *see* European Union
euro 148, 151, 152, 155, 161, 162
Eurodollar market 132, 134
Europe: currency crisis 152–4; currency
    union 145, 146–8, 150–2, 154–5,
    157–62; economic polarisation 116;
    foreign direct investment 113; inflation
    81; integration 104–6, 109, 110, 114,
    116–18, 121; oil **179**; reforestation
    246; *see also* European Union
European Central Bank (ECB) 128, 148,
    151, 152, 155
European Currency Unit (Ecu) 147
European Free Trade Area (EFTA) 107,
    108
European Union (EU) 94, 95, 106, 107–8,
116–21, 123; Common Agricultural
    Policy 59–60, 110–11; currency union
    145, 146–8, 150–2, 154–5, 157–62;
    diversity 111–12, 116; economic
    polarisation 116; labour productivity
    112; nuclear power 170; transition
    countries 42; unemployment 73; *see
    also* Europe
Exchange Rate Mechanism (ERM) 144,
    146–7, 148, 152, 154, 162
exchange rates 41, 128, 136–7, 138, 201,
    229; adjustable pegs 146, 162; Asian
    financial crisis 196–7; fixed 145–6,
    147–8, 152–4, 162, 196, 204;
    Gresham's law 126; income
    measurement 209; managed floating
    146, 164; purchasing power parity 209,
    231; stabilisation 214; tied floating
    146–7; uncertainty 151; volatility 134;
    see also currency
exchange restrictions 146, 162, 218
expectations 80–1, 86, 87
exports: Argentina 199; Asian
    'dragons' 91, 224–5, 226, 227; China
    45, 50, 91; currency appreciation 134;
    Europe 157, 158, **158**; exchange rates
    214; foreign trade multiplier 164;
    growth in sales 253; Japan 67, 103,
    104, 254; macroeconomics 63, 64, **64**;
    Mexico 99, 100, 101; monetary policy
    137; oil **179**; primary produce 216;
    stabilisation policies 192; *see also*
    trade
extended family ethic 13, 14
external economies/diseconomies 115,
    123
Exxon 172, 180, 244

fallacy of composition 62, 68, 256
FDI *see* foreign direct investment
Federal Reserve 128, 132, 146, 189
feudal society 32–3
financial crises 188–9, 194–9, 202;
    Argentina 149, 189, 198–9; East Asia
    13, 24, 127, 188, 190, 195–8, 227;
    Europe 152–4; Mexico 138, 188,
    194–5; Russia 49, 188, 190, 198
financial globalisation 131–7, 140, 254
financial intermediaries 48, 53–4, 129,
    130, 141; *see also* disintermediation
financial markets 22–3, 113, 128–40, 150,
    196, 254
Finland 107, **117**, **158**
fiscal policy 81, 151
fiscal transfers 162

fixed exchange rates 145–6, 147–8, 152–4, 162, 196, 204
floating exchange rates 146–7, 164
foreign direct investment (FDI) 123, 202; China 44; Europe 113; Mexico 101
foreign exchange 132, 137
foreign trade multiplier 100, 157, 164
formal sector 20, 28, 29, 207, 223
fractional reserve banking 127, 141
France: currency speculation 154; European Union 107; exports **158**; financial deregulation 133; GDP **117**; GNP **207**; inflation 84, **86**; nuclear power 170; population **117**; unemployment 84, **86**, **161**; wage growth **161**
free goods 234, 250
free riders 92, 106, 244
free trade 25, 91–106, 192, 253; comparative advantage 97–9; costs of 99–100; Mexico 100–2; NAFTA 95–7; protests against 26; strategic trade policies 102–4; trade agreements 94–5; traditional societies 32; *see also* market systems; trade
free trade areas (FTAs) 44, 94, 95, 108
free-market systems *see* market systems
Friedman, Milton 80, 82, 84, 86
FTAs *see* free trade areas
futures 141, 151

Gaidar, Yegor 51
Galbraith, John Kenneth 15, 186, 254
Gandhi, Mahatma 210
gas 169–70, 171, 177, 183–4, 239
GATT *see* General Agreement on Tariffs and Trade
GDP *see* gross domestic product
General Agreement on Tariffs and Trade (GATT) 92–3, 96
Germany: Bundesbank 127–8, 153; currency union 143–4; development indicators **208**; European Union 107; exports **158**; GDP **117**; GNP **207**; inflation 84, **85**; monetary discipline 150; population **117**; unemployment 84, **85**, **161**; unification 143–4, 153, 158, 162; wage growth **161**
Germany, East 50–1, 153
GHGs *see* greenhouse gases
global warming 245–6, 250
globalisation 72, 88–90; employment 73; finance 131–7, 140, 254
GNP *see* gross national product
gold 126

gold standard 211, 231
Goodhart, Charles 141
Goodhart's law 136, 141
Gorbachev, Mikhail 36, 39, 54
government intervention 10, 21, 26, 217, 218, 257; Asian financial markets 196; environmental issues 244; Keynesian economics 65, 66, 67, 74, 76; Singapore 228; strategic trade policies 102; *see also* regulation
Great Depression 24, 64, 66, 202; 'beggar-my-neighbour' policies 72, 92; wage cuts 60, 61
Greece 107, **117**, 158, **158**
greenhouse gases (GHGs) 246, 250
Greenspan, Alan 190
Gresham's law 126
gross domestic product (GDP) **46**, 67, **208**; Asian 'dragons' **225**; China 43, 45, **45**; East Asian financial crisis **197**; Europe **117**; India **219**; Mexico 101; Russia 47, **47**
gross national product (GNP) **207**; measurement 209–10; Soviet Union 36–7, **37**

Harrod, Roy 215
Harrod-Domar growth model 215–16, 218–20, 231
HDI *see* Human Development Index
Heavily Indebted Poor Countries (HIPCs) 194, 202, **204**
hedge funds 188–9, 190, 204
hedging 34, 151
herd instinct 22–3, 24
HIPCs *see* Heavily Indebted Poor Countries
Holmes, Sherlock 8
Hong Kong 225, 228; clothing exports 91; GDP **225**; GNP **224**
horizontal integration 187
household responsibility system 44, 54
human capital 61, 68–9, 90, 222, 258
Human Development Index (HDI) **208**, 210–11
Hungary: agriculture 17, 158; EU accession 108; GDP **117**; investment **49**; population **117**; transition process 42
hyperinflation 143, 150, 164, 198
hysteresis 87, 90

ICOR *see* incremental capital-output ratio
IMF *see* International Monetary Fund

import-substituting industrialisation 216–18, 220, 224
imports 63, 64, **64**, 67, 134; exchange rates 214; monetary policy 137; oil **179**; quotas 93, 106; *see also* tariffs; trade
income elasticity of demand 167
incomes **46**, 70, 209–10, 211; inflation 88; macroeconomic theory 62–4, **63**, 64, **64**, 65; Mexico 101; oil demand 184; polarisation 255; Russia 49
incremental capital-output ratio (ICOR) 216, 218, 231
India: capital-labour ratio 218; coal consumption 171; development indicators **208**; economic growth 219; GDP **46**, **219**; GNP **207**; income per head **46**; industrial growth 168, 218; nationalism 216; oil 167, 168; outsourcing to 91, 219
Indonesia: coal consumption 171; debt 196, **201**; financial crisis 23, 127, 195, 197, **197**; industrial growth 168; investment **49**; nationalism 216; oil 167
industrial disinvestment 104
industrialisation 71, 168; import-substituting 216–18, 220, 224; political independence 216
inequalities 83, 101, 257; *see also* dualism
infant industries 102, 216, 217–18
inflation 6, 24, 41, 88, 90, 258; aggregate demand 62; Chile 79; Dutch Disease 214; European currency crisis 154; expectations 80–1, 86; government spending 67; Japan 66, 67; Phillips curve 74–5, **77**; real rate of interest 205; Russia 47, 49; supply-side economics 76, 81, 82–3, 84, 87; unemployment 73–5, 80–7
informal sector 20, 28, 29, 207, 209–10, 222–3
information: asymmetric 40, 53, 54; perfect 22
innovation 33, 51; endogenous growth model 221; financial 133; Japan 103
institutions: banking 129, 135, 136; economic prosperity 34, 35; European Union 162; international financial 199–202; transition economies 46, 50, 51
interest rates 82, 131, 135, 229; debt crisis 191; European currency crisis 152, 153, 154; monetary policy 137; oil

prices 175, 241; real 189, 191, 205; volatility 134
intergenerational equity 241, 250
international financial institutions 198–202
International Monetary Fund (IMF) 194, 198–202, 204–5, 258; Asian financial crisis 197; critics of 192, 203; stabilisation policies 192, 205; supply-side economics 87
investment: borrowing 191; capital mobility 113–14; cross-country comparisons **49**; endogenous growth model 221; incremental capital-output ratio 216; informal sector 223; inward 115; Japan 103; macroeconomic theory 63, **63**, **64**; oil 175, 179; primary production 213; risk 54; Russia **47**; shareholding 17–18; short-termism 30; Stages of Economic Growth model 215; transition economies 51; *see also* foreign direct investment
'invisible hand' 12, 16, 56, 258
Iran 179, 180, 181
Iraq 179, 180, 181, 183
Ireland 107, **117**, 157, **158**
Italy: European Union 107; exports **158**; GDP **117**; GNP **207**; inflation 84, **86**; monetary union 158; population **117**; unemployment 84, **86**, **160**; wage growth **160**

Japan: coal consumption 171; comparative advantage 98; development indicators **208**, 211; entrepreneurs 229; export earnings 254; financial crisis 127; financial deregulation 133; financial trading 133–4; GDP **46**, 67; GNP **207**; income per head **46**; land reforms 225; macroeconomics 66–7; oil 166, 167, **179**; pension funds 135; strategic trade policy 102, 103–4; unemployment 73
joint profit maximisation 180, 186
joint stock companies 33–4
joint ventures 176, 177, 217
junk bonds 134, 142

Keynes, John Maynard 24, 56–7, 62, 65, 72, 255
Keynesian economics 62–7, 68, 72, 74, 75–6, 81, 215
kleptocapitalism 51–3, 54
Kornai, Janos 38
Krugman, Paul 66, 196

Kuwait 181, 184, 214
Kyoto treaty (1997) 246

labour: common markets 113; competition
    19; feudalism 32; less developed
    countries 218; mobility 24, 25, 76, 88,
    112, 113, 256; participation rate 112,
    121, 123; price of 50–1, 229;
    productivity 112, 123; Taiwan 227; *see
    also* employment
labour markets: Argentina 199;
    deregulation 82, 87; Europe 157;
    flexibility 155, 156, 157;
    microeconomic theory 60–1
land 32, 33; East Asian reforms 225–6;
    occupational mobility 121, 123;
    privatisation 40
language issues 120
lateral integration 187
Latin America 99, 191, 192, 194, 222
Latvia **49**, 107, **117**
Lawson, Nigel 82
LDCs *see* less developed countries
lender of last resort 201–2
less developed countries (LDCs): debt
    crises 191–4, 199–200, 202–3, **204**;
    development 207, 211–12, 215,
    216–18, 224; export growth 253;
    imperfect markets 229;
    industrialisation bias 220;
    monocultures 213; oil consumption
    171, 172; positive feedback 228; *see
    also* developing countries
Lewis, W. Arthur 207
liberalisation 39, 228, 229; Chile 79;
    financial crises 199; financial markets
    196, 254; Mexico 101; Poland 42;
    Russia 47; stabilisation policies 192;
    Taiwan 227–8; *see also* deregulation;
    privatisation
Libya 180–1
life expectancy 49, **208**, 210–11
limited liability 18, 29, 34
liquidity 135, 142
literacy **208**, 211
Lithuania 108, **117**
local monopoly 177, 186
Long Term Capital Management (LTCM)
    190
Luxembourg 107, **117**, 143, **208**

Maastricht Treaty (1991) 145, 152
macroeconomics 56–7, 62–7, 68, 70;
    European currency union 155, 162;
    global demand management 258; oil

prices 166; unemployment/inflation
    relationship 73, 74, 88
Maddison, Angus 43, 44
Madrid, Miguel de 96
Mahathir Mohamed 138
Malaysia: capital controls 200; debt **201**;
    development indicators **208**; financial
    crisis 195, 197, **197**
Malta 108, **117**
Malthus, Thomas 233, 250
managed floating 146, 164
manufacturing 112, 119–20, 176, 218,
    227, 236
maquiladoras 99, 100
marginal costs 175, 176, 177
marginal propensity to consume (mpc) 65,
    70
market entry 41
market failure 21–5, 193, 235, 255
market forces 19, 88, 114, 116
market surveys 247–8
market systems 9, 29, 229; consumer
    sovereignty 11; environmental issues
    244, 249, 250; industry 19–20; price
    mechanism 15–16, 234, 235–6;
    resource ownership 17–18; self-
    interest 12–13; system failure 22–5,
    235; transition economies 39–40, 42,
    50, 51; *see also* free trade
markets: decentralised 26; efficient 22;
    financial 22–3, 113, 128–40, 150, 196,
    254; government relationship 24, 257;
    less developed countries 217, 228,
    229; microeconomics 56, 57–62;
    multiasset 135–6; price mechanism
    15–16; secondary 135, 141, 142
Mauritania **214**
maximum carrying capacity (mcc) 242,
    242, 250
Meadows, D. H. 233
Menem, Carlos 198
mercantilism 92, 93, 106, 123, 253
Mercosur 99
mergers and acquisitions 136, 172
merit goods 22, 29
Merton, Robert 190
Mexico 100–2; comparative advantage
    97, 98–9; debt 191, **201**; financial
    crisis 138, 188, 194–5; GNP **207**;
    NAFTA 96–7, 101; outsourcing to 91
microeconomics 56, 57–62, 70, 88, 257;
    European currency union 155, 156,
    162; oil 165–6, 172–3
Middle East 178–9, **179**, 180, 182
Mobil 172, 180

monetarism 6, 137, 191
monetary policy 81, 128, 135, 137, 138;
    central banks 129, 131; currency union
    145, 151, 161; economic union 95;
    European Central Bank 155; Exchange
    Rate Mechanism 147
monetary union *see* currency union
money 125–7, 128, 143; creation 130,
    150; international flows 131, 132
money supply 41, 67, 82, 148–50;
    aggregates 135–6; banking 129, 130–1,
    137; endogenous 126, 141
monocultures 213, 231
monopolies 29, 83; local 177, 186; natural
    176, 187, 212; state 19, 29, 41
monopsony 177, 186
moral hazard 196, 202, 205
mortgage rates 158
mpc *see* marginal propensity to consume
Mulroney, Brian 96
multinational corporations: economic
    power 11–12; employment-for-life 14;
    finance 128, 136; foreign direct
    investment 113; global reach 258;
    globalisation 88; joint ventures 217;
    mining companies 244; oil 175, 184;
    resource flows 25
multiplier effect 64, 65, 70, 100

NAFTA *see* North American Free Trade
    Agreement
national interests 118–19, 152
nationalisation 77, 78, 180, 181
nationalism 72, 92, 216
natural monopoly 176, 186–7, 212
natural regeneration rate 238, 241–2, **242**,
    250
Nayyar, Deepak 202
neoclassical economics 60, 65, 193, 208,
    255; efficiency 235; government
    intervention 244; growth model 220–1,
    221, 224–5, 228, 231
Netherlands: European Union 107;
    exports 157, **158**; GDP **117**; population
    117; unemployment **160**; wage growth
    160
New Zealand 166, 167
newly industrialised countries: export
    growth 253; extended family ethic 13;
    strategic trade policy 102; *see also*
    Asian 'dragons'
Niger **208**
non-price competition 177, 186
non-tariff barriers 94, 96, 118, 120–1,
    145, 253

normative economics 22, 26, 30, 88
North American Free Trade Agreement
    (NAFTA) 95–7, 99, 101, 121, 194
North Korea 35
Norway 107, 158, **208**, 249
nuclear power 170

occupational mobility 121, 123, 155,
    156
OECD *see* Organisation of Economic
    Cooperation and Development
Ofer, G. 38
offshore banking 132, 133, 189
oil 6, 49, 165–87, 233–4, 238;
    consumption 166–9, **167**, 184–6, 189;
    crises (1973/1979) 76, 81, 96, 181,
    189; distribution 176–8; exploration
    173–4; Kuwait effect 214; optimal
    depletion rate 241; producer countries
    178–9, 180, 181, 182–3; production
    174–5; refining 176; reserves **174**;
    revenues 212–13; struggle for control
    of supplies 179–82; substitutes
    169–72; transport 175–6
oligarchy 50, 51, 54
oligopolies 19, 20, 23, 30; joint profit
    maximisation 186; non-price
    competition 186; oil industry 166, 177,
    178, 180
OPEC *see* Organisation of Petroleum
    Exporting Countries
open market operations 130–1, 137, 141
opportunity cost 1, 8
optimal currency areas 156–7, 164, 199
Organisation of Economic Cooperation
    and Development (OECD) 155, 187;
    oil consumption 166, 167, 181;
    substitute fuels 169, 170, 171
Organisation of Petroleum Exporting
    Countries (OPEC) 132, 146, 166,
    181–2, 184, 189
outsourcing 91, 219

Pakistan **208**
Pangloss values 196
Paraguay 99
participation rate 112, 121, 123
perestroika 36, 39, 54
perfect competition 11, 22
perfect information 22
petrodollars 132
Phelps, Edmund 80, 86
Philippines 195, **201**
Phillips, A. W. 74–5, 90
Phillips curve 75, **77**, 80;

expectations-augmented 80–1, **80**, 87; short-run 84
Pinochet, Augusto 77, 78, 138
planning: central 14–15, 21, 28, 35, 36, 37–9; corporate 15
Poland: agriculture 17, 158; coal 171; economic crisis 36; energy prices 41; EU accession 108; GDP **117**; investment **49**; market reforms 42, 50, 100; population **117**
political freedom 210
political issues: China 44; command economy ideology 35; European currency crisis 152; international finance 140; oil 173, 180, 183; sovereignty pooling 95
pollution 236, 243, 245–7
Polo, Marco 33
Portugal 107, **117**, **158**
positive economics 4, 22, 26, 30
positive feedback 228, 231
poverty 207, 215, 254; dualism 11, 28; lack of property rights 18; Russia 49
PPP *see* purchasing power parity
predation 34, 49, 51
predictions 2, 6, 233
price-inelastic demand 181, 187
prices 15–16, 29, 56, 229; aggregate demand 62; agricultural 58–60; arbitrage 140; asymmetric information 53; cigarettes 61; collusion 20, 30; corporate planning 15; currency union 150–1; dual track pricing 44, 46, 53; energy 240, 254; environmental issues 235–6, 243, 247; exhaustible resources 241; full market pricing 43; LDC industrialisation 217, 220; microeconomics 57, 58; oil 165–6, 170, 173–5, 181–3, **182**, 186, 212–13, 233–4; pollution permits 246, 247; substitute fuels 169; system failure 22, 23–4; transition economies 40–1, 50; *see also* inflation
principal-agent problem 40, 54
private enterprise 17–18, 27, 76, 83; *see also* entrepreneurs
private sector: Chile 78; China 44; Russia 46, 48; supply-side economics 76, 78, 81; transition economies 50
privatisation 54, 133, 255; China 43; Mexico 101; Russia 47; stabilisation policies 192; supply-side economics 76; transition economies 40; United Kingdom 83; *see also* deregulation; liberalisation

production: diminishing returns 53; dualistic systems 11–12; neoclassical growth model 220–1, **221**; primary 212–16, 236; Soviet central planning 37, 38–9
productivity: agricultural 220; China 44, 54; Europe 112; labour 112, 123; Mexico 101; Soviet Union 37–8, **37**
profit maximisation 13, 18, 23, 180, 186
progressive tax 83, 90, 231
property rights 13, 18, 24, 30, 229, 257; entrepreneurial culture 222; formalisation 51; informal sector 222–3; natural assets 243–4; privatisation 40; Russia 48, 49
protectionism 77, 92–4, 121, 155, 192, 217–18, 227
public goods 22, 30
public procurement 119
public sector 44, 150, 258
purchasing power parity (PPP) 209, 210–11, 231
Putin, Vladimir 49

quasi-rents 213, 232
questionnaires 248–9
quotas 93, 106, 218

Reagan, Ronald 77, 133
real rate of interest 189, 191, 205
recession 62, 64, 81, 84, 134, 154, 189–91
recycling 236, 245
regional trade blocs 93–4, 121, 123, 253
regulation: business 223; environmental 24, 243–7; financial 128, 129, 132, 133, 200; market failure 193; *see also* government intervention
renewable resources 171, 238, 239, 241–3, 250, 252
rent 232
rent-seeking 48, 54
reserve ratios 131, 141
resources: allocation 14–16, 68, 110, 217, 229; core/periphery flows 115, **115**; depletion of exhaustible resources 240–1, 250; dualistic systems 11, 12; ownership 16–18, 40; primary production 212–16, 236; renewable 171, 238, 239, 241–3, 250, 252; rents 232; supply-side economics 65; sustainable development 238, 239; traditional societies 32–3; unequal flow of 25; valuing 247–9
Ricardo, David 97–8
risk 34, 35, 54, 134

Romania 108
Romer, Paul 221
Rostow, Walt 215, 216
Russia: capital flows **48**; coal 171; debt **201**; development indicators **208**; financial crisis 49, 188, 190, 197–8; GDP **46**, **47**; income per head **46**; investment **49**; oil 172, 178, **178**, 179, 182, 183; rouble devaluation 49, 125, 143; transition 46–50, 51–3; *see also* Soviet Union, former

Sachs, Jeffrey 40, 42
Salinas, Carlos 96
Samarec 184
Samuelson, Paul 11
Saudi Arabia 178–9, **178**, 180, 181, 182–4, **208**
savings 63, **63**, **64**, 215, 216
Scholes, Myron 190
Schumpeter, Joseph 72
science 3–4, 5, 6
secondary markets 135, 141, 142
self-interest 12, 25, 53, 255
SEZs *see* special enterprise zones
shareholding 17–18, 29
Shell 180, 184
short-termism 25, 30, 34, 257
signalling 15, 16, 24, 57, 217, 235
Singapore 225, 228; development indicators **208**; entrepreneurs 229; financial markets 202; GDP **225**; GNP **224**; strategic trade policy 102
Single European Act (1985) 118, 119
skills 60, 61, 88, 115
Slovakia 42, 108, **117**
Slovenia 108, **117**
Smith, Adam 12–13, 57, 258
social costs 243–4, 247–8, 255, 257
social science 3, 4, 5, 6
social structures 34, 258
social welfare legislation 157
society 3, 4, 12, 25
SOEs *see* state owned enterprises
Solomon, Robert 134
Solow, Robert 220, 221
Soto, Hernando de 223
South Africa **208**
South Korea: clothing exports 91; debt 191, 196; economic growth 226–7; entrepreneurs 229; financial crisis 127, 195, 197, **197**; GDP **225**; GNP **207**, **224**; land reforms 225–6, 228; strategic trade policy 102
sovereignty 95, 151–2

Soviet Union, former: capital investment 216; COMECON 39, 53; command economy 9, 10, 14–15, 17, 21; dissolution 125, 143; economic decline 36–9; environmental degradation 235; GDP **46**; GNP 36–7, **37**; income per head **46**; oil 166, 178, **179**; oligarchy 54; transition 35, 39–41, 42–3, 51; *see also* Russia
Spain 107, **117**, **158**, **160**
special enterprise zones (SEZs) 44
specialisation 15, 72; customs unions 111; free trade 97; primary produce 215, 216
speculation 138, 154
stabilisation policies 43, 192, 205
Stages of Economic Growth 215
stagflation 81, 133, 181, 189
standards of living 210, 211, 215, 235, 236, 257
state owned enterprises (SOEs) 17, 51, 54; China 45, **45**, 46; manufacturing 218; Russia 48
state (public) monopolies 19, 29, 41
stock markets 190
'storming' 38
strategic trade policies 102–4, 217
subsidies 40, 41, 93, 102, 104; Common Agricultural Policy 123; environmental policy 245; Europe 118, 119
substitute goods 169, 186
supply: aggregate 67, 74, 76; labour market 60; market systems 29; microeconomics 57–8; oil 174, 183, 184
supply-side economics 65, 70, 76–7, 81, 87; Chile 77–9; government spending 67; United Kingdom 77, 82–3, 84
sustainable development 24, 212, 235, 237–40, 252
Sweden 107, **117**, **158**, **208**, 211
Switzerland 107

tacit collusion 19, 20, 30, 61
Tadzhikistan 43
Taiwan: clothing exports 91; economic growth 227–8; financial markets 202; GDP **225**; GNP **224**; import barriers 216; land reforms 225, 228; strategic trade policy 102, 103
tariffs 93, 96, 106, 145, 218; Chile 78; common external tariff 94, 108, 110–11, 113, 118, 123; Europe 118; foreign direct investment 113; free trade areas 108; Japan 103; Mexico 99;

reduction 94, 253; stabilisation policies 192

taxation: business 223; environmental control 245; Europe 119; feudal society 33; progressive 83, 90, 231; public goods provision 30; UK reforms 83

technical standards 119–20

technology: energy 239; financial markets 133–4; flexible 112; Japan 103; neoclassical growth model 220–1, 231; oil industry 184; traditional societies 32

TEV *see* total economic value

Texaco 172, 180

Thailand: debt **201**; financial crisis 127, 188, 195, 196–7, **197**

Thatcher, Margaret 12, 77, 82, 133, 146

tied floating exchange rates 146–7

Total 172

total economic value (TEV) 248

town and village enterprises (TVEs) 44, 45, **45**, 46, 54–5

tradable goods 156

trade 71–2, 144–5, 253; China 44, **45**; colonies 211–12; customs unions 94, 108–13; globalisation 88; growth **93**; institutional foundations 33–5; international finance 132; non-tariff barriers 94, 96, 118, 120–1, 145, 253; strategic trade policies 102–4, 217; *see also* exports; free trade; imports

trade agreements 94–5

trade creation 109, 110, 121

trade diversion 109, 110–11, 121, 123

trade-offs 73–4, 84, 86, 87, 90

tradition 16

'tragedy of the commons' 173

training 68, 88, 258

transactions costs 133–4, 142, 150, 222, 244, 245

transition economies 32–55; command system inefficiencies 35–6; economic decline 36–9; EU membership 107–8; reforms 39–41, 50

transparency 200

transport 23

Treaty of Rome (1957) 95, 107, 118

Turkey 108

TVEs *see* town and village enterprises

Ukraine 171

UN *see* United Nations

uncertainty 6, 34, 55, 254, 258; exchange rates 151; natural environments 239–40

underdevelopment 100

unemployment 4, 5, 67–8, 71, 88, 256; aggregate demand 62; Chile 79, **79**; circular flow model 64; cyclical 68; definition 70; Dutch Disease 214; Europe 153, 157, 158, **160**, **161**; expectations 80–1, 86; inflation 73–5, 80–7; Keynesian economics 65–7, 68, 72, 74; labour market flexibility 156; market 'solutions' 24; microeconomic theory 60–1; Phillips curve 74–5, **77**; reducing 258; structural 68, 158; supply-side economics 76, 81, 82–3, 84, 87; United Kingdom 116, **159**; United States **159**

United Kingdom (UK): Bank of England 127–8, 132, 133, 211; Common Agricultural Policy 110–11; deforestation 239; development indicators **208**; European Union 107; exports **158**; financial trading 133–4; free trade 102; GDP **117**; GNP **207**; industrial decay 116; industrial revolution 71; inflation 81, 84, **85**, 154; mortgage rates 158; outsourcing 91; pension funds 135; population **117**; pound sterling 126; supply-side economics 77, 82–3, 84, 87; unemployment 74–5, **75**, 84, **85**, 157, **159**; wage cuts 60; wage growth 157, **159**

United Nations (UN) 194, 203, 210–11

United States (US): Argentina peg to the dollar 199; budget deficit 192; coal consumption 171; development indicators **208**; Federal Reserve 127–8, 132, 146, 189; financial trading 133–4; free trade 102; GDP **46**; GNP **207**; Great Depression 60, 61, 64, 66; income per head **46**; inflation 81, 84, **85**; Kyoto treaty 246; Mexican peso crisis 195; Mexico relationship 97, 98, 99; NAFTA 95–7; oil 166, 168, 173, 178–9, **178**, **179**, 181; outsourcing 91; pension funds 135; South Korea 226; supply-side economics 77, 87; Taiwanese students 103; unemployment 73, **75**, 84, **85**, 157, **159**; wage growth 157, **159**

Uruguay 99, **208**

utility 13, 235, 236, 237

values 4, 248

Venezuela 181
vertical integration 176, 177, 180, 184, 187

wages: cuts 24, 60, 61, 62; Europe 157, **160**, **161**; fallacy of composition 68; labour market flexibility 156; macroeconomic theory 62, 64; microeconomic theory 60; United Kingdom **159**; United States **159**
Walker, Martin 38
Washington consensus 87, 194, 205

waste 236, 238
welfare state 255, 257
World Bank 194, 199, 202, 204; critics 203; GNP measurement 209; supply-side economics 87
World Commission on Environment and Development 237
World Trade Organisation (WTO) 92–4, 97, 145, 203, 258

Zaire **214**
Zapatistas 101, 102, 195, 257